PURDUE'S FEMALE FOUNDERS

THE FOUNDERS SERIES

The Founders Series publishes books on and about Purdue University, whether the physical campus, the University's impact on the region and world, or the many visionaries who attended or worked at the University.

OTHER TITLES IN THIS SERIES

A Spirit of Service: Purdue University and the United States Military
John Norberg

Purdue Memorial Union: The First 100 Years, 1924–2024
Robert L. Mindrum

Forging the Future: A History of the John Martinson Honors College, 2013–2023
Emily Allen, Jannine Huby, and Pulkit Manchanda (Eds.)

Boiler Up: A University President in the Public Square
Mitchell E. Daniels, Jr.

The Rocket Lab: Maurice Zucrow, Purdue University, and America's Race to Space
Michael G. Smith

Planting the Seeds of Hope: Indiana County Extension Agents During the Great Depression and World War II
Frederick Whitford

Queen of American Agriculture: A Biography of Virginia Claypool Meredith
Frederick Whitford, Andrew G. Martin, and Phyllis Mattheis

WBAA: 100 Years as the Voice of Purdue
Angie Klink

Pledge and Promise: Celebrating the Bond and Heritage of Fraternity, Sorority, and Cooperative Life at Purdue University
Angie Klink

Wings of Their Dreams: Purdue in Flight, Second Edition
John Norberg

Ever True: 150 Years of Giant Leaps at Purdue University
John Norberg

Purdue at 150: A Visual History of Student Life
David M. Hovde, Adriana Harmeyer, Neal Harmeyer, and Sammie L. Morris

Memories of Life on the Farm: Through the Lens of Pioneer Photographer J. C. Allen
Frederick Whitford and Neal Harmeyer

Also by Angie Klink
www.angieklink.com

- *Forging Ahead*
- *WBAA—100 Years as the Voice of Purdue*
- *Pledge and Promise: Celebrating the Bond and Heritage of Fraternity, Sorority, and Cooperative Life at Purdue*
- *The Deans' Bible: Five Purdue Women and Their Quest for Equality*
- *Kirby's Way: How Kirby and Caroline Risk Built Their Company on Kitchen-Table Values*
- *Bridges and More: Celebrating 25 Years of Purdue Civil Engineering*
- *Divided Paths, Common Ground: The Story of Mary Matthews and Lella Gaddis, Pioneering Purdue Women Who Introduced Science into the Home*
- *I Found U*, Lift-the-Flap Children's Book
- *Purdue Pete Finds His Hammer*, Lift-the-Flap Children's Book

PURDUE'S FEMALE FOUNDERS

*The Untold History of
Trailblazing Women Faculty*

ANGIE KLINK

Edited by
JENNIFER L. BAY

Copyright © 2025 by Angela R. Klink. All rights reserved.

Cataloging-in-Publication Data on file at the Library of Congress.

978-1-62671-176-1 (hardcover)
978-1-62671-177-8 (paperback)
978-1-62671-178-5 (epub)
978-1-62671-179-2 (epdf)

Cover image: Annie Smith Peck, Professor of Latin, Purdue University, 1881–1883. Record-breaking mountain climber. Courtesy New York Herald Syndicate, May 24, 1911.

*To my grandmother, Della Dove Lawhead,
who did not have the opportunity of an education.
(1890–1969)*

Let it fly.
—HELEN BASS WILLIAMS,
FIRST BLACK FEMALE FACULTY MEMBER,
PURDUE UNIVERSITY, 1968–1978

Climbing is unadulterated hard labor.
The only real pleasure is the satisfaction
of going where no man has been before
and where few can follow.
—ANNIE SMITH PECK,
PROFESSOR OF LATIN,
PURDUE UNIVERSITY, 1881–1883,
AND RECORD-BREAKING
MOUNTAIN CLIMBER

CONTENTS

Foreword   xiii
KATEY WATSON

Preface   xv
ANGIE KLINK

Introduction   1
JENNIFER L. BAY

1   Purdue's Feminine Roots   5
2   Health Starts at Home   25
3   Home Economics Powerhouses   37
4   A "Room" of One's Own   41
5   Late to the Game—Physical Education   49
6   Indiana's First Nursery School   55
7   Art, the Hoosier Salon, and Historic Fashions   62
8   Amelia Earhart and Lillian Gilbreth   67
9   World War II Survivors and Thrivers   80
10   Women Who Enriched Family Life   97
11   New Home Economics Dean and Pioneers in Brazil   102
12   Influencers in Liberal Arts and School of Science   109
13   Research Horizons in Beulah Land   121
14   Lone Woman in Agriculture   131
15   Women in Engineering   142

16	Physical Education for Women and Title IX	156
17	Nursing, a Sleeping Giant	167
18	Home Economics Reordered for the Times	177
19	Comforting the Afflicted and Afflicting the Comfortable	190
20	Helen Schleman Fights for Female Faculty	199
21	The 1970s and the Women's Liberation Movement	208
22	Krannert Trailblazers	215
23	Rats Help Better Babies' Lives	224
24	Diets and Skeletons	234
25	The World Needs Educated Women	251
26	Strides for Minorities and Community	265
27	Historic Treks in Speech and Hearing	274
28	Forging New Fields of Study	286
29	Fashion Design, Historic Costumes, and the Purdue Tartan	295
30	Family First	300
31	Rising through the Ranks and Creating a New College	312
Postscript		321
Notes		323
Index		377
About the Author		403
About the Editor		405

FOREWORD

Engineers, pilots, nutritionists, cattle breeders, nurses, international researchers, entomologists, mountain climbers, home economists, early childhood educators—Angie Klink's newest book, *Purdue's Female Founders: The Untold History of Trailblazing Women Faculty*, brings together stories of significant women from across Purdue University. This extensively researched volume gives recognition to women faculty for their influence and work in building the university, departments, programs, and student body into the world-class institution we know today.

Unlike previous histories of the university or its colleges and departments, this work focuses specifically on female faculty who have shaped our campus. It also shows the breadth of women's impact by branching out from the university's typical focus on agriculture, science, engineering, and math (STEAM) fields to include home economics, nursing, early childhood education, and liberal arts, giving these rigorous disciplines the recognition and respect they deserve. This book not only features well-known names on Purdue's campus like Amelia Earhart and Dr. Lillian Gilbreth, but also shines a light on lesser-known women who have shaped our campus and the nation.

Read about women like Katherine Bitting, a female faculty member in biology, who invented shelf-stable, preservative-free ketchup with her husband right here in Lafayette; Edith Gamble, a home economics professor, who established what would become Purdue's globally renowned hospitality and tourism program in 1918; and Dr. Avanelle Kirksey, professor of foods and nutrition, whose nutrition research revolutionized our understanding of maternal and infant health.

Using extensive archival research, Klink weaves together biographical information, professional accomplishments, challenges, and personal stories for each of the women featured. This is no easy feat. Klink spent eight years conducting extensive research to first identify these women and learn about their life, work, struggles, and successes. Archival research is painstaking work. In libraries, each book or item is individually described. However, in archives, due to the sheer volume of materials we collect, materials are kept together by the person or organization who created them and described in groupings, usually by topic or type of materials. Therefore, researchers must first comb through our catalogs and detailed finding aids to identify relevant collections before spending hours and days digging through dozens of boxes to find the information that they are seeking.

The research necessary for this publication would not have been possible without the creation of the Susan Bulkeley Butler Women's Archives in 2006 and nearly twenty years of collecting efforts by archivists and supporters. The Women's Archives was established to address the absence of women's stories in the Purdue Archives. This would not have been possible without the financial support of Susan Bulkeley Butler, Dr. France A. Córdova, and many other Women's Archives donors who supported this endeavor financially and through the donation of their papers. The Women's Archives now holds over 230 collections documenting 149 years of women's history at Purdue and is used by researchers around the world.

This work demonstrates the value of specialized collecting efforts like the Women's Archives to address past discrimination and oversight. If not for the Women's Archives and researchers like Klink dedicated to telling their stories, many of these women might never have made it into our history books. As Klink mentions throughout, many of these women endured discrimination in hiring, fair wages, and access to equitable opportunities. It is important for us to remember that the women who made it into this book are the women who succeeded in their fields, but we should also recognize that the barriers they faced likely prevented many other women and minoritized groups from pursuing or succeeding at Purdue.

I hope you enjoy reading this wonderfully researched book and learning about some of our amazing female faculty, both past and present.

—Katey Watson, Clinical Assistant Professor
and France A. Córdova Archivist
Susan Bulkeley Butler Women's Archives,
Purdue University Archives and Special Collections

PREFACE

For eight years I conducted research and wrote about "Purdue's Female Founders." When I mentioned my book title to a friend, her response was, "Are there any?"

No doubt she was thinking of the men who began the university in 1869, including benefactor John Purdue, of course. But also the first presidents, trustees, and professors. All men. Women became founders later, beginning in 1875 when Sarah Allen Oren, the university's first female professor, began teaching. Perhaps you do not think of her as a founder. However, I see any woman who is the first to work in a male-centric arena—the classroom, research laboratory, boardroom, or administration—as a founder of female possibility.

The only woman in a room full of men is brave. She is setting the footpath, marking her place as a female voice, mustering her courage to speak out with the feminine point of view that is so important for full participation of both women and men in all theaters of life. The women of this book were faculty who walked the Purdue campus beginning when it was just a smattering of buildings surrounded by dirt roads and ink-black wrought iron fences and into the twentieth century when much of the heavy lifting and great strides for women's rights occurred in the United States.

Decade after decade, the women in this book endured discrimination. Through the 1900s, many of the professors and researchers were looked down upon, sequestered in the Department of Domestic Science, which became the School of Home Economics and then the College of Consumer and Family Sciences. It was thought women belonged away from the "manly" areas such as engineering, agriculture, and the sciences, even though the women's research and teachings were very much scientific and vital to the health and well-being of society. Home Economics deserves its place in the sun, as do the women who taught, conducted research, and obtained degrees under that dynamic umbrella.

Read about female faculty who were told they could not work once they married or became pregnant. Virginia Ferris wanted to continue her research on nematodes, her passion, so she hid her pregnancy for as long as possible behind a lab coat.

The stories of artists (Laura Anne Fry and Laurentza Schantz-Hansen) in Purdue's history give a balance to the narratives we hear most often in the university's longtime, repeated chronicles about males in the "hard sciences." Yet, women were there in the sciences, too, making history. Dean of Engineering Leah Jamieson, cofounder and director of EPICS, Engineering Projects in Community Service, and Martha Chiscon, a lone female professor of biology and the first female administrator in the College of Science, for example.

Edith Weisskopf-Joelson is a name long forgotten by Purdue. A professor of psychology from 1949 to 1962, she was a friend of author and Holocaust survivor Viktor Frankl. She lived and taught Frankl's theory that finding meaning in life correlates with better mental health. She herself was a survivor of schizophrenia. Her methods and philosophies conflicted with her Purdue male colleagues' rigid and pragmatic approach to psychology, and she felt isolated and alone in her belief in logotherapy. Frankl devoted a postscript to Joelson in his 1984 edition of *Man's Search for Meaning*.

With great fortitude, trailblazing faculty of color chiseled passageways for both women and minorities. Helen Bass Williams was Purdue's first Black female faculty member, and Clara Bell founded the Minority Students in Nursing organization.

I thank Katharine "Katey" Watson, clinical assistant professor, France A. Córdova Archivist with Susan Bulkeley Butler Women's Archives at Purdue University for her early reading and meticulous fact-checking of the manuscript. Over the years, Katey has helped me in countless ways, answering questions and pulling out archival papers when I conduct research for my books, essays, articles, and more. Richard Bernier, processing and public services archivist with Purdue University Libraries, was diligent and cheery as he helped me track down photos for the book.

I give a hearty acknowledgment to Kelly Lippie, curator at Tippecanoe County Historical Association, who helped me dig up additional photos of some of the women featured within these pages. I thank the faculty connected with the Women's Global Health Institute (WGHI) who supported me along the way as I birthed this tome into existence. The vision of the WGHI is to improve the quality of life for women around the world through the prevention and early detection of disease. It was founded through the foresight of Dr. Connie Weaver, renowned nutrition researcher who made profound discoveries of the importance of calcium to women's health.

An enthusiastic dose of gratitude goes to Jennifer Bay, my editor who came on board in the last stretch of the book with good cheer and insights and wrote about a couple more women in the area of my beloved liberal arts, particularly Muriel Harris, founder of Purdue's globally renowned online writing lab, OWL.

I concentrated mainly on female faculty for this book. Nearly seventy women who were "firsts" or "the only" in their realms and began their professorships at Purdue during the nineteenth or twentieth centuries are included. The book is not intended to be exhaustive. Many of the featured women were selected because of the availability of sources to write their stories. Undoubtedly readers will think of someone who is "left out," and perhaps one day a volume II will be created.

My book *The Deans' Bible: Five Purdue Women and Their Quest for Equality*, published by Purdue University Press in 2014, highlights the stories of Purdue's deans of women and deans of students of the twentieth century. Some of those five are mentioned in this book, but I did not include their full stories because *The Deans' Bible* gives an account of their contributions to the university.

I wrote *Purdue's Female Founders: The Untold History of Trailblazing Women Faculty* to enlighten and inspire. Above all, I penned this tome to give those chronicled the spotlight they deserve in the scripts the university writes for generations to come in speeches, marketing materials, and tales told at alumni reunions. Often, the same male-centric history is told and retold, as if women never existed in the nooks and crannies of Purdue.

My hope is that future illuminations of Purdue's bygone days include the women within these pages—founders of female possibility.

—Angie Klink

INTRODUCTION

What does "found" mean? Usually, we use the word to indicate that we have located a lost object or come across something new. Figuratively, it means to establish or start a program, business, or institution. For Purdue's female faculty, the word operates in both senses of the word.

Not only were women faculty discovering new knowledges and ideas that had been lost or overlooked, but they were also participating in the art of discovery, or what today we might call research. Moreover, in discovering new ideas and creating new knowledge, they often founded programs, departments, and larger institutional structures that allowed them to pursue the codification and circulation of that knowledge.

In short, Purdue functioned as a sort of "foundry" for the women profiled in this volume, a place where it was possible to create something out of nothing or at least create a field, vision, department, institution where none had existed before. These are truly "first" women.

But how did it all happen? How did Purdue become a place where women could flourish? Most institutions of higher education were dominated by men, especially when Purdue was founded in 1869. But there were bright spots where women crept in and were able to plant small seeds that could blossom and sustain future female students and faculty.

The Midwest has always been known as a farming region engaged in agricultural and mechanical production—a special place where regular people just did the work that was needed without complaint or comment. Indeed, in some ways, this is the hallmark of a Boilermaker: Do more with less. Boilermakers have grit and just get it done. That kind of Hoosier mentality was a driving force for many of these women, even if they were not native to the state.

Take, for instance, Annie Peck, the mountain climber professor who graces the cover of this book. Peck risked arrest and jail for wearing pants while climbing the Matterhorn in the Swiss Alps in 1895. Her grit and determination fueled her to do what men had been doing to achieve their goals and not feel ashamed of it. Peck's "firsts" broke barriers that allowed other women to follow suit, perhaps most famously Amelia Earhart in her wearing of pants and eschewing what had previously been considered the province of men.

While we have many examples of women who bucked tradition and forged a path, we also have many examples of women who faced discrimination but persevered and thrived in the face of prejudice. Virginia Ferris, for example, suffered through graduate school where no men wanted to be her lab partner, was berated for taking the place of a man as a teaching assistant, was made to feel embarrassed for accepting a prestigious National Science Foundation fellowship, hid her pregnancy for seven months, was forced to resign or be fired after the birth of her child, and took up using initials in publications and consulting work rather than her full name to disguise that she was a woman. After all of this, she finally got hired as a faculty member at Purdue (after her husband) and was able to be a pioneer in entomology. What she is remembered for is not just her perseverance, but her mentoring of other women who needed help and advice.

Indeed, mentoring might be seen as the most important impact made by some of the women featured in this book. It's not just that they were visionary leaders who founded disciplines, degrees, and programs; they also mentored and stood as models for other women who wanted to succeed in the university. These women understood what it meant to face resistance and wanted to ensure that future women had an easier path to success.

Laurentza Schantz-Hansen, for instance, hand selected female students for advanced courses in art so they could achieve bachelor's degrees in that discipline. Violet Haas mentored female students in Purdue's chapter of the Society of Women Engineers, and her advocacy, along with that of other women, eventually led to Purdue developing the Women in Engineering Program. Haas's work promoting women led to the Violet Haas award to honor women who have advanced the cause of women at Purdue. Likewise, Leah Jamieson helped raise the status of women at Purdue, working to hire more female faculty in engineering so that female students had mentors and role models. In the English department, Janice Lauer founded an informal mentoring program for Rhetoric and Composition, a field that has been historically dominated by women, to support students in the new doctoral program she developed. All these women and more knew that in order to advance as a university, women had to be involved at every level, and as such, they had to be supported and treated equitably and fairly.

While Schantz-Hansen, Haas, Jamieson, and Lauer developed more formal mentoring structures, some women just stood as models to be emulated because they served as "firsts." Emma Ewing was the first female department head at Purdue. Helen Golden was the first female professor of engineering. Virginia Meredith and Mary Lockwood Matthews, of course, stand out for their ability to recruit and develop women in extension and home economics. These women served as luminaries for the young women they would teach and the female faculty who would follow in their footsteps.

More recently, Christine Ladisch occupied multiple administrative roles at Purdue, showing that women could still rise to the highest positions. She earned her graduate degree at Purdue, then went on to serve in prominent faculty roles at the university, including vice provost of Academic Affairs and as the inaugural dean of the College of Health and Human Sciences. Purdue and female faculty also have Ladisch to thank for the "stop the tenure clock" policy; she was one of the first women to balance her personal life and academic life through that initiative. Until the 1980s, female faculty had to balance the demands of achieving tenure with caregiving and child-rearing, and many did not make it to tenure.

Carolyn Woo rose up from an undergraduate degree at Purdue to dean of the Krannert School of Management and then went on to serve as dean of Notre Dame's Mendoza College of Business and head of Catholic Relief Services. Woo is a good example of a female faculty achiever who fought discrimination on more than one front. Woo came from China without knowing much about Purdue or how she would fund her education beyond her freshman year. She studied night and day to achieve her goals, living as a "church mouse" at St. Thomas Aquinas church in lieu of rent.

Likewise, Helen Bass Williams was relentless in her pursuit for justice and a place for Black women at Purdue. Williams recruited more Black students to Purdue than anyone prior to her arrival in 1968. She was Purdue's first female Black faculty member. Williams had a background in social justice advocacy, serving on the board at Highlander Research and Education Center, which she brought to Purdue. She sat on a committee to bring more minority students and faculty to Purdue, and she did, helping to house and support them monetarily and emotionally. She saw the need for more formal mentoring and was able to secure support for Purdue's Learning Center, which could help students who needed additional preparation or support to understand the culture of higher education and succeed in it. Williams developed more programs to help support minority students and faculty such as the African American Studies program and the Black Cultural Center.

All of these initiatives came out of her own understanding of what we now would call "intersectionality," a term coined by Kimberlé Crenshaw. Crenshaw proposed that women of color experienced "intersecting" patterns of racism and sexism.[1] That is, we can't understand a woman of color's experiences of discrimination only through race or only through sex; rather, we must understand that discourses of racism and sexism overlap, and we must take those overlaps into consideration when understanding the experiences of women of color. Helen Bass Williams understood intersectionality all too well, even though she may not have had Crenshaw's language.

Thus, when we think of Purdue's female founders, we cannot only think of their accomplishments in terms of gender. We must consider these women with respect to all of the multidimensional aspects of their identities: race, class, sexual orientation, motherhood, rural life, physical ability, and more. Women are not just defined by their gender, but by all of the ways that gender intersects with the various aspects of their lived experiences.

The women in this book who have been identified as Purdue's female founders only provide a glimpse of the radical potential of women at the university. May Purdue continue to nurture and cultivate more female faculty who can break barriers we have yet to identify and continue to push the university toward a more equitable future.

—Jennifer L. Bay, Professor of English,
Purdue University

1

PURDUE'S FEMININE ROOTS

SARAH ALLEN OREN, "FEMALE TEACHER OF THE UNIVERSITY" AND STATE LIBRARIAN

Sarah Allen Oren was the first woman to be appointed a faculty member at Purdue University when she was hired in July 1875, the same year female students were first admitted.

Oren's title was "female teacher of the university," pointing to the obvious as she began her position surrounded by a conclave of male colleagues. Thankfully, President Abraham Shortridge found her title awkward and soon changed it to assistant professor of mathematics. Oren was paid $1,000 per year. However, in August the board of trustees also appointed Oren to be a professor of botany, so today she could be considered Purdue's first female faculty member in agriculture. She also received a raise in salary to $1,500. Most of the male professors were paid $2,000 annually.[1]

In the 1876 to 1877 Annual Register of Purdue, Oren is listed under "Faculty" as "Associate Principal of Academy."[2] Nine women students were enrolled when Oren was hired. While all courses were open to women, the registrar steered them away from engineering and agriculture.

Oren was thirty-nine, widow of a Civil War army captain, and mother of one daughter when she came to the young Purdue campus dotted with a smattering of buildings erected since the university was founded in 1869. She was a native of Clinton County, Ohio, and educated at Antioch College in Yellow Springs where she was influenced by the first president of the college, the famed American educator Horace Mann.

Mann was a well-known abolitionist and social reformer who is considered the founder of public education in the United States. In his first graduation speech, Mann implored the Antioch graduates to "be ashamed to die until you have won some victory for humanity." Coeducational from the outset, Antioch was a leader in progressive thought and innovation and was the first college in the United States to have a female faculty member who was considered equal to her male counterparts. It also offered a universal curriculum for men and women.[3] Oren stepped into her Purdue classroom emboldened by Antioch's enlightened philosophies.

Before her appointment at Purdue, Oren held several impressive positions for a woman of the era that formed a firm foundation for her to become a Purdue faculty member. In 1868, she was named preceptress of the City Academy in Indianapolis and a year later joined the faculty at Indianapolis High School, later named after its former superintendent, Purdue President Abraham C. Shortridge. She taught there until 1873 when the Indiana legislature selected her as the first female state librarian. Her work to reform a badly neglected library facility was said to be of "heroic proportions."[4]

Oren's selection as state librarian was "more than a relief; it was a revolution."[5] She may have been elected because she was a soldier's widow, yet Oren was qualified. She exuded common sense and a head for business to master the complex position, bringing about numerous reforms, not just in the library proper, but also in the entire state building.

At that time, the librarian was also the legal custodian of the State House, a Greek revival building built in 1835 to resemble the Parthenon in Athens, Greece. The structure had been deteriorating since the 1860s, and Oren worked to improve its condition.[6] It stood in the footprint of the present Indiana State House.

Oren had the building scrubbed and disinfected. Under her supervision, the blocked chimneys and flues were opened and cleaned; the grimy walls were papered; the steps and pavements of the porches were repaired; the legislative papers that had not yet been eaten by mice were taken from musty cupboards and packed into tin boxes. She organized the books, recovering missing volumes that had been borrowed and never returned. She rearranged the volumes on the plan of the Boston Public Library, in departments by subjects and alphabetically by authors' names. Labels were pasted on the books to designate their locations on

Sarah A. Oren became Purdue's first female faculty member in 1875. Courtesy Tim Oren and family.

the shelves. When purchasing new tomes, Oren kept a careful eye on the needs of "the laboring people," who could not afford to purchase costly reference books.[7]

Oren held the office of state librarian for two years; then the political composition of the legislature changed and her position as librarian was not renewed.[8] A January 23, 1875, story in the *Indianapolis News* advocated for the legislature to vote for Oren to continue in her position. Of course, Oren could not vote in political elections. Most American women would not receive suffrage until 1920.

Oren lost her post as the Indiana state librarian to Lycurgus Dalton, a Democrat from Bedford.[9] Oren persevered and headed to Purdue where she dug in and made her mark. Less than one month after she arrived, she presented a plan to the board of trustees to create an orchard on campus for experimental work. The board approved the plan and designated about one acre northeast of Purdue Hall for the plantings.¹⁰ Purdue Hall was an original campus building that housed male students and stood north of University Hall.

In April 1876, Oren was asked to serve as "oversight" (faculty sponsor) for Purdue's first women's literary society, which focused on literature, music, and debate. The group was known as the Cereal Society until female students petitioned for the creation of a literary club sanctioned by the university and the group became the Philalethean Literary Society. At the time, it was the only Purdue-sponsored extracurricular activity for women.¹¹

In November 1876, Oren became the first "matron" in charge of the female students who lived in the Boarding House (later named Ladies Hall), one of the first three buildings erected at Purdue. Oren lived there in two rooms with her daughter Cata, a Purdue student.

A *Purdue Exponent* article stated that at that time the "girls were not allowed to go to the village, leave the campus, nor stay in the village over night with any friend or relative, except by special permission. About 1890, with the further expansion of the university and increased enrollment of coeds, the girls were given more freedom; they were allowed to come and go during the day as they wished."¹²

Built in 1874, the Boarding House was a stately, red brick building with twin towers and a porch. As the first permanent building north of State Street, it stood sentinel between what is now Matthews Hall and Stone Hall. In the early years, it contained the college dining room, living quarters for faculty and their families, and the office of Purdue's president. For most of its existence, the building would serve as a women's residence, laboratory, and classroom.¹³

Oren resigned from Purdue in 1878 when she married Wesley Haynes and moved to his farm near Peru, Indiana. She was the first faculty member, man or woman, to receive a board of trustees citation in appreciation of her work on behalf of the university.¹⁴ Olivia T. Alderman was her successor.¹⁵ Oren's husband died one year after their marriage, and she moved to Sault St. Marie, Michigan, to live with Cata until her own death on April 21, 1907, at the age of seventy-one.

ANNIE SMITH PECK, LATIN PROFESSOR AND RECORD-BREAKING MOUNTAINEER

Annie Smith Peck climbed to the summit of the Matterhorn in the Swiss Alps in 1895, and the world was up in arms. Not because she was one of only three women who had accomplished such a feat, but because during her climb she wore pants.

As Peck celebrated her successful climb on one of the most dangerous peaks in Europe, people wondered if she should be arrested. At that time, some women who wore pants in public were taken to jail.

By then, Peck, age forty-four, was an accomplished mountaineer, author, and academic who had spent two years on the faculty at Purdue. She fought for the life she wanted in a time when women were not expected to seek adventure or higher education. She wore pants out of practicality and did not let the public's outrage trouble her. Peck knew of stories of women tripping on their long skirts and falling into large crevasses as they climbed mountains. She thought, "Why not wear what men wear and be safe?"[16] A photograph of her wearing pants (like the one featured on the book cover) was published in several newspapers and became an instant sensation. Peck would go on to break mountain climbing records while wearing pants.

She was born in Providence, Rhode Island, in 1850, the youngest of five children in a prominent family. As a teenager, she regularly attended lectures on women's rights and racial justice. Despite her family's initial objections, Peck chose to pursue higher education in a time when many people believed that it was physically dangerous for women to participate in schooling. This hazard to women's health brought on by education was "scientifically proven" by Edward H. Clarke, a member of the Massachusetts Medical Society, fellow of the American Academy of Arts and Sciences, and medical professor of Harvard College.

Following the theory of Darwinism that deemed men as more fit than women, who had less developed brains, Clarke wrote *Sex in Education or A Fair Chance for the Girls,* an 1873 treatise against coeducation. It became a bestseller. Clark explained in his volume that women who were educated would have a future with "uterine disease, hysteria, and other derangements of the nervous system."[17] He claimed that women would use all of their energy on their brains, and that energy would be drawn from their reproductive systems, eventually, in essence, rendering all women in the United States infertile.[18] This was the societal poppycock that Peck bucked.

Peck received a teaching certificate from the Rhode Island Normal School in 1872, taught high school in Providence, and then moved to Saginaw, Michigan, to teach at the high school.[19] Yet she desired more education. Peck's father and her three brothers attended Brown University, and she wanted to follow in their footsteps. She wrote to Brown President Ezekiel G. Robinson, and his response followed suit with Clarke's book. The president wrote, "Women are not encouraged to seek education."

However, the University of Michigan encouraged women and first admitted females in 1871, so she headed there and studied Greek, Latin, public speaking, rhetoric, and algebra. After graduation, she was disheartened that the only teaching job she could find was at Bartholomew's school for young women in Cincinnati as an assistant instructor in algebra, rather than as a full instructor of the classics that she knew well and yearned to teach. After less than a year in Cincinnati, she found another position teaching boys algebra and Greek in New Jersey.

Peck had an opportunity to obtain a master's degree in classical languages from the University of Michigan in 1881, and that led her to Purdue where she landed a job as an instructor in Latin and elocution.[20] At Purdue, she was finally teaching what she loved.

Author Hannah Kimberley wrote in her book *A Woman's Place Is at the Top* that Peck was successful in her teaching at Purdue, but she "was decidedly miserable in Lafayette." Kimberley wrote, "In fact, Annie's go-to adjective for many things about Lafayette was 'wretched.' Goods were much more expensive there than in the East. If she needed to purchase material for a dress, she had to send to New York for it, as it was twice as expensive in Indiana, 'a wretched place to get anything.'"[21]

Peck endured a rough winter of rain. The Wabash River rose over the levee three times, forcing her to cross in a boat as she traveled to and from campus. To make matters more dire, smallpox was prevalent, and Peck saw a homeopath to be vaccinated. He also prescribed medicine for malaria. On top of fearing disease, she had health problems that included a severe pain in one eye, blisters on her skin, kidney ailments, and severe fatigue. Perhaps all of these maladies stemmed from her unhappiness with her location. Kimberley wrote, "And the only relief she found for that [fatigue] was in northern New York's Adirondack Mountain area, where she spent at least a month each summer."[22]

The mountains were calling. Peck left Purdue in 1883. She would later return as a celebrated mountaineer.

Immediately after she left Purdue, Peck pursued advanced studies in Germany, studying German and French, and became the first woman admitted to the American School of Classical Studies in Athens, Greece. Traveling from Germany to Greece, she saw the Matterhorn and was enchanted. She began to scale increasingly technical peaks and mountain passes while in Europe. When she returned to the United States, she accepted a teaching position at Smith College, but once she was well-known enough to support herself through public lectures, she resigned and focused on mountain climbing.

Peck wore leather boots four sizes too large to accommodate four pairs of woolen socks, and she hammered nails onto the soles for traction on the ice.[23]

She tackled Mount Shasta in California, and her ascent of the Matterhorn in 1895 brought her wide celebrity. Two years later, she climbed Mount Orizaba in Mexico, breaking the women's world altitude record. Yet even then, she faced discrimination. At the end of a long climb, she was the one expected to spend hours boiling snow, cooking, and cleaning up. Men continually questioned whether she knew what she was talking about.[24]

On December 15, 1907, after a climbing expedition in South America the week prior, Peck was the guest of honor at the annual dinner of the Purdue Alumni Association of New York. When she spoke at the dinner, she said her desire to climb the Matterhorn had first come to her while she was at Purdue, and after hearing a lecture on the subject by Professor Jordan. A *Purdue Exponent* story reported that "ever since that time, she has been casting about the globe looking for new worlds to conquer in the shape of unclimbed peaks."[25]

By the time she spoke at the Purdue dinner, she had made her mark in mountain climbing. However, it was the following year when her greatest triumph occurred—her record-breaking 1908 ascent of the north peak of Peru's 22,205-foot Mount Huascaran at the age of fifty-eight. It had taken her a decade and several attempts to achieve this goal. As the first person to scale Mount Huascaran,[26] she was awarded a gold medal from the president of Peru in recognition of her accomplishment. The country even named the North Peak of Huascaran "Cubre Ana Peck."[27]

Peck's great feats brought notoriety and her name and/or image appeared in advertisement campaigns. Makers of the Featherweight Blickensderfer typewriter mentioned her in a 1907 ad with the headline, "Blick Typewriter Carried by Famous Explorer." The copy read, "Portability and durability were the essential reasons why Miss Peck selected a Blick."[28]

In 1910, every Singer sewing machine came with a package of photographs and postcards of Annie Peck. One of the packs was titled "World Famous Explorers" and contained cards depicting twenty-five male explorers and Peck. A color illustration of Peck appeared on a Hassan cigarette card with the headline, "The World's Greatest Explorers." The short bio on the card mentioned that she was professor of Latin at Purdue.

Peck wrote several books about South America in hopes of furthering diplomatic relations between North and South America. She lobbied the US government to appoint her as an ambassador to South America, but was rejected for being old and a woman. In 1911, at age sixty-one, she climbed Mount Coropuna in Peru and planted a "Votes for Women" pennant on behalf of the Joan of Arc Equal Suffrage League. Later, she became president of the league.[29]

Peck returned to Purdue in 1913 to speak in the Lecture and Concert Course at Eliza Fowler Hall (demolished in 1954). Her talk was titled "The Story of the Conquest of Huascaran." The *Purdue Exponent* headline read, "The world's greatest woman mountain climber to give illustrated talk." At the lecture, Peck recounted her harrowing descent of Mt. Huascaran and said, "Had I not had my climbing irons, I doubt if I should have gotten out alive." She presented 150 lantern slides showing the ascent.[30] One of the men on her team lost a hand and half of his foot to frostbite, an incident she described as a "horrible nightmare." Peck published a book about the climb titled *The Search for the Apex of America*.[31]

Toward the end of her life, Peck returned to Athens and climbed to the top of the Acropolis in what would be her last ascent. While in Greece, she became ill, so she returned to New York where she died on July 18, 1935, at the age of eighty-four. The *New York Times* quoted the magazine *Athenaeum* in her obituary, which stated, "She has done all that a man could, if not more. She had sagacity, and with it 'nerve' and 'grit.'"[32]

EMMA PIKE EWING, FIRST FEMALE DEPARTMENT HEAD

Emma Pike Ewing was known as "the woman who would have taught America to make good bread if America could have been taught."[33] Ewing did, in fact, teach America to bake good bread and much more before coming to Purdue as the university's first female department head.

Ewing believed that good food was an important factor in the development of the individual, morally, mentally, and physically, and she strove to improve people's diets by introducing better and more economical methods of cooking. Originally from New York State, Ewing gained national recognition as a cooking instructor after the Civil War and authored several books prior to arriving at Purdue.

She recorded her acquired knowledge in the form of a story, and James R. Osgood & Co. of Boston published *Cooking and Castle Building* in 1880. Reviewers said it was "well calculated to popularize cookery in its scientific aspects."

The year after her book was published, she became the superintendent of the Chicago Training School of Cookery, opened under the auspices of sixty prominent Chicago women. Ewing gave lectures in some of the most prominent schools for young women in Chicago. These lectures were promoted in the

An 1893 advertisement for the "Art of Cooking" taught by Emma Pike Ewing at the Chautauqua Assembly. Courtesy Purdue University Archives and Special Collections.

newspaper with such headlines as "Scientific Cooking," fostering Ewing's reputation as a scholar of cooking principles.

In 1882, Ewing published a series of short works covering soup making, salads, breads, and vegetables. A volume combining the four individual works was published in 1891 under the title *Cookery Manuals*.[34]

Ewing headed the domestic economy department at Iowa Agricultural College (today Iowa State University) before she arrived in a horse-drawn carriage and stepped her high-buttoned shoes onto Purdue soil in 1887 as the newly appointed head of the new Department of Domestic Economy in the School of Science. She taught a series of domestic economy courses[35] in Ladies Hall to the smattering of women students on campus. All wore dresses with high-standing collars and long draping skirts that skimmed the dusty roads of the university.

She resigned from Purdue two years later and went to Kansas City, Missouri, to organize a school of household science. Within a year, she left Kansas City because she was receiving numerous requests from across the United States to deliver lectures and lessons on culinary topics.[36]

Domestic economy, later termed "home economics," courses were women's foot in the door to academia. Many universities and colleges were developing domestic economy programs for women, and Kansas State was ahead of the game, having created such a program in 1875.[37]

It appears that Purdue's domestic economy classes were offered from 1887 to 1889, then took a hiatus. In 1890, "An Epitaph" appeared in Purdue's *Debris* yearbook conveying, in poetic form, that the courses in domestic economy were "lying in peace—though the pieces still lie."[38] Perhaps this hiatus occurred when Ewing left Purdue. In 1891, she became the dean of the Chautauqua Assembly in New York and a traveling lecturer.[39] Her *A Text-Book of Cookery for Use in Schools* was published in 1899.

LAURA ANNE FRY, GROUNDBREAKING ROOKWOOD POTTERY ARTIST

When she became a Purdue art professor in 1891, Laura Anne Fry was one of the most gifted artists of the nineteenth-century Women's Art movement and a patent holder for a revolutionary ceramic glazing technique used by Rookwood Pottery in Cincinnati.

Quiet and unassuming, Fry had studied in England and France and was a founding member of the first women's pottery organization in the United States, the Cincinnati Pottery Club established in 1879. The club rented a room for their workshop at the Rookwood School for Pottery Decoration.[40] In her twenties, Fry opened her own studio where she worked in carving, furniture design, and china painting, but it was not a financial success, and she had to close.

Fry became a designer and teacher at Rookwood the year after Maria Longworth Nichols Storer founded the company in 1880 in an old schoolhouse her father owned on the Ohio River. He would continue to help Storer financially. Looking back decades later at age eighty-three, Fry wrote, "Mrs. Storer asked me to be one of the decorators for which I was paid $20.00 a week [very good wages], and there with 6 or 7 others, [I] worked in a large room formerly used for the school."[41]

Fry became an integral part of Rookwood when Storer did something that no American woman had done before—she launched the first female-owned and female-founded manufacturing company in the United States. Businessmen scoffed at Storer's audacity in opening her own business, and they predicted she would fail. Undaunted, Storer declared, "The potter's wheel will be turned by woman power."[42]

Within a decade, Rookwood was considered the country's top pottery studio. Fry's own woman power transformed glazing at Rookwood when she conceived a new method to apply the delicately graded backgrounds she wanted for her pottery. She wrote, "After two or three years of mottled or clouded backgrounds manipulated like oil color [and] ... sponged backgrounds made by dipping a fine sponge in color and applying it to the moist body of the piece to secure an even surface of color, one day the idea came to me to blow the colors on in the same way that I used my atomizer to keep my work moist."[43]

After hearing a "voice from the air" that said, "Why not blow the color on?" Fry repeated her idea to the (male) head decorator who told her it would never work. The next day he left for vacation, and Fry successfully tried her experiment on several pieces. These were later exhibited in the Cincinnati Exposition. Her process was soon adopted by every decorator in the room.[44]

Fry's atomizer technique provided Rookwood with new blended colors that helped propel the company's pottery to international fame. In 1885, a number of female decorators complained that the mouth atomizers caused throat irritations. Rookwood's manager, William Watts Taylor, had a piping system installed to supply steam pressure for mechanical atomizers, but the steam diluted the slips, making them difficult to control, so a transfer to air pumps was made and the system became an airbrush operation.

The following summer, Fry left as a regular employee of Rookwood but continued on a freelance basis. In 1888, Taylor wrote to Fry suggesting that she take out a patent on her method of decorating with the atomizer or airbrush. He pointed out that if she could obtain a patent covering the application of colored slip to pottery, "it would be useful to the pottery to hold such a patent as an obstacle to dishonorable competition by former employees, from which the pottery had already suffered." He promised that Rookwood would pay all expenses necessary for her to obtain the patent. Fry expressed willingness to have the process patented if she might continue to use it, as she was no longer officially employed at Rookwood.

However, when she was asked to sign the patent application and a paper assigning her interest to the pottery for a nominal consideration, she declined to do so, and instead applied for the patent in her own name through New York lawyers.[45] Fry was awarded a US Patent in 1889 for an "Improvement in the Art of Decorating Pottery-Ware."

While Fry's invention contributed to Rookwood's rise to fame and increased profitability, Taylor was reluctant to recognize her impact on the pottery's success. In 1890, Storer retired and signed Rookwood over to Taylor, giving it to him as a gift. Rookwood was subsequently incorporated, with Taylor, the majority shareholder, as president and treasurer.[46] Now, the potter's wheel turned by manpower.

Meanwhile, Fry turned to other artistic callings and was studying in the New York Art Students League, aspiring to become a landscape painter. However, her direction changed when at age thirty-four she received an offer to teach art at Purdue. She would become head of the Industrial Arts Department in 1906.

Simmering in the background of Fry's life at Purdue would be her nearly eight-year fight to protect her atomizer technique. Taylor still refused to honor Fry's patent, and in 1893, she sued Rookwood for patent infringement. The lawsuit split the Cincinnati art community, with artists, art dealers, and museums taking sides in a debate on the business of art.

Judge William Howard Taft issued a final opinion in the case in 1898—in Rookwood's favor. He decided that the process was not patentable on the grounds that while it was a new use for an old tool, the process was not a new one. The blowing of color on pottery had been practiced by the Chinese centuries before. Fry appealed, but in 1900 Taft's decision was upheld.

Nonetheless, Fry's genius had a far-reaching influence on ceramic production in America. Her underglaze spraying process became almost universally used in the ceramic industry.[47] She went on to concentrate her imaginative mind on teaching and championing art at Purdue and in the Lafayette community.

Said to have a keen sense of humor, Fry wrote that at Purdue she "took charge of classes that had made life miserable for the young man who had been in charge." That man was Prof. Ernest Knaufft, who resigned. Fry taught classes in drawing and china painting. She penned:

> The china painting attracted outsiders besides the regular students and our Art Department soon brought the enrollment of the university to a point where we outnumbered our rival—Indiana University.... While at Purdue, I had some very fine students, young women who could do almost anything I asked of them.... Several young women learned that difficult and dangerous process of "etching" which required a strong acid to cut the glaze. For all this work during all the years, I personally did the firing: at first in a charcoal kiln then in a kerosene oil kiln. This is where the enchantment comes. To see a piece go into the kiln dull and come out bright—brings a thrill without compare.
>
> The slogan "Keep the fires alive" appeals to all ceramists, be they potters or decorators.... The uncertainty of what prank the fire will play lures every ceramist on to pursue the undiscovered.[48]

Fry lived in an apartment in Ladies Hall where she also conducted her classes in industrial arts and held a student art exhibit each year for the public. Industrial Arts focused on teaching students practical skills and hands-on learning for careers in woodworking, pottery, upholstery, needlecraft, china painting, and more. There was a suite of rooms for the school of Industrial Arts, including a lecture hall, four rooms for modeling in clay, an office, a library, and two basement rooms for additional work.[49]

Not far from campus was her 1857 birthplace on, as she said, "the edge of the prairie in White County, Indiana." Both her father and grandfather were professional artists who taught her wood carving. She and other women students of her father's carved a screen for the organ built in the Cincinnati Music Hall. Her grandfather Henry carved the throne used by Queen Victoria. Fry had nine siblings, and her family moved to Cincinnati so that her father could teach at the McMicken School of Design where she began training at the age of twelve.

Fry left Purdue in 1892 to work for Lonhuda Pottery Company in Steubenville, Ohio, but returned to the university to teach industrial arts the following year. She exhibited some of her work at the 1893 Chicago World's Fair where she received two medals. She later served on the committee to select work in the style of the Arts and Crafts movement for the Panama Exposition held in San Diego, California, from 1915 to 1917. It was the first time that a Purdue professor had served on such a committee.[50] For several years, Fry taught wood carving each summer at the Chautauqua Institution in New York.

At Purdue, Fry taught with Professor Anna Embree Baker, instructor of wood carving, who married Purdue alumnus and famed type designer Bruce Rogers. One of Fry's students was Lyla Marshall Harcoff, who became a renowned artist in Santa Barbara, California.[51] Fry's sister Lillie Fry Fisher taught art at Purdue from 1917 to 1922. While teaching, Fry continued to exhibit her pottery and other works in exhibitions throughout the country, particularly at the Cincinnati Art Museum and the St. Louis Art Museum. Today, some of Fry's pottery and paintings are preserved in the Smithsonian Institution.

Fry looked beyond campus to bring art to her community and was the guiding light in establishing the Lafayette Art League, holding a meeting to organize the new group in Ladies Hall on September 23, 1898. Prior to the first gathering, she made detailed plans and already had two hundred paid members, a slate of proposed officers, a suggested constitution, and an art exhibit in the works. In 1900, the name of the organization changed to Art Club.[52]

In April 1909, members of the Art Club met to form the Lafayette Art Association.[53] The following month, the association's first annual exhibition, which Fry had secured, was held at the YMCA on Seventh Street in Lafayette, featuring works from the Society of Western Artists.

Fry was elected vice president and Purdue alumnus Judge Henry H. Vinton was president. Board members affiliated with Purdue included President Winthrop E. Stone; Nellie P. Samson, art teacher specializing in wood carving; and Carolyn E. Shoemaker, an English literature professor whom Stone would name Purdue's first dean of women in 1913. Later, William M. Hepburn, dean of Purdue Libraries, served on the board. The Art Club would eventually become today's Art Museum of Greater Lafayette.

In 1918, at the height of World War I, the Purdue Girls' Club decided to purchase a University Service Flag and conferred with Fry about the design. The Purdue Girls' club had been founded by Professor Emma Montgomery McRae in 1907 for female students to "further the Purdue Girl spirit" by holding social

When Laura Anne Fry became a Purdue art professor in 1891, she was one of the most gifted artists of the nineteenth-century Women's Art movement and a patent holder for a revolutionary ceramic glazing technique used by Rookwood Pottery in Cincinnati. Courtesy Public Domain.

events such as luncheons, picnics, and dances.[54] For the flag's design, Fry conceived the idea of having those serving in the war represented by one large blue star and the letters "P.U." with the number of Purdue men who had enlisted indicated below. Gold stars symbolized each Purdue man who had lost his life. President Stone accepted the flag in a ceremony on March 7 in Eliza Fowler Hall. Two men in uniform pulled the Purdue Service Flag over the pipe organ where it was displayed.[55]

By 1922, the university had grown to the extent that not all Purdue faculty knew one another. Some women had a vision for a women's club to foster close relationships. Fry persuaded Lucy Post Coulter, wife of Purdue Dean of the School of Science and Dean of Men Stanley E. Coulter, to call a meeting of the women on campus.

About 125 women, faculty members as well as wives of faculty, met in the Purdue Library on March 16, 1922. By unanimous vote, an organization to promote sociability among the women of the university was approved with Lucy Coulter as president pro tem. She appointed a committee to frame a constitution, create a name, and establish officers. On April 22, 1922, the Purdue Women's Club was founded and still thrives today.[56]

A few months later, Fry retired from Purdue at the age of sixty-five and moved to Terrace Park, a suburb of Cincinnati. Perhaps in reaction to her own struggles for credit and professional recognition, Fry ardently supported other female artists throughout her life. In her writings and lectures, she championed women who spearheaded new developments and experiments in American ceramics.

Three years before her death in 1943 at age eighty-five, Fry wrote of her life's work to the wife of Ross C. Purdy, general secretary of the American Ceramic Society, and said, "I really tried to do only what hundreds of women have done better, i.e. tried to help along. By doing the things that came to my brush and my hand, I had lots of fun and never felt it a burden. It took me many places both here and abroad on journeys of investigation."[57]

HELEN GOLDEN, FIRST FEMALE FACULTY IN ENGINEERING

When Professor Helen Golden left Purdue in 1920, a story in the *Indianapolis News* stated, "Miss Helen Golden, the only woman who ever held a professorship in the engineering department at Purdue University, has resigned as assistant professor of mechanical drawing."[58] Helen taught descriptive geometry[59] where problems are solved in three dimensions by generating two-dimensional views.

Helen began her instructorship in 1906 when the Practical Mechanics Department was headed by her brother Michael Joseph Golden. The Goldens were from a Stratford, Ontario, family of poor Irish immigrants, and they spoke with thick brogues.

Helen Golden, Purdue's first female professor of engineering (*left*), with her brother Michael Golden and sister (*right*) Katherine E. Golden Bitting, who was an 1892 alumna of Purdue and professor of biology. Courtesy Purdue University Archives and Special Collections.

Helen's brother Michael, athletic and fiery with a shock of red hair, came to Purdue in 1884 and struck fear into every freshman mechanics student he taught. Yet, he turned out to be a beloved faculty member. After Michael passed away in 1920, the Practical Mechanics Building at the corner of Northwestern and Grant Streets was renamed Michael Golden Shops. Later it was renamed Michael Golden Laboratories. However, engineering students nicknamed the building "Mike's Castle." The main part of the building was razed in 1982 to build the Maurice G. Knoy Hall of Technology.

Helen and her sister Katherine, who also went by "Katie," walked in the shadow of their flamboyant brother, yet his notoriety must have helped them in obtaining their positions at Purdue. The trio had another sister, Josephine, who was living in West Lafayette for a time, but she passed away in San Francisco, California, in 1935.[60]

Helen and Katherine followed their brother to Purdue where they both earned bachelor's and master's degrees in 1890 and 1892, respectively. Katherine's degrees were in biology, and her graduate degree thesis topic was "Fermentation of Bread." While a student in the School of Science,[61] Helen was on the editorial staff of the *Purdue Exponent*. Her thesis was titled "Germination of Seeds."[62] After graduation, Helen became the assistant principal of a high school in Lawrence, Massachusetts.[63]

Helen returned to Purdue in 1906 to join the faculty. In 1919, she resigned to join the research laboratory of the newly founded Glass Container Association where she utilized her mechanical drawing artistry to illustrate numerous articles. Her sister Katherine Golden Bitting and her husband Arvil worked there as well. Today the association is named the Glass Packaging Institute, the trade association representing the North American glass container industry.[64]

After a lifetime of research and collecting cookbooks, Katherine published her book *Gastronomic Bibliography*. In the book's dedication to her sister Helen, Katherine wrote, "Clean-souled, clear-eyed, unspoiled, discreet, Thou gavs't thy gifts to make Life sweet."[65]

KATHERINE GOLDEN BITTING, KETCHUP RESEARCHER AND GASTRONOMIC BOOK COLLECTOR

Katherine Golden Bitting and her husband conducted groundbreaking research on ketchup to determine how it could be preserved naturally without benzoic acid or sodium benzoate. Former Purdue Professor of Chemistry and Indiana's first state chemist Harvey Wiley charged Katherine and her husband Arvil Bitting with the task of making preservative-free ketchup. He advocated for the passage of the Meat Inspection Act[66] and is known as the father of the Pure Food and Drug Act.

Born in Stratford, Ontario, in 1869, Katherine immigrated to the United States with her family, including her siblings Michael and Helen, who became Purdue renowned. She received her bachelor's degree from the State Normal School in Salem, Massachusetts, studied bacteriology at Massachusetts Institute of Technology, and received a Purdue master's degree in 1892. As a student, she was editor-in-chief of the *Debris* yearbook and president of her class.

While completing her master's thesis, a study on the use of pure yeast in bread, she worked at the Indiana Agricultural Experiment Station at Purdue as an assistant botanist and was hired as an instructor in 1893. Katherine was eventually promoted to assistant professor of biology in 1901, a position she kept until 1904.

Professor Katherine E. Golden Bitting with her colleagues in the School of Science, 1901. Courtesy Purdue University Archives and Special Collections.

When she married her colleague Arvil Bitting, a graduate of Purdue who taught veterinary medicine, Katherine was propelled into a successful personal and professional partnership that lasted four decades and was unusual for a woman of her time. She became a fellow in the American Association for the Advancement of Science, the most prestigious honorary scientific society in the country.

Wiley had been recruited in 1883 to become head of the Division of Chemistry in the US Department of Agriculture. There, he fought for the first federal law to protect the safety of the food supply and to protect the public from dangerous substances then often found in common medicinal elixirs and food preservatives.[67]

In 1906, Arvil Bitting became a special agent for the US Department of Agriculture, stationed in Lafayette. He then became an inspector for the US Bureau of Chemistry, and in September 1907, Katherine was appointed to the position of microanalyst with the bureau and was assigned to work with her husband. Their first joint project was to determine how to make ketchup without added preservatives.

The Bittings created a lab in their home in Lafayette where they used a variety of techniques to examine ketchup made commercially, analyzing more than sixteen hundred bottles. They visited numerous factories that made tomato pulp and ketchup. When they discovered that homemade ketchup survived much longer after opening than did commercial ketchup, the Bittings began collecting ketchup recipes from magazines, journals, and cookbooks to test in their laboratory. They found that homemade ketchup had a heavier body and contained more vinegar, sugar, and spices.

The Bittings concluded that the process for making preservative-free ketchup was simple: Carefully select ripe tomatoes, handle them in a sanitary manner, increase the amount of vinegar, increase the body of the ketchup, and sterilize the finished product. Arvil published their initial findings, "Experiments on the Spoilage of Tomato Ketchup," in January 1909 as the Bureau of Chemistry's *Bulletin 119*. Six years later the couple published two monographs bound together: Arvil's "Ketchup: Methods of Manufacturer" and Katherine's "Microscopic Examination." The end result of their numerous experiments was a preservative-free ketchup that would keep almost indefinitely after opening.[68]

Between 1913 and 1918, Katherine was a microanalyst for the National Canners Association. When World War I began, she collaborated with her husband for one year working in food specifications with the Subsistence Division of the War Department before becoming a bacteriologist with the Glass Container Association.[69] Katherine authored nearly fifty pamphlets on the subject of food preservation, including a forty-nine-page piece titled "The Olive" for the Glass Container Association. Purdue awarded honorary doctor of science degrees to both Katherine and her husband in 1935.

Throughout her life, Katherine collected rare and extraordinary cookbooks. When she died at age sixty-eight in 1937 at her home in San Francisco, her collection of gastronomic literature in a dozen languages from the fifteenth through the twentieth centuries numbered an astonishing 4,346 volumes.[70]

Two years after her death, Arvil finished Katherine's *Gastronomic Bibliography* as a memorial to her. The 750-page book was beautifully printed by the Halle-Cordis Composing Room of San Francisco and sold for $8.50, a top price for the day. He donated her collection to the Library of Congress where it was deemed one of the largest and most exclusive private libraries on a single field of study. Recognizing its great importance, the Library of Congress established the Katherine Golden Bitting Collection of Gastronomy as a separate element among its collections, and it remains as such today.[71]

2

HEALTH STARTS AT HOME

THE VIRGINIA C. MEREDITH INFLUENCE

At the turn of the twentieth century, an unconventional and determined woman was behind the scenes attempting to convince Purdue President Winthrop Stone to offer courses in home economics to bring more women students and faculty to campus. She was Indiana's nationally known "lady farmer," renowned speaker, and prolific writer, Virginia Claypool Meredith.

Meredith led an astonishing life for a woman of her era, or even for a woman of today. She would become the first woman to be appointed to Purdue's Board of Trustees in 1921 and hold significant sway upon the direction of the university.

Meredith's rare early life laid the fertile groundwork for the profound mark she would later make on Purdue, discussed in later chapters, and the state of Indiana. She was born on Maplewood Farm near Connersville, Indiana, in 1848. Her father believed that his daughters should receive the same educational opportunities as his sons. She accompanied her father on horse and wagon rides to his fields and learned about his successful farming and business practices. Little did she know then that she would run a farm on her own.

In 1866, she graduated with honors from Glendale Female College in Glendale, Ohio, a premier private school where wealthy families sent their daughters. Four years later she married Henry Clay Meredith, son of Civil War general

Solomon Meredith, and moved into the general's home, the famous Oakland Farm near Cambridge City, Indiana, today designated a historic landmark.

Within a twelve-year span Meredith's in-laws and husband passed away, leaving her, at age thirty-four, with a choice. She could do what convention suggested for that time and return to her father's home, or she could choose the radical route and carry on the operations of Oakland Farm. She chose the farm, and her path would catapult her into national recognition.[1]

Meredith was a conspicuous sight when she exhibited her livestock at county and state fairs. A woman stockbreeder was unheard of, and sometimes her presence was met with ridicule. Yet, her animals competed well against the livestock bred and shown by men, and she became nationally known for her crop production and livestock operation. Her accomplishments opened doors to speaking engagements at agricultural meetings.

During this time, the education of the farming community was becoming a priority of the Indiana State Board of Agriculture, once served by Meredith's father and husband. The board decided to offer programs called Farmers' Institutes, the forerunner to programs provided later by the Cooperative Extension Service to offer university knowledge to Indiana citizens.

The Indiana General Assembly passed the Farmers' Institute Act of 1889 giving management of the program to Purdue under the leadership of Professor of Agriculture William C. Latta. He was a proponent of women's education and included topics of importance to women at the Farmers' Institutes, inviting women such as Meredith and Purdue Professor of Domestic Economy Emma Pike Ewing to speak.

Meredith is considered the first woman to be hired by Purdue's Agricultural Extension Department, and she became Latta's close colleague. The Farmers' Institutes launched her career as a speaker and writer on topics related to agriculture, the farm home, and community.

Latta wanted to pay Meredith for her speaking engagements, but he was not permitted to do so because of a decision made by the Purdue Board of Trustees. Meredith said, "One of the board members protested against paying any woman for any kind of work." However, eventually she was paid for her contributions.[2]

In 1889, another event occurred that changed Meredith's world dramatically. At the age of forty, Meredith, a widow with no children, adopted her deceased best friend's two children, seven-year-old Mary Lockwood Matthews and her two-year-old brother Meredith, named after Virginia. Mary would grow up to become Purdue's first dean of the School of Home Economics.

Meredith gained national prominence in 1893 when she was appointed vice chair of the Board of Lady Managers for the World's Columbian Exposition, also known as the Chicago World's Fair. The board determined how contributions by women would be managed at the exposition and bestowed awards upon women.

Three years later, Meredith joined governors and other dignitaries to speak at the Inter-State Agricultural Institute at Vicksburg, Mississippi. Her speech was groundbreaking because before that time in the South, it was considered inappropriate for a woman to speak in public. Meredith's speech captivated the audience, and during the final ceremonies she was given a gold medal engraved with the words "Queen of American Agriculture." It was a "crowning" that would remain with her for life, as she would often be introduced with this regal nomenclature.[3] Today that medal is preserved in Purdue University Archives and Special Collections.

Land-grant universities were among the first institutions to offer home economics and domestic science programs in the 1890s. Latta enlisted Meredith to help garner backing for such a program at Purdue. When Meredith spoke at Farmers' Institutes, she made appeals for special training for homemaking. Her words were a revelation to the farm women in the audience who thought of their daily tasks as merely toil and not something that could be studied at a university for the betterment of society.

Latta thought that if he offered what were called "Winter Short Courses" at Purdue with topics of importance to women and they attended, President Stone would be convinced that there would be interest in a home economics department at the university. But, alas, the courses were not well attended, and the idea backfired. Stone was still hesitant to establish the department.[4]

In 1897, Meredith and her two children headed to the University of Minnesota, where she became the preceptress of the School of Agriculture and started a home economics program. Fifteen-year-old Mary and ten-year-old Meredith moved into a new women's residence hall with their adoptive mother. Mary Matthews became the first woman to earn a bachelor's degree in home economics from the University of Minnesota in 1904. Meanwhile, while Purdue had a Department of Domestic Economy, it had not yet established a home economics program as so many land-grant universities were doing in the United States.

The synchronicity of events regarding home economics was buzzing around the country with the formation of the historic Lake Placid Conferences, a national, yearly conference held from 1899 to 1908 designed to help establish home economics as a field of study. The first conference, held in New York's Adirondack

Mountains, was attended by Ellen Swallow Richards, the founder of "home economics"—a term coined there.

In years to come, Richards would have a special connection to Purdue. As an international expert in water quality, Richards was the first woman instructor at the Massachusetts Institute of Technology, teaching there until her death. She taught Purdue's Andrey Abraham "A. A." Potter during her time there. Affectionately referred to as the "Dean of Deans,"[5] Potter arrived at Purdue from Kansas State Agricultural College in 1920 and became a legendary dean of the School of Engineering.

Potter often told stories of what it was like to be entertained in the Richards's household as a student. He held the study of home economics in high regard because of his esteem for Richards and the fact that his wife had a degree in domestic science. Thus, later, Potter and Mary L. Matthews developed a special kinship, and he was her avid supporter as she developed Purdue's Department of Home Economics.[6] In 1968, Potter's daughter Helen would be appointed professor in the Department of Home Management and Family Economics at Purdue.[7]

Those who attended the Lake Placid Conference began a study of home sanitation. They wanted to develop a body of knowledge for new domestic science departments that were forming at colleges, and they believed that home economics should not be confused with "household arts," such as dusting, cleaning, and mending.[8] Meredith spoke at the Lake Placid Conferences in July 1900. Her speech was titled "What Agricultural Colleges May Do for the Farmer's Daughter."[9]

Many land-grant universities followed the recommendations of the Lake Placid Conferences to create departments of home economics. The conferences spawned the founding in 1909 of the American Home Economics Association, a national umbrella organization for home economics subgroups that would be started in each state.[10] Today, the organization is named the American Association of Family and Consumer Sciences.

By 1902, Latta had attempted and failed at numerous strategies to form a home economics curriculum at Purdue, and he was becoming discouraged. Meredith aided Latta by lobbying President Stone using her past professorship in home economics at the University of Minnesota as leverage. Finally, Stone reconsidered, and Purdue's Department of Household Economics in the School of Science was created in 1905. It is not known what finally swayed Stone, but conceivably he was experiencing political pressure to establish a home economics course, as Purdue was one of the last land-grant institutions to do so.

Virginia Claypool Meredith became the first female member of Purdue's Board of Trustees in 1921. She advocated for Purdue to establish courses in home economics to bring more women students to the university. She was the adoptive mother of Mary Lockwood Matthews, first dean of the School of Home Economics, a root of today's College of Health and Human Sciences. Courtesy of Purdue University Archives and Special Collections.

Ivy F. Harner, a graduate of the School of Domestic Economy at the Kansas State Agricultural College, was named director. The four-year course led to a bachelor of science degree, and, according to Stone, the instruction was "comparable in scope and thoroughness with the scientific and engineering school of the university."[11]

A brochure outlined the curriculum that included chemistry, bacteriology, and physics, all taught in relation to their application in running a household.

Academic subjects included sanitary science, industrial biology, geology, physiology, hygiene and nutrition, economics, dietetics, and textiles, among others.[12]

Members of the faculty were trailblazing, early Purdue female leaders, including Emma Montgomery McRae of the Department of Literature, Pauline Mariotte-Davies of the Department of French, Laura Anne Fry and Nellie Phillips Samson of the Department of Art, and Caroline Shoemaker of the Department of English who in 1913 would be appointed Purdue's first part-time dean of women.[13]

The early home economics courses laid the groundwork for future academic and research at Purdue that are vital today: nutrition science, hospitality and tourism management, consumer science, family and child development, public health, nursing, psychological sciences, art and design, apparel design, and more.

Household economics was a rigorous study of the sciences balanced with art, language, literature, history, and English. The curriculum also offered training to meet the demand for teachers.[14] A laboratory equipped for the study of food materials and food preparation was located in a wing of Ladies Hall. Each student was assigned a desk supplied with water, gas, and utensils for use in experiments. Coal and gas ranges were provided.[15]

Students also spent time in art studios, where they learned drawing, sketching, china decoration, and wood carving. The department's brochure stated: "The work in this department is calculated not merely to train in execution but also to cultivate artistic taste and discrimination."[16]

MARY LOCKWOOD MATTHEWS ARRIVES

Today, home economics tends to be disregarded as a serious discipline, but that's partly because its founder, Ellen Swallow Richards, was so effective in achieving her objectives in establishing prevalent standards for health, nutrition, and sanitation. Standards we may take for granted now.

Richards had "'faith in science as a cure-all' and believed that the application of scientific principles to domestic life would improve living conditions, especially for the working class."[17] In essence, if the homemaker understood the scientific principles of nutrition and sanitation, then humanity would be healthier and more productive. Health started at home.

Professor Mary Lockwood Matthews was hired as an instructor in home economics extension in 1910. She became the first female academic dean at Purdue when she was named dean of home economics in 1926. Courtesy Purdue Archives and Special Collections.

Richards wrote, "The quality of life depends upon the ability of society to teach its members how to live in harmony with their environment—defined first as family, then the community, then the world and its resources."[18] Her statement, written in the late 1800s, resonates still in the mission of Purdue Extension.

The Cooperative Extension Service is one of the nation's largest providers of scientific research-based information and education that takes the university to the people, extending academic knowledge into the state. Extension is a network of colleges, universities, and the US Department of Agriculture, serving communities and counties across America.

Mary Lockwood Matthews was a grand follower of Ellen Swallow Richards's philosophies. Tall and raven haired, Matthews first brought her deep reverence for home economics to Purdue as an extension agent. She was born in Pewee Valley, Kentucky, in 1882 and adopted at age seven by Virginia Meredith.

In 1906, the School of Agriculture, across the street from Ladies Hall on Purdue's young campus, was organizing its outreach efforts of Farmers' Institutes as extension work within the Agricultural Experiment Station. George I. Christie was named director and, with his booming voice, was said to be "the preacher of the gospel of the science of agriculture."[19] He did not need the era's traditional megaphone when speaking to a large group. Matthews had become acquainted with Christie while working with her mother at Farmers' Institutes.

In 1910, Christie hired Matthews, age twenty-eight, as an instructor in home economics extension within the School of Agriculture. In the first year, there were thirty-three domestic science demonstrations conducted throughout Indiana that reached four thousand Indiana women.[20] The next year, Matthews stayed on campus to teach home economics during summer school. There were about forty female students at Purdue.[21]

When the Clore Act of 1911 was passed by the Indiana General Assembly, it established the Department of Agricultural Extension at Purdue and became a defined program within the Agricultural Experiment Station. It also brought an end to Farmers' Institutes.[22] The department began informal education programs off-campus with field demonstrations for farmers and home management demonstrations for rural women.

Purdue's first head of the Department of Household Economics, Ivy Harner, had resigned in 1908 to serve as head of the Domestic Science Department of the Louisiana Industrial Institute. Henrietta Calvin, from Kansas Agricultural College, succeeded Harner as head. When she arrived at Purdue, she was a widow raising five children.[23] In 1912, Calvin moved on to become dean of home economics for Oregon State University, and Mary Matthews was appointed head of Purdue's Department of Household Economics in the School of Science, beginning her forty-one-year career at the university.[24]

Matthews would lead the charge to educate females and hire female faculty, while another woman would soon lead the way to reach rural wives and mothers through the backroads of Indiana—Lella Reed Gaddis.

LELLA REED GADDIS, A STOLEN SPARKLER

With her perfect posture, can-do spirit, and direct manner, Lella Reed Gaddis was destined to be handpicked for a singular role at Purdue. Described as "a real sparkler," Gaddis was appointed Purdue's first state leader of home demonstration in the Agricultural Extension Department in 1914.

Gaddis had taken Purdue summer school short courses organized by Mary Matthews in 1910. Originally from a farm in Rossville, Indiana, Gaddis and her sister Bertha "Kate," a Lafayette schoolteacher, were good friends with the director of the Department of Agricultural Extension, George Christie.

The year Matthews became head of the Department of Household Economics, Gaddis, age thirty-five, enrolled at Purdue. The interweaving of longtime, close relationships between Christie and Matthews and Christie and Gaddis may have "stirred the pot" of hard feelings about where the jurisdiction of household economics belonged when it became a part of Agricultural Extension. At this time, Purdue's campus was prime green pasture dotted with a few redbrick buildings; the faculty was small in number; and the climate was fresh with growth and possibilities as each department defined its purpose.

The reserved Matthews and the dynamic Gaddis had a working relationship. In 1914, Gaddis helped Matthews with summer school classes to train the first home economics vocational teachers in Indiana.[25] Matthews assigned Gaddis the task of setting up an exhibit at the Indiana State Fair in September. That same month, President Winthrop Stone offered Gaddis the position as Purdue's first state leader of home demonstration in the Agricultural Extension Department. Gaddis and the agents she hired would travel the state's backroads to take the knowledge of Purdue's Department of Household Economics to isolated, rural Indiana women by conducting home demonstrations. She accepted the position, even though she had been offered the same post at Pennsylvania State University for more money.[26]

The Smith-Lever Act signed by President Woodrow Wilson in 1914 authorized the establishment of extension programs at the county, state, and federal levels and held a mandate to give instruction in home economics across the nation. The act required matching funds from state and local sources as a form of cost sharing. Thus, it became known as the *Cooperative* Extension Service. It was a partnership between the US Department of Agriculture and land-grant universities. Wilson deemed it "one of the most significant and far-reaching measures for

Lella Reed Gaddis was appointed the first state leader of home demonstration when Purdue's Agricultural Extension Department was established in 1914. Gaddis and the agents she hired traveled the Indiana countryside taking the teachings of Purdue to women, many of them isolated on rural farms. Courtesy Purdue University Archives and Special Collections.

the education of adults ever adopted by the government." The foundational idea was to "help people help themselves" by "taking the university to the people."[27]

Matthews assumed Gaddis, her newly created position, and its funding would be under her Department of Household Economics; after all, she had trained Gaddis. But her thinking was forcibly changed one clandestine night.

The story weaves like a fable as told in 2010 by Purdue Dean Emeritus of the School of Home Economics Eva Goble,[28] then age one hundred. One night in 1914, while the campus slumbered, the "Purdue Ag Boys" hooked up a team of horses to a wagon, climbed aboard, and trekked north across the dirt thoroughfare that was State Street to where Ladies Hall towered like Rapunzel's castle.

The Ag Boys entered Ladies Hall and found the office they wanted. To the wagon they carried out the furniture, files, and records they believed should belong on "their side" of State Street. They hurried aboard the wagon, gave a yank to the reins, and the horses moved the office of Lella Gaddis, the new state leader of home demonstration, to the "Ag side."

The following day, Gaddis reported to the Department of Agricultural Extension. She no longer worked for the Department of Household Economics headed by Mary Matthews. Matthews was incensed; Gaddis had been stolen from her. It is then that the paths of Matthews and Gaddis were divided. They would go forth with the same mission to educate women, but in different Purdue realms—Matthews on campus and Gaddis throughout the Indiana heartland.

Women in the United States did not yet have the right to vote in political elections. The positions held by Gaddis and Matthews within the uniquely American trifecta of the land-grant university, Agricultural Experiment Station, and Cooperative Extension Service were made possible by a government in which they had no say.

More than fifty years after the Ag Boys allegedly "stole" Gaddis from Matthews, home economics extension would return to the School of Home Economics in 1967, the year before both Matthews and Gaddis passed away.[29]

Today, Purdue Extension continues to influence countless lives by providing education to people of all ages throughout Indiana. Portraits of both Mary Lockwood Matthews and Lella Reed Gaddis[30] are displayed in Matthews Hall, formerly known as the Home Economics Building, renamed in honor of Matthews in 1976.

A NETWORK FOR INDIANA WOMEN

Once Mary Matthews was appointed head of the Department of Household Economics in 1912, she worked to bring more women to Purdue and cultivate her program. Matthews was an early feminist before the term was coined and a protagonist for women's suffrage.

Matthews and her mother, Virginia Meredith, wanted to bolster interest in the home economics program throughout Indiana and at the same time better women's lives through a network of support. Thus, they created the Indiana Home Economics Association (IHEA) on January 17, 1913, during the annual Agricultural Conference at Purdue.

Matthews and Meredith called a meeting of a small group of women to discuss the possibility of organizing the IHEA to encourage more county educational groups for homemakers and to promote the teaching of domestic science in public schools. They met in Professor of Agriculture William Latta's office. Meredith was elected president and Matthews was on the executive committee. Fifty-eight women who were attending the Agricultural Conference became members that day.[31]

Members of the IHEA petitioned for legislation that established funds and offices for the early extension workers in each county. The IHEA became a lobbying force for females, extension, and home economics, while providing rural women with an educational and social group to which they could bond, often for a lifetime.

Meredith was president of the IHEA until she was succeeded by Matthews in January 1917. Matthews was president until 1920 when for the first time someone other than a staff member of Purdue was elected. From that year forward, women from various Indiana counties have been elected president of the IHEA.[32]

The IHEA was a groundbreaking, profoundly influential entity for women that would grow monumentally for decades, launching thousands of Home Economics Clubs in Indiana, many of which still exist today. The IHEA is now called the Indiana Extension Homemakers Association.

Each year after the IHEA was founded, members of Indiana's Home Economics Clubs traveled from throughout the state to Purdue to attend the annual Home Economics Conferences originally held for a week in January. The meeting was later named the Home and Family Conference and held in the summer.

For many women who attended during the first part of the twentieth century, the meeting was their only time away from home and family the entire year and their first experience with a university environment. Meredith, Matthews, and Gaddis all spoke at the conferences. Meals were served in the Home Economics Cafeteria, which was novel for many women who rarely ate anything but home-cooked meals. The women marveled at such exotic dishes as tomato aspic. Today, the annual Home and Family Conference is held near Indianapolis.

3

HOME ECONOMICS POWERHOUSES

EDITH GAMBLE, EDUCATING WOMEN IN INSTITUTIONAL MANAGEMENT

Mary "Edith" Gamble was appointed an assistant in home economics in 1911 and would become pivotal in the development of Purdue's Institutional Management Department, which would become the School of Hospitality and Tourism Management within the College of Health and Human Sciences. Gamble was from Logansport, Indiana, graduated from Purdue in 1913, and earned her master's degree from Columbia University.

Through Gamble's providence, the pedigree of Purdue's Institutional Management Department was established in 1916. New courses in home economics were announced "for those girls who wish to make a special study of food and nutrition, thereby becoming fitted for such positions as dietitians in hospitals, managers of school lunch rooms, and specialists in food analysis work."[1]

The new curriculum was the launch of careers for women in service to the community by teaching management skills for institutions rather than just the home. While today it may look like a natural step to extend the skills in managing a home to be used for the public good, it was no small step for the time. Few careers were open to women, and this new idea of community involvement as a profession, rather than volunteer work, opened a new world of opportunities.

Dean of the School of Home Economics Gladys E. Vail, *right*, honors Professor Mary Edith Gamble with the first "Distinguished Alumni" distinction presented by the school on May 2, 1964. Gamble was the first head of the Department of Institutional Management, beginning in 1926. Courtesy Purdue University Archives and Special Collections.

In 1918, Gamble persuaded President Winthrop Stone to allow her to organize classes in foods that emphasized "group feeding," leading to the establishment of laboratory programs known as the Home Economics Food Service in Ladies Hall, the ancestor of today's John Purdue Room in Marriott Hall.[2]

Stone told Gamble that she could offer a course in group feeding only if it did not cost the university "one cent." The class of students served two lunches per week and never once operated at a loss. Each student was required to sell forty tickets per meal at a cost of forty cents each.[3]

As the new group feeding endeavor perked along, Gamble taught a course in elementary principles of dietetics to a junior class of nurses from Lafayette Home Hospital.[4] She became an assistant professor in 1919, and then took a leave of absence the following year to co-manage the Anchorage Tea House in Eugene, Oregon.[5] Gamble partnered with Mary S. Kieffer, who had opened the tea room "on the millrace."[6]

The millrace was a flowing stream at the center of the University of Oregon that originally powered a flour mill, sawmill, and furniture factory.[7] Gamble honed her skills and offered her proficiency in institutional management at the Anchorage Tea House, then brought her experience back to Purdue in 1925. Three years later, she was made full professor and head of the Institutional Management Program and would remain in that position until her retirement in 1953. She and Dean of Home Economics Mary Matthews were good friends as well as colleagues.

Gamble celebrated her ninetieth birthday with a cake-cutting ceremony on September 19, 1972, where she lived in Comfort Nursing Home in Lafayette. She was visited by close friends, relatives, and members of the Purdue women's choir, the Purduettes, who fêted her in song. Later that day Mary Edith Gamble passed away, having made her mark on Purdue and the lives of its students that still resonates today in the School of Hospitality and Tourism Management.[8]

HOME ECONOMICS ANSWERS NEEDS DURING WORLD WAR I

Virginia C. Meredith moved from her farm in Cambridge City, Indiana, to 356 West State Street in West Lafayette to live with her daughter Mary L. Matthews, then the head of the Department of Household Economics. It was 1916 and Meredith was sixty-seven.[9] Her relocation marked the turning point of the unprecedented Purdue accomplishments as a woman (and an "older" woman, as well) that she would make in the following two decades.

The conservation of food at the family table was lauded as key in helping win World War I. The rally cry on propaganda posters was "Food will win the war! Don't waste it!" President Woodrow Wilson said, "To provide adequate supplies for the coming year is of absolutely vital importance to the conduct of the war, and without a very conscientious elimination of waste and very strict economy in our food consumption, we cannot hope to fulfill this primary duty."

As the state leader of home demonstration in Purdue's Agricultural Extension Service, Lella Gaddis hired emergency agents to help teach Indiana women how to conserve food and "serve the cause of freedom." The essential foods to conserve were wheat, meat, fats, and sugar.

The war brought extension agents across the country together with a unified national agenda as the patriotic leaders of a vital war campaign. Conserving food and using every drop and morsel was preached across the United States. In a time when a family's food—home-baked bread, preserved vegetables from the garden, for example—was prepared from scratch rather than purchased in a grocery store, Gaddis and her agents made it known in Indiana that waste was a no-no; utilizing the leftovers was mandatory.

Mary Matthews was also in the food conservation trenches through her Department of Household Economics. She was named director of home economics for the Indiana Food Administration and chair of the Home Economics Committee under the Indiana State Council of Defense.[10] Her students arranged a food exhibit for a war conference given at Central Presbyterian Church in Lafayette on Valentine's Day, 1918, to "illustrate the use of substitute foods in order to meet the requests of the food administration."[11]

Edith Gamble's students conducted research in the home economics laboratory on recipes that used substituted foods, and she created a series of bulletins known as *Emergency Food Leaflets*. The first, titled "Liberty Breads," included bread recipes that used substitutes for flour, such as cooked potatoes. All recipes were tested in the home economics laboratories because many of those that appeared in magazines and newspapers of the time were incorrect and produced a cooking failure. Other leaflets in the series were "Use of Less Sugar," "Substitutes for Meat," "The Use of Fish," "Menus for Meatless Days," and "Menus for Wheatless Days."[12]

Matthews oversaw the implementation of a tuition-free, five-day "war school" for women through Purdue's home economics department in June 1918. She invited Indiana women who were "anxious to carry out regulations regarding food substitution, canning, drying, and preserving." Held on campus, the course also taught women ways to manage their households so they could devote more time to outside activities such as Red Cross relief work. There were courses on how to make over garments, remove stains, and clean and dye material for make-over purposes.[13]

Months before World War I ended, the United States and the world experienced another kind of battle—the most serious flu epidemic of the twentieth century that killed more people than the Great War itself.[14] Purdue's Extension home demonstrations agents took the lead to aid county health departments during the 1918 influenza emergency (akin to the COVID-19 pandemic that hit more than one hundred years later in 2019). In many cases, they served as nurses and dietitians. Lella Gaddis was in charge of a health campaign that included training women in the care of the sick and better nutrition for children.

4
A "ROOM" OF ONE'S OWN

THE BEST IN THE COUNTRY!

By 1919, Purdue's female students were disheartened by the poor classroom conditions they endured in Ladies Hall. They had outgrown the space; it was unsafe; plaster was falling from the ceiling; and the lighting was dismal. Dean of Women Carolyn Shoemaker wrote an essay for the *Debris* yearbook commending the "promise of a Woman's Building." Shoemaker was referring to the new Home Economics Building that would be constructed under Mary Matthews's leadership in 1922 at the corner of West State and University Streets, today known as Matthews Hall.

Virginia Meredith would play a key role in advocating for a new Woman's Building and the Department of Physical Education for women after she received her historic appointment as the first woman to serve on Purdue's Board of Trustees in 1921, the year the Indiana General Assembly passed a bill requiring the governor to select at least one woman among the six appointments.

Meredith attended her first board meeting in July 1921 already knowing many of her male colleagues, including Purdue alumnus and benefactor David E. Ross. Meredith's first meeting proved momentous because one of the agenda items was a vote to authorize the plans for the construction of the Home Economics

Building—the structure that fifty years later would be renamed after her daughter.[1] Construction began that fall on a site just west of Ladies Hall and partly occupied by a greenhouse, which was relocated. The cost of the building was about $200,000, which would be about three million dollars in 2024.

An *Exponent* story stated, "The building will be a three-story structure of brick, finished in terra cotta and stone. The cafeteria will be in the north end, with the auditorium above.... Such a building with its increased and modern facilities and equipment is greatly needed and should prove to be an indispensable asset to the course in Home Economics at Purdue. Present conditions are too unfavorable for the inducement of more coeds for the course, and it is expected that the building to be erected will undoubtedly prove to be a stimulant to coed enrollment here."[2]

As the foundation was built, Mary Matthews's book *Elementary Home Economics* was published in 1921 by Little Brown and Company. It was a highly successful textbook and the only one adopted in Indiana for the teaching of seventh- and eighth-grade domestic science classes for more than twenty years. Matthews wrote the book's preface on October 13, 1920, her thirty-eighth birthday. After the book's success, Matthews said, "My royalties amounted to more than my salary, but of course salaries were small then, and I had little competition for there were only a few home economics books to be had."[3]

The Classical Revival–style Home Economics Building opened in 1922. The auditorium had seating for three hundred. Today, it's the oldest auditorium on campus. The cafeteria, named the Spruce Room after the spruce trees that grew outside its doors, served as a training laboratory for students in Edith Gamble's institutional management courses. At that time, Purdue was one of few colleges and universities to offer a food service enterprise providing students with real-world experience.[4]

The Board of Trustees enjoyed the first lunch served in the Spruce Room, prepared and served entirely by students in lunchroom management.[5] Dean of Engineering Andrey Abraham (A. A.) Potter was the first to give a lecture in the auditorium on November 8, 1922. Arranged by the Home Economics Club, the address was for all women students. Potter spoke on "How to Get the Most Out of College."[6]

The public opening of the building was held the following spring. The *Exponent* touted the building as "the best of its kind in the country!" The day was brimming with lectures on home furnishings, demonstrations of modern labor-saving devices, and delicious food. A fashion show was given by students wearing coats and gowns they had made themselves, and students in the millinery department exhibited their hat creations.[7]

One can imagine Matthews, Meredith, faculty, and students beaming with pride and anticipation as the doors were thrown open to the brick structure with the words "Home Economics Building" carved in stone above its entrance. Today, those words that meant so much to so many women are covered by a stone slab, presumably placed there when the building was renamed Matthews Hall in 1976. However, in the annals of Purdue history, home economics and the name Matthews are essentially interchangeable, forever tied.

MARY MATTHEWS OPENS PURDUE'S FIRST PRACTICE HOUSE

In the fall of 1919, Purdue saw the largest enrollment of women in its history. Of the 260 on campus, 240 were enrolled in home economics. Of the twenty non–home economics women, four majored in agriculture, one in civil engineering, and the remainder in pharmacy and chemical engineering.[8]

Also that year, Purdue's master's program in home economics began, and Matthews debuted a new way of learning for home economics students emerging in universities across the country called Practice House.

The Practice House was a full-fledged house that acted as a laboratory where senior students in home economics could practice the management of a home. Also known as Home Management House, it provided a hands-on environment for the student to apply what she had learned in the classroom. Today, the experience might be termed a "clinical." Purdue rented a nine-room, two-story house with a front porch that had previously been occupied by Alpha Chi Omega Sorority at 115 Waldron Street, down the street from where Matthews and Virginia Meredith lived. Students planned and purchased the furnishings with many pieces donated.

Every thirty days, a different group of six students and a chaperone lived in the Practice House and acted in six rotating capacities—hostess, housekeeper, assistant housekeeper, cook, assistant cook, and waitress. The supervisor checked the work performed each day. Laura J. Cheney was an early overseer. The women paid $10 monthly rent plus the cost of their meals at twenty-three cents each and continued to take classes while living in the Practice House. Mathews believed that the students' class/lab workload would not "wear them out" because the house

Professor Mary Louise Foster (*right*), much-loved supervisor in the Practice House on Waldron Street, demonstrates a vacuum to one of her students in 1956. Courtesy Mary Louise Foster.

had many labor-saving appliances, such as "a fireless gas stove, a kitchen cabinet, a high stool, a wheel tray, and a suction sweeper."[9]

Professor Mary Louise Foster was a much-loved supervisor in the Practice House on Waldron beginning in the 1950s and until the concept's demise in the late 1970s. Many students dreaded their time in the house because they had to temporarily move out of their residence hall or sorority. They did not like leaving their friends and daily lives or the added expense.

If a student was married, she left her husband and children to live in the house. In the 1960s that changed with an "innovative" idea by Professor Cleo Fitzsimmons, who was head of the Department of Home Management and Family Economics. Married women were allowed to attend lectures, meet in small-group discussion seminars, and then apply the principles they learned in class to manage their own homes.[10]

Foster predicted the future in a 1968 *Indianapolis Star* article. By that time there were four houses on campus. Foster said, "Studies indicate that young women of this age group will have household help a good many years of their married lives. They will not only be the homemaker, but will also be a wage earner, away from home and finding it necessary to employ someone to follow their directions for caring for their homes."[11]

In fall 1978, a stay in a Home Management House or the "residency requirement" was no longer compulsory. By then, the School of Home Economics was renamed the School of Consumer and Family Sciences.[12]

NO PRACTICE BABY AT PURDUE

On campuses across the country, Practice Houses were opening as new educational ventures. Time, motion, and fatigue studies within the homes examined such tasks as making beds and ironing cloth napkins. Matthews embraced the latest teaching methods in home economics, but there was one "clinical experience" common at other universities that she did *not* implement at Purdue—the "practice baby."

Many Home Management Houses at other universities, such as Cornell, had a resident baby that was the center of the household called the "practice baby." For thirty days, a senior woman, the "practice mother," was in complete charge of the baby, kept records of his or her development, and did the child's laundry.

After that student's time was finished, another student became the child's practice mother for thirty days. Essentially, the practice baby had a new mother every month. A university psychology instructor visited the Practice House regularly to observe the baby and determine if he or she was on track developmentally.[13]

Local orphanages and child welfare organizations loaned the practice babies to the universities for a year or more. After their practice time, the children were returned to their orphanages for adoption. Cornell University began incorporating practice babies into their curriculum in 1919. Prospective adoptive parents desired practice babies because presumably they had been raised according to the most advanced scientific principles. The practice mothers kept scrapbooks with photographs of the baby's milestones. The babies often arrived at the house ill or undernourished and left healthy—at least physically.[14]

In years to come, research in early childhood development would prove that a baby needs a primary bond with a single caregiver. In 1954 the child welfare officials at the Illinois Department of Public Welfare declared that the practice house was not a "normal setting" for a baby. Babette Penner, director of the Women's Service Division of United Charities, said, "Imagine what anxieties there are in a child who is given a bottle in twelve or more pairs of arms."[15]

It is not known why Matthews did not incorporate a practice baby in the Practice House experience at Purdue. One can speculate that as an adopted child herself, she had an intuitive sense of its inappropriate nature. She did add a new course in 1922 titled "Home Nursing and Child Care" taught by Laura Partch.[16]

MATTHEWS, FIRST FEMALE DEAN OF A SCHOOL

The Department of Home Economics separated from the School of Science in 1926 to become the School of Home Economics. Mary Lockwood Matthews was named the first dean of the new school, and any school on campus. At the time, there were 13 faculty members, 368 undergraduate students, and 3 graduate students.[17] No doubt Virginia Meredith was proud of her daughter, who would lead the school she had spent so many years striving to establish. Home Economics would make its mark for decades to come in the areas of foods and nutrition, child development, clothing and textiles, institutional management, and more. Under Matthews's leadership, Purdue's School of Home Economics would become the second largest in the nation.[18]

School of Home Economics powerhouses gather under the portrait of Virginia C. Meredith. *Left to right*: Professor of Institutional Management Mary Edith Gamble; Professor of Clothing and Textiles Amy L. Howe; Professor, Head of Foods and Nutrition, creator of the famous Purdue Recipe File Amy Irene Bloye; Mary Lockwood Matthews, the first dean of the new school, and, thus, the first female dean of any school on campus; Head of the Department of Applied Design Laurentza Schantz-Hansen. Courtesy Mary Louise Foster.

AMY BLOYE, CREATOR OF THE RECIPE FILE AND INDIANA'S FIRST DIETETICS MAJOR

Amy Irene Bloye came to Purdue as a home economics instructor in 1918 and headed Foods and Nutrition until 1953. Under Bloye's direction, the dietetics program began in 1923 and offered the first dietetics major in Indiana.

Bloye created the famous Purdue Recipe File, a beautifully crafted oak box with a hinged lid and dovetailed corners that held the collection of 400 recipes used by the students and faculty of the School of Home Economics. The recipes were printed on index cards and divided among twenty-four subjects from "breads" to "vegetables." The file was copyrighted by Bloye in 1927 and revised in 1936.[19] Women purchased the Purdue Recipe File at Southworth's Book Store in West Lafayette.[20]

5

LATE TO THE GAME—
PHYSICAL EDUCATION

GERTRUDE BILHUBER, FIRST INSTRUCTOR OF WOMEN'S PHYSICAL EDUCATION

The Athletic Conference of American College Women (ACACW) was founded in 1917 through the Women's Athletic Association at the University of Wisconsin. Interest in athletics had greatly increased for women, yet the development of women's athletics was still incomplete. Delegates convened from twenty colleges at the first National Conference of the ACACW in March.[1] Purdue was not represented, as it did not yet offer physical education for women. One of the resolutions passed by the organization was that the Women's Athletic Association in universities and colleges have a close relationship with the departments of physical education for women.[2]

Virginia Meredith, who had become the first female member of Purdue's board of trustees in 1921, advocated for physical education for women at Purdue as ardently as she pushed for the establishment of home economics courses. In 1923, Purdue's new president was Edward C. Elliott, who was appointed after Winthrop Stone's shocking death from a fall atop Eon Mountain in the Canadian Rockies.[3] Elliott proposed that the Purdue Board of Trustees make a plan for the physical welfare of all students, and a new male staff member had been hired in the Department of Physical Education to establish physical education for women.[4]

Yet, Meredith could see that another male instructor was not the answer to lead women in the area of physical education, and board minutes from June 12, 1923, stated, "Mrs. Meredith said that there should be a woman director of physical education for women students."

Purdue was the only institution of its size that did not provide organized physical education for women.[5] Dean of Women Carolyn Shoemaker wrote a letter to President Elliott dated April 9, 1924, stating, "The girls are anxious to have compulsory physical education next year. This means that the basement of Ladies Hall must be put in shape; and also, that a woman be in charge of athletics."[6] Meredith and Shoemaker continually and tirelessly advocated for female students to be offered opportunities at Purdue.

After Shoemaker's letter was read and discussed at the trustees' meeting, Virginia Meredith, the lone female voice on the board, offered a resolution to authorize a credited course in physical training for women students be established and be taught by "a competent and experienced woman director."

Meredith was a wise woman and her resolution outlined how she wanted each aspect of the program to equal that of the men's physical education department, which had been established ten years earlier. The parity of the program she wanted included the compensation of the women's director, who she said "shall be paid a salary the same as that paid to men for similar service."[7]

The motion was not seconded. Alternatively, Trustee David Ross moved that President Elliott submit plans at the next meeting for the physical education of women. Ross's motion was carried unanimously. Six months after Meredith's thwarted resolution, Elliott presented plans for remodeling the former Electrical Engineering Building for use as a women's gymnasium. Meredith moved to accept the plans to be completed by the opening of school in 1925. It was seconded and unanimously approved. Gertrude Bilhuber was appointed Purdue's first Associate Professor of Physical Education for Women, and she would lead the program in its infancy.[8]

HELEN W. HAZELTON AND WOMEN'S PHYSICAL EDUCATION

In the first year of women's physical education at Purdue headed by Professor Gertrude Bilhuber twelve activities were offered including rifle shooting, "natural" dancing (dancing that emphasizes the body's natural capabilities and emotional expressions, rather than rigid techniques), clogging, fencing, and quoits (a game, similar to horseshoes, in which a ring is thrown to encircle a stake). The "We Girls Rifle Team" competed in intramural contests in the armory under the auspices of the Field Artillery Reserve Officers Training Corps.[9]

By 1928, all freshmen and sophomore women were required to take physical education and a one-semester course in hygiene. Two staff members taught a total of 500 students.[10] That year the department conducted the first High School Play Day in Indiana. More than one hundred women participated from neighboring high schools. Two weeks later, Purdue hosted ten colleges in the state at its first All-College Play Day, which included intramural sports and games, a banquet, dance, teachers' conference, and a meeting of the State Association of the Women's Athletic Association (WAA). Purdue's WAA possessed the largest membership in the state.[11]

After four successful years of building the department, Bilhuber resigned, and Helen W. Hazelton was appointed head in the fall of 1929. Students called her "Haz." She was said to be one of those teachers "who scared the devil out of students."[12]

Yet in her photos, Hazelton had a pleasant smile and an attractive swoop of bangs. She could easily walk down a twenty-first-century street and look of the time. Under her headship, the department flourished for thirty-four years. She established herself as a leader in her profession both nationally and internationally until her retirement in 1963.

Hazelton added courses in applied kinesiology to the curriculum. In 1929, physical examinations became a requirement for all new women students, and a course in physical education leading to a bachelor's degree was inaugurated.

Swimming was popular, yet female students were at a disadvantage with no pool of their own. They used the men's pool in the Memorial Gymnasium, which presented a sticky wicket—the only entrance to the pool was through the men's dressing room. This dilemma was solved in 1931 when a women's dressing room was constructed on the south side of the building.

Purdue's chief financial and business officer, Robert Bruce (R. B.) Stewart, donated a cabin on his property for the exclusive use of women students. Barbara Ellen Joy, a well-known camping specialist, came to Purdue to offer an intensive week-long workshop.[13] Joy founded and co-directed Joy Camps, a summer camp near Hazelhurst, Wisconsin. Joy believed in the importance of practical life experience. Her camps trained women in the use of hatchets and

Professor Helen Hazelton, head of the Department of Physical Education for Women (1929–1963), *left*, confers with Dr. Lillian Gilbreth, renowned industrial psychologist, industrial engineer, and inventor, who was hired as a professor of management within the School of Mechanical Engineering in 1935. Courtesy Purdue University Archives and Special Collections.

axes; how to pitch tents and construct shelters; how to build fires; and how to cook over campfires.[14]

The women's program grew steadily with course and staff additions. A state law was passed making physical education in high school mandatory, and Purdue met the need by training women to teach physical education in schools. In 1933 Purdue students began their teaching training in physical education at Jefferson High School in Lafayette.

PURDUE WOMEN LOSE THEIR FIERCE ADVOCATE, VIRGINIA CLAYPOOL MEREDITH

The Queen of American Agriculture and matriarch of Purdue, Virginia Claypool Meredith passed away at age eighty-eight on December 9, 1936, in the home she and Mary Matthews shared on Waldron Street. Meredith had been ill for three months following a heart attack. The previous July she had been reappointed to continue her service as a trustee.

A newspaper story stated, "Mrs. Meredith had been especially active in the cause of women students and was one of the first supporters of the move for a department of physical education for women and also for the women's residence halls. The Virginia C. Meredith club, an organization of home economics students, was named in her honor."[15]

Held in her home, Meredith's funeral was as she had requested—"free of all ostentation," and as a newspaper article stated, "its simplicity reflecting the gentle nature of the woman who had earned a state's gratitude for outstanding civic service." Among the distinguished pallbearers were President Elliott and Dean A. A. Potter. At 9:30 a.m. buglers stationed at various locations on campus played taps. Home economics classes were dismissed for the morning. The campus flag was at half-staff.[16]

Meredith was taken to Cambridge City, Indiana, to be buried alongside her husband and family. University officials accompanied the body to Riverside Cemetery. On its way through Indianapolis the funeral party was provided with a police escort. Today, a historical marker honoring the life of Virginia Claypool Meredith is displayed on Main Street (U.S. 40) in Cambridge City.

One month after Meredith's death, a memorial was held at Purdue's Eliza Fowler Hall as part of the annual Agricultural Conference. Several speakers paid tribute to Meredith, and their remarks were published in a small book with a foreword by President Elliott. He wrote, "Whenever and wherever there is a character such as Virginia Claypool Meredith the world will be levelled upward."[17]

The Indiana Federation of Clubs created the Virginia Meredith Memorial Forest near Shoals, Indiana, in 1938 as a living tribute to the woman who made monumental contributions to agriculture, stock raising, and homemaking in Indiana.[18] Meredith was a founder of the Indiana Federation of Clubs and had been made honorary president.

Meredith's name continues to live on with Purdue's Meredith Residence Hall named in her honor. In 1974, Helen Clark, groundbreaking early nutrition science researcher, was the first woman to be recognized as a Distinguished Professor at Purdue with the title of Meredith Distinguished Professor.

FEMALE STUDENTS RECEIVE HAND-ME-DOWN GYMNASIUM

When the men moved out of the Memorial Gymnasium and held their physical education classes and athletic events in Purdue's new Fieldhouse and Gymnasium in 1938, female students moved from the former Electrical Engineering Building to the hand-me-down Memorial Gymnasium for physical education classes and athletic meets. Yet they had to share their building for other events, World War II needs, and more. Had Virginia Meredith been living, she more than likely would have bristled at this move, which might have looked like a step up for women but had its share of inconveniences, and expressed her disapproval in Board of Trustees meetings.

The Memorial Gymnasium was used for university convocations until 1940 when the Hall of Music (now Elliott Hall of Music) was built. The women were bumped out of the gym during and after World War II so that the building could house military training classes, student barracks, and a furniture warehouse. The women had to seek other space to hold their gym classes, such as in the Purdue Memorial Union ballrooms.[19]

After the war, a new floor was installed in the Memorial Gym, and a wall was constructed to provide a dance studio. More offices, a staff dressing room, and a lecture room were added, and the Memorial Gymnasium finally took on the character of a physical education facility.

Physical Education for Women remained in the Memorial Gymnasium for nearly forty years until the men's and women's departments merged after the passing of Title IX, a federal civil rights law of the Education Amendments of 1972. Title IX protects people from discrimination on the basis of sex in any federally funded education program or activity.[20] In 1975, the Men's and Women's Physical Education Departments would be, for the first time, housed under one common roof. Purdue was forced to fund women's intercollegiate athletics. Prior to Title IX, women athletes at Purdue participated in intramurals and largely funded their own travel and equipment. (Read more about this in Chapter 16.)

6

INDIANA'S FIRST NURSERY SCHOOL

LAURA PARTCH AND INDIANA'S FIRST NURSERY SCHOOL

Mary Matthews enlisted Laura Partch to create and direct the Purdue Nursery School in 1926. It was the first nursery school in Indiana and the first of ten university-based nursery schools in the United States.[1]

A graduate of the Indianapolis City Hospital School of Nursing, Partch taught classes in child care and home nursing. This was before the advent of antibiotics and vaccines, when polio was feared by parents. Health care was uppermost in their minds, and Partch's nursing training for students who worked in the nursery school was an added appeal.

The nursery school was housed in Building Two, so named because it was the second building constructed on campus. It stood where Beering Hall is today. Sixteen children between the ages of three and five attended the first classes. The school served as a laboratory for undergraduate students in child development courses, a research laboratory for graduate students, and a center for training those who wanted to become nursery school teachers.[2] Today, the Ben and Maxine Miller Child Development Laboratory School at Purdue carries on the original mission of the nursery school to educate students in child development.

The children who attended the Purdue Nursery School were selected from a long waiting list and each was required to pass a physical examination. Teachers

In 1926 Laura Partch, shown here in 1917, was asked by Dean of Home Economics Mary L. Matthews to create and direct Indiana's first nursery school located at Purdue University. Courtesy Purdue University Archives and Special Collections.

wore white lab coats and carried clipboards. A well-known early childhood educator and psychologist, Katherine Haskell Read, taught at the nursery school from 1929 to 1931. After doing graduate work at the University of Chicago and Purdue, she earned her master's degree from Purdue in 1938 and served as a Purdue instructor from 1935 to 1940.

Read influenced the field of early childhood education worldwide for more than a half a century. In 1950, she wrote the first textbook preparing college students to teach young children, entitled *The Nursery School: A Human Relationships Laboratory*. Read died in 1991, and the ninth edition of her book was printed posthumously in 1993 with an updated title, *Early Childhood Programs: Human Relationships and*

Learning. The book was printed in seven different languages. Read's "Guides to Speech and Action" have endured and most are still relevant today.³

In 1930 the American Home Economics Association reorganized and designated nine official professional departments, two of which were family relations and child development. During this decade Dean Mary Matthews established a playground east of the Home Economics Building where the Loeb Fountain flows today. Apple trees shaded the play area, and a railroad track ran alongside where trains carried coal from the south end of campus to the power and heating plant near the Engineering Administration Building on the north side where the Wilmeth Active Learning Center stands today.

A streetcar ran down the middle of University Street on the other side of the Home Economics Building. In warm weather months when the windows were open in the building, professors had to pause in the middle of their lectures as the trolley screeched and clanged on one side of the building and the train rumbled down the tracks on the other, drowning out their voices.

Professor Mary Louise Foster was on staff with the child development program and remembered the challenges of the passing train. "The problem was to get the children into the playground before the train would come, one way or the other," she recalled. "The train engineer would honk the horn and wave at the kids on the playground. He would stop and talk to them, and he got to know their names. It was a fun time to be working with the child development program."⁴

Amelia Earhart visited the playground during one of her stays as a visiting professor and women's advisor. Helen Dawson Miller, who graduated in home economics in 1939, remembered bumping into Earhart. When asked about her favorite campus recollection in 1998, Miller said:

> You asked, "What is your favorite Purdue memory?" Mine would be the day I was just leaving the home economics building when Miss Bloye asked me where I was going. I told her that I was on my way to the library, so she asked me if I would drop off some papers at the Dean's office for her. As I approached the door of Dean [Dorothy] Stratton's office with the papers, who should be coming out but Amelia Earhart! She spoke to me and shook my hand. This was not long before her fatal flight. If I had known how famous she was about to become, I would have hesitated to wash my hand.⁵

Eventually, there were two Purdue nursery schools equipped to care for thirty children. Graduate assistants in the Department of Foods and Nutrition served

Amelia Earhart (*third from right*) and students Gabrielle Miles and Edna Hutson observe children on the playground of Indiana's first nursery school, created at Purdue by Professor Laura Partch in 1926. Courtesy Purdue Archives and Special Collections.

as nursery school dietitians. Parents were expected to keep an "elimination chart" for their children.[6] Marion Mattson, who had a PhD from the University of Minnesota's Institute of Child Welfare, became director of the Purdue Nursery School. During World War II, she was a member of the Indiana State Committee on Care of Children in Wartime, which worked with the Indiana State Defense Council and the Indiana State Nutrition Council to prepare a guide entitled *Feeding Children in Group Care*. Two other Purdue faculty members were on the committee: Assistant Professor of Foods and Nutrition Cecelia Schuck and Associate Professor of Institutional Management Ruby Clark.

As mothers went to work in factories and offices while fathers were serving in World War II, there was concern about nutritious meals for children in day care. The guide read, "While mothers work in our war plants, their children must be afforded the same care and consideration they would have under a normal home atmosphere." The guide promoted what was then deemed the basic seven food groups:

1. green and yellow vegetables
2. oranges, tomatoes, grapefruit
3. potatoes and other vegetables and fruits
4. milk and milk products
5. meat, poultry, fish, or eggs
6. bread, flour, and cereals
7. butter and fortified margarine[7]

HARRIET EASTERBROOKS O'SHEA AND INDIANA'S EMERGENCY NURSERY SCHOOLS

President Edward Elliott's foresight brought the brightest stars to campus from other universities and the country at large. He fostered the foundation of numerous departments during the 1930s when enrollment was, at the most, 7,000 students.[8] Elliott was a liberal arts man, a big thinker with an open mind. He hired many of Purdue's extraordinary women in a time when it was difficult for women to find significant faculty positions.

Elliott brought Harriet Easterbrooks O'Shea to West Lafayette after she received her PhD in clinical psychology from Columbia University in 1931. She taught child psychology in the Department of Education, and she devoted one third of her time as a psychologist for the Purdue Nursery School, replacing Katherine Read.

O'Shea wore several hats and her Purdue career touched many areas of the university. Before arriving at Purdue, she worked in the nursery school at Mills College in California where she was also in charge of personnel work, so Elliott also appointed O'Shea as personnel director for women students.[9] Academia was in O'Shea's blood, and the World Book Encyclopedia was nearly a member of her family.

She grew up with the University of Wisconsin as a backdrop to her childhood. Her father, Michael Vincent O'Shea, was a professor of education there. Michael O'Shea had been hired in 1915 as editor-in-chief by Chicago publishers J. H. Hansen and John Bellows to revamp the World Book Encyclopedia to make it engaging and easy to read. Hansen and Bellows realized that the encyclopedias were off-putting to young readers. Michael O'Shea reworked the text, adding thousands of illustrations to capture a child's imagination. The new edition was immediately successful.[10]

Like most of Purdue's female faculty, Harriet O'Shea was not married. Societal expectations of the day stated that women could not be married and also have their careers. Back then it was presumed that once a woman married, she would quit her job (or be "let go") because she had a husband to support her. Sadly, this is why so many of Purdue's accomplished early female leaders had no children to carry on the legacy of their lives.

The early 1930s were dismal years for teachers. The Great Depression caused many citizens to be unemployed or survive on reduced incomes, and they could no longer pay their property taxes, which paid for schools. Budget cutbacks resulted in reduced hours for schools, an increase in class sizes, and a decrease in teachers' salaries. Poor school districts closed their doors.[11]

The Purdue Nursery School was used as a training site for emergency nursery school teachers as part of Indiana's federal emergency education relief project of the Civil Works Administration. The Works Progress Administration created a program of Emergency Nursery Schools to offer jobs to unemployed teachers. Unlike earlier nursery schools which were largely private and charged fees, the government-sponsored schools were free and available for all, not just the middle class.[12] These newly formed nursery schools needed trained teachers.

Unemployed teachers enrolled at Purdue for an intensive eight-day training to direct emergency nursery schools established in Indiana. Teachers began drawing salaries when they enrolled.[13] Purdue staff members donated their time to conduct the classes, and Harriet O'Shea headed up the effort. O'Shea was appointed chairman of the advisory committee for emergency nursery schools in Indiana in December 1934.[14] The following year, her co-authored book *Essentials of Nursery Education with Special Reference to Nursery Schools* was published by the National Association for Nursery Education.

Garnering national attention that same year, O'Shea was chosen to be a consultant for the Educational Policies commission by the National Education Association and the Department of Superintendence to develop long-range planning for the improvement of American schools.[15] Four years later, she was invited by Grover Whalen, president of the New York World's Fair[16] Corporation, to be a member of one hundred women to advise the fair. She also became the president of the Indiana Association of Clinical Psychologists.

O'Shea was active as a therapist and psychologist in the University Psychological Services. She trained clinical psychologists from 1946 to 1960, following the Boulder Conference model, also known as the scientist-practitioner model. Before 1949, individual psychology departments in universities throughout the

Harriet Easterbrooks O'Shea, *second from right*, received the Order of the Delta Gamma Rose at a banquet of the Delta Gamma sorority in 1953. The award was given to women who were outstanding nationally in their field. Courtesy Tippecanoe County Historical Association.

United States ran their training programs with individual freedom. There were no set standards. The Boulder Conference at the University of Colorado in Boulder was the first national meeting to discuss standards for doctoral training in psychology. Part of the impetus for the conference was related to the federal government's desire to provide adequate mental health services to the veterans of World War II. The Boulder model underscored the idea that clinical psychologists should be competent in both conducting research and providing professional psychological services.[17] O'Shea was at the forefront of advocating for the Boulder model.

7

ART, THE HOOSIER SALON, AND HISTORIC FASHIONS

LAURENTZA SCHANTZ-HANSEN
REFINED ART AT PURDUE

Her name alone was exotic: Laurentza Schantz-Hansen. She was an artist and head of the Department of Applied Design in the School of Home Economics from 1929 to 1955. Applied design was, essentially, the art department. Purdue would not have a liberal arts program until 1963, when it split from the School of Science.[1] Thus, Schantz-Hansen's Department of Applied Design was relegated to the School of Home Economics.

From Danish ancestry, Schantz-Hansen grew up in Iowa. Short and solid in stature, Schantz-Hansen was lively and refined.[2] She attended the Stout Institute, a practical manual training school in Wisconsin that offered applied art as one of its focuses.[3] She graduated from the University of Chicago and obtained her master's degree at Teachers College, Columbia University. Schantz-Hansen also studied at the Art Institute of Chicago and in a school near Copenhagen, Denmark.[4] For Schantz-Hansen to have a position in a university other than a women's college, particularly one that emphasized engineering and agriculture, was an anomaly.

Patricia Albjerg Graham, Purdue alumna who today is the Charles Warren Professor of the History of Education emerita at Harvard University, was Schantz-Hansen's goddaughter. Graham said, "She was a woman who was devoted to her students at Purdue and the School of Home Economics but who had a much broader vision of society than we typically associate with early mid-twentieth-century home economics. She was a cultured, sophisticated person in Tippecanoe County when that kind of culture was in short supply."[5]

Schantz-Hansen's office and charming home on Waldron Street were filled with art. She displayed her collection of Madonna and Child pieces in December 1952 in the music room of the Purdue Memorial Union.[6] She organized campus art exhibits, including the famed Hoosier Salon in the Purdue Memorial Union. She sparked students' creativity and nurtured her own artistic yearnings. Schantz-Hansen was a renegade in a school bustling with home economics primacies.

Schantz-Hansen taught applied design classes with such topics as "analysis of line within the field of the practical arts" that opened students' eyes to the lines in the design of bed linens, furniture, hats, shoes, china, glassware, and nature.[7]

Helen Thompson Terry, a 1948 Purdue alumna, said, "I did have a favorite professor who developed my lifetime interest in art and design. She was anxious to turn the small applied design department into an important area within the home economics school. To accomplish this goal she selected eleven students in our junior year to become a test case for advanced courses in art history and design. As a result, I graduated with a bachelor of science degree in art! She was a most remarkable woman, an outstanding teacher, and a dear friend. Her name was Laurentza Schantz Hansen."[8]

The Applied Design Department was in Building Number Two where the nursery school resided, north of the Home Economics Building (Matthews Hall). Freshmen in Schantz-Hansen's classes made posters for campus activities,[9] such as women's athletic events, the horticultural show, and happenings in the nursery school.[10] During World War II, students made posters that were displayed throughout Indiana to advertise the war training program, encouraging women to take courses in radio work, electricity, engineering drawing, rubber and plastic work, and metallurgy.[11]

Schantz-Hansen was elected president of the Art Section of the Indiana State Teachers' Institute in 1933.[12] With her new post, she was invited to speak at the art conference at Ball State Teachers College (Ball State University). Her talk was on art and its importance to industry. She said, "An appreciation of everyday things from the standpoint of design and color will lead to the growth of good taste, and eventually, to a renaissance of art in the United States." She displayed various containers of popular advertised products and photos of furnishings, and then said, "Art has been applied to manufacturing and selling as a solid business proposition. Business men have summoned artists to their factories because their touch turns products to gold."[13]

Schantz-Hansen studied painting in Woodstock, New York; Taxco, Mexico; and throughout Europe. In the summers of 1936 and 1938, she was awarded a Carnegie Art scholarship for study in the history and appreciation of art at Harvard University.[14]

Applied Design was renamed Art and Design and in 1963 became part of the newly established School of Humanities, Social Science and Education (College of Liberal Arts).[15] Schantz-Hansen retired in 1956 after serving for a quarter of a century as head of Applied Design.

She admired fine book illustration and design, and throughout her life collected children's books from around the world, as well as books on art.[16] At retirement, she donated approximately 650 children's books to the Purdue Nursery School. Today, those books and her collection of art books, nearly 1,000 volumes worth nearly $4,000 dollars in the 1950s,[17] are preserved in the Purdue University Archives and Special Collections rare book collection. In 1974 Schantz-Hansen passed away at age eighty-five in Iowa.

FERN RUPEL, HISTORIC COSTUME CURATOR

The Virginia C. Meredith Home Economics Club hosted a historical style show on October 1, 1952. Professor Marian Willoughby, head of the Clothing and Textiles Department, supervised the event. A paper summarizing the style show and the department's historical costumes stated, "The School of Home Economics has what is probably the largest and best collection of historic costumes of any school in the United States."

The first and most prestigious gift of opulent fashions was made by Ophelia Fowler Duhme around 1927. Duhme was the daughter of Moses and Eliza Fowler. Moses had been a business partner and friend of John Purdue. In 1901, Eliza gave money to build the first assembly hall on campus, named Eliza Fowler Hall. It was demolished in 1954. Today, Eliza Fowler Hall in Stewart Center is essentially on the same footprint as the former building.[18] Ophelia Duhme donated farm land to Purdue where the first women's residence hall was built, now named Duhme Hall as part of Windsor Halls, and where Amelia Earhart and Lillian Gilbreth lived when on campus.

Duhme's fashion donation was extraordinary. It included a lace ball gown with jewels and a four-foot train of ruffles, silk and taffeta dresses with hand-embroidered details, a wool dressing gown with rabbit fur lining, capes, silk and lace parasols, a fan, and slippers made in Paris in the 1890s. Through the years, many other fashion donations were made by prominent women dating from the Civil War days through the late twentieth century.

President Frederick Hovde's wife, Priscilla, donated a collection of her unusual and colorful hats. A lace-trimmed, brown silk gown with a velvet collar and a bustle belonged to the grandmother of John DeCamp, once the sportscaster and general manager of WBAA Radio who was known as the "Voice of Purdue."[19] The collection included clothes for children and folk costumes. All were used in clothing classes as examples of textiles, design, and workmanship and in discussion of the history of costume design.[20] Faculty often used the collection in talks or art exhibits.

A rare collection of antique lace was donated in 1961 at the request of the late Jessie Yost Berry of Fowler, Indiana. Three generations of women in Berry's lineage had created and/or collected ninety-six pieces of exquisite lace.[21] The collection, valued at $4,000 at that time, was presented to Purdue by her son, Burton Berry, and included a lace baby cap made by Yost in 1906, handkerchiefs of Chantilly and Valenciennes lace, a half-dozen fans decorated with mother of pearl encrusted with gold and ivory, and a tablecloth of handmade needlepoint lace from the nineteenth century.

The Berry Lace Collection was exhibited during the third annual Purdue Arts Festival in 1966 in the lobby of the Home Economics Administration Building (Stone Hall). Leola K. Decker, a graduate student, catalogued the collection. Using a microscope, Decker identified the types of lace, patterns, and method of construction and then conducted research on the periods in history in which each type of lace originated. Decker used her findings as basis for a master's degree thesis in clothing and textiles.[22]

By the 1980s, Purdue's historic costume collection was housed in climate-controlled storage in Matthews Hall. In 1988, Purdue alumna and former member of the home economics education faculty Delpha Jeanette Parvis donated the 1897 graduation dress worn by her aunt, Delpha Ann Eva Orem, to

Professor Esther Fern Rupel was the historical costume curator who preserved Purdue's historic costume collection. As a member of the Church of the Brethren, she wrote her doctoral dissertation in the early 1970s on the symbolism reflected in Brethren dress. Courtesy Purdue University Archives and Special Collections.

the Consumer Sciences and Retailing Historic Collection. Delpha Orem was the only woman in her Purdue pharmacy class and served one year as its vice president. She authored the class poem. After her death, the dress had been given to her niece and namesake who bequeathed it to Purdue.[23]

Dr. Esther Fern Rupel was the historic costume collection curator and looked after the collection for many years. Rupel earned a bachelor's degree in home economics in 1947 from Manchester College in North Manchester, Indiana. She received her master's degree in clothing textiles from Purdue's School of Home Economics in 1957 and began teaching in the Department of Clothing and Textiles that September under department head Amy L. Howe. Rupel taught her first class in historic costume two years later.

In 1965, Rupel was one of seven professors at Purdue cited through write-in votes by Purdue junior and senior students as "most appreciated."[24] Rupel received a $3,000 General Foods Fund fellowship to earn her doctorate degree at the University of Minnesota while on sabbatical in 1971. As an active member of the Church of the Brethren, she wrote her doctoral dissertation on the symbolism reflected in Brethren dress.[25] Rupel retired from Purdue in 1989.[26]

8

AMELIA EARHART AND LILLIAN GILBRETH

AMELIA EARHART AND HER "DEPARTMENT OF ADVENTURE"

Purdue President Edward C. Elliott was the father of two daughters, and he was exceptionally interested in the education of women. Female faculty members at most American universities were scarce in the 1930s. Elliott believed that if there were more professional women to revere and admire on campus, more female students would be attracted to Purdue. If those role models were world-famous, that would be an added coup.

Elliott inspired two globally recognized women to come to Purdue as visiting instructors—renowned industrial psychologist, industrial engineer, and inventor Lillian Gilbreth, who was later hired as a professor of management in the School of Mechanical Engineering in 1935, and famed aviatrix Amelia Earhart. A chance meeting with Earhart sparked a flash of brilliance for Elliott, and he invited her to be a consultant in careers for women and advisor in aeronautics beginning in 1935.

Elliott and Earhart were both speakers at the 1934 annual Women and the Changing World Conference sponsored by the *New York Herald Tribune* in New York City. By then, Earhart had claimed many flying firsts. She piloted over the Atlantic alone, and she became the first person, male or female, to cross twice. Additionally, she set the women's record for fastest nonstop transcontinental flight. She was a successful author and little-known poet, who took Eleanor Roosevelt on a night flight to go "skylarking." Her record-setting flights and singular example of what women can do, along with her humble, down-to-earth personality, made her a beacon of hope to unemployed, struggling families during the Great Depression.

Elliott happened to be seated next to Earhart at the luncheon where they both spoke. The master of ceremonies introduced Earhart by saying she "has worked, and is working, and will continue to work hard to further the science to which she has dedicated her life."[1]

From the podium Earhart, age thirty-seven, said that she had been asked to direct her talk to youth; however, she did so with trepidation because it occurred to her that "the ancients, such as I am, should be listening to young ideas rather than point up opportunities in a world which has the elders decidedly on the run!"[2]

In his book *Soaring Wings*, Earhart's husband, George Palmer Putnam, who referred to his wife as "AE," recalled, "I wonder if that was not the point at which Dr. Edward C. Elliott, President of Purdue University, who was in the audience, got the idea which crystallized not long after into AE's association with his institution."[3]

That evening Elliott dined with Earhart and Putnam at the Coffee House Club located in the Hotel Seymour where the couple lived when in New York. Putnam and Earhart sat on a clubhouse couch while Elliott sat in a chair facing the couple. He smiled and got to the point: "We want you at Purdue."[4]

"I'd like that," Earhart said without hesitation. "If it can be arranged. What do you think I should do?"[5]

Elliott told Earhart that Purdue had six thousand enrolled students, of whom eight hundred were women. He said, "We've a feeling the girls aren't keeping abreast of the inspirational opportunities of the day nearly as well as might be."[6]

Putnam wrote of Earhart's reaction. "AE's eyes shone, as they always did at the suggestion of a challenge—not in the excited way of an anticipation that burns itself out of its own fire before it can produce anything lasting, but with a certain steady glow."[7]

The three discussed the idea of Earhart coming to Purdue and how she could work with the female students and the plan was settled. She would spend as much time on campus as she was able, which for such a busy woman would total about six to seven weeks out of the academic year. Earhart was attracted to Purdue because it was the only university in the United States with its own airport.[8]

In a letter to Earhart in May 1935 outlining what she might do at Purdue, Elliott wrote, "The university intends to set up a new center of interest—call it a department, if you will—for the study of Careers for Women. Through this Center will be attempted the stimulation and orientation of women (and men?) students, as to the new conditions and opportunities produced in our changed world."[9] Elliott mentioned a name he had first suggested for the center—the "Department of Adventure"—and added, "Whatever the name, the idea is the same."[10]

In June 1935, Elliott announced the appointment: "Miss Earhart represents better than any other young woman of this generation the spirit and the courageous skill of what may be called the new pioneering. At no point in our educational system is there greater need for pioneering and constructive planning than in education for women. The university believes that Amelia Earhart will help us to see and to attack successfully many unsolved problems."[11]

The January before she started as a Purdue faculty member, Earhart flew from Honolulu, Hawaii, to Oakland, California, in her Lockheed Vega in eighteen hours and fifteen minutes, the first person to make this flight. A few months later, she flew from Burbank, California, to Mexico City, Mexico, in thirteen hours and thirty-two minutes for a new record. When she arrived at the university in November 1935, Earhart drove her Palm Beach Tan[12] convertible Cord onto Purdue's campus with her neck scarf billowing and two newly acquired world records.

After conferring with students and faculty, Dean of Women Dorothy C. Stratton wrote Elliott a letter outlining how Earhart could be of service when she arrived. Earhart's desk would be headquartered in the Office of the Dean of Women and the two women would become good friends.

Stratton suggested that Earhart make informal student contacts, and the best way to do that would be for her to stay in the Women's Residence Hall (later named Duhme as part of Windsor Residence Halls).[13] There was a high demand for individual consultations, and Stratton did not want Earhart to be overwhelmed. Stratton wrote, "It might be best if only those students particularly interested in some phase of aeronautics, dress designing, or other fields with which Miss Earhart is particularly familiar were urged to take advantage of these conferences."

Stratton mentioned dress designing because Earhart had started her own fashion line in 1934 when she was in need of funds. She designed and selected fabrics for "Amelia Fashions," carried exclusively in fine department stores in metropolitan cities across the country, although the endeavor only lasted for one year. "Amelia Fashions" resembled Earhart's easygoing, outdoorsy, classic style with a touch of aviatrix details, such as buttons shaped like an airplane rivet.[14]

She and a single seamstress created samples of her clothing in her suite in the Hotel Seymour. She was the first to popularize the concept of "separates." Each garment featured a label depicting a tiny red plane darting from left to right with a crimson contrail zipping across Earhart's signature rendered in black thread.[15] Unfortunately, "Amelia Fashions" did not take off, largely because of the Great Depression. The business venture ended about the time that Earhart came to Purdue.

Purdue's first annual career conference for female students, titled "Conference on Women's Work and Opportunities," was held in spring 1935. Speakers included Earhart, President Elliott, Professor of Child Psychology Harriett O'Shea, Dean of Women Dorothy Stratton (who was also an associate professor of psychology), Dean of Home Economics Mary Matthews, Professor of Institutional Management Edith Gamble, and Professor of Women's Physical Education Helen Hazelton.[16]

Before the conference, Earhart sent out a questionnaire to women students to explore their postscholastic plans. O'Shea assisted Earhart in creating the questionnaire. Earhart wanted to help Purdue's faculty develop appropriate courses for women and help female students clarify their goals. Earhart spoke on the findings from her questionnaire at the conference.

She said that 92 percent of the women who answered planned to work after leaving college, and the reasons given for seeking employment were not economic necessity, as one might think during the Great Depression years, but to achieve professional success. The second most popular reason for working after college was to attain personal independence; and the third was economic necessity.

Earhart also sketched notes on her idea for a "Handyman's Course" for women where female students would learn how to repair electrical fixtures, leaking faucets, gas burners, clogged drains, typewriters, doorknobs, doorbells, and more. Since childhood, Earhart had been a self-professed tinkerer, and the course spoke to her desire to give women opportunities to explore self-sufficient accomplishments outside of what was considered women's realms. By all indications, the course did not materialize.

Women students came to know Earhart personally during mealtimes in the Women's Residence Hall. According to her husband, who also stayed in her suite, she enjoyed every minute of her time with the students. Sometimes she absent-mindedly broke the rules. Female students and staff were not allowed to

Amelia Earhart (*second from left*) encouraged women students to consider occupations beyond the traditional expectations of homemaker, teacher, or nurse. She emphasized scientific pursuits. Courtesy Purdue Archives and Special Collections.

wear slacks on campus, yet, she came to dinner once in her flying clothes, and the freshmen waited to see if she would be sent back to get properly dressed. Of course, she was allowed to wear whatever she wanted, pants and all.

After dinner, many students followed Earhart to a lounge, and the young woman gathered around her as they all sat on the floor to talk. The conversations invariably centered on Earhart's conviction that women had choices about what they could do with their lives and that men needed training in domesticity and child-rearing.

Student Marian Frazier painted a picture of what it was like to live in the same dormitory as Earhart. Frazier said, "One night I was sitting in my room studying, and Miss Earhart stuck her head in the door and asked if she could borrow my pen. She said, 'I'll bring it back in a sec,' just like any girl would do. I guess I couldn't keep it to myself, because, when she did bring it back, there was a bunch of girls in my room—just to get another look at her. But really, you know, I don't think she gets enough sleep. She's terribly busy. I often hear her typewriter clear up to midnight."[17]

Earhart was a poet and a writer. She savored words as much as she did soaring airborne. When she wrote of flying, she melded her loves: "After midnight the moon set, and I was alone with the stars.... The lure of flying is the lure of beauty, and I need no other flight to convince me that the reason flyers fly, whether they know it or not, is the esthetic appeal of flying."[18]

By the time she was at Purdue, Earhart had written two nonfiction books, chapters for several children's tomes, and stories on aviation for numerous magazines and newspapers. For a short interval, she was aviation editor for *Cosmopolitan* magazine, answering readers' questions about flying. But her poems and short stories were her heart's fancy.

At Purdue, Earhart especially valued how conclusions from laboratory tests conducted in the aeronautics department could be immediately put into practice at the airfield southwest of campus. In Putnam's *Soaring Wings*, Earhart is quoted: "You see, my interest in aviation goes into every part of the industry. It isn't flying alone.... It takes from forty to a hundred men on the ground to keep one plane in the air. That is from forty to a hundred jobs per plane—and I don't think all those jobs need forever be held by men!"[19]

President Elliott asked Putnam what he thought Earhart desired most in the field of research and education beyond the classroom. Putnam recounted, "I told him she was hankering for a bigger and better plane, not only one in which she could go to far places farther and faster and more safely, but to use as a laboratory for research in aviation education and for technical experimentation."[20]

Earhart yearned to pilot the longest flight of her aviation career, a world flight. While on the expedition, she wanted to test human reactions to flying—responses involving diet and altitude, fatigue, the effect of the stratosphere on people conditioned to lower altitudes, and the differences in the reactions of men and women to air travel, if any.

In fall 1935, Elliott held a dinner party at the university-owned president's home located on South Seventh Street in Lafayette. At the party with several Purdue-connected guests, Earhart talked of her dreams for women and aviation. Before the evening was over, David Ross, a Purdue alumnus and trustee who led the founding of the Purdue Research Foundation, offered to donate $50,000 toward the cost of a plane that would be Earhart's flying laboratory.

Additional donations in cash and equipment were received from Josiah K. Lilly of Eli Lilly Drug Company, a member of the Purdue Board of Trustees; Vincent Bendix; and manufacturers Western Electric, Goodrich, and Goodyear.

A total of $80,000 comprised the Amelia Earhart Fund for Aeronautical Research. The manufacturers hoped Earhart's flight would help their cause in promoting aviation to women, who at that time displayed "sales resistance" to air travel.[21]

Amid the clouds, Earhart recalled her quest for the very airplane from which she wrote: "Where to find the tree on which costly airplanes grow, I did not know. But I did know the kind I wanted—an Electra Lockheed, big brother of my Vega, with, of course, Wasp engines.... Such is the trusting simplicity of a pilot's mind, it seemed ordained that somehow the dream would materialize. Once the prize was in hand, obviously there was one flight which I most wanted to attempt—a circumnavigation of the globe as near its waistline as could be."[22]

Earhart took delivery of her Lockheed Electra in California on July 24, 1936, her thirty-ninth birthday. It was a standard commercial plane that she had modified to her specifications. "It's simply elegant," Earhart said to mechanics who crowded around the gleaming all-metal craft, with its smooth curvatures and duel propellers poised like graceful butter knives. "I could write poetry about this ship."[23]

President Elliott traveled to Los Angeles for a scheduled inspection of the flying laboratory in August. There was tremendous excitement on campus about Earhart's plane, repainted in Purdue's colors of gold and black, and when she flew it in to the Purdue Airport, students gathered to greet her. In March 1937, Earhart left Purdue for California and then on to Honolulu to begin her world flight.

However, she, mechanic Fred Noonan, and Harry Manning, a close friend of Earhart's who acted as radio operator and navigator, experienced a false start on March 20. A tire blew, a strut collapsed, and Earhart crashed taking off in Hawaii, headed for Howland Island. Manning did not join Earhart and Noonan when they took off for a second time. She returned the plane to the Lockheed factory in California for repairs. Then she reversed the route of the flight, and on June 1, 1937, Earhart and Noonan took off again to circle the globe.

The mood on the Purdue campus was electric. It was, in a sense, Purdue's plane. Purdue's Amelia. Purdue's world flight. Elliott sent a telegram of encouragement. On March 25, he wrote a letter to Putnam, who was at Union Air Terminal in Burbank, California. Evidently, to help buoy his wife, Putnam had suggested the telegram idea to Elliott. By this time the two men had become close, as indicated by the salutation of familiarity:

My dear G.P.:

Thanks for the clippings and for the suggestion of a special message for A.E. when she lands today. This has gone and reads as follows:

YOU ARE COMMISSIONED AND CHARGED TO GIVE A.E. A SPECIAL PURDUE GREETING WHEN SHE LANDS TODAY STOP HER COURAGEOUS EXPLOIT HAS GIVEN THRILL TO EVERY MEMBER OF THE BOILERMAKERS GUILD STOP THEY ARE ALL WITH HER TO THE SUCCESSFUL END OF THE FLIGHT[24]

I hope it contains pep for her.[25]

Four months later, Lae, New Guinea, would be Earhart's final stop. On July 1, 1937, she wrote, "The Lockheed is smooth and to the native resembles tins in which certain biscuits are shipped from England. Therefore it is known as the 'biscuit box.'"[26]

Earhart and her biscuit box would attempt to cross eastward over the Pacific to land on Howland Island, along a route never traveled before by airplane. Before taking off, she wrote, "Shall be glad when we have the hazards of its navigation behind us."[27]

Rather than behind her, the hazards would forever be Earhart's mystery and legacy.

On July 2, Earhart's final radio message came. It was picked up by a New Guinea radio station: "Circling ... cannot see island ... gas running low."[28]

Reportedly, the tragedy was the result of a communication failure with the Coast Guard cutter *Itasca* stationed near Howland Island. The commander expected Earhart to broadcast in code on 500 kilocycles. However, Earhart had scrapped her 500-kilocycle equipment in an effort to streamline, thinking she did not need it. The commander of the *Itasca* was unaware that Earhart could not receive the signal sent from his ship.

On July 2, 1937, Dean of Women Dorothy Stratton was at a meeting in the Purdue Memorial Union when word came—Amelia Earhart was lost at sea. Those in the meeting sat dazed, then mechanically and without a word, they gathered their papers. In silence, Stratton and the group left the room, walked down the hallways of the Union, where Earhart had once walked, and out into the summer sunshine.[29]

On July 16, Elliott sent a telegram to Putnam, which read:

SHE WOULD NOT WANT US TO GRIEVE AND WEEP YET WE ARE IN THE DEEPEST DEPTHS OF SADNESS STOP WE SHALL LONG MOURN THIS GALLANT ONE WHOSE LIFE WAS A COURAGEOUS ADVENTURE SHE WOULD HAVE A HEROINES PART IN ANY AGE STOP WHEN YOU ARE ABLE PLEASE LET ME KNOW YOUR PLANS SO THAT WE MAY MEET TO CONSIDER HOW TO CARRY ON

Earhart was writing a book titled *World Flight* and along her route had mailed her writings to her husband because she had promised her publisher that she would produce her manuscript promptly. When her plane vanished, Putnam already had a written account of Earhart's journey, and the book was retitled *Last Flight*. It was written nearly entirely by Earhart from journals, logbooks, and letters scribbled in the cockpit.

Earhart wrote about why she wanted to circle the world. "Here was shining adventure, beckoning with new experiences, added knowledge of flying, of peoples—of myself. I felt that with the flight behind me I would be more useful to me and to the program we had planned at Purdue."[30]

LILLIAN MOLLER GILBRETH, THE ONE BEST WAY

The same year Amelia Earhart started at Purdue, another famed woman also joined the faculty roster—Lillian Moller Gilbreth. President Edward Elliott heard Gilbreth speak at the same Women and the Changing World Conference where he met Earhart.

Gilbreth and Earhart often found themselves in the same spheres, as both were admired around the world. They appeared together in Ida Tarbell's September 13, 1930, "Fifty Foremost Women of the United States," a list of women defined as having done the most to advance the country's welfare. Gilbreth was nearly twenty years Earhart's senior. Long before Earhart herself became famous, she was a fan of the Gilbreths and had pasted a photograph of the couple in her 1924 scrapbook.

Many accounts of Gilbreth initially focus on the fact that she and her husband Frank had twelve children; however, while loving and rearing her gaggle of Gilbreths, Gilbreth also birthed extraordinary milestones in engineering, even by today's standards. The Gilbreths' organized and regimented family life, a reflection of their work, was light-heartedly depicted in the best-selling books *Cheaper by the Dozen* and *Bells on Their Toes*, written by two of their offspring.

Lillian Moller was born in Oakland, California, in 1878. She convinced her father, who was initially opposed to her education, to let her attend college and earn a bachelor's degree in literature in 1900 from the University of California–Berkeley. She was selected as the commencement speaker, becoming the first woman to speak at the university's graduation ceremony. She attended Columbia University but when she became ill returned home and earned her master's degree in literature from Berkeley in 1902.[31] Gilbreth already had seven children when she earned a PhD in psychology from Brown University in 1915.

Thin, yet vigorous, with red hair and a compassionate smile, Gilbreth is credited with being the person to bring engineering and psychology together for the first time. She was a proponent of using psychology as a management tool. Her approach was to adjust the workplace to fit the needs of the worker. She focused on reducing worker fatigue, improving worker satisfaction, and providing workers with incentives and advancement in the workplace,[32] what is referred to as human factors or ergonomics. Her work in applied motion improved efficiency in the workplace and the home.

From 1911 to 1920, between having her twelve babies[33] (actually, she gave birth to thirteen children, but only eleven survived to adulthood), she collaborated with her husband Frank to write several classic books on management, incorporating their combined knowledge of psychology along with engineering. Frank shopped for publishers for their books, such as *Motion Study*, *A Primer of Scientific Study*, and *Fatigue Study*. But he came to resent the fact that the manuscripts with only his name were quickly accepted, but manuscripts with both his and Lillian's name found no market. Macmillan finally published their co-authored books, provided Lillian's name was represented only by initials and the publicity would not include the fact that she was a woman.[34]

Gilbreth was a model of acumen and caring as one of the world's few female authorities in industrial engineering and management. She was internationally known for her breakthrough contributions in the field of motion study, work simplification, and psychology as it applied in industry, the home, and the world of the physically disabled. Her focus was on worker satisfaction and reducing worker fatigue. "Anyone can make a problem complicated," Gilbreth said. "The real achievement is to make it simple."[35]

The Gilbreths were good friends with Purdue Dean of Engineering Andrey Abraham "A.A." Potter, and he invited Frank to lecture at the university. Frank

When Lillian Gilbreth (*second from right*), shown here with students in 1957, was appointed a professor of management in Purdue's School of Mechanical Engineering in 1935, she became the first woman in the United States to hold such a title. Courtesy Purdue University Archives and Special Collections.

brought gifts to Potter's daughter, Helen, who later became a Purdue Professor of Home Management and Family Economics.[36]

The Gilbreths' work was motivated by their calling to contribute to the well-being of all people everywhere. They originated their concept of "therbligs," a term they invented by spelling "Gilbreth" backward. A therblig is the smallest unit of work motion. For example, to check off a box on a form, one needs to look for a pencil, reach for the pencil, pick it up, adjust the grip, move the lead to the paper, make a check mark, move the pencil to its resting place, and put it down. Each of these tiny steps is a therblig.

They were the first to use motion pictures to study timed units of work and find ways to eliminate unnecessary therbligs from tasks.[37] Purdue University Archives and Special Collections holds the Gilbreths' original motion study films, the only known collection of its kind.

After Frank's sudden death from a heart attack in 1924, Lillian focused on improving efficiency in women's spheres. Her efficiency kitchen was revolutionary, and many of her innovations are now standards in today's kitchen, particularly the "workplace triangle"— optimizing the efficiency and functionality of a kitchen by organizing the refrigerator, sink, and stove in a triangular layout. She also redesigned sanitary napkins for Johnson and Johnson and advised large companies like Macy's and the Girl Scouts of America.

In 1935, President Elliott hired Gilbreth, age fifty-seven, as a professor of management in the School of Mechanical Engineering, and she was the first female engineering professor in the United States.[38] In 1941, she was promoted to full professor.[39] At her request, she also taught at Purdue in the areas of psychology, education, and home economics. Like Earhart, Gilbreth also lived in the Women's Residence Hall.

Also like Earhart, Dean of Women Dorothy Stratton became a good friend of Gilbreth, whom she called "Dr. G." Stratton said that Gilbreth's hands were never still. "She was always knitting, crocheting, or tatting something for someone's birthday or anniversary."[40] She kept an extensive birthday book and sent notes to an astonishing number of people. According to Stratton, Gilbreth had a great capacity for caring.

She would rise early in the morning and send postcards to her children before breakfast. Students learned that they could enjoy time with her if they, too, arrived when the Women's Residence Hall dining room doors opened at 6:30 a.m. For most of her life she walked a mile a day, and she never learned to drive. If Gilbreth met a student who wanted to talk to her in the Purdue Memorial Union, she said, "Walk with me. I need to pace my daily number of steps."

It was not always easy for Lillian as the only female in Purdue's male engineering environment. She collaborated with a younger professor, Marvin Mundel, who was an abrasive character. He repeatedly attempted to embarrass her in front of other engineers, calling on her to complete mathematical calculations. Math was not her strong suit. Frank had always done the calculations needed for their motion studies. However, there may have been more personal reasons as to why Mundel caused difficulty for Gilbreth. She had liked Mundel's first wife and was affronted by his divorce. Yet, on the whole, Gilbreth's Purdue experience was a happy, successful one—so much so that she donated both her personal and professional papers to Purdue where they are preserved today.

Dean of Engineering A. A. Potter described Gilbreth as "a master of the art of conducting free discussion until mutual understanding was achieved."[41] Her natural gift of free discussion was recognized, and she served on presidential committees during the administrations of Hoover, Roosevelt, Eisenhower,

Kennedy, and Johnson. The committees included civil defense, war production, women in the services, aging, and rehabilitation and employment of the physically disabled.

During the Depression, President Hoover asked her to join the Emergency Committee for Unemployment where she created a nationwide program called "Share the Work" that created new jobs. During World War II, Gilbreth worked as a government consultant overseeing the conversion of factories to military bases and war plants. She is credited with numerous inventions, including the foot-pedal trash can, refrigerator door shelves, and the electric mixer.[42]

When she retired from Purdue in 1948, Gilbreth, age seventy, was awarded an honorary doctor of industrial psychology degree and named professor emeritus.[43] She continued to make yearly visits, giving lectures at Purdue for many years, and carried on her work with General Electric and other manufacturers to improve the design of kitchens and household appliances before she passed away in 1972.

Gilbreth broke the glass ceiling of honors that had been bestowed only on men. In 1965, Gilbreth was the first woman elected to the National Academy of Engineering. The next year, she was the first woman, and until 2005 the *only* woman, awarded the Herbert Hoover Medal recognizing outstanding civic or humanitarian service. The award citation noted: "Her unselfish application of energy and creative efforts in modifying industrial and home environments for the handicapped has resulted in full employment of their capabilities and elevation of their self-esteem."[44]

In 1984, the US Postal Service issued a forty-cent stamp posthumously in Gilbreth's honor as part of its "Great Americans Series."

9

WORLD WAR II SURVIVORS AND THRIVERS

ANNA AKELEY, PHYSICS PROFESSOR WITHOUT A DEGREE AND ART BENEFACTOR

Anna "Anni" Mandler Akeley from Vienna, Austria, was a small dynamo of a woman who became a Purdue physics professor without a physics degree during World War II. At under five feet tall with black, wavy hair and dark eyes, she was diminutive, yet her presence was large.

At age thirty-six, Akeley escaped the Nazis, who eventually took the lives of her mother and sister, by leaving Austria for America in 1940. The fact that Mussolini had closed the Atlantic to all passenger ships did not stop her from making her way to Purdue where her American sweetheart waited.

Akeley telegrammed her future husband whom she admired for his intelligence, brooding good looks, and six-foot stature, Purdue Physics Professor Edward Stowe Akeley. He was ten years older than she and more than a foot taller. She wrote, "Can't come. Atlantic closed."

He sent a simple reply: "The earth is round."[1]

"My God, that man is crazy," Akeley recalled in her 2000 memoir she titled with Edward's succinct declaration: *The Earth Is Round*.

"He says that the earth is round," she continued. "I know the earth is round. That's the man I might marry? This is ridiculous. Then I thought, *No. I know about Edward, that he would not write or send a senseless telegram.* It occurred to me that he wanted to tell me that in order to go west, I should go east."[2]

With the help of a network of Quakers using their contacts throughout Europe and the Orient, Akeley made a long, arduous, but safe solo journey of escape through Russia, Korea, Japan, and across the Pacific, landing in California. After working in California to pay off her debts to the Quakers, Akeley traveled by train to Lafayette in 1942 and married Edward.

The couple first met a few years before Akeley fled Austria when Edward had visited Europe and at the request of his boss, Karl Lark-Horovitz, head of the Physics Department, agreed to call on Akeley's sister, whom Lark-Horovitz knew. In turn, Akeley's sister asked Edward to go see Akeley in Vienna. The Nazis had restricted normal communication channels, and she wanted to know how Akeley was faring. Akeley knew nothing of this arrangement when Edward knocked on her door.

"He came to me and introduced himself as Edward Akeley from Lafayette, and I thought, You are a dirty liar, because Lafayette must be in France, and you have the wrong accent," Akeley recalled. She thought he was a spy. Later she learned he was a physicist from America. They saw one another during two visits Edward made to Europe, communicating by cobbling together three different languages they both knew. On his second visit he proposed marriage.[3]

Akeley's sister and her husband had fled to Prague after Hitler came to Vienna in 1938 for a speech at the Heldenplatz, the central square, where 300,000 citizens had been ordered to attend. Akeley was there and recalled, "I was some distance from Hitler, but I could see him standing in the car and then on the balcony of the chancellery. When he arrived the people were jubilant.... I was amazed that the people were jubilant!"[4]

When Akeley arrived home that day, her sister and her husband were packed to leave immediately for Prague where they thought they would be safe. Akeley's sister did not want to go to America where she thought immigrants became maids. That was the last time Akeley saw her sister, who later died at the hands of the Nazis.

Akeley was born in 1904 to an affluent Jewish family. She said they were "Jews but non-religious Jews." She attended a Catholic school and celebrated Christmas with the family's servants who were Catholic. Her well-educated mother, an accomplished pianist, came from a family of Moravian textile barons. Akeley grew up in a household with a cook, chauffeur, maids, and a French governess.[5] She was fluent in French by age four. Akeley was athletic and took instructions in swimming, fencing, gymnastics, and skiing.[6] In high school she took drawing lessons with the famed Austrian artist Oskar Kokoschka.[7] In 1918 when she was fourteen, her father died from tuberculosis and cancer. Her family's well-heeled lifestyle ended when Hitler took Austria.

In the early 1920s, Akeley studied comparative philosophy of religion at university and took courses in physics with a study of X-rays at the Roentgen Institute.[8] She conducted research on how to reduce patients' exposure time to an X-ray machine's radiation. She said:

> We tried all kinds of silly things on the machine until I went to our major professor and told him the following thing: "I know that there is a man by the name of Eastman in a firm called Kodak in America who was able to reduce the exposure time of ordinary films. Why don't we ask him if he can give us a tip on how he did that, and we can then change it a little and apply it to X-rays." He did that.... We were able to really reduce the exposure time to a certain extent, although not to the same extent as now. Therefore I got my diploma as a licensed X-ray machine technician.[9]

In 1940, Akeley wanted to escape Austria, but because of her job working in a hospital she was not allowed to go to Berlin to obtain a passport and leave for America. She was advised to break a bone in her right hand, because as a right-handed person she would then be unable to work and be free to go to Berlin. The advisor gave her a name of a doctor who could put her finger in a vice and turn it a bit.

"What kind of anesthetics will you use?" Akeley asked the doctor.

"I can't give you any anesthetic because it might be detected," he replied.

Akeley wrote in her memoir, "I put my finger in the vise, and he quickly broke my finger. I screamed.... [He] told me to say that I had broken it by stumbling and landing on it when I tried to catch myself. He then made holes in my stockings and put dirt on my dress to make the story more convincing."[10]

She traveled to Berlin where she obtained papers to enter the United States as an immigrant. Once she arrived at Purdue, Akeley was in awe. "When I saw West Lafayette, a stone fell from my heart," she said. "It looked wonderful, especially

Anna Akeley, shown here in 1947, fled Austria to escape the Nazis. She became a popular Purdue professor of physics even though she did not hold a PhD in physics. Courtesy Purdue University Archives and Special Collections.

with all these enormous trees on the campus. I had not seen any campus like that. European campuses are very different. All that space!"[11]

After Akeley married Edward, they lived in his tiny apartment on Hayes Street. She looked at the two dramatic pen-and-ink drawings Edward had on the wall by artist Guillermo Meza titled *Dream of the Dance*. At first she thought they were reproductions that Edward had purchased at S. S. Kresge or Woolworth's. She asked if the paintings were real. Edward said that yes, they were real. He had purchased them in Mexico.

That was Akeley's first glimmer of knowledge that Edward was a self-made, savvy art collector. By skipping lunch when he was at the University of Chicago, he could afford to visit art museums where he trained his eye to identify significant works. He often traveled to Mexico where he purchased art at little cost, and he rescued noteworthy pieces from the hands of the Nazis who destroyed art across Europe.

Shortly after Akeley arrived in West Lafayette, she received a phone call from Lark-Horovitz, head of Purdue's Physics Department and Edward's boss, who asked her to send her resume to him right away. Edward immediately hand-delivered Akeley's credentials. Two hours later, the phone rang for Akeley and Lark-Horovitz said, "You are going to teach the laboratory class for the first engineering course."

She said, "In what field?"

"In physics," he answered.

"Sir, I haven't had physics for sixteen years and never in English," Akeley said.

"You have a husband," Lark-Horovitz replied. "He will teach you in two weeks or less."[12]

There was a shortage of professors due to the war, so Akeley's help was sorely needed. When Edward came home that night, she said, "Your boss is crazy. I have forgotten my physics, because I learned about X-rays.... Surely I will be completely lost."[13]

Nevertheless, every night after dinner, Akeley went to the physics laboratory where Edward taught her about the equipment and how to conduct experiments. She also sat in on physics lectures to soak up as much knowledge as she could. She then began teaching students in the Reserve Officers' Training Corps (ROTC).

"I was supposed to call them 'gentlemen' when I addressed them," Akeley recalled. "They had to call me 'madam' and stand up when I talked to them.... I went to class and said 'good morning' and they all stood up.... I said I am sorry that I have an accent, but you will get accustomed to it. I heard a little voice say, 'When?'"

One day her use of the wrong word brought about a humorous situation. "I mixed up a term in electricity," she explained. "Instead of 'induced current,' I said, 'Gentlemen, today we are going to discuss '*seduced* current.' They all laughed. I asked, 'What's wrong?' There stood a boy, ... at least 6'5" or 6'7", way above me and he said, 'Does madam want an experimental or a theoretical explanation?'"

A little Jewish student came to Akeley's rescue. He said, "We are going to discuss *induced* current. Sit down." That student was Ben R. Mottelson, who would be awarded the Nobel Prize in physics in 1975.[14]

Soon, Akeley was asked to teach in the physics lab for home economics students, all female. Many of the women had no prior experience in physics and struggled. "Most of my students took half an hour just to use a slide rule," Akeley recalled. "The lab was a continuous stream of tears. They had hoped I would change that. I had one good idea in my life—change the course completely."[15]

Akeley's good idea was that while teaching the women physics, she would also teach them about the famous scientists who were mentioned in the course, bringing them to life. She said, "How many of them knew that Isaac Newton thought he was going to be a great religious writer, or that Galileo was threatened with excommunication for his scientific theories? You see, the students began to see these men as real people, not just scientists."[16]

Akeley admitted that not having a physics degree was at times problematic. "It was sometimes very tough, because the more I taught, and the more that physics developed, the more I realized how little I knew," she said. "Students would ask me about the atomic bomb or the evolution of the universe, and I would have to admit to them, I am not a physicist, I am just a simple physics teacher."[17]

However, to her students Akeley was much more than "just a simple physics teacher." In 1966 she was surprised with the Best Instructor Award by Purdue Student Government in recognition of her outstanding classroom work and her rapport with students. The student body had voted for Akeley to receive the award, which also reflected her popularity as a counselor for women's residence halls.

In 1969 Akeley was the second woman, after Helen Blanche Schleman herself, to receive Purdue's Helen B. Schleman Gold Medallion Award established upon Schleman's retirement as dean of women (1947–1968). Still awarded today, it annually honors a female faculty member or administrator who encourages women in academic and professional areas within the university.

After twenty-nine years of teaching at Purdue, Akeley retired with tenure as instructor emerita in 1971. Edward died in 1984. She continued to live in their small home at 525 Meridian that she good humoredly called "le shack." Unbeknownst to many, that unassuming home was filled with some of Edward's vast collection of Latin American, German, and Japanese art he had quietly amassed for fifty years.

Before he died, Edward told Akeley that she was to use his collection of paintings to ensure her lifestyle, but if she didn't need them, she was to give them away. He did not want his collection given to major museums, such as the Art Institute of Chicago, because he feared they would end up in storage. "I don't want them in drawers," he told Akeley. "I want them in institutions where they might hang them up."[18]

For ten years, Akeley continued to live among Edward's acquisitions, but when her accountant told her in 1994 that she was financially secure through age 100, she knew the moment had come to give the 144 paintings away to four museums and Edward's two nephews.

She asked Sharon Theobald, then executive director of the Greater Lafayette Museum of Art, to appraise Edward's collection. Edward had served as chairman of the collections committee at the museum. It would be Theobald's first major appraisal and catapult her career as an evaluator of fine art. Today she is president of Appraisal Associates International LLC.

While part of the collection was displayed on the walls of "le shack," a large number of Edward's paintings had been stored for years in a padlocked, four-foot wooden crate painted battleship grey and kept in a storage room he had secured on the fourth floor of Purdue's Stewart Center. Theobald created an inventory of the works and hired a photographer to take pictures of each piece, compiling the photos on CDs, which she still has today. Then she created a catalog.

Lisa Palmer, head of the Latin American department of Christie's, the respected New York art auction house, helped Theobald set values for the paintings. Theobald also worked with a representative from Sotheby's, the oldest and largest internationally recognized firm of fine art auctioneers in the world.[19]

A work by Diego Rivera, *Cabeza de Tehuana: Tehuantepec*, was valued at $130,000 in 1994. Rivera was the husband of artist Frida Kahlo. Two *Dance of the Dream* drawings that Edward had purchased for $15 from the artist in 1941 were worth $2,500.[20] The entire collection was valued at $1 million back then, and in 2023 Theobald said it would be worth $10 million.[21]

The institutions that would receive the art were the Smart Museum at the University of Chicago where Edward received his PhD, the University of South Dakota where his father had been dean of science, the Purdue Galleries, and the Art Museum of Greater Lafayette. Edward's two nephews also received works.

Theobald collaborated with Mona Berg, then director of Purdue Galleries, to assemble representatives from the institutions in a room in Purdue's Krannert School of Management where the collection was privately exhibited for the selection process. Each representative was given Theobald's appraisal catalog and a CD of photographs of each work.

"It resembled the NFL draft," Theobald recalled. "The representatives from the University of Chicago were number one, and they could chose any work they

Professor Anna Akeley in 1995 at her home she affectionately called "le shack" surrounded by some of the valuable artwork collected by her husband Edward Akeley and donated by the couple to Purdue University Galleries and other art institutions. Courtesy Purdue University Galleries.

wanted. Number two was Purdue University, then University of South Dakota, then the Art Museum of Greater Lafayette, and finally the Akeleys' two nephews. We went for thirty rounds until the entire collection was given away."

It was a thrill for Akeley to see Edward's collection finally go to museums after most of it had been locked away in a storage room for so long. The Art Museum of Greater Lafayette chose the mysterious and symbol-filled *Annunciation* painted in 1959 by Leonora Carrington, a British-born Mexican artist, surrealist painter and novelist. The painting instantly became the prized piece in the museum's collection. "It is probably one of the most iconic paintings that Leonora Carrington ever did," Theobald said in 2023. "And [it] may turn out to be the most valuable painting in the entire collection. It must be worth four to five million dollars today."[22]

In 2024, Purdue Galleries has 534 works donated by the Akeleys in their collection, and that number continues to grow as new discoveries are made and works are transferred to them from Purdue University Archives.[23]

Akeley also sold some of the collection to create a scholarship for art students at Purdue. Looking back, Theobald said, "There will never be any other appraisal assignment that will rival the Akeley collection in my mind. Such iconic works in so many different areas from a man who really studied, learned, and trained his eye as a connoisseur to acquire the very best works."[24]

When Akeley turned 100 in May 2004, an open house was held at Heritage Healthcare where she lived. At the event, Purdue President Martin C. Jischke awarded her with the Order of the Griffin, one of Purdue's highest honors recognizing outstanding service by those who have gone beyond the call of duty to benefit Purdue. Akeley died less than two months later.

Akeley had gone beyond the call of duty to escape the Nazis, teach her physics students, lift up the art world, and love and honor Edward. In essence, Akeley's 100 years were a metaphor for Edward's declaration—the earth is round.

EDITH WEISSKOPF-JOELSON, FUSING KNOWLEDGE AND FEELING

Edith Weisskopf-Joelson was born in Vienna, Austria, in 1910 to educated and cultured parents and lived an astounding life as a Jewish woman who escaped persecution, became an unconventional (by her Purdue male colleagues' standards) psychology professor, and survived tuberculosis and schizophrenia. Joelson endured a lonely career and health challenges, yet, in the end, led a life of triumph.

Joelson was a professor of psychology at Purdue from 1949 to 1962, bringing to the department her avant-garde spirit and knowledge of logotherapy, a form of psychotherapy that her friend Dr. Viktor Frankl developed as a survivor of the Holocaust. Frankl was a famed neurologist and psychiatrist who wrote the international best-seller *Man's Search for Meaning*. He wrote his book in nine days, and it was first published in German in 1946. The original English title was *From Death-Camp to Existentialism*.

Joelson was greatly influenced by Frankl's theory that finding meaning in life correlates with better mental health. She taught and lived this theory, even when her methods and philosophies conflicted with her Purdue male colleagues' rigid and pragmatic approach to psychology. Even when she fought her own psychological trepidations.

Joelson studied psychology at the Philosophical School of the University of Vienna. In 1932, she was one of the first women in the world to have her nose "fixed" by Dr. Jacques Joseph of Berlin who developed the plastic-surgery procedure. Joelson's reconstructed nose may have saved her life. She first admitted that she underwent plastic surgery out of a desire to look pretty, yet decades later she said, "It is ironic that I might not be alive today had I not had my nose changed from its original shape and its stereotypic Jewish curve."[25] Six years after her surgery, Adolf Hitler ordered the seizure and confinement to concentration camps of people of Austria who "looked Jewish."

She was only thirty-nine when she arrived at Purdue as an associate professor, yet Joelson had already amassed a bevy of courageous life and career experiences. Diminutive at five foot, three inches tall, she fled Austria on a ship and arrived in New York City in 1939. Despite not speaking English and being a refugee during the Depression when many could not find work, she quickly obtained a position as an instructor in the Department of Psychology at Briarcliffe College on Long Island, New York. She had no teaching experience but since childhood had ardently wanted to teach.

In her autobiography, Joelson wrote, "It was my special ambition to bring the material [I] taught close to the experience of my students. I wanted to help them overcome the split between knowledge and feeling which had plagued me all my life, and at the same time I wanted to overcome my own split. And I believe that I succeeded later on."[26]

Joelson's quest to meld knowledge and feeling speaks to one of the differences between women and men and how they view and experience the world. Women are more likely to lead through inspiration, transforming people's attitudes and beliefs, and aligning people with meaning and purpose. Women lead with their hearts and souls. Men tend to be self-focused and lead in a more competitive manner. Joelson worked with male colleagues and with theories devised by men. She felt alone in what she sensed in her gut was important research and credo to "overcome the split between knowledge and feeling."

Joelson had to teach herself American psychology before she could teach her students at Briarcliffe. She wrote, "American psychology was so different from the psychology I had learned in Vienna, that I failed to find any connection between the material I was supposed to teach and my inner world—my thoughts, fantasies, and wishes. The books described complex theoretical schemes which seemed to have been constructed for the purpose of making psychology look like

Shown here in 1976, Professor of Psychology Edith Weisskopf-Joelson brought her avant-garde spirit and knowledge of logotherapy to Purdue; however, her direction did not sit well with her male peers. Courtesy University of West Georgia, Ingram Library, Special Collections, Edith Weisskopf-Joelson Papers, MS-0006, Box 12.

an exact science rather than a tool for increasing our understanding of human beings' thoughts, feelings, attitudes, and behaviors."[27]

Later, Joelson became an assistant professor of psychology at Indiana University and a clinical psychologist at the Indiana State Department of Public Welfare, before she came to Purdue and undertook new endeavors—research and publishing as an associate professor of psychology in the graduate program.

Her first published research at Purdue involved a test consisting of a series of pictures to evaluate a subject's personality. The subject was asked to tell a story about each picture to reveal his or her preoccupations, worries, joys, and hopes. Joelson published several articles in a short time, made a name for herself, and was appointed a full professor of psychology at Purdue in 1958. Yet, she felt she made concessions. She had followed the trend of psychology at that time to show an abundance of computations in research. She wrote, "Strangely enough I was rather depressed during this time of success.... I had conformed in order to become well known and respected."

In "The History of Psychology at Purdue," Professor James C. Naylor wrote, "[Joelson's] European style and psychodynamic orientation conflicted somewhat with the hard-nosed empirical approach of the remainder of the faculty, many of whom had roots in the Iowa school. She considered it her mission in life to persuade experimentally oriented students to consider alternative approaches to viewing the complexities of human existence"[28]

This is when Joelson discovered the works of Dr. Viktor Frankl. Frankl's experience in Auschwitz solidified one of his central ideas: logotherapy, from the Greek word *logos*, which denotes "meaning."[29] According to logotherapy, the striving to find a meaning in one's life is the primary motivational force in all humans.

Joelson was drawn to Frankl's logotherapy because it aligned with her own professional theories of a therapy being closer to philosophy than to science. Logotherapy supported her "hunch that psychotherapy works because the therapist helps the patient develop a philosophy of life that dares to go beyond the body and the psyche."[30] She decided to do a new kind of research and writing not based on numbers and computations but on intuition. She incorporated logotherapy theory into her teaching. However, her new direction did not sit well with her peers at Purdue.

Joelson said, "A number of psychologists in the western states gave me some recognition, but at that time, those I worked with at Purdue were strict experimentalists who vehemently rejected my new approach. Thus, my position among my colleagues dropped within a short time from stardom to complete rejection and isolation. At that time it seemed to me that if you wanted to live in a society, you had to disregard your inner promptings and follow the common trend. In order to live, you had to become an as-if person, a pretense person, a pseudo person."[31]

At the same time that Joelson was rejected by her Purdue contemporaries, her marriage fell apart, and in 1962 when she was fifty-two, she was diagnosed with tuberculosis and hospitalized. She said, "My physicians believed me to be very close to death. They told me that I had been dying gradually during the past years, that I had been dying in the midst of a college campus in full view of my students and colleagues."[32]

After two years in a TB sanatorium, Joelson's tuberculosis was completely arrested and she was released. However, it was there that she began to experience hallucinations, which may have been drug-induced. Her physicians felt she was too weak to return to the pressures of teaching at Purdue, so she found part-time work at St. Mary-of-the-Woods, a Catholic College near Terre Haute, Indiana. Her hallucinations worsened to the point that she thought she was to play the role of Jesus Christ in a performance of a passion play that would be presented at the college. To the contrary, such a performance was not planned.

Joelson, age fifty-five, was admitted to Central Louisiana State Hospital, a psychiatric facility in Pineville, Louisiana, and diagnosed as suffering a schizophrenic episode. Her estranged husband continued to advocate for her, refusing to give permission for Joelson to receive electric shock treatments. Of her husband's decision, she wrote, "Should I receive a sizeable number of shock treatments, he argues, I might not be able to say smart things to students, which I will have to do until the age of sixty-seven, when I retire."[33] Instead of shock treatments, she was prescribed Thorazine.

Joelson kept a diary during both of her hospital stays. She wrote about a particular physician at the psychiatric hospital who was a beacon of hope for her. He was the only one who called her *Dr.* Joelson. One day when she was in occupational therapy making a potholder, the bearded Dr. Tom Sorcy joined her to see how she was doing. She confided in him, speculating that her vision might not have been a breakdown but a *breakthrough*.[34]

"Everyone thinks it is so dreadful to have hallucinations or—as you call them—visions," Joelson said to Sorcy. "But it is one of the most beautiful gifts I have ever received—the gift to see the world quite differently than I saw it all my life."

"Your rapture is not accepted in the world in which we live," Sorcy reassured her. "You know that Faulkner wrote, 'Craziness ain't so much what a fellow does, but it's the way the majority of folks is looking at him when he does it.'"

Sorcy further consoled her by saying, "But you'll recover.... You will have moments when everything around you becomes enthralled and glorious. There'll still be many mysteries for you to solve."

Joelson was puzzled by Sorcy's statements and said, "Why are you so different from all these doctors?"

"I took a class which made me see the world of mental illness in a new light," Sorcy confessed.

"A class in a medical school?" Joelson asked.

"No," Sorcy said. "In the Department of Psychology at Purdue University. Abnormal psychology taught by Dr. Joelson."

Sorcy pulled a photo of himself as a Purdue student out of his wallet and showed it to Joelson. While at Purdue, Tom Sorcy had short hair and was clean shaven so Joelson had not recognized her former student, the doctor who sat before her.[35]

Joelson was astounded. "Tom, is that you?"

Nearly in tears, Sorcy answered, "Yes."

More good fortune occurred in July 1966. Joelson received a phone call from the chair of psychology at Duke University offering her a position as a visiting professor. Joelson had sent letters to various universities in search of a post upon her discharge from the hospital. Sorcy helped her prepare to leave and take the position at Duke.[36]

During her time at Purdue, she had felt isolated and alone in her belief in logotherapy, yet Joelson had, unknowingly, greatly influenced Sorcy, her student who years later became her mentor, friend, and life-affirming doctor.

After teaching for one year at Duke, Joelson accepted a position as a professor of psychology at the University of West Georgia where she remained until her death in 1983 at age seventy-three. Her papers are preserved in University of West Georgia Special Collections.

Before her death, Joelson had placed her diary in a locked safe intending never to take it out again, but she changed her mind and exhumed the journal to include excerpts in her memoir, *Father, Have I Kept My Promise?* The book was her legacy to the Institute of Logotherapy and was published posthumously by Purdue University Press in 1988. Willis C. Fink, executive director of the Institute, wrote the foreword, stating, "You could not be around Edith without realizing that she was the embodiment of logotherapy. It was difficult to distinguish where logotherapy ended and her personal lifestyle began.... Logotherapy worked for Edith, and she worked for logotherapy."

Frankl wrote the afterword for Joelson's book, stating, "To me, it was gripping and moving, and I could not help but be reminded of the best-selling old-timer *Lost Horizon* by James Hilton."[37] Frankl devoted a postscript to Joelson in his 1984 edition of *Man's Search for Meaning*. It read, "Dedicated to the memory of Edith Weisskopf-Joelson whose pioneering efforts in logotherapy in the United States began as early as 1955 and whose contributions to the field have been invaluable."[38]

The year she died, Edith Weisskopf-Joelson's last authored work was published in *The International Forum for Logotherapy Journal of Search for Meaning* produced by the Institute of Logotherapy. It was titled, "Remarks of a Free-Floating Spirit."[39]

GERTRUDE SUNDERLIN AND MIRACULOUS MASTER MIX

While World War II raged in Europe, Professor Gertrude Laura Sunderlin and her research students developed the internationally famous recipe for Master Mix, a revolutionary baking blend that took America's kitchens by floury storm.

Sunderlin had a slim face and a wide, toothy, infectious smile. Raised in Iowa City, she graduated from the College of Home Economics at Iowa State in 1919. She earned both her master's and doctorate in bacteriology and was the first woman to earn a PhD from Iowa's College of Home Economics.[40] She received financial support from Ball Fruit Jar Company to pursue her doctorate.[41]

Sunderlin arrived at Purdue in 1931 and advanced to full professor in foods and nutrition by 1946. She led a clutch of research students in her experimental foods class to develop the Master Mix recipe that became famous throughout the country. For months, Sunderlin's class created and tested the mixture that could be made in large batches in the home kitchen and used as needed for a variety of baked goods. Master Mix was a substitute for the flour, salt, baking powder, and shortening used to make breads, cakes, cookies, desserts, and more. It would keep up to six weeks without refrigeration.

Commercial mixes such as boxed cake mixes were just beginning to be developed.[42] With the first announcement of Master Mix, more than 150,000 copies of the recipe were sent throughout the United States by Purdue's Cooperative Extension Service. Sunderlin and her students created a recipe booklet with special cake and cookie mixes, and it was distributed throughout Indiana, the United States, and several foreign countries.[43]

In 1948, a 4 x 6-inch recipe booklet with a spiral binding was created and bore these words: "The Master Mix recipes are time savers and reputation builders. The siftings and measurements of the dry ingredients and the blending of the fat can be done at one time for a dozen bakings."

A few of the recipes from the booklet were published in the January 1948 issue of *Better Homes and Gardens* magazine. Margaret Billings and Lucy Goetz, two of Sunderlin's students who had helped test and create Master Mix, were given a byline in the magazine. Black-and-white photos of food made with Master Mix were described as "speedy pancakes," "golden-top muffins," and "fluffy dumplings."

Once the word was out, many newspapers across the country ran a story about Master Mix accompanied by the recipe. The *Noblesville Ledger* stated, "Master Mix saves time. For biscuits, it takes only three minutes from the time the lid is taken off the Master Mix canister until the oven door closes."[44]

The *Muncie Evening Press* extoled Master Mix with this hook line: "Every homemaker, young and old, is constantly looking for time savers, bargains and knacks that will enrich her reputation with the family for being able to accomplish miracles."[45]

On October 1, 1949, Gertrude Sunderlin was a guest on the *National Farm and Home Hour* to tell the story of Master Mix. The *National Farm and Home Hour* was a national radio variety show produced by the US Department of Agriculture that ran from 1928 to 1958 and featured farm news and events, agricultural and home advice, as well as live music. Everett Mitchell was the show's host, and his signature opening line became a popular catchphrase: "It's a beautiful day in Chicago!"[46]

After Sunderlin spoke about Master Mix on national radio, interest in the recipe soared. Cards and letters from every state poured into Sunderlin's office at Purdue.[47] More newspapers ran stories of the baking time-saver. The Master Mix leaflet produced by the Purdue Agricultural Extension Service was mailed out by the thousands. By 1952, the bulletin had become the fourth most popular publication of the Extension Service. An article titled "Master Mix in Quantity" was published in the *Journal of the American Dietetic Association*.[48]

After Master Mix was formulated, Sunderlin and her students developed special cake and cookie mix recipes, which were also distributed to several hundred thousand people. Yet, Sunderlin did not rest on her baking laurels. She and a graduate student moved on to freezer jam, another innovative cooking concept developed in the Purdue Home Economics laboratories. Mary Akers Kramer conducted her master's thesis work on the recipe that revolutionized "home jamming."[49]

Traditionally, jams and jellies were prepared with the canning method—glass canning jars (often referred to as Ball or Mason jars) were filled with cooked fruit, topped with lids, placed into a canning pot, covered with water, and boiled until the lid was safely sealed so the product could sit on a shelf for months before eaten. Sunderlin and Kramer's new and speedy method that did not require cooking the fruit was announced to hundreds of home economists attending the 1952 American Home Economics Association annual meeting in Atlantic City with several of Purdue's home economics professors in attendance.

Kramer presented her paper about her research on uncooked fruit jams at the convention, and the rest was freezer jam history. The following month Kramer demonstrated "Uncooked Jams from Frozen and Fresh Fruit" to homemakers attending the annual Indiana Home Economics Association conference at Purdue.

The key ingredient was pectin. Pectin is a starch that occurs naturally in the cell walls of fruits and vegetables. Commercial pectin is sold as a powder or liquid and is a gelling agent. Kramer's research focused on combining pectin in a bowl with fresh fruit and sugar to produce a no-fail jam to be eaten immediately or placed

At a dinner in her honor, Professor Gertrude Laura Sunderlin holds up a Mix Master hand mixer, presumably a nod to Master Mix, the internationally famous baking blend Sunderlin and her students developed that was the originator of all baking mixes today. Courtesy Purdue University Archives and Special Collections.

in the freezer where it could be stored for months. Because it was uncooked, the jam tasted like just-picked berries. Freezer jam is still popularly made today.

Another student of Sunderlin's was Ruth M. Siems who graduated with a bachelor's degree in home economics in 1953. Siems worked for General Foods in Evansville, Indiana, conducting research on flour and angel food cake mixes. Her claim to fame came in 1971 when she helped develop Stove Top Stuffing while working at General Foods in White Plains, New York. She was listed first among four inventors when the patent was awarded four years later. After her success, Siems wrote a note of appreciation to Sunderlin. Stove Top Stuffing continues to be popular today as a quick and easy way to make stuffing without actually stuffing a turkey.[50]

Sunderlin retired from Purdue in 1954 and moved back to her roots in Iowa City. Nearly twenty years later, the *Des Moines Tribune* ran a springtime story with the headline, "At Strawberry Time, We Honor Professor of Jam." The article read, "Thank you, Miss Sunderlin. We wouldn't dream of letting the strawberry season slip by without donning our apron and doffing our bonnet to Miss Sunderlin."[51]

10

WOMEN WHO ENRICHED FAMILY LIFE

When World War II ended, fathers came home, women left factories and offices—most were let go to give men back their jobs—and couples were together again. Time to delight in and emphasize the family. Dean of the School of Home Economics Mary Matthews saw a need and took action. In 1946, she strengthened the focus on child development and family relations by establishing the Department of Family Life, the seed of today's Human Development and Family Science at Purdue. It was part of what was called "postwar expansion of the School of Home Economics."[1]

Matthews divided her Department of Home Administration into two units: Home Management and Family Life. She appointed Cleo Fitzsimmons of the University of Illinois as head of the Home Management Department. The director of the Purdue Nursery School, Margaret Nesbitt (later Murphy), was made head of the Department of Family Life.

Nesbitt's academic background was in educational psychology and child development.[2] She headed the Department of Family Life when a cooperative nursery school was formed in 1947 called the Associated Parents Nursery School, later developing into the Nimitz Drive Cooperative Nursery School in 1958. It integrated childcare and schooling for young children of Purdue's faculty, staff, and students into the nursery school coursework. For ten years the nursery school was held in a building on Memorial Drive West in what was called the "experimental housing" part of campus.

Many married students with children relied on the play groups and nursery school offered by the Department of Family Life as their day care while they were in class or needed time to study. In 1959, the building was torn down to make way for a new water tank that was part of a power plant expansion. The Associated Parents Nursery School moved off campus for the first time and set up operations in the Unitarian Fellowship building at 489 Harrison.[3]

ISABELLE DIEHL FIRST TO TEACH NURSING

A hint of Purdue's future School of Nursing that would be founded in 1963 came to Purdue in 1939 in the form of Isabelle Diehl. Diehl was a registered nurse with a degree from Johns Hopkins University when she joined the School of Home Economics staff to teach nursing subjects and serve as a nurse for the Purdue Nursery School. Diehl took a leave of absence during World War II to become a member of the Army Nurses Corps and was stationed at a hospital in the Fiji islands.[4]

When she returned to Purdue, having been discharged with the rank of captain, Diehl established innovative programs for infants and toddlers involving their mothers and Purdue students. Diehl would be instrumental in guiding the formation of Purdue's two-year nursing program as a member of the community advisory committee on nursing education that guided the establishment of an associated degree in 1963.[5] (Read about the founding of Purdue's School of Nursing in chapter 17.)

IDA B. KELLEY, FIRST PROFESSOR EMERITUS OF PSYCHOLOGY

Psychology and Family Life intertwined as Ida B. Kelley of the Psychology Department held a joint appointment in both disciplines. The basic course in family relationships was offered in both departments.[6] Kelley's interest in human behavior led her to psychology. She obtained all three of her degrees from Purdue and was a member of the International Mental Health Association. She lectured in Germany in 1948 as a part of the group's program.[7] Kelley was director of the Purdue University School Psychology Clinic for children and adolescents. In the mid-1950s there was a waiting list of more than 150 children. Kelley said, "The aim of the clinic is reconstructing and rechanneling the child's behavior; not to find out what the child must do to be 'normal,' but to find out what he can do reasonably well and with a feeling of satisfaction and social approval."[8] Kelley retired in 1959 and was the first psychologist at Purdue to receive the title of professor emeritus.[9]

ELAINE T. DOLCH, FOUNDER OF PURDUE CHILD CARE

Chats About Children was a Cooperative Extension Service newsletter written by Professor Elaine Thome Dolch. Throughout her career, Dolch chatted about children in a monumental way at the podium and throughout the Purdue and local communities facilitating small steps toward the establishment of child care and research laboratories in early childhood education. Dolch led the charge to create the Purdue Child Care Program in a vacant West Lafayette school, the precursor to today's Ben and Maxine Miller Child Development Laboratory School.

When Home Economics Extension moved to the School of Home Economics from the School of Agriculture in the mid-1960s, Dolch was the extension specialist in family life and child development. After the move, the Department of Child Development and Family Life became more closely related to the Cooperative Extension Service, even though the department was not part of the School of Home Economics at the time.

Dolch studied, taught, wrote, counseled, formed student organizations, and started Purdue's first day care during her thirty-nine-year career at Purdue. She had earned a bachelor's degree in textile chemistry from Purdue in 1948. After she received her master's degree in child development from the university in 1951, she served on the faculty of the Purdue child development and family life clinic.[10] For twenty years, Dolch was an advisor for the Nimitz Drive Cooperative Nursery School, which later became the Purdue Village Preschool. She was on the Board of Directors of Tippecanoe County Child Care, a service that provided child care to low-income families.

Dolch was the energy behind the formation of the Purdue Child Care Program in the former Burtsfield Elementary School in West Lafayette. It was a cooperative venture between West Lafayette Community School Corp. (WLCSC) and the university that started in 1983 for children of Purdue and WLCSC employees. This was an era when more and more women were joining the workforce, and families needed quality day care. The Greater Lafayette community was in dire need of child care facilities (as it still is today). The new program did not begin to meet the demand, but it was a small start.

At first, the facility was looked upon by some as not "necessary," and it was not strongly supported.[11] A Purdue Research Foundation (PRF) fund drive had gathered pledges for an infant-toddler center to be started in a house owned by PRF the year before the opening of the Purdue Child Care Program, but the center never materialized.

The Purdue Child Care Program grew from twelve children in 1983 to more than seventy children in 1988.[12] It provided Purdue students with opportunities to observe and participate in a model child care program and conduct research in the fields of early childhood education, just as Indiana's first nursery school did after it was started by Mary Matthews in the 1930s.

In 1981, Dolch co-founded the Purdue Association for the Education of Young Children (PAEYC), a student organization that ended in 2012. In 1986, she wisely pushed for accreditation for the Child Development Laboratories and the Purdue Child Care Program with the National Association for the Education of Young Children by seeking funds to initiate the application process.[13] Dolch served twice as acting director of the Child Development Laboratories and Purdue Child Care Program.[14] She conducted a joint research project with Lee Kruel of the Department of Restaurant, Hotel, and Institutional Management on the feasibility of establishing child care facilities in hotels and motels sponsored by the Institute for Consumer and Family Studies.[15]

Legislation was passed to protect those with disabilities, particularly children, and Dolch had a professional and personal interest. The Education for All Handicapped Children Act of 1975 (renamed the Individuals with Disabilities Education Act in 1990) declared that a child could not be excluded from a public school because of a disability, and school districts were required to provide special services to meet the needs of children with disabilities.

Dolch spoke to groups on topics such as "The Handicapped Child in the Family and Community" and "Developing Skills in Parenting the Handicapped Child." Dolch spoke as an expert in the field of child development but also as a parent of a child with a disability. Her son Eric had cerebral palsy and was in a wheelchair. He attended the Purdue Nursery School as a preschooler.

The Purdue Child Care Program moved to temporary buildings near the Horticulture Park at the west end of Purdue's campus in 1988. The buildings were custom-designed for what was then named the Department of Child

Development and Family Studies. The new location was more convenient for students who worked at the center and for the Purdue staff members whose children were enrolled.[16]

Dolch's love of children's literature was evident in her work and life. Two of the courses she taught were "Music and Literature for Young Children" and "Books and Pictures for Young Children." Her authored piece "Books for the Hospitalized Child" was published in the *American Journal of Nursing* in December 1961.

Upon her retirement in 1990, Dolch made a monetary gift to the Department of Child Development and Family Studies (now Science) for a lounge and resource center to be used by the faculty and staff. The Parent Advisory Council and the Child Development staff honored her by creating the Elaine T. Dolch Children's Library in the Child Development Laboratories. Each book donated held a specially designed bookplate with the donor's name. The books were presented to Dolch at the dedication of the library on March 19, 1991, and she herself placed them upon the bookshelves.[17]

11

NEW HOME ECONOMICS DEAN AND PIONEERS IN BRAZIL

MATTHEWS RETIRES, BEULAH V. GILLASPIE NAMED DEAN

It was announced that Mary Lockwood Matthews, seventy, would retire as the founding dean of the School of Home Economics, and in December 1951 the *Exponent* devoted an entire issue to Matthews and the school. The following January, a banquet was held in her honor in the Purdue Memorial Union to commemorate her forty-one years of service.[1]

Margaret Nesbitt Murphy acted as toastmistress. President Frederick Hovde commended "our gracious and distinguished lady," and President Emeritus Edward Elliott paid tribute. Longtime friend and colleague A. A. Potter made remarks ending with a nod to the "atomic age." He said:

> The type of education which is represented by the Land-Grant Institutions has developed in thousands of our citizens the power of analysis so that they approach problems with an open mind without prejudice and preconceived notions.... The home economics programs have definitely resulted in improving the homes of the Nation.

All curricula of the Land-Grant Colleges have always stressed the art, as well as the science, of their respective fields, and few have contributed more richly to the art of home economics education, the country over, than has Mary L. Matthews.

Atomic scientists speak of chain reactions. Dean Matthews has started a Home Economics chain reaction at Purdue University, which will be felt through the years in better and happier living for humanity, and—we hope—in a world at peace.[2]

Matthews was honored with the title of Dean Emeritus. The Mary L. Matthews Club was founded that March, and Edith Gamble and Ruth Jordan, co-chairs of the club, established the Mary L. Matthews Scholarship Fund.[3] The club remains active today. Matthews received an honorary degree of doctor of laws at the May 1953 commencement.[4] Today, the Mary L. Matthews Outstanding Undergraduate Teaching Award is bestowed annually on a member of the faculty of the College of Health and Human Sciences.

President Hovde considered appointing William E. Martin as Matthews's successor. Martin was head of the Department of Child Development and Family Life. Regarding home economics, Hovde admitted, "It was the one academic area at Purdue that stumped me."[5]

When the home economics faculty heard that Hovde might hire a man, they were not supportive of the idea.[6] Dean of Women Helen B. Schleman spoke out about the need for a woman to lead the School of Home Economics as a role model for women students. If a man had been appointed, there would have been all male academic deans on campus and not a single female dean. Hovde changed course and, while he did not hire a man, he appointed a woman very different from Mary Matthews—Beulah V. Gillaspie.

As much as Matthews was reserved with tightly coifed hair and sensible shoes, Gillaspie was said to be forward in a "New York" way. She liked jewelry and fashion. She came to Purdue from the University of Arkansas where she had been head of the Department of Home Economics. In the 1930s, Gillaspie worked as a food research editor and director for the Laboratory Kitchen of *McCall's Magazine*. She was also the director of the Sealtest Laboratory Kitchen, and her recipes were printed in newspapers across the country.

The Sealtest symbol was much like the Good Housekeeping Seal of Approval. A brochure listing the ice cream brands that bore "the coveted Sealtest Symbol"

Beulah V. Gillaspie, *second from left*, visits with students. She succeeded Mary L. Matthews as dean of the School of Home Economics in 1952. Courtesy Purdue University Archives and Special Collections.

stated, "Visit the Sealtest Laboratory Kitchen when you are in New York. And, if there is any way in which the Kitchen can help you with your food problems, drop a note to Miss Gillaspie, 30 Rockefeller Plaza."[7]

Gillaspie's style appealed to the students. She had an astute business sense, and she encouraged students in home economics to enter the business world. The year Gillaspie became dean, Purdue took home economics education to South America.

ANITA DICKSON, AMERICAN PIONEER, IN BRAZIL

A team of home economics faculty members moved to Vicosa, Brazil, in 1952 to establish a School of Home Economics at the Rural University of Minas Gerais (UREMG). It became the first university in South America to grant a bachelor's degree in home economics.

The Purdue-Brazil Technical Assistance Program was funded by the US Agency for International Development (AID).[8] Purdue's School of Agriculture also sent faculty to establish programs and teach. The collaboration took the Vicosa university from being essentially a vocational school to a prestigious Latin American university that would be put under federal control in 1969 and renamed the Federal University of Vicosa.[9]

The goal of the Purdue team in Brazil was to help UREMG become a land-grant type of organization. Purdue took their land-grant mission of extension to Brazil to help the country help themselves in improving their agricultural practices (including home economics) by assisting them in educating their people. The objectives were to increase the supply of trained scientists through a graduate program, train technicians, spread information through an extension program, and gain public support.

Purdue hoped to help UREMG become as useful to the state of Minas Gerais as Purdue is to the state of Indiana, and it met that goal. A 1964 report stated, "The ability to 'stick its nose into other people's business,' so well-learned and well-practiced at home, makes the land-grant concept a useful tool in many aspects of agricultural development, not limited to the colleges themselves."[10]

When the Purdue-Brazil program began in 1952, Anita Dickson was appointed as technical assistance advisor to the project, and she established the Superior School of Home Economics or Escola Superior Ciencia Domestica in Vicosa. Dickson was perfect for the position because she had served thirty-two years in the USDA Agricultural Extension Service before coming to Purdue. In 1964, she returned to Vicosa for a second tour of duty to serve as a home economics extension technician.[11]

When Dickson first arrived in Brazil, only four young women were enrolled in home economics and facilities to house the new endeavor were practically nonexistent. Eventually classes were held in a remodeled warehouse. The former residence of the university president was converted into an overcrowded dormitory. By the end of the Purdue-Brazil tour fourteen years later, the UREMG had a school of home economics, an academic building, a four-year curriculum, and 106 women enrolled.[12] Early graduates became instructors. Many graduates became welfare extension workers in several regions of Brazil.[13]

In the beginning, there were some skeptics among the faculty of UREMG, but that attitude changed for the most part to one of pride and enthusiasm. At the ten-year anniversary of the Superior School of Home Economics, nearly an entire issue of the Vicosa newspaper was devoted to commemorating the school's

Anita Dickson, *right*, with student Shane Jackson in 1960. Dickson established the Superior School of Home Economics as technical assistance advisor to the Purdue-Vicosa project in Brazil, South America, beginning in 1952. Courtesy Purdue University Archives and Special Collections.

milestone. In a progress report, Dickson wrote, "Better than acceptance, adoption of practices that were clearly identifiable with the teachings of the Home Economics School is now evident in the homes of residents of Vicosa."

Yet, there were challenges. There was a need for more teaching material in Portuguese and more home economics textbooks. Teachers needed training in writing and presenting.[14] There was lack of research on Brazilian foods, Brazilian living conditions, and Brazilian family life that would have helped with creation of instructions and extension programs. The small town of Vicosa was isolated from the rest of the state until 1965 when a paved road was completed.[15]

UREMG President L. Menicucci Sobrinho said this about Anita Dickson's leadership at his university:

> The University was lucky, because it received among its members one of the most dedicated, most able, and most distinguished home economists, Miss Anita Dickson, who knew how to start the School on the right foundations....

Simple, kind, understanding, besides being able and competent, she knew how to gain the confidence, the admiration, and the respect of all the ones who came close to her. She didn't ask for too much, she didn't impose any conditions, but on the contrary, she organized the School with the existent resources, making adjustments and improvisations, crossing any obstacle.[16]

In the summer of 1959, Purdue's Dean of the School of Home Economics Beulah Gillaspie traveled to Brazil to be a consultant for a clothing workshop, nutrition workshop, and a regional home economics meeting at the UREMG. The impetus for the regional meeting was to establish a national home economics association in Brazil. Gillaspie had been president of the American Home Economics Association for two years, so she was a prime candidate to help Brazil establish their own association.[17]

Other faculty members who taught and consulted in Brazil were Mary Louise Foster of the home management and family economics department and Gladys E. Vail, a renowned researcher and head of the department of foods and nutrition who would succeed Gillaspie as dean. Purdue President Frederick Hovde visited the Purdue-Brazil project in 1965.[18]

Tables were turned and seven Brazilian women students arrived at Purdue in 1962 as undergraduates in home economics through scholarships provided by the Purdue-Brazil Project. They attended Purdue to fulfill a need for trained home economics teachers in their home country. When asked how campus life compared with that in Brazil, the women said the most noticeable difference was the "constant rush" of everyone at Purdue. A newspaper article stated that the women went to some dances, and "they even admit to attending some 'twist help-sessions'—but felt the 'twist' was just a fad."[19]

In 1966, after fourteen years of working with the UREMG, Purdue's faculty in Brazil abruptly returned to the United States on a month's notice when funding stopped.[20]

Fast forward to 1992, and a letter arrived at Purdue from Maria de Fatima Lopes, a professor in the Department of Home Economics at the Federal University of Vicosa, formerly UREMG. Lopes was working on her doctoral thesis in social anthropology. She addressed the letter to "Family and Friends of Anita Dickson."[21] Dickson had passed away at age seventy-seven from brain cancer in 1989 in her home in Albuquerque, New Mexico.[22]

In her letter, Lopes explained that her plan of study for her thesis included the historical origin of the courses defined as home economics and agricultural engineering and the biographies of Americans who founded home economics in Brazil. She was writing her thesis on the Purdue trailblazers who founded home economics in Brazil. She wrote, "Please, kindly provide your knowledge of people, dates, history, and other information about the American pioneers in the creation of home economics in Brazil. This is a vital part of institutional history that I intend to study and report."

Anita Dickson and the Purdue home economics faculty who created a School of Home Economics in Brazil were, indeed, American pioneers.

12
INFLUENCERS IN LIBERAL ARTS AND SCHOOL OF SCIENCE

MARGARET CHURCH, FIRST FEMALE FULL PROFESSOR IN LIBERAL ARTS

Like the opening of a novel, Margaret Church wrote of driving into Lafayette, Indiana, for the first time on a September morning in 1953 "with my car and trunk piled high with almost all my belongings, and a cashier's check, representing whatever money I could draw on, tucked carefully in my handbag."[1]

"Lafayette, with its Victorian angularities, its gingerbread, is a Grant Wood original," she penned at age thirty-three. "But what struck me first was its flatness. The town sits on the banks of the Wabash, east and west, but beyond its outskirts lie seemingly endless stretches of flat farmland, divided at intervals by gravel roads, designed originally to follow boundary lines between properties. Thus in traveling them one is frequently subject to right-angle turns for no apparent reason."[2]

Church made a right-angle turn onto the Purdue campus to be an instructor in Modern Fiction and for nearly thirty years made her mark on the literary community at the university and globally. She said that Purdue and Lafayette were her destiny. When she became a full professor in 1965, she was the first woman in Purdue's College of Liberal Arts, then called the School of Humanities,

Social Science, and Education, to do so.³ That same year, she became chair of the newly established program in comparative literature. She helped to found the internationally known journal *Modern Fiction Studies*, chaired Purdue's distinguished Literary Awards banquet, and was a trustee of the International James Joyce Foundation, founded in Dublin, Ireland.

A Bostonian with short dark hair and a warm smile, Church was born in 1920. She received a master's in English from Columbia University (1942) and a PhD in English from Radcliffe College (1944). She taught English and comparative literature at Temple and Duke Universities before arriving at Purdue. She said, "I retain memories of Philadelphia in the war years and night classes at Temple, when it was still safe to walk on Broad Street at 11 p.m. and ride the subway home; and I remember riding the Philadelphia subway to work the April morning that FDR died, and seeing the quiet weeping of fellow passengers."⁴

When she taught at Duke in the late 1940s and early 1950s, female students and faculty were segregated to the East Campus, men to the West. She became a role model for women entering the field of English and literature professorship. Church wrote three books and more than two dozen articles and reviews on modern fiction and on James Joyce, Virginia Woolf, and other great twentieth-century fiction writers. She also wrote poetry.

In his eulogy for Church, her colleague Hugo Reichard said, "She was a private, independent person, with a mind that was not only gifted but her own. She stood up fearlessly against snakes in the basement, hunters in the nearby woods, and adversaries in meetings she attended. She was always in a meeting, as in the class and living room, fair and cooperative. She was ever sensitive to another's misgivings, another's pain, another's grief, and went out of her way inconspicuously to ease, if not to share, the distress."⁵

Church received numerous grants to present papers and conduct research abroad. She presented reviews and also served as chair of the English Department's "Books and Coffee" series where Purdue faculty members reviewed current popular books.

Church founded Purdue's doctoral program in Comparative Literature and served as its first director. Her student Joanne Trautmann was the first recipient of a Purdue PhD in English in 1967.⁶ Also that year, Purdue's Mortar Board Honor Society named its four-year freshman scholarship after Church. Yearly, Mortar Board, then an all-female organization, named the scholarship in honor of an outstanding woman on campus.⁷ She was also honored with the Helen B. Schleman Gold Medallion Award for her support of women.

Also in 1967, the James Joyce Foundation was established at the first International James Joyce Symposium to encourage scholarship, criticism, and study of the life, work, and career of writer James Joyce and Church would become a trustee of the foundation. The symposium continues to be held each year around Bloomsday, the day in fiction—June 16, 1904—that Leopold Bloom spent wandering the streets of Dublin in Joyce's *Ulysses*.

Church was the coeditor of the journal *Modern Fiction Studies* from 1969 until her death in 1982. However, Church had been involved as a member of the journal's editorial board beginning when it was first published at Purdue in 1955 by the Modern Fiction Club in the Department of English. Then mimeographed on letter-size paper, it was the first journal devoted exclusively to criticism of contemporary American, English, and European fiction.[8] For decades, Church was the only female professor associated with the quarterly. By 1975, the editors received as many as 700 manuscripts, and from those forty to fifty were selected for publication.[9] It evolved into a major journal with worldwide circulation, and today it is published by the Johns Hopkins University Press.[10]

When Church chaired Purdue's 1972 Literary Awards Banquet (still an annual event), held in the Purdue Memorial Union ballroom, which culminated in the annual literary awards contest for students with cash prizes and gift certificates, the American playwright Tennessee Williams was the event's speaker. Williams wrote, among other works, *The Glass Menagerie* and the Pulitzer Prize–winning dramas *A Streetcar Named Desire* and *Cat on a Hot Tin Roof*, all later made into movies.

She became chair of the Comparative Literature program at Purdue and was elected vice president and president of the Midwest Modern Language Association from 1975 to 1977.[11]

Church loved the outdoors, sports, and gardening. In his eulogy, Reichard said, "She supplied advice to inept gardeners as if she were Heavilon Hall's resident agent of the extension service."[12] She rode her horse every day for decades. She played tennis, went skiing, and jogged up and down County Road 400 West near her home in all kinds of weather. She traveled broadly, including a trip up the Nile.

Many of her trips were in connection with the James Joyce Foundation, attending symposia in Dublin, London, Trieste, Paris, and Zurich where she presented papers and chaired panel discussions. She was always thrilled when she spied a copy of *Modern Fiction Studies* in a foreign library. "But in September," she wrote shortly before her death, "when 32,000 students converge on Lafayette

In 1965, Margaret Church was the first woman to become a full professor in the College of Liberal Arts. She was a founder of the journal *Modern Fiction Studies*, chaired Purdue's Literary Awards banquet, and was a trustee of the International James Joyce Foundation, Dublin, Ireland. Courtesy Purdue University Archives and Special Collections.

(by moped, bicycle, rail, car, and plane), I, too, return to its familiar and comfortable confines."[13]

On the afternoon of Sunday, August 29, 1982, workmen were repairing the roof of Church's one-story home and she climbed up. As she descended the ladder, she fell onto a concrete driveway, hit her head and shoulders, and was flown to Methodist Hospital in Indianapolis by Life Line helicopter. Church, age sixty-two, died the following day. She was survived by two sisters and was buried in Hanover, Massachusetts.

A memorial service was planned for the East Meadow of Purdue's Horticulture Park (apropos given that Church loved the outdoors); however, due to rain, it took place in Stewart Center. A number of her colleagues spoke or gave readings. Reichard described his colleague and friend: "She loaded and unloaded the suitcases of ailing friends with trips to make. She broke bread with many of us, and watched movies, and exchanged letters or phone calls or visits with zest. She was a many-sided person living and helping others to live a rich full life."[14]

Church's former graduate student of comparative literature, Leila Berberovic, donated a portrait as part of the Margaret Church Memorial Fund that was painted by Leila's father, O. Berberovic from Croatia, Yugoslavia. The portrait is part of the collections in Purdue Galleries, and digital photos of the artwork are preserved in Purdue University Archives.

The Margaret Church Modern Fiction Studies Memorial Prize was established in 1984 in memory of Church. Winners of the annual prize are announced in the summer issue of each volume. The Purdue Board of Trustees named a distinguished professorship in her honor in 1998.

At the time of her death, Church had completed a manuscript for a book titled *Structure and Theme: "Don Quixote" to James Joyce*. Her colleague Thomas P. Adler finished the page proofs and index, and the book was published in 1983 by Ohio State University Press. In the book's foreword, Adler wrote, "In the dozen years since I arrived at Purdue, I came to know Margaret Church as a warm and witty colleague, and I feel fortunate to be able to repay her friendship and support.... I am thankful for this opportunity to reaffirm something to which Margaret Church devoted her professional life: the existence of a community of scholars and teachers. The sadness of loss is tempered by this book, through which she continues to teach us all."[15]

Church ended her entry for the Radcliffe College fortieth reunion yearbook with this: "I know the Midwest as well as I know the books I teach. It is a lesson in life; hard and cantankerous in January and February; scorching and dust-filled in July and August; but conciliatory in the fall, with day after day of brilliant color and high blue skies."[16]

MARTHA OAKLEY CHISCON, WONDER WOMAN OF SCIENCE

As a young girl growing up in Chicago in the 1940s, Martha Oakley Chiscon read *Wonder Woman* comic books. The caped woman with her lasso of truth and superhuman powers exemplified fortitude, perseverance, and compassion. She was one of Chiscon's heroines, and her attributes describe Chiscon and her trajectory at Purdue as a lone female professor of biology who cared deeply for students and became the first female administrator in the College of Science.[17]

Throughout her career, she was a role model for female science students and in the late 1970s a voice for drafting guidelines to integrate women's sports into the Big Ten conference, all while she and her husband, a white couple, raised two adopted biracial children. Dean of Science Harry Morrison called her "a teacher's teacher and a dean's dean."[18]

Born on August 27, 1935, Chiscon absorbed a love of science, technology, and tailoring skills from her mother, a secretary who could do anything—repair a broken toaster, install an electrical outlet, sew, and knit. (Following suit, Chiscon made her own formal wedding dress.) Her father was a pianist, singer, and composer who wrote motivational manuals and developed and presented sales seminars. During the war he ran a major service center in Chicago for service members.

Chiscon was influenced by her seventh- and eighth-grade teacher, Miss Schultz, age sixty-two, who wrote daily mottos on the chalkboard such as "Perseverance counts!" and "Reach for the stars!" She told young Chiscon that she "could do something special."[19] And she did. Through example and deed, Chiscon lifted women students and faculty up to show them how they could raise the bar on what they thought they could become.

Her parents did not have college degrees, but they encouraged their three children to obtain a higher degree, even though funds were scarce. Chiscon attended a junior college, then received a scholarship that paid the $100 per year it cost to attend Western Illinois University. She would be the only child in her family to earn a degree.

"I was vacillating between chemistry and biology [as a major]," Chiscon recalled. "I decided there might be a woman or two in biology, so I chose biology. But I was wrong. I was the only woman in all of my science classes going through college."[20]

When she graduated in 1956, Chiscon had many offers for high school teaching positions. She chose Anchorage High School in Alaska. "I just wanted to do something different," she said of her willingness to move to Alaska from the Midwest. She was there for three years during a historic time. "I voted for statehood,"[21] Chiscon said proudly.

She returned to Illinois in 1959 and taught for two years at Bushnell High School while she completed her physics teaching concentration and then at

Maine West High School. In 1963, needing a master's degree to maintain her teaching certification, she enrolled at Purdue in a four-summer National Science Foundation (NFS) program. She had looked at University of Arizona, but knew it would be hot there in the summer. Purdue was close to Chicago but not too close. She knew nothing about Purdue and at first thought it was an Ivy League, private men's school. At the end of her first summer, the head of the Department of Biology, Henry Koffler (later president of the University of Arizona), called her in for a meeting.

"You didn't always know what Henry was really saying," Chiscon recalled.[22] She left the meeting wondering what it was all about, so she asked one of her professors who speculated that Koffler was offering her a graduate teaching assistant position. She told him she couldn't do that because she had a townhouse in Chicago that she had to pay for, so she returned to her high school teaching position. However, the following spring she received a call from Joseph D. Novak, a Purdue biology professor, who asked, "Are you coming this next year?"

"Nobody told me what the offer was," Chiscon replied. Novak explained that the offer was for a position as a full-time, tenure track instructor in the Biology Department. The salary was more than what she made at the time. "I said, 'Why not?' I was adventuresome. That was the momentous decision that I [made]—the choice between Arizona and Purdue, first of all, and then the decision to just pick up and come to Purdue to be an instructor. I didn't even know what I was going to be teaching. I found out much later that Henry Koffler was recruiting what he thought were talented high school teachers who were in the NSF program."[23]

As Martha *Oakley*, she taught the introductory principles of biology course with professor J. Alfred "Al" Chiscon. Martha and Al worked together for several years. "He was an incredible mentor and role model about how one should treat students, how one can reach students in different ways," Chiscon recalled. "During this time there was never any social interaction that occurred between us. In fact, I always wondered why he never took me home for dinner. He took everybody else home for dinner, but he never took me home to meet his mother."[24]

Later he told her, "You were the one I was going to marry."

"Well, I didn't know that." she replied.

When Al went on sabbatical to Washington, DC, their relationship changed. "We both decided we missed one another for more than just collegial reasons," Chiscon said. She traveled out to visit him and they took off for Maine and visited Mount Desert Island, home of Acadia National Park, where he asked her to marry him.

"We had never dated," Chiscon said. "We had never gone out, and so it was an interesting situation. I said we had to talk to Henry [Koffler] to see whether he would allow us both to continue [working together] because we worried about the nepotism issue. Henry gave his blessing, and so, indeed, we did marry the following May and invited all of our colleagues."

The wedding was held at the University Presbyterian Church Chapel with the reception at Morris Bryant Inn, a popular restaurant on Morehouse Road known for its lavish smorgasbord. By then, Chiscon was working on her PhD in immunobiology, which she received in 1971. She had not finished her master's, but the biology department did not a require one to have a master's to obtain a doctorate. She worked full time teaching for six years while earning her PhD.

"Then I applied for an NSF predoctoral grant followed by a two-year postdoctoral grant," Martha said. "It isn't common that you're allowed to stay where you got your PhD, but NIH allowed me to do that. At the end of the first year, Henry [Koffler] stepped into the picture again and offered me an assistant professor position. So I did not finish the second year of my postdoc."

Chiscon and her husband had side-by-side offices and shared a secretary during their tenures. Each had files filled with index cards providing details on every student who passed through their classrooms. The card included the student's photo, grade report, and observations about the student. They received hundreds and wrote thousands of letters over the years to students and recommendations for current and former students. Both the Chiscons were known for taking very good care of their students.[25] "You have to know when to pull out the handkerchief, pat them on the hand, or kick them in the rear," Chiscon said upon retirement. "We have, figuratively, done all of those."[26]

Chiscon said that her path to professorship and Purdue "emphasizes the fact that if you go through life with blinders on and don't take advantage of opportunities that pop up in places that you don't expect them to, then you might miss out."

Purdue was the first institution of higher education to offer a Women in Science Program (WISP) in the School (College) of Science. Around the country, a few had been offered in liberal arts or women's studies programs. "But nobody in any school of science or college of science was willing to admit that there was an issue that needed to be addressed," Chiscon said.[27]

Felix Haas (husband of Violet) was the dean of the School of Science then and he encouraged the writing of an NSF grant for postsecondary education to fund the WISP from 1974 to 1975. The course was funded by the School of Science for

Martha Chiscon's office was next to her husband's. She joined Purdue's Department of Biological Sciences as an instructor in 1964 and during her tenure became the only female professor of biology and the first female administrator in the College of Science. Courtesy Tippecanoe County Historical Association. Photo by Frank Oliver.

a second year and then was developed into a WBAA radio version and an independent study course.

"Lynne Harrington Brown [a counselor] ... and [I] had an incredibly fantastic experience," Chiscon recalled. "Because the course was unique in that the young women were freshmen ... and they had an opportunity to meet women scientists who were in their early, mid, and late career stages who we invited to come in pairs throughout the semester for two days."

Chiscon and Brown wanted to "erase the 'mad scientist' image."[28] The visiting women met with female students, gave presentations, and ate dinner with them. They met in Chiscon's home to sit in her living room and chat. The following morning, Chiscon interviewed the visiting women on videotape. One woman spoke of how difficult it had been to become an astronomer because she was not allowed to use the telescope.[29]

The students also had an opportunity to work in a laboratory and receive hands-on mentoring. "The whole experience was a very positive one for not only us—we learned a lot—but also for the young women [students]," Chiscon said. "Many of them went on to reach higher than they had thought about reaching."

Chiscon was often the only woman professor her students had. "They [female students] did not see any other women doing what they wanted to do," Chiscon said. "They were saying, 'I want to be one of those, but I don't see any.' But then they saw that I was married. They saw that I wasn't really too weird. I wasn't the stereotypic view of what a woman scientist might have been depicted as in the sixties and seventies. And not only that, but we adopted two children."

The Chiscons often hosted "Student, Faculty, Staff, Community Parties" with seventy to one hundred people in their home. "The people from the community were doing what our students said they wanted to do," Chiscon said. "So they were able to talk with those kinds of folks in a social environment."

Chiscon's female students who had come in as freshmen aiming for a goal saw the accomplishments of women in science—more than what they thought they could do—and, thus, raised the bar on their original ambitions. They saw a higher goal as "an okay thing to do and it's doable," Chiscon said. "You don't have to be a total superwoman."

Chiscon made presentations in Indiana, nationally, and internationally about the success of the program, and many similar programs began across the country. Everything Chiscon did for the WISP was in addition to her duties as a professor.

When the NSF grant and additional year of science funding ended Brown and Chiscon had a meeting with the department head and dean and told them that the program took a great deal of time. They enjoyed leading it but they could not commit to it "forever" because it was overwhelming. "And the response was, 'Well, gee. Your results are wonderful,'" Chiscon recalled. "The women's attrition rate in science now is basically equivalent to that of men."[30] (It had been much higher when women did not have the attention that WISP offered.)

From the late 1970s to the mid-1990s WISP lay dormant because of lack of funding until the School of Science and Schools of Engineering (both now colleges) joined together with a grant for a mentoring and residential program for undergraduate and graduate women. Chiscon hired Barbara S. Clark as director of the program. It grew to be successful and self-supporting. Dean Harry Morrison placed money into an endowment to ensure that it had sustaining funds, and it became an important program for women and persons of color.

Clark, a Purdue graduate, became the director of the College of Science's Science Diversity Office.[31] In 1999, she was a founding member of the Computer Science Women's Network, a student-led organization.

A longtime commitment that serendipitously came into Chiscon's life was her service on the Athletic Affairs Committee, which led to her being a faculty representative to the Big Ten and the National Collegiate Athletic Association. "It was an opportunity that arose, and I said yes," Chiscon recalled. In the late 1970s, President Arthur Hansen called Chiscon and asked her if she could complete the term of the first and only female member of the seven-person Athletic Affairs Committee who had just passed away. "This was all during the time of Title IX and the university was trying to figure out what we are supposed to be doing, and what we are willing to do. What can we afford?"

Title IX prohibits discrimination based on sex in any education program that receives federal funds. Chiscon helped draft guidelines for the integration of women's athletics into the Big Ten conference. "As the only woman on the Athletic Affairs Committee, I was put on this task force of twenty," Chiscon recalled in 2008. "Here I was, this neophyte. I wasn't an athlete." (In college she had earned a silver medal in synchronized swimming.) "I wasn't a jock," she added. "I was a scientist."[32]

By 1981, women were more integrated into the Big Ten. "There were a number of years of serious battles," Chiscon said. "Basically what had to happen was the old athletic directors had to retire. The new, younger athletic directors, who were still mostly men, had grown up in an environment in which they shared responsibilities with their female counterparts and therefore were not so threatened by the women coming into their sport."[33]

Chiscon remembered it as a fascinating period in her life, yet wrought with anxiety. "I would come home from some of the local Athletic Affairs meetings, and I would say to Al, 'Why am I doing this?' I would be so upset by the conversation. I knew my male colleagues were upset because the hair on the back of their necks was standing up straight just like they were a cat.... But ultimately, it all worked out in the proper way."[34]

Some of the men feared that the aspects of sports that they dearly loved would disappear. "In reality, the sports sphere has expanded and become more inclusive and has done all sorts of positive things for both men and women," Chiscon surmised.

Chiscon served two terms on the University Senate and on a number of committees. One that was particularly important to her mentoring of women was the nominating committee. As chair of the nominating committee, she encouraged women faculty to request to be considered for the promotions committee. Members had to be full professors, and at the time not many women held that title.

"In many cases women did not put their names forward ... and as a result their voice was not heard," Chiscon said. "One of those places was on the university promotions committee that for too long had either none or very few women faculty members. Lots of women have blanks in their careers for one reason or another," Chiscon explained. "There has to be somebody on the promotions committee who understands that and can speak to those issues."[35]

In 1982 to 1983, Chiscon was a member of the committee to select a new president, Steven C. Beering. She was an assistant dean of the School of Science from 1988 to 1998 and associate dean from 1998 to 2000 where she focused on undergraduate issues.

Chiscon was chosen ten times as one of the School of Science's top ten outstanding teachers for science majors. For all she did to help women, she was given the Helen B. Schleman Gold Medallion and the Violet Haas Awards. She received the Murphy Award, the highest honor for undergraduate teaching, the first year it was given and named Indiana Professor of the Year in 1993 by the Council for the Advancement and Support of Higher Education.

The Indiana Commission for Women bestowed the Torchbearer award on Chiscon, the highest honor given by the state for women who had overcome barriers to equality. In 2000, Chiscon was honored with the Sagamore of the Wabash Award. Upon retirement, she and Al created the Chiscon Award to honor outstanding teachers in the biological sciences. The Chiscons were named the first recipients.

Robert Ringel, then executive vice president for academic affairs, said, "Martha Chiscon is a spectacular teacher and administrator, a mentor to students and other faculty, and an unbelievably good citizen of the university. We will only need three or four people to replace her."[36]

Chiscon summed up her career: "I've spent my academic life fighting for women to be able to do things with their careers, whether they are engineers, doctors, lawyers, or agricultural scientists," she said. "Many of the women came to Purdue with lower academic goals and saw a professional woman like me. They looked at me and said, 'She has two kids, is married, and isn't too weird. Maybe I can do it.'"[37]

13
RESEARCH HORIZONS IN BEULAH LAND

BEULAH V. GILLASPIE AND THE OPENING OF STONE HALL

Dean of the School of Home Economics Beulah V. Gillaspie was wooed to Purdue in 1952 with the promise of new construction, the Home Economics Administrative Building she planned and guided to fruition. When it was renamed in 1976, some thought the building should have been named after Gillaspie; however, it was renamed Stone Hall after the late President Winthrop E. Stone.

During construction, two large mountains of soil stood at the site. Students playfully named the mounds of dirt "Mount Hovde" for then President Frederick Hovde and "Mount Stewart" for Vice President R. B. Stewart. "They said you could walk between the mountains into Beulah Land," Gillaspie recalled. "I thought it was great. I even received mail addressed that way."[1]

Built where Ladies Hall once stood, the three-story red brick Home Economics Administration Building opened at the corner of State Street and Oval Drive in August 1957. The Home Economics offices and staff moved to the new building so that renovation could begin on the old building, which was renamed Home Economics II. In 1976, it was renamed Matthews Hall after Mary Lockwood Matthews.

Over the main entrance of the new building facing State Street, an aluminum art piece was fashioned depicting the Betty Lamp, the iconic image representing home economics. An *Indianapolis Star* story about the opening of the building stated that the foyer held "Herman Miller modern, black leather sofas with accents of red and chartreuse in the molded plastic chairs and enormous modern ash trays."[2]

The foyer and vestibule marble came from French Morocco. The interior was designed by Gillaspie, Margaret Beeman, assistant to the dean, and Dick Rankin of the Art and Design Department in tandem with the Purdue Purchasing Department.[3] It housed administrative offices, the "air conditioned Home Economics Library of 7,000 volumes," the departments of Foods and Nutrition and Institutional Management, and the Purdue Graduate Women's Club.[4]

The building was the only academic structure on campus that also included a residence for students. The Purdue Graduate Women's Club was located on the top floor and offered rooms for seventy-four female graduate students. Many majored in institutional management.[5] Yet, students were not required to be in the home economics field to live there. After it opened, a student from every school on campus except Veterinary Science was represented. The "metabolism suite" was also on the third floor to house students serving as subjects for dietary studies.[6] When Purdue's Graduate House was constructed in 1963, the third floor was converted to offices and laboratories.[7]

Laboratories for teaching and research in foods and nutrition were located throughout the building. There were nine home-sized " dream kitchens," each with a different arrangement, equipment, color scheme, and price range—"even the new electronic oven that turns out a cake in three and a half minutes."[8] A closed-circuit television studio broadcasted live demonstrations conducted in a kitchen on a platform in the east wing of the basement.[9]

Before the new building opened, the new Department of Equipment and Family Housing was created and Kathleen Johnston was appointed as professor and head. She arrived at Purdue from Pennsylvania State University where she had been director of Housing Research with the Agriculture Experiment Station. Her research had been in the area of space saving in the home.[10]

The Oval Room, so named because the new building was on what was known as the Oval, today's Memorial Mall, was the formal dining room, referred to as "the tea room," on the first floor. Also on that floor was the Spruce Room, a learning cafeteria. Its huge kitchens were called "large quantity food laboratories,"[11] and it was where future restaurant managers, dietitians, teachers, and home economists obtained practical experience in operating equipment, planning menus, ordering food, managing the preparation and service, and balancing the books.

Two of the most popular dishes from the Spruce Room were Hunter's Dinner, a combination of lima beans, spaghetti, pork, tomatoes, and other vegetables, and a recipe for baked chili that made 100 servings.[12]

GLADYS E. VAIL AND HELEN CLARK, NUTRITION LEADERS

Two brilliant researchers in foods and nutrition came to Purdue in the mid-1950s. They were scientists who happened to be women in a man's world.

Gladys E. Vail became the head of Purdue's Foods and Nutrition Department (now Nutrition Science), replacing Amy Bloye who stepped away from administrative duties in 1953, yet continued as a professor. Vail arrived from Kansas State where she had also been head of foods and nutrition. Helen E. Clark was an assistant professor of foods and nutrition at Kansas, and the two women began a lifelong friendship there. After Vail came to campus, she invited Clark to also join the Purdue faculty. Clark moved to West Lafayette in 1954, and the two women elevated foods and nutrition science at Purdue.

Before arriving on campus, Vail had received the National Christie Award in 1950 for her work on poultry products. Sponsored by the Poultry and Egg National Board,[13] the $500 award along with a "scroll" was presented each year to the individual who made the most significant contributions in poultry and egg research during the previous ten years.

Once on faculty, Vail participated in the annual "Egg Day" sponsored by the Purdue poultry department, the agricultural extension service, and the Indiana State Poultry Association. In 1957, Vail was an Egg Day panelist on the topic, "What can we do to stimulate egg consumption?"[14] Throughout her tenure, Vail participated in poultry and egg events sponsored by Purdue's agriculture department, intertwining the research and initiatives of home economics and animal sciences.

Both Vail and Clark were listed in *American Men of Science*. The standard, multivolume directory of scientists would not change its title to include women until 1971 when, as the *New York Times* reported, the directory "bowed to the feminist movement."[15] The *New York Times* story about the title change to "American Men and Women of Science" stated that of the total 185,000 names in the directory of American scientists, "only a relatively small percentage of those listed are women."

Vail and Clark were honored as fellows by the American Institute for Nutrition (AIN). In 2005, the American Institute for Nutrition, the American Society for Clinical Nutrition, and the Society for International Nutrition merged to form the American Society for Nutritional Sciences.[16] An AIN fellow was designated as a person sixty-five years of age or older who had a distinguished career in nutrition. No more than three were named each year. Vail received her honor in 1958,[17] and Clark was recognized in 1979.[18] Vail was also elected as a fellow of the American Association for the Advancement of Science.[19]

Vail grew up in Plains, Kansas. She was soft-spoken with a dry sense of humor. She became head of the Department of Foods and Nutrition at Purdue with plans to expand the graduate and research opportunities. Her PhD from the University of Minnesota was in biochemistry. Her successful, coauthored textbook, *Foods: An Introductory College Course*, was first published in 1933 and reprinted for thirty years.

Vail was a charter member and only woman of the Institute of Food Technologists (IFT), the influential organization for food professionals and educators that advances the science of food across the globe. Today the motto for IFT is "feeding the minds that feed the world."[20] Vail became a fellow of the IFT in 1971.[21]

HELEN CLARK, METICULOUS NUTRITION RESEARCH

Gladys Vail built a national and international reputation for the Department of Foods and Nutrition. When she invited Helen Clark to Purdue, Vail brought a woman who would quietly become one of the giants in human nutrition and metabolic research. Clark's research on adult requirements for lysine has been used by national and international policy makers to formulate changes for better nutrition that benefit world food problems. Her groundbreaking work in protein metabolism and amino acids is still referenced by researchers today.

Born in 1912 in Edam, Saskatchewan, Canada, Clark was educated in a one-room schoolhouse. She grew up about three hundred miles north of the US border. She eventually became a naturalized citizen of the United States. After she graduated from high school, Clark taught in one-room schools in her hometown until she earned enough money to enroll in the University of Saskatchewan. In 1939, at the age of twenty-seven, Clark earned her bachelor of science degree with distinction.

Clark took a leap into her future that would ultimately impact Purdue when she chose to seek graduate education at Iowa State University because of their nutrition program. A big breakthrough came when Clark was asked by her doctoral professor Pearl Swanson to coauthor an article on the metabolism of proteins and amino acids. It would be Clark's first scientific publication and numerous more would follow. Clark greatly admired her lifetime mentor Swanson, a woman also listed in *American Men of Science*.[22]

After earning her doctorate at Iowa in 1950, Clark joined the faculty at Kansas State University, and there she met Gladys Vail, who came to Purdue in 1953 and brought Clark to the university the next year. The female lineage of influence in foods and nutrition at land-grant universities raised the bar for all.

Clark was among the world's top leaders in her field and was at the cutting edge of human metabolic research in relation to amino acids and protein nutrition for a period of about twenty-five years beginning in the late 1950s. She established a human nutrition research metabolic unit when few institutions had such a component. Her investigations were part of what came to be known as the Green Revolution. The term Green Revolution refers to the renovation of agricultural practices to produce high-yield, nutritionally rich crops during the mid-twentieth century.

Clark was revered for her meticulous attention to detail in planning and conducting human experiments. Her research focused on two amino acids—lysine and methionine, which were critical in developing countries where the primary sources of proteins were cereals and legumes. Clark's findings unveiled many of the mysteries related to lysine that led to more effective use of plant proteins. Her research to genetically improve cereals and legumes contributed to both basic nutrition knowledge and to the solution of world food problems.[23]

Clark conducted research and published findings with Edwin T. Mertz, professor of biochemistry, on high-lysine corn at Purdue's Agricultural Experiment Station in the late 1950s. High-lysine corn is a hybrid that was developed through a breeding program at Purdue to improve the protein levels in corn. Purdue first announced its discovery of high-lysine corn as a valuable livestock feed in 1963. High-lysine corn was developed to be an improved food source over ordinary corn.

Through Clark's research, high-lysine corn held exceptional promise in human nutrition because it had the potential for eliminating kwashiorkor—a protein deficiency in children living in countries where corn is the primary diet, which leads to bloated stomachs, large livers, red hair, and unexpected death. Although

Helen Clark, one of the nation's leaders in the study of the world's nutrition problems, stands in front of students participating in her diet research program to study lysine requirements of men and women in October 1968. Courtesy Purdue University Archives and Special Collections.

regular corn provides plenty of calories, it is inadequate in amino acids, particularly lysine. Amino acids are the building blocks of all protein. Essential amino acids are those that cannot be made in the body but must be supplied by the diet for good nutrition.

High-lysine corn nearly doubled the effective protein content of normal corn—almost as much as meat and more than milk. Clark's trials with graduate students proved that the corn protein could be effectively digested by humans. To make the corn appetizing to her students, it was prepared as grits, cornbread, or in a casserole.[24] She proved that high-lysine corn was digestible and utilizable—that the nutrients did not remain in the corn, and thus could be used nutritionally.

Clark built the foundation for Purdue's current graduate program in nutrition. She inspired hundreds of students who became leaders in the field throughout the world. She was a stickler for excellence in her own research and teaching, and in what she expected of her students who, in turn, respected and valued her personal and professional advice.[25] She may have been looked upon by students as demanding, yet Clark demanded no less of herself. She insisted on quality work. She said, "Sometimes, I get impatient, especially when I realize how much needs to be done."[26]

During her career and after retirement, Clark, who remained single, corresponded with many of her students who frequently visited her home in West Lafayette. She genuinely cared for students' welfare and career development. Clark's first graduate student, Jean Howe, became an assistant professor in Foods and Nutrition and worked alongside Clark in her research.[27] A suite on the ground floor of what is today Stone Hall was used exclusively for nutrition research with seniors or graduate students as volunteer subjects.[28] Howe and Clark led comparison studies between diets where rice supplied all the protein and those where both chicken and rice were protein sources.[29]

Clark's research helped to solve the problem of adequately feeding the exploding world population by determining that protein balance could be maintained with consumption of various types of foods containing no animal protein. Since meat was a scarce commodity for much of the world, the findings were groundbreaking. She read the report she coauthored with two faculty colleagues and a graduate student at the fifth International Congress on Nutrition in Washington, DC in September 1960.[30]

The Food Science Institute was established on campus in 1968 to provide coordinated management for interdisciplinary research and educational and extension programs in food sciences. A newspaper story about Clark, age fifty-six, with the headline "A Hungry World Is Her Stage," described her as a "silver-haired professor" and "one of the nation's leaders in the study of the world's nutrition problems." She was "vibrant, dedicated, self-questioning and self-disciplined." The reporter wrote, "Most of her daylight hours and many evenings are spent in the somewhat less than aesthetic environment of test tubes and calibrated machinery. 'Many persons, especially children in the developing countries, will die of malnutrition this year, and even the survivors may be stunted or particularly susceptible to disease and infections,' she explains."[31]

Clark never lost sight of the cost for a woman to excel in science. She demanded that her women students attain and keep higher standards than their male counterparts, believing they would never be recognized with parity. To achieve success, they had to be better.[32]

Yet, Clark had outside interests. She was an elder at Central Presbyterian Church. She read historical novels and biographies and had an extensive record album collection of classical and Big Band music. Clark broke ground for women in science, and she served on the University Committee on the Status of Women. Often the only female member of professional groups, she was concerned about the "chilly climate" for women on campus and contributed to a report the Committee on the Status of Women prepared for the university.

Clark was a woman of many firsts. She participated in the first White House Conference on Food, Nutrition and Health in 1969. The following year, she served as the only female member of a committee appointed jointly by the US Department of Agriculture and the National Academy of Sciences to make recommendations concerning research in food science and nutrition.

In 1973, Clark was acting head of the Department of Foods and Nutrition until Paul Abernathy was hired the following year. When Clark was briefly interim head, she visited every person in every office in the department and said, "Welcome. We're going to have a great semester."[33]

The School of Home Economics designated a distinguished chair in Virginia C. Meredith's name nearly forty years after Meredith's death. In 1974, Helen Clark was the first woman to be recognized as a Distinguished Professor at Purdue, and she was given the title of Meredith Distinguished Professor. Clark was described as having "intellectual skills and evangelical zeal" for a better use of available food sources for the world. Purdue awarded Clark an honorary doctorate degree in 1994.[34]

Decades before in 1968 when Clark received the coveted Indiana Home Economics Association Borden Award for Outstanding Research, the nutrition field's highest recognition, her acceptance speech was a profound and eloquent homage to the great value of home economics and nutrition research. She said:

> Home Economics can be likened to a tree, standing among other trees.... Home Economics has many roots. One of these is its heritage, the years of progress and service since Ellen Richards stated that Home Economics stands for, among other things, "the utilization of all the resources of modern science to improve the home life."
>
> Another root is research, which has been defined in many ways but in the final analysis is the search for and discovery of laws written into the Universe by its Creator.
>
> ...This tree [Home Economics] stands among other trees—such as the supporting sciences, education, communication, and the social sciences.

Nutrition research *can* improve the well-being of man, in this nation and around the world, but only if it is interpreted in a reliable and meaningful way and if people are motivated to apply its findings. The new knowledge from the root of research must rise through the trunk and spread through the branches to be used by people everywhere. This is one of the great challenges of our time.[35]

GLADYS VAIL NAMED DEAN

Beulah Gillaspie retired as dean of the School of Home Economics in 1962 and became head of the Department of Home Economics at California State. Gladys Vail was named the third dean of Purdue's School of Home Economics, and she was given an honorary Doctor of Science degree from Kansas State the following year.

Even when she was dean, Vail continued with her research. In 1966 she received the Indiana Home Economics Association Borden Award for Outstanding Research, cited for her contributions in experimental foods through studies of beef tenderness and other quality characteristics of meat and poultry.

Vail established the Purdue Home Economics Alumni Organization with an inaugural Home Economics Alumni Day in 1965. Her impetus was to provide continuing education for alumni and promote interest in the academic and research programs of the school.[36]

The New York editor Zoe Coulson, a 1954 Purdue graduate who edited "What's New in Home Economics," was the speaker at the third annual Alumni Day in 1967 and jarred her audience into thinking pragmatically about the future of home economics. Coulson said, "Do we become outcasts working in isolation? Or do we become converts to other disciplines, leading to loss of identity?" Faculty from other schools within a university, she said, sometimes "look down" on home economics, adding, "They think we're cooking over Bunsen burners and drying fruits for the cellar."[37] The *Journal and Courier* paraphrased Coulson's visionary words, stating:

> This attitude strikes a sensitive chord in professors who are training highly skilled dietitians, institutional food managers, fashion retailers and candidates for other good-paying professions. They are trying desperately to meet the challenges of the 70s. To combat this, Miss Coulson said some schools are

now changing their names to School of Human Development, Environmental Sciences or Human Welfare.[38]

Purdue's School of Home Economics celebrated its fortieth anniversary in 1966. Home economics had come a long way since the days when Virginia Meredith and William Latta struggled for the discipline to have a respected place on Purdue's campus. Yet, the same year the school celebrated its fortieth anniversary, President Frederick Hovde appointed a committee to study the reorganization of the Schools of Agriculture and Home Economics. The executive committee of the Purdue Home Economics Alumni Organization sent Hovde a letter expressing their desire for the administration to continue their support of home economics as a separate school.[39] Hovde replied to the letter stating that "no unanimity of agreement on the part of those who made this study could be achieved."[40] The School of Home Economics would remain a viable, separate school at that time.

14

LONE WOMAN IN AGRICULTURE

VIRGINIA FERRIS

As a girl growing up in the 1930s in Abilene, Kansas, Virginia Rogers Ferris was interested in plants and meandering streams. She walked the creek that ran behind her family's home, picking leaves and flowers to take home for identification. As a Girl Scout, she earned every biology badge. Her childhood love of flora and fauna became her lifelong passion and prolific career as a nematologist. Despite countless obstacles because of her gender, she became one of the world's leading experts on the soybean cyst nematode, a destructive plant parasite that cost producers millions of dollars in crop damage.[1]

In 1965, Ferris made history when she was hired as an assistant professor and the first female faculty member in Purdue's Department of Entomology. She would become Purdue's first female assistant dean of the Graduate School and first female assistant provost.[2]

Ferris became an internationally known researcher in the field of nematology, the study of nematodes—microscopic, slender, translucent roundworms found in soil and water. Some are good for the ecosystem and others are parasites of animals and plants, particularly corn and soybeans. She and her husband John, also a nematologist, conducted research to keep the harmful nematodes from taking over. Farmers sent the couple soil samples for their help in determining how to counteract harmful nematodes.

What became her lifelong nematode adventure began when, as a young girl, Ferris built her own experimental water "laboratory." She recalled:

> I dug a pond in our backyard ... and I went to the junk yard by myself and found some metal rods, and ... I got a bucket and I mixed up concrete in this bucket [laughs] and lined my little pond with the concrete and put in metal rods because you know, I could read and find out all the things you had to do. The rods were to keep it from fracturing in the wintertime if it freezes.

> I filled it with water and went back to my creek and snared some fish which I brought home and put into this [container] and grew little plants in there. And of course, all this time I was reading books about this kind of stuff. It just kind of grew naturally. Then my folks gave me a tiny little microscope for Christmas one year so I could haul out pond scum and look at it through the microscope. [laughs]

> I talked my family doctor into putting some harmful bacteria under a real microscope, and he showed them to me. I thought that was pretty exciting. So it was pretty well settled that I was going to do something in biology when I grew up. [This] was all self-generated. Nobody said, "Hey, this would be a good thing for you to do."[3]

Abilene was a small town and Ferris, her parents, and her brother were a traditional unit. "The men ran everything," she recalled. "The women pretty much cooked and cleaned, and took care of the household and deferred to the men. I felt something stirring within me even then, [because I] didn't think that was such a great idea. Not much I could do about it in Abilene."

However, there was much she could do once she left for Wellesley College, an all-female institution in Massachusetts where she received a bachelor's degree in botany and Phi Beta Kappa membership in 1949. Wellesley boasts many well-known alumnae, including Hillary Clinton, Madeleine Albright, Ali McGraw, and Nora Ephron.

"That was sort of a turning point," Ferris recalled, "because I found out that women could run for office and be elected. But we only had women, so for instance, we had to edit our newspaper. Anything that we did, the women had to do it. It was very competitive to get into Wellesley."

The head of the Botany Department and a professor of bacteriology, two "top-notch women," one later awarded a Nobel Prize, took Ferris under their wing and encouraged her, gave her research opportunities, and assured her that she would be able to obtain an assistantship for graduate work at a university.

"They gave me the courage to persevere," Ferris said. Another female professor had ties with Harvard botanists and took her to Cambridge to learn about research there. The experience was an example of established women cheering on younger females coming up through the ranks, an unusual situation in the 1940s. The intrepid Ferris would pay it forward and throughout her career encourage generations of women to pursue their passions and explore nontraditional paths of work and study. In 1988 she received Wellesley's Alumnae Achievement Award.

Ferris was accepted into Cornell's PhD program. "There were twenty of us," Ferris said, "and needless to say, I was the only female.... There were only about three people [who] didn't drop out or flunk out. I was one of them. I stuck in there and got my degree. I thought that was pretty neat. I didn't find Cornell nearly as difficult as Wellesley, which I thought was kind of interesting because I was usually the only woman in any of the classes."

None of the male PhD candidates wanted Ferris as their lab partner. "I was always the last person chosen," she recalled. "But usually I did better than any of them. Little by little they began to find out that being my lab partner was not all that bad. That was uphill work."

Ferris's future husband, John, was one of the "hapless lads" that got "stuck" with her as a lab partner and they began to date. He would become her colleague, major collaborator, and best friend until his death in 2000. They were a team in marriage and at work, coauthoring papers under "Ferris and Ferris" and taking turns as to whose name was listed first. John had been in the army so he was two years behind her. They married the year before she obtained her PhD, and he helped her type her thesis. "We didn't have computers," Ferris said. "You just typed this thing a million times 'til you got it right."

She had a teaching assistantship (T.A.) instructing men who were at Cornell on the G.I. Bill. Her job was to pass out small boxes of lab equipment at a window. For two years, many of the male students took the opportunity when they approached the window to tell her she did not belong. "[They] would berate me for taking a job of an able-bodied male," Ferris remembered. "'What are you doing here? You shouldn't even have this job because some guy would want that job and really deserves it. You're just going to get married and have kids and drop out anyway.'"

Then she applied for a National Science Foundation (NSF) predoctoral fellowship. "To my utter surprise, I got one of those [fellowships] and there were not very many awarded then, but it was a full ride for the rest of my PhD period. They even offered extra money for your spouse. I believe they said, 'for your wife.'"

At the time she was taking an advanced course in plant physiology. "I'll never forget this," she said decades later. "I told my professor about this [fellowship], and he said, 'Well, you're not going to accept that fellowship, are you?' And I said, 'Why not?' He gave me that old story again about how I was taking the place of an able-bodied male who would put it to much better use than I would, and I really should decline to accept it. But I didn't. I accepted it because I liked the idea of a full ride; I didn't have to do a T.A. This was wonderful!"

Nevertheless, the professor's words tainted the great pride Ferris should have felt for her accomplishment, and she did not apply for the additional money for her spouse because "I was so embarrassed even accepting the fellowship. Isn't that crazy?"

When the professor posted grades on his door that semester, Ferris was the top name, but still he discouraged her from taking the prestigious fellowship. "That's the kind of stuff we ran into," she recalled in 2007. "In retrospect, it hardly seems possible."

In 1954 with a newly minted PhD in plant pathology and a new husband, Ferris wondered what was next when the professor who ran the nematology lab at Cornell left for sabbatical, and she was asked to be an acting assistant professor and run the nematology program at full salary. Ferris told Cornell she had to think about it. "I was playing hard to get in those days," she remembered. "Isn't that amazing considering what I had been through?"

She decided that if she was going to do the work, she should be an assistant professor, not "acting" assistant professor, so she told Cornell she would do the work but only if they removed the word "acting" from her title, and they agreed.

Nematology was a brand-new discipline at the time, and Ferris admitted she did not know anything about it. "The guy I was replacing didn't know an awful lot either. In fact, I learned what he knew in about an afternoon.... It wasn't hard to catch up."

Ferris's husband was finishing his PhD in the nematology program, so he was her student when she first started as an assistant professor. In her second year of teaching at Cornell, she became pregnant with their first child. This led to a distressing event that was common then for employed women everywhere because it was before the Pregnancy Discrimination Act of 1978 outlawed sex discrimination on the basis of pregnancy.[4] Ferris explained:

> Do you want to hear another horrible story? This [pregnancy] was a definite no-no. So I kept it concealed under a big lab coat for seven months. Finally, I had a little illness and they discovered this terrible truth. The department head called the professors together to take a vote on whether I would be allowed to go to faculty meetings in my condition. Have you ever heard of such a thing? [laughs]
>
> I didn't know whether to be angry or whether to assume that this is the way the world was. But I promised to wear my lab coat so they wouldn't have to look at it. They finally decided I could come to meetings but then the department head said, "The minute that baby arrives, I want a letter of resignation on my desk the very next day, or I'll have to fire you and that won't look good on your C.V." So that's what we did.

The next hurdle was nepotism. John finished his PhD, and she helped him type his thesis, as he had helped her. Their son was a year old when they both looked for jobs. In 1956, John found a position with the Natural History Survey in Urbana-Champaign, Illinois. "During this time nobody would touch me," Ferris said. "I mean, goodness gracious, we had nepotism.... It's when they won't hire a husband and wife in the same department. It was supposed to have been a law. Turned out in Indiana it really wasn't a law, but the department heads used it. It was a very convenient thing to say, 'No, I can't hire you because of the nepotism rule.'"

Not to be thwarted, Ferris began a successful private consulting business in the couple's spare bedroom where she set up a laboratory under the name V. R. Ferris so people wouldn't know she was a woman. She purchased a microscope with her last month's salary from Cornell. "I was pretty good now at finding these little critters [nematodes] in the soil, and so people that were going to be sued because of their pesticides, or whatever, would have me look at the soil to determine if there were any other things in there that could be causing the trouble that they were being sued over."

She was also hired by a USDA soybean breeder in Illinois to look at his breeding plots to determine what nematodes were in the soil affecting his results when he tested new lines of soybeans. It was a lucrative venture. In 1958, John obtained his professorship in the Entomology Department at Purdue, and they moved to West Lafayette. Ferris set up her freelance consulting business in a new home they built. The first finished room was her basement laboratory. She would become internationally famous under the name V. R. Ferris.

Ferris and nematology grew up together, as it was a young science then. She worked diligently, conducting research, editing professional journals, lecturing, and networking with other scientists. "I started off being an agricultural nematologist. In other words, I would go out and find out what was the matter with somebody's crop and see if nematodes were involved," she said. "But soon thereafter, I moved into the field of ecology because we became very interested in why certain nematodes are some places and not others. So we would collect in stream areas."

The couple and their two children traveled extensively in a small travel trailer that housed lab equipment. The family slept and ate in the trailer as they stopped at interesting spots, including every state and national park in the country, to collect different species of nematodes. "We discovered that each little child equipped with a knapsack could hold thirty-five pounds of soil on [their] little back," she said. "So we could collect these soil samples and load the kids up with them. Then some years later we wondered why neither of them wanted to go into science."

They began to find nematodes they did not recognize. "We didn't know what they were, and it would turn out that they had not ever been described," Ferris said. "I went gradually into nematode systematics, so we could describe these nematodes, and this was a whole new ballgame." Nematode systematics is the study of the classification of nematodes: microscopic worms. By 1969, more than 50,000 permanently mounted nematode specimens were in Purdue's collection, curated by Ferris and her husband,[5] and it would become one of the top four largest in the nation, used by visiting scientists and for classroom instruction.[6]

Ferris continued to work with the USDA soybean breeder in Illinois, and they began to publish papers that had to be approved by the USDA. The moguls there asked why he was working with "this woman." "So he wrote them back that there weren't any men to work with," Ferris recalled. "There weren't that many nematologists kicking around loose. They said, 'This is terrible. We're going to have to put a man out there.'"

The USDA established a station in Urbana-Champaign and hired a professor and staff to run it. "Which meant I was going to be out in the cold," Ferris remembered. "I just threw a fit. It made me so angry. I was being replaced by a whole station over there. So I was raising such a fuss that they decided to throw me some kind of a sop."

The USDA posted a position for the program tailored to Ferris, she applied, and got the three-year contract contingent on her being hired as an assistant professor. She went to the head of the Department of Entomology and showed him the position's requirement. Ferris recalled his response:

> He said, "Oh, I can't hire you because of this nepotism thing," which he'd been using all along.... I said, "Okay. I would take this contract to this other department. Then I would spend my time competing with Entomology, and my husband and I [would] give them a run for their money."

> So within twenty-four hours, the nepotism rule had disappeared. Later I investigated it, and it really wasn't a rule per se. The rule is that you can't hire your relative, but my husband wasn't hiring me, so it evaporated, and that was probably good because there are a lot of women that got to be hired afterwards, after I demolished the nepotism rule, which wasn't there anyway.

Ferris was already one of the foremost experts on nematodes when she was appointed as an assistant professor in the Department of Entomology in Purdue's School of Agriculture in 1965. Thin with dark hair coifed in the era's bouffant style, she arrived on campus as a founding member of the Society of Nematologists, associate editor of its publication, and its newly elected secretary. By the end of the 1960s, she would serve as vice president and president. In 1985 she would be named a fellow of the society for her contributions to nematology, and in 2001, Ferris received the highest honor bestowed by the Society of Nematologists—the Honorary Member award.

Ferris was hired as a half-time employee in entomology at Purdue. Later, when she received an NSF grant, much to the surprise of the men in the department, she was still paid half-time. In 1970, she was promoted to associate professor with tenure and, astonishingly, even then remained a half-time faculty member. "I don't think this has ever happened before or since," Ferris said years later.

Then in 1971, Ferris said Purdue suddenly realized that they had no women in administration, and she was appointed assistant dean in the Graduate School. This was the year that the Labor Department, under President Richard M. Nixon, revised Order No. 4 of the Affirmative Action Policy to include women

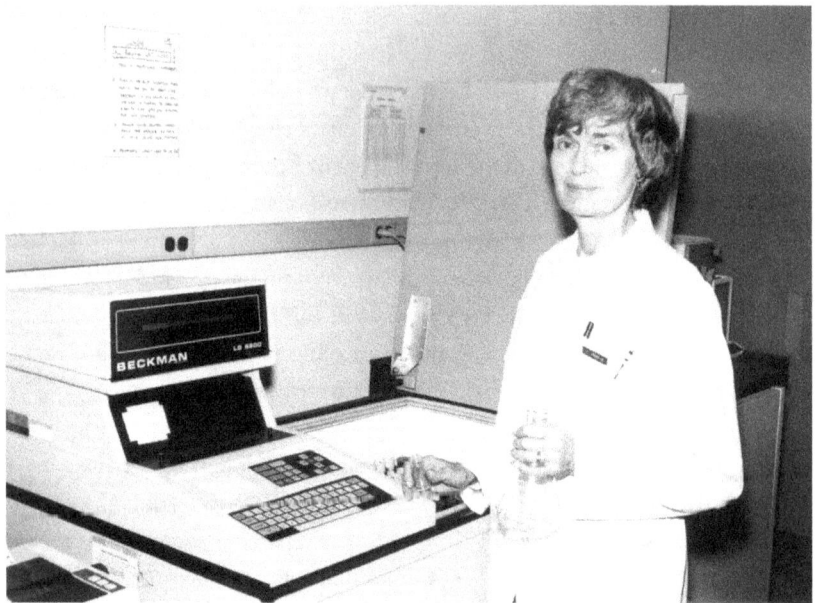

Virginia Rogers Ferris was an internationally known researcher in the field of nematology, the study of nematodes. She made history in 1965 when she was hired as the first female faculty member in Purdue's Department of Entomology. Courtesy Susan Ferris Edgell.

in authorizing flexible goals and timetables to correct "underutilized minorities by federal contractors."[7]

Frederick N. Andrews was dean and was heard to say that women belonged in the Graduate School, "but not in my deanery." Decades later, Ferris laughed at the memory and said, "He and I became very good friends, and while I was appointed originally for three years, I stayed on an extra year at his request." Ferris's brilliance, good nature, and diplomacy often won others over. Once they worked with her, the men in power realized that her leadership was a valuable asset.

Soon after, she was asked to be an assistant provost, again because Purdue needed female representation. After bargaining, Ferris accepted the position because she wanted the experience. She said she didn't want to just be the "Woman Assistant Provost"; she "wanted the whole smear just like the guys." Two others were hired, as well. "They were what they called their Black, their woman, and their regular person," Ferris said. "I always thought that was a riot, but the three of us got along really well." The other assistant provosts were David Kessler in chemical engineering and Luther S. Williams in biological sciences.

Ferris was the only female faculty member on campus who was a member of Phi Beta Kappa when she was invited to be on the steering committee to establish the honor society at Purdue in 1971. Phi Beta Kappa Society is the oldest academic honor society in the United States and the most prestigious, honoring the best and brightest liberal arts and sciences undergraduates. Only 10 percent of US colleges and universities have Phi Beta Kappa chapters, and they only select about 10 percent of their arts and sciences graduates to join.[8]

Ferris served in offices for the local chapter and was elected for three terms as a senator for the National Phi Beta Kappa. One year she was on the ballot against the president of Wabash College, an all-male institution in Crawfordsville, Indiana. The males thought he would surely win with his cachet and notoriety, but the women members voted for Ferris and, much to her astonishment, she won. In 1997 the Purdue chapter of Phi Beta Kappa renamed its literary awards in her honor: the Virginia R. Ferris Phi Beta Kappa Literary Awards.[9]

Ferris received the Helen B. Schleman Gold Medallion Award in 1973 for her encouragement of women in academic and professional areas and for her university leadership. By then Helen B. Schleman had retired as the dean of women but she continued to encourage women on campus.

"Helen Schleman had a huge effect on me," Ferris said. "She was such a positive force. There were very few women I could talk to, but the Dean of Students' office when Helen was there, and Bev Stone, and Barb Cook [deans of Women/Students]—they would have a little dinner about once a month [and] scoop up all of us—there were only a handful of faculty types on campus that were women.... It was a good time to network with these people. Helen [would] say, 'Keep up the good work.'"

The following year, she was promoted to full professor. She was one of less than half a dozen female full professors in the university and the only one in the College of Agriculture.[10] "But, throughout this whole thing I was still only paid half-time," Ferris recalled with chagrin. "A rationale for this was that the state doesn't like to pay two people in the family full-time salaries."

Once her provost position ended, Ferris returned to the Department of Entomology full-time, although she had never really left because she continued her research while holding her other positions. This is when she turned on her "full-court press" to demand an equitable wage for her work. Finally after nearly ten years at Purdue, Ferris was paid a full-time salary for the full-time work she had always been doing.

Before anyone at Purdue was researching molecular biology, Ferris wanted to "jump right into DNA." She said, "I took this up with some of the people in my department. They said, 'Huh, we don't do DNA. That's for people a lot smarter than us.'" So Ferris worked with proteins instead of DNA for about ten years.

In the late 1980s, she began to teach herself about DNA, getting up in the wee hours of the morning to read how to make a genomic library. Her daughter Susan Ferris Edgell, who like her mother went to Wellesley College and then on to Cornell Law School, said, "When people stopped looking through microscopes and started looking at DNA and how to extract it from nematodes, nobody knew how to do it yet. It was cutting edge. My mother would get up at three in the morning every single day to study and learn."[11]

After she received an NSF career advancement grant for DNA research, she rarely looked through a microscope again, because lab research relied on molecular data. This led to her identifying genes in soybeans that provided resistance to the cyst nematode, and ultimately a patent. Discoveries in molecular biology made it possible to obtain vast amounts of DNA from a single nematode. Still, Ferris kept her microscope as a reminder of the device that first fascinated her as a youth.

For decades, Ferris conducted research that combined traditional science methods and advances made possible by genomics, along with fellow researchers that included her husband, lifelong lab partner and best friend John Ferris, also a nematologist; Jamal Faghihi; and Rick Vierling. They identified genes in soybeans that provided resistance to the cyst nematode, a pest that cost farmers millions in crop losses. The Purdue-patented technology, CystX, is commercially available in many soybean varieties. Ferris and the group earned the 2001 Purdue Agriculture Team Award honoring achievements of faculty and staff who collaborate on interdisciplinary teams.[12]

The Council on the Status of Women honored Ferris in 2006 as one of fifteen women Pioneers of Purdue. The annual accolade had been created the year before to raise awareness of female contributions at the university. Ferris was in her seventies and still teaching. Her students loved her for her mentorship, exemplary work ethic, kindness, and compassion. She mentored many young women, and she and her husband were faculty fellows at Earhart Residence Hall for thirty years. When they had dinner there, young women poured their hearts out to the couple. Ferris continued to conduct research into her nineties and passed away in 2017.

"Since my parents passed, I have heard so many stories from so many young women who were from Earhart Hall, remembering the advice they received," Susan Ferris Edgell recalls. "Sometimes if it was a problem with a professor or a class, they would have a quiet phone conversation and help the student's situation."

At the end of her Purdue Archives oral history interview, Ferris summed up her career and time at Purdue: "There were a lot of obstacles, and there were times when I felt like giving up, but this is where I wanted to be."

15

WOMEN IN ENGINEERING

VIOLET BUSHWICK HAAS, BALANCING THE EQUATION

Violet Bushwick Haas had been a professor of electrical engineering at Purdue for four years when a story was written about her for the February 1966 issue of *The Purdue Engineer*. Student writer Chuck McWilliams began his article stating that Haas was working to find the best computational methods to determine how to make a soft landing on Mars, factoring in the optimization of time, payload, and fuel. Referring to Haas as "Mrs." rather than "doctor" or "professor," McWilliams wrote:

> The life story of Mrs. Haas reflects her feelings about the position of women in society.... Although fields of science and engineering have long been alien to women, Mrs. Haas deplores this situation. Women tend to ignore engineering because society does not expect them to become engineers, but aptitude and ability in science and engineering have little relation to sex.
>
> Since one of the greatest pleasures in life is the sense of satisfaction after solving a difficult problem, the women who avoid these problems are not getting as much as possible out of life.

IN ENGINEERING?

Dr. Violet Bushwick Haas became a professor of electrical engineering in 1962. In 1990, Purdue's Council on the Status of Women established the annual Violet Haas Award to recognize individuals, departments, or programs that have promoted women's rights at Purdue. Courtesy Purdue Archives and Special Collections.

To those who raise the objection that technically oriented women have disagreeable personalities, she replies that there are some women whose personalities are disagreeable no matter what they do.[1]

McWilliams's words beg for the counterpoint that perhaps "technically oriented women" had "disagreeable personalities" because in 1966 they were weary and angry about being seen as a freakish anomaly and having their brilliance diminished by society's low expectations of what females could do. Haas diplomatically dealt with this sort of bias toward women in the sciences for her entire life, which was sadly cut short in 1986. The photo that accompanied the article shows Haas standing at the blackboard, chalk in hand, writing out an equation for her students. As if Haas is an oddity, the caption asks, "In Engineering?"

Haas was born in Brooklyn, New York, in 1926 and received an AB degree in mathematics and the equivalent of a physics degree from Brooklyn College in 1947. She majored in math because it "was just a lot of fun."[2] When she was a freshman in high school, her counselor suggested she go into engineering on the basis of her interests. However, Brooklyn College had no engineering program, plus she knew nothing about the work of engineers, so she ignored the suggestion. At the time of her 1966 interview, she was hoping more high schools offered engineering courses. By 1995, Purdue's recruitment programs began as early as grade school.[3]

Haas earned her master's and doctoral degrees at Massachusetts Institute of Technology (MIT) where she met her husband, Felix, also in mathematics. On her first day at MIT she had a chance meeting with a professor who greeted her by name, as if he already knew her. Haas was surprised, but soon learned that she was known simply because she was the only woman among all the students and faculty in the entire math department.

Her first couple of years of graduate work at MIT were difficult. She was not given an office with the other graduate students and she felt segregated. "Men do not visualize women as playing the role, as they see an engineer," she once said, looking back. "I learned quickly to rely on myself."[4]

Hass's dissertation was titled *Singular Perturbations of an Ordinary Differential Equation*. During this time, women were not allowed to teach at MIT. They could grade papers and conduct labs but were not permitted to give lectures. However, when her thesis supervisor was appointed department head, Haas was eventually permitted to lecture to undergraduates.[5]

Once she completed her doctorate, she considered attempting to work in industry, but it was hard for women to find jobs in manufacturing in the 1950s, and many companies blatantly said, "We don't hire women." Haas also knew she wanted a family, and there was no accommodation in industry for a flexible schedule, so teaching looked favorable.[6]

Haas received a Vassie James Hill one-year fellowship from the American Association of University Women in 1951 and began teaching at Immaculata University, then a small Catholic women's college in Pennsylvania, today considered to be the birthplace of modern college women's basketball.[7]

Haas and her husband then went to the University of Connecticut, and according to McWilliams's article in *The Purdue Engineer*, they were not happy there. McWilliams continued his story, addressing Felix as "doctor," but Violet as "Mrs." He wrote, "Dr. Haas got a position at Wayne State University, and

Mrs. Haas worked at the University of Detroit."[8] She was a faculty member at Detroit from 1957 to 1962.[9]

The issue of *The Purdue Engineer* in which Haas was profiled also included an advertisement for Douglas Aircraft Co. that is indicative of the pervasive sexism that prevailed during that time. The ad is a cartoon showing a man sitting at a drafting table with a drawing of a naked woman sketched as if she is flying, face down, arms out to the side with a serene look on her face. The headline reads, "Intrigued by exotic designs?" The man looks at his drawing, bugged-eyed with his tongue licking his lips lasciviously. "Come to Douglas," the copy reads. "We have a lot to intrigue you ..." Incongruously, under the Douglas logo are the words, "An Equal Opportunity Employer."[10]

Haas received a National Science Foundation fellowship to work at the University of Michigan on the calculus of variations and differential equations. When her husband was offered a plum position as head of the Division of Mathematical Sciences at Purdue in 1962 and charged with building the department, she was the "trailing spouse," and once the couple arrived on campus, she had to switch from teaching math to teaching electrical engineering because of the university's anti-nepotism rule. Just like Virginia Ferris in entomology, Haas had to readjust her career desires because of Purdue's rule that a husband and wife could not work in the same department. At the time, 1 percent of Purdue's engineering students were women.[11] As of fall 2022, there were about 4,200 women engineering students, with women making up 26 percent of the total undergraduate and graduate engineering enrollment.[12]

Within a year after arriving on campus, Felix became Purdue's first dean of the School of Science and eventually became executive vice president and provost. The Memorial Gym would later be renamed in his honor. In an *Exponent* story on anti-nepotism rules, Violet, the voice of experience, said, "The husband is always free to choose the best job available, but his wife usually must take what comes along."[13]

At the beginning of her teaching career, when students entered her classroom and saw her, Haas often heard questions such as, "Are we in the wrong room?" or "Is this a Home Ec class?" In 1974, she was one of only three women who taught engineering at Purdue. By this time she had published nine research papers on the topics of optional control and differential equations.[14]

Ultimately, during her career Haas would publish more than thirty journal and conference papers and author the *Analog Computer Handbook*. She was instrumental in developing five new courses. Another *Exponent* interview gave a

Intrigued by exotic designs?

Come to Douglas. We have a lot to intrigue you: extensive and exceptional Southern California facilities, where there are many independent research and development programs underway; engineering design problems to challenge the most creative minds; encouragement to publish. Why not find out about Douglas? Contact your placement office or send a resume to L. P. Kilgore, Box 701-Y, Corporate Offices, Douglas Aircraft Co., Inc., Santa Monica, Calif.

DOUGLAS
An equal opportunity employer

This ad for Douglas Aircraft ran in the February 1, 1966, issue of *The Purdue Engineer* magazine that also featured a story about Dr. Violet Haas. It is an example of the ubiquitous sexism in the culture as she and all women at that time attempted to live out their dreams and goals. Courtesy Purdue University Archives and Special Collections.

glimpse into her playful personality. She said, "We always have to stand at the blackboard and write equations, which proves to be boring. So I try to throw in a joke or two."[15]

When asked about possible discrimination in the School of Electrical Engineering, Haas told the reporter that none existed. Yet, she mentioned the faculty's weekly "Thank-God-It's-Friday" gathering, an entirely "stag" get-together. She had convinced another woman on the staff to accompany her to boldly crash the all-male revelry.[16]

After teaching math for nine years at other universities, it was difficult at first for Haas to teach electrical engineering at Purdue in the era of the slide rule. She began as an assistant professor with basic courses and discovered that her math and physics background really helped her with theory. "If I combined math and physics, I found EE was just playing games," she said.[17] She was promoted to associate professor in 1965 and to full professor in 1977. Throughout her career, control systems theory remained her major interest.

Haas was also a counselor for the Purdue Student Section of Society of Women Engineers (SWE), founded at Purdue in 1954 and today the oldest continuously chartered SWE section in the United States.[18] When she was first contacted about helping with the organization, she thought it was a group of housewives because the advisor was a housewife who had graduated with an engineering degree but never practiced the profession. Once she determined it was a student group, Haas became involved and was an important mentor and role model for women students and faculty in engineering.[19]

Her concerns about professional challenges for women in nontraditional fields led her to also become active in the American Women in Science association and the Association for Women in Mathematics. She spoke regularly to a seminar of freshman women engineering students, sharing her experiences and helping them to recognize their own capabilities.

In 1969 when only forty-seven women were enrolled in engineering,[20] Purdue's Women in Engineering Program was founded, the first program of its kind in the country. The following year Haas and other influential university women were sent a memo inviting them to a luncheon by the program's founding director, Donna Frohreich McKenzie, who wrote, "The purpose of the luncheon is to make these new students feel welcome at the university and to indicate to their parents that we feel that engineering is a very appropriate, acceptable career for women! Many parents seem to disapprove of their daughters studying engineering—too unfeminine."[21]

One of McKenzie's first projects as director was to create a map of the restrooms available to women in Purdue's engineering buildings. Often there were none because when those structures were originally built, administrators, professors, architects, and planners (all male) did not fathom that females would ever spend time there.

Haas was recognized for her leadership on behalf of women students and staff when she was selected as one of five "Very Important Women" on campus by the Purdue Association of Women Students in 1976. The following year, she received the D. D. Ewing teaching award and received $800. In 1978 she received the Helen B. Schleman Gold Medallion Award, presented annually by Purdue's Mortar Board chapter to a faculty member or administrator who has helped with the advancement of women students and women's issues on campus.

Outside of academia, Haas raised three children and enjoyed swimming, tennis, drawing, oil painting, sculpture, and pottery. From 1983 to 1984, she was a visiting professor at MIT through the National Science Foundation visiting professorships for women program investigating control theory and infinite dimensional control problems. Eight months after leaving MIT, Haas was diagnosed with a brain tumor and soon became unconscious, remaining so for nearly one year until her death at age fifty-nine on January 21, 1986.[22]

A service was held in Fowler Hall of Stewart Center, and a Memorial Resolution was written by three of Haas's electrical engineering colleagues, Raymond A. DeCarlo, John C. Lindenlaub, and Stanislaw H. Zak. They wrote, "Her goodwill, enthusiastic energy, superior sense of ethics, and commitment to excellence made her a highly regarded person professionally and socially."

In 1990, Purdue's Council on the Status of Women established the annual Violet Haas Award to recognize individuals, departments, or programs that have promoted women's rights at Purdue. Nominations were accepted from anyone on campus or throughout the community.

Two years earlier, the council had been founded, independent of the university, to provide a space for female students, faculty, and staff to network and advocate for women. Its mission was to create a voice for all women in the university, and it was instrumental in the founding of the Women's Resource Center and the Office of Human Relations. The group met monthly and worked for the advancement of women and other minorities, afforded input on job searches, provided mentorship, and offered seminars. However, the Council on the Status of Women may best be known for its sponsorship of the Violet Haas Award, which continues today even though the council dissolved in 2011.[23]

The first recipient of the Violet Haas Award was Purdue Professor of Sociology and Anthropology Carolyn C. Perrucci. Perrucci helped establish Purdue's Women's Center on Andrew Place at the edge of campus in the late 1970s. She was a founding member of the Purdue Committee on Women's Studies and served as the program's first chair.[24]

In 1984, Perrucci and Haas co-edited a book titled *Women in Scientific and Engineering Professions*. The volume spawned from the lectures given at a national conference they co-chaired on Women in the Professions: Science, Social Science, Engineering held at Purdue in March 1981.

The conference was academic and action-oriented, examining career opportunities and the status of women. Perrucci wrote the introduction for the book, ending it with a quote from conference lecturer Lilli Hornig: "Equality in education and work has turned out to be a moving target, but women have learned to take much better aim."[25]

Haas wrote the epilogue comparing past women's conferences. She began with a 1964 MIT symposium when the proportion of women in science professions was at "an all-time low," wrote of two New York conferences held in the 1970s, and included the 1981 Purdue Conference where lecturers sounded "a clarion call for a reorganization of society in order to make men's and women's participation in all aspects of life more equal."[26] Haas could have reached back to 1935 when Amelia Earhart spoke at Purdue's first annual career conference for female students titled "Conference on Women's Work and Opportunities." Earhart's lifelong clarion call echoed forth in 1981 and is still ringing out for change today.

In 2007, nearly twenty years after Violet Haas passed away, her husband Felix, then retired from Purdue, was interviewed for a Purdue Archives oral history. When asked about his three grown children, he said, "Much of what I did with them was related to my late wife, Violet, who was a professor of electrical engineering. When I think of the impact we had on the institution, it was a joint impact, not just my impact."[27]

LEAH HOPE JAMIESON, ENGINEERING WITH A SOCIAL CONSCIENCE

"Engineering is about what can be."[28] Those words were from a "stunning speech" given by Neil Armstrong at Purdue, his alma mater, as part of the dedication of the new Neil Armstrong Hall of Engineering named in his honor. They became Dean of Engineering Leah H. Jamieson's personal favorite definition of the discipline she loves.

In her own speech, Jamieson added, "Engineers imagine a future different than where we are. It's about solving human problems."[29] Jamieson's middle name, Hope, essentially defined what she became—an engineer who spent much of her career working to solve human problems, including the human problem of gender equity in engineering and science, both at Purdue and globally. She held hope that more women would enter engineering and the sciences and succeed on an equal playing field in the classroom, laboratory, and workplace.

After receiving her bachelor's degree in mathematics from the Massachusetts Institute of Technology in 1972, she earned an MA, MSE, and PhD in electrical engineering and computer science from Princeton University. At Princeton she was shown "a richness of context" where "engineering connected not only with math, but math with philosophy and her engineering research with music."[30]

Jamieson also liked this description of how an engineer thinks: "Some people see the glass as half-empty, and some see it as half-full. An engineer always wonders why the glass is twice as big as it has to be."[31]

Born in 1949, Jamieson grew up in New Jersey an only child whose mother had been a nurse in World War II and whose father was a controller for Crane Company. A first-generation college student, Jamieson said, "I chose electrical engineering because it looked like it would provide many ways to apply math. Heading into my second year in grad school, after looking at many facets of electrical engineering with the help of my advisor, I chose speech processing for the dissertation topic."[32]

Her early research was in developing high-accuracy techniques to analyze speech, characterizing the motion of the vocal cords and labeling the basic sounds called phonemes in continuous speech. She then worked on measuring and using information such as duration, rhythm, intensity, pitch, and intonation to facilitate more accurate speech recognition systems.

When Jamieson, age twenty-seven, joined the Purdue faculty in 1976 as an assistant professor of electrical engineering, she continued her work in speech processing through both research and teaching, taught algorithm complexity, and added a research program in algorithms and software for parallel computers. Parallel computing is the study, design, and implementation of algorithms to use multiple processors to solve a problem faster or a bigger problem in the same amount of time by using more processors to share the work.

In the 1990s, she said, "I've continued working in both speech and parallel processing because I enjoy the variety. One of the things that I've always liked about working in the area of speech recognition is that I can talk about my work to anyone, including my parents, and . . . my seven-year-old daughter."[33]

Perhaps Jamieson's greatest legacy at Purdue is her co-founding (with Professors Edward Coyle and Hank Dietz) and directing of EPICS, Engineering Projects in Community Service. At the time of its birth in 1995, EPICS was an innovative, essentially unheard-of approach to undergraduate engineering education. EPICS was created because the engineering education community was drawing fire from industry for graduating students who had strong technical backgrounds but few other skills necessary for successful careers. It matches teams of engineering students with local nonprofit agencies to define, design, build, test, and support projects that improve the community. The nationally award-winning program has also played a role in increasing the number of women and minorities in engineering. EPICS has been adopted by numerous universities around the world and became a K–12 approach for introducing engineering through service-learning.

Early EPICS teams advised by Jamieson included students from electrical, mechanical, environmental, and computer engineering; child development; sociology; and professional writing. They developed software to address homelessness, new toys for children with disabilities, and tactics for environmental cleanup. In a 2001 interview she said, "I want to create good, real world solutions and give students from lots of different disciplines the skills to work well together."[34]

For her work in EPICS, Jamieson was named the 2002 Indiana Professor of the Year by the Carnegie Foundation and the Council for Advancement and Support of Education. The following year, the EPICS program was awarded the Indiana Governor's Award for Outstanding Volunteerism,[35] and in 2005, Jamieson and colleagues Ed Coyle and Bill Oakes were awarded the Bernard M. Gordon Prize for Innovation in Engineering and Technology Education by the US National Academy of Engineering for their work with EPICS.

During her Purdue tenure, Jamieson also devoted time to advocate for the university's female faculty. In 1998 the "Status of Women at Purdue" report commissioned by Purdue President Steven Beering and conducted by the University Task Force on Women's Issues was released. Jamieson was a member of the task force made up of fifteen women from Purdue's faculty, staff, and administration.

Dr. Leah Jamieson joined the Purdue faculty in 1976 as an assistant professor of electrical engineering. She cofounded and directed EPICS, Engineering Projects in Community Service. Courtesy Purdue University Archives and Special Collections.

The report, based on 1995 data, stated that male engineering faculty outnumbered female faculty 251 to 13. There was one male professor for every twenty male undergraduates, but only one female professor for every 109 women.[36] It meant that female engineering students lacked the same-sex mentors and role models that their male counterparts used for guidance, inspiration, references, and job contacts.

Overall, there were 326 female professors at Purdue in 1995 vs. 1,359 male professors. Only 55 women had the rank of full professor, compared with 660 men.[37]

The report stated, "Because society comparatively undervalues women's careers, women's need for mentors to help identify strengths and resources may actually be greater than men's... thus it is not surprising that many young women would prefer a woman mentor."[38]

Women faculty are important for both male and female students so that both see women in leadership roles and see differences in communication styles. At the time of the report, 43 percent of Purdue's student population were women, but most were in the schools of education, consumer and family sciences, and the humanities.

Jamieson became the founding chair of the Purdue Women Faculty in Engineering Committee in 1999. Also that year, she was awarded the Helen B. Schleman Gold Medallion for her advocacy for women. When asked what challenges she had to overcome as a woman leader in engineering, she said, "A sense of isolation has probably been the most constant challenge. When I was a grad student, sometimes feeling different from everyone around me and wondering what in the world I was doing. Over time, feeling a part of multiple communities—my department, my research communities, IEEE, Computing Research Association–Widening Participation [CRA-WP]; then as dean, once again finding myself in meetings where I'm the only woman in the room. It's a reminder that we still have a ways to go."[39]

The Violet Haas Award was bestowed upon Jamieson the following year by the Council on the Status of Women for her impact on the advancement of women both nationally and at Purdue through the EPICS program and as a facilitator for workshops aimed at fostering a climate of gender equity in the classroom.[40]

In 1993 Jamieson was elected a Fellow of the Institute of Electrical and Electronics Engineers (IEEE) for her contributions to the design and characterization of parallel algorithms for speech, image, and signal processing applications. In 2007, she became the second woman in the history of IEEE to be elected its president since it was founded in 1963. At the time only about 10 percent of professors in engineering departments across the country were women.[41] She later served as president of the IEEE Foundation.

Jamieson, the Ransburg Professor of Electrical and Computer Engineering, was named dean of the College of Engineering at Purdue in 2006, succeeding Dean Linda P. B. Katehi, who held the position for four years as the university's first female dean of engineering. The year prior, Jamieson had been inducted into the National Academy of Engineering.

One of Jamieson's goals as dean was for Purdue to be a leader in embracing changes in engineering education that were embodied in reports such as "The Engineer of 2020"[42] and the radically updated accreditation criteria that had been instituted in 2020 by the Accreditation Board for Engineering and Technology

(ABET).⁴³ Jamieson explained, "These included increasing students' experiential opportunities such as co-op and internships in industry, study abroad and international experiences, entrepreneurship opportunities, service learning, and research."⁴⁴

She saw the need for engineering students to have a broad background to work in a global world and to come up with open-ended solutions that stretch creativity. She strove to change the Purdue curriculum to answer those needs, although some students and faculty were wary, claiming that curriculum changes had been rare in engineering.⁴⁵ Of course for centuries, men led the way in creating the curriculum aimed at male students. Jamieson saw engineering from a broader perspective. Research was showing that women engineers like to know they are contributing to the greater good.⁴⁶

Jamieson was inducted into the 2011 class of the American Academy of Arts and Sciences, one of the country's most prestigious honorary societies, bringing Purdue's number of members to ten at that time.⁴⁷

Under Jamieson's tenure as dean there were record enrollments in engineering—a 40 percent increase from 2006 to 2017. In that same period, the number of female engineering students doubled to almost 3,000, and underrepresented minorities nearly doubled to more than 750. With regard to faculty, there was a 46 percent increase in the number of underrepresented minority professors and a 90 percent increase in the number of female faculty.⁴⁸

After eleven years as the dean of the College of Engineering, Jamieson completed her term in 2017. She was asked if serving as dean was different from what she had expected. "The first surprise was the pace of decision-making," Jamieson said. "I was floored by the sheer number of decisions that had to be made every day—some of them small, but some really big—and nearly all with incomplete information. But often in engineering you make decisions with incomplete information, and you have to weigh a variety of factors.... There is risk-taking every day."⁴⁹

The following year, the directorship of Purdue's Women in Engineering Program (WIEP) was named after Jamieson. When she was honored at a retirement dinner, the College of Engineering secretly had a silk scarf and necktie designed in her honor. Created by Harris Made, the rectangular scarf in shades of gold incorporated the text of Jamieson's final remarks given at a homecoming dinner along with her signature. The College of Engineering logo subtly floated in the underlying pattern of the scarf and tie.

In 2020, Jamieson received yet another impressive award, the IEEE James H. Mulligan, Jr. Education Medal given for her contributions to the promotion, innovation, and inclusivity of engineering education. As Neil Armstrong said, "Engineering is about what can be." Jamieson saw what could be at Purdue and ran with it, solving human problems while loving the discipline and the "extraordinary people" of Purdue Engineering.

16

PHYSICAL EDUCATION FOR WOMEN AND TITLE IX

MARGUERITE CLIFTON ESTABLISHES KINESIOLOGY

Professor Marguerite Ann "Mickey" Clifton transformed Purdue's Department of Physical Education for Women by offering kinesiology, the study of the anatomy in relation to movement. She established an undergraduate program in the study of human movement that was the first of its kind. Many universities followed Purdue's lead.

Clifton was the department head beginning in 1964 and served during a time when the climate of inclusion for women, not just in sports but in all of academia, began to change on university campuses across the country. Clifton spoke out for intercollegiate sports opportunities for women. She blazed her own trail along the way. Clifton was the first woman to be appointed a member of Stanford University's Athletic Board in 1973.[1]

When Professor Helen Hazelton retired as head of the Department of Physical Education for Women in 1963, there were twelve instructors teaching more than two thousand students each semester in thirty different courses.[2] Students were required to wear gym uniforms they purchased at the women's fashion store, the Elsalyn Shop, which first opened on Northwestern Avenue, then moved to

State Street across from Harry's Chocolate Shop.[3] This was close to where Hazelton lived in Varsity Apartments, the only apartment building in West Lafayette at the time, which still stands today.[4]

Clifton was hired as head of the department the following year, coming from the University of California. Her degrees were from University of Redlands, University of Southern California, and Stanford. Clifton would help change the face of the Department of Physical Education for Women at Purdue and throughout the United States.

She was at the cusp of developing a new discipline for physical education (PE). Traditional PE taught women to play sports and to dance. Under Clifton's watch, the emphasis at Purdue would be on research and the science of human movement, her specialty. The new curriculum taught how the body performs as well as why. She explained that the complexities of modern living had created a need for investigating, for example, the relationship of mental health and physical activity.[5] In fall 1964 the university requirement of two years of physical education was reduced to one year and the first PhD candidate began.[6]

Clifton hired eight new faculty members, most with extensive backgrounds in various phases of the science of body movement. Professor Hope Smith was hired as an associate professor with a background in the study of perception and body movement. Smith was Clifton's lifelong colleague and friend. Enrollment was at capacity for the size of the cramped Memorial Gymnasium where the women's physical education classes were still held since the department moved there in 1938 (see chapter 5).

A human movement course for Purdue freshmen women was first offered in fall 1966. A group of female faculty volunteers worked for two years to design the course as a study of human movement in relation to a variety of physical and social forces that affect movement behavior. The course was based on the understanding that from birth a person manifests behavior toward or away from, with or against the forces that exist in the environment. Patterns of response develop and are reinforced as the person interacts with these forces.[7]

The Human Movement Research Laboratory was located on the lower floor of Memorial Gymnasium and was used extensively for cinematographic studies of movement behavior and undergraduate classes in kinesiology.[8] The study of human movement became an undergraduate major and a graduate program under Clifton's leadership.

Faculty members wrote a book to accompany the course published in 1968. *Introduction to Human Movement* was edited by Hope Smith, written by five instructors, and contained a foreword by Clifton. She wrote, "This particular book is timely, however, in that it symbolizes a faculty commitment to a focus of study that sharply departs from the traditional ideas of physical education. The faculty is to be commended for its dedication to a conceptual scheme, for its flexibility in thinking, and for courage in innovation. The freedom of the department to assume a nontraditional focus of study was made possible, however, only through the understanding and support of the administration. For this we are indeed grateful to Purdue university."[9]

The cover image of *Introduction to Human Movement* is a free-form painting in red and forest green that conceptually depicts a person in movement. Clifton and Smith requested that one-third of the royalties from the book went to the expansion of the Department of Physical Education for Women. Skeptics of the new major predicted that the woman student would be "turned off" by the novel study, but to the contrary. In 1970, the undergraduate major in human movement drew the largest entering freshman class in the history of the department.[10]

Clifton was installed as an Active Fellow of the American Academy of Physical Education in March 1966. At the time, she was the only member of the Purdue physical education staff, male or female, who was a fellow of the academy. She was selected for her scholarly contributions to the literature of the field of physical education, her leadership, and her eminence as a teacher and administrator. By then, Clifton had authored five textbooks, produced educational films on physical education, and received several research grants.[11] The second member of Purdue's Department of Physical Education to be elected a Fellow of the American Academy of Physical Education was Clifton's colleague and friend Hope M. Smith in 1970.[12]

The department recommended that the university requirement for physical education for women be eliminated in 1968. Physical Education for Women became a highly successful elective program with women students picking and choosing from the array of classes offered.[13]

CLIFTON'S UNPARALLELED STUDY ON CHILDREN

Marguerite Clifton was chairman of the Perceptual-Motor Symposium held in Washington, DC in May 1968. The symposium was sponsored by the American Association for Health, Physical Education and Recreation (AAHPER) to develop revised physical education programs for children in elementary schools.[14]

From the symposium and other conferences, Clifton determined that it was imperative to study early motor development in children.

There was concern that children were confined in playpens, glued to chairs watching television, carted around in cars, and were in, as one newspaper stated, a "sit-and-atrophy environment."[15] Clifton began the Development Movement Education (DME) Program at Purdue with Professors Jane Maver and Ray Anne Shrader (two of the co-authors of *Introduction to Human Movement*) to study preschool children.[16] With little precedence, the program focused on developmental levels of performance in perceptual processing and motor behavior exhibited by each child. The children attended twice a week and spent twenty-five minutes each in the women's gym and pool. Each child enrolled with a parent who stayed with the child during the activities.[17]

The children played games such as "Cross the Crick." They threw beanbags at a "Face Board," walked through a tire maze, worked on a balance beam, and more. Each game had a purpose to help children with different types of movement. Most of the equipment was built by Purdue. The children were supervised and instructed by students.[18]

During this time, school districts had been given federal grants to improve academic achievement through improvement in young children's perceptual motor skills. Clifton said, "We found physical education being besieged by requests from teachers about what to do. Their own professional preparation really had not included this kind of training."

Clifton's study was unprecedented. There had been studies of the relation of motor development to learning in children with learning disabilities. However, no one in the United States had studied preschool children in the normal learning range. The DME served as an intensive training ground for students in physical education and elementary and kindergarten education. Half of the students were PE majors and the other half were in education. The DME also served Clifton's research efforts.[19]

Clifton subscribed to the theory that one cannot separate mind and body, and by 1972, she saw several movement problems for children. One was inactivity, which affected the entire learning process. Another was fear of failure, and yet another was the demands imposed by parents that caused a child to withdraw when the going got tough.[20]

As the 1970s rolled out, Clifton's influence on physical education grew with momentum. Vice President of the United States Spiro T. Agnew spoke at the 1972 convention of AAHPER in Indianapolis. He spoke out about drugs and

America's youth, stressing that athletic and physical education programs should not be reduced because of financial pressures in the nation's school districts. As outgoing president of the AAHPER and an accomplished golfer herself, Clifton presented Agnew with a lighthearted trophy depicting a golfer with the inscription, "Our Straightest Hitter," in reference to the vice president's occasional wayward golf shots.[21]

NUDE POSTURE PHOTOS

A peculiar photographic session for every physical education woman student occurred during the 1950s to 1960s and came to light in the 1990s. In the basement of the Memorial Gymnasium was the "posture picture" room where each woman in physical education was photographed individually in the nude. (It is not known if male Purdue students were also subjected to nude posture photos.)

A February 1995 story in the *New York Times Magazine* titled "The Great Ivy League Nude Posture Photo Scandal" shed heartbreaking light upon the matter. The "posture photo" had been a routine part of freshman orientation week to check for curvature of the spine and assign those in need to remedial posture classes at many Ivy League and Seven Sisters schools across the country, from Harvard and Yale to Vassar and Wellesley. Students who later became many of our nation's leaders or famed journalists, such as George Bush, Bob Woodward, Hillary Rodham Clinton, Diane Sawyer and Nora Ephron, for example, had all dutifully obeyed the requirement of a nude posture photo.[22]

In reality, the photos were part of an anthropological research study by E. A. Hooton of Harvard and W. H. Sheldon who directed the institute for physique studies at Columbia University. Unfortunately, Sheldon convinced many elite schools that his research was pressing, cutting-edge innovation rather than the pseudo-science it has since been deemed. The original photographs were eventually given to the Smithsonian's National Anthropological Archives and subsequently destroyed.

After the *New York Times Magazine* story broke, it was determined that female students at Purdue and Indiana Universities were among scores of college students across the nation who were photographed nude for posture studies. A newspaper story quoted Pat Grabill, a 1965 Purdue graduate. Grabill said, "I just remember enormous trauma, these poor girls, 17–18-year-old girls and fresh out of high school. There were very few things more humiliating than parading around naked in front of a bunch of strangers. I was never convinced what it was for."[23]

Jeanne Norberg, then director of Purdue News Service, said the physical education instructor checked the film for posture problems and threw it away without making prints. By the 1970s, the "posture picture" room had been renovated to become the Movement Sciences Research and Learning Center.[24]

Physical education for women remained in Memorial Gymnasium until 1985, when the building was remodeled to house the Department of Computer Science. The women moved into Lambert Fieldhouse. A women's PE faculty member heard about the upcoming move from a custodial worker. The department had not been made privy to the planning or formally notified by the administration that the move would take place.[25] The Memorial Gymnasium, originally built in tribute to the football players, students, and alumni who lost their lives in the 1903 Purdue train wreck, was renamed in 2006 to honor Felix Haas, former dean of the School of Science and husband of Professor of Engineering Violet Haas.[26]

TITLE IX TURNS THE TIDE

Marguerite Clifton was one of the first women to meet with the National Collegiate Athletic Association (NCAA) and participate in a study of women in intercollegiate sports. In 1964 she presented a paper to the organization titled "Extending the Horizons for Interscholastic Sports Competition."[27] She was also president of the division of girls' and women's sports of the American Association for Health, Physical Education and Recreation (AAHPER) and helped develop the first guidelines for intramural and intercollegiate competition for women.[28] Clifton said, "The researchers may even find why there is a 'cultural expectation' which keeps many girls from stimulating and healthful physical activity."[29] That was an understatement that exploded with Title IX.

Title IX of the education amendments of 1972 was enacted into law, and Clifton was at the helm as landmark changes evolved for women in physical education and athletics at Purdue.

Title IX states, "No person in the United States shall, on the basis of sex, be excluded from participation in, be denied the benefits of, or be subjected to discrimination under any education program or activity receiving Federal financial assistance." In short, all public schools from elementary to university level must provide fair and equal treatment of the sexes in all areas, including athletics.

Title IX created a sea change for women students and faculty. However, it was not a tidal wave of instant change but more like a faucet drip of slow transformation. At the time, the NCAA offered no athletic scholarships for women and held no championships for women's teams, although women across the United States and at Purdue had been involved in athletics for decades. Women had participated in competitions at Purdue since the 1920s, with the Women's Athletics Association chartered at Purdue in 1921. Women's facilities across the country were lacking. As a result, when Title IX became law, there were just 30,000 women in NCAA sports, compared to 170,000 men.[30]

Yet, the women had the Association for Intercollegiate Athletics for Women (AIAW), founded in 1971 by female professors and coaches from an outcry for women's athletics to have opportunities to compete. Wanting more than intramural sports for girls and women, the AIAW wanted what the men had—standards, national championships, and true competition among colleges and universities. Purdue Professor Carole Oglesby served as the first president of the AIAW. Oglesby earned her PhD in physical education at Purdue, was on the faculty from 1964 to 1972, and coached several sports, taking the softball and gymnastics teams to national championship tournaments. Oglesby was awarded Purdue's Title IX Distinguished Service Award in 2017.[31]

The university's Title IX Distinguished Service Award recognizes those who demonstrate sustained accomplishments in one or more of the following areas:

- Maximizing institutional and/or societal resources to broaden access and opportunity to women in higher education.
- Expanding the range and quality of the female undergraduate or graduate student experience at Purdue.
- Contributing to the achievement of gender equity at all levels of the academic community.
- Contributing to the advancement of women in intercollegiate athletics.
- Providing local and/or national leadership on issues related to gender equity in education at all levels.[32]

The AIAW expanded quickly, and in the 1970s a struggle took place between the AIAW and the NCAA to control women's athletics. The AIAW focused on the female student-athlete's education, not on athletic performance. The AIAW

Marguerite Clifton after she left Purdue for California State University, Long Beach, California. Courtesy California State University, Long Beach Library—Special Collections and University Archives.

emphasized participation in sport and deemphasized winning.[33] Yet, when the NCAA began to offer championships for women, many schools left the AIAW for the NCAA. The AIAW disbanded in 1982.[34]

Although Title IX did not require that women's athletics receive the same amount of money as men's athletics, it required equal access and quality. Women's and men's programs were mandated to dedicate the same resources to locker rooms, medical treatment, training, coaching, practice times, travel allowances, equipment, practice facilities, tutoring and recruitment. Scholarship funds were to be budgeted on a commensurate basis.[35] All of these mandates did not happen overnight and caused a flurry of questions, hope, skepticism, and fear.

Purdue was the first major university in Indiana to offer a series of coaching courses for women[36] when the Department of Physical Education for Women created a series of eleven different courses designed to prepare women to coach girls and women.[37] In 1975, the department celebrated its fiftieth anniversary with a commemorative newsletter featuring a detailed history of its progress. A festive gathering was held for alumnae in Memorial Gymnasium on homecoming weekend. The celebration marked a turning point of grand measure. Women's physical education and athletics were about to forge new territories.

The men's and women's physical education departments at Purdue consolidated on July 1, 1976. The combined unit was named the Department of Physical Education, Health and Recreation Studies. Dale Lester Hanson from the University of New Mexico was appointed head of the new department by a unanimous vote of the search committee. Marguerite Clifton, having lost her position as a department head, continued for a couple of years as a professor of physical education and conducted research. In 1978 she became president of the American Academy of Physical Education.[38] Soon after, Clifton left Purdue and became department chair of Physical Education at California State University, Long Beach, where she was awarded Professor Emeritus status in 1987. She passed away on September 9, 2009.

CAROL S. MERTLER, FOUNDER, WOMEN'S INTERCOLLEGIATE SPORTS

On August 22, 1975, Purdue President Arthur Hansen appointed three men, including Athletic Director George King, to develop a plan for implementation of a women's intercollegiate sports program at the university. The group worked in conjunction with the Athletic Affairs Committee composed of three men and one woman—Professor Jo-Ann Price of Physical Education for Women. Price was the first woman at Purdue to be selected to the University Athletic Affairs Committee for a four-year term, and she would serve as chair from 1976 to 1977.[39]

After many meetings and hours of work, a report was given to the president. Price said, "The report is somewhat favorable to the women's point of view, but I still feel it was unwise that the coordinator of women's intercollegiate sports was not appointed as a member of the three-man group."[40]

Price was referring to Carol S. Mertler, Purdue's new assistant athletic director and coordinator of women's intercollegiate sports, appointed in July 1975 to start a women's program from scratch. She also coached field hockey. Mertler had just obtained her doctorate degree from Ohio State when Title IX was passed. She had been director of physical education for women at Ashland College in Ohio. Mertler grew up in Mansfield, Ohio. In the 1940s when she was a young girl, her elementary school coach started a football team, and she asked the principal if she could play. Even though she was the biggest kid in the class, the answer, of course, was no.[41]

Mertler's office was in Lambert Fieldhouse. An avid golfer, she was often asked by male reporters, "Why do women compete?" Her response was, "Why do men compete?" Even the smallest requests for the women's program was a fight in the male-dominated institution. Purdue hosted cross-country meets at the golf course with no women's restroom. Across the street was a gas station with one restroom, and women lined up to use it before the race. Mertler suggested a portable toilet for the meets.

"You'd have thought I asked for the moon," she said in a 2014 newspaper interview. She was told that it was not a problem for the men. "There's a little difference there," she pointed out. She got her way and the portable toilet was provided. When she requested hair dryers for the women's locker room, she was told the men don't have hair dryers in their locker room. When female garments started showing up in the laundry, the men who cleaned the uniforms balked at washing them, and Purdue hired a woman to do the women's laundry.

But Mertler had bigger challenges to focus upon as she hired coaches for six new female sports teams, made schedules for each, lined up officials, and purchased uniforms. In 1977, she offered her first athletic scholarship to Sue Fackler, a 6-foot, 3-inch center on the women's basketball team. Mertler had been assistant athletic director for six years before the Big Ten recognized women's athletics in 1981 and took over conference scheduling. Before then, Purdue played teams within driving distance in Indiana, as women's athletic directors got together at a central location and made up schedules for the year. That year, Purdue hosted the first Women's Big Ten Basketball Tournament that Carol helped organize.

By the mid-1980s, budgets were bigger and women's athletics was more organized, especially when the NCAA won governance over the Association for Intercollegiate Athletics for Women. It was slowly gaining more mainstream audiences through better promotion and improved athletes. Mertler hired Carol Dewey as the women's basketball coach, established the volleyball program, and created the foundation for both to become national powers before leaving her position in 1988. In 2013, Mertler was inducted into the Purdue Intercollegiate Athletics Hall of Fame.[42] She passed away on November 16, 2020.

SALLY DODDS COMBS ELLIOTT, FIRST DIRECTOR OF PUBLIC RELATIONS FOR WOMEN'S SPORTS

After Title IX was passed, Sally Dodds Combs Elliott was named director of public relations and promotions for women's intercollegiate athletics. She shared an office in Mackey Arena with announcer and journalist John DeCamp. DeCamp was in charge of promoting men's athletics. He generously mentored Combs as she navigated advancing Purdue's new feminine athletic terrain.[43]

Combs had been an instructor in Purdue's Department of Physical Education for women from 1958 to 1967. She also was coordinator of women's athletics in the recreational gymnasium (Co-Rec).[44] She left Purdue in 1967 to work for the West Lafayette School System where she wrote a health education curriculum, taught physical education and health, and organized a program for girls' athletics as the girls' sports director.[45] Combs was married to Loyal William "Bill" Combs, Purdue's football team physician and director of the Purdue Student Hospital. After his death, Sally Combs married Edward Elliott, son of former Purdue University President Edward C. Elliott.

Combs established the Purdue Sportswomen Society, the women's counterpart to the John Purdue Club, the organization responsible for raising the funds needed to support male student athletes. Both women and men could be members in both clubs; the difference was the destination of the donation. The Purdue Sportswomen Board sponsored the annual Schleman-Hovde Jubilee golf outing named after longtime Dean of Women Helen B. Schleman and Purdue President Frederick Hovde, colleagues, friends, and avid golfers.

A callout for Purdue women students interested in participating in fall sports was issued.[46] Professor Deborah L. Gebhardt, who had taught physical education at Purdue since 1973, was named Purdue's first women's basketball coach.[47]

When Sally Combs retired in 1988, she advised Athletic Director George King to merge the Sportswomen Society with the John Purdue Club to eliminate duplication of activities. Nancy Cross replaced Sally Combs and became assistant director of the John Purdue Club. The Sportswomen Society had served its purpose.

17
NURSING, A SLEEPING GIANT

HELEN JOHNSON, MANNA FROM HEAVEN

When Helen R. Snyder Johnson was six, she broke her leg and had to have surgery. While in the hospital she grew to adore her nurse. "She was so pretty in her uniform, so good to me," Johnson said. "I decided then and there that I would be a nurse, and I never changed my mind."[1]

Today, students become nurses at Purdue because Helen Johnson never changed her mind. Her belief in nursing coursed in her blood, and she built the institution's nursing program from a mere idea in the ether.

The ebony-haired Johnson was born in 1914 and grew up with her six siblings in the small town of Fritchton, near Vincennes, Indiana, where she helped her parents run a general store. After her stay in the hospital as a child, she read every Clara Barton and Florence Nightingale book she could find. She obtained her nursing degree from Indiana University and became a head nurse and instructor at the Indiana University Medical Center.

As a mother of two sons, Johnson often took night duty to be home during the day. Throughout World War II, Johnson served as director of the Indianapolis Chapter of the American Red Cross of Volunteer Nurses Aides. She was chief of nursing for Richard Roudebush Regional Veterans Administration Medical Center and then became an assistant professor of nursing at Indiana University's Indianapolis campus before arriving at Purdue. Twice she was president of the state nurses' organization. While she was in office, the organization strove for better working conditions and salaries for nurses, and looked at facilities in Indiana for training more nurses as there was an acute shortage.[2]

Early on, Johnson was well connected in her profession as she sat on the boards of the Indiana Heart foundation and the Public Health Association. She was on the executive committee of the State Board of Health for sixteen years, which served to give her a deep understanding of the need for nurses who could foster superlative health programs.[3] When her husband died suddenly from a heart attack in 1954, Johnson faced the challenge of raising her two sons alone. She continued to work and further her education.[4] Without knowing it, Johnson primed herself to be the perfect person to create and lead Purdue's nursing program.

In the 1950s, Charles H. Lawshe, Purdue alumnus and former professor of industrial psychology who was dean of university extension, was aware of the dire need for nurses in Indiana and the necessity for students to have educational opportunities. Health care organizations and hospitals were nearly begging universities to design curriculums that would provide well-educated nurses.

Lawshe sat on the board of Lafayette Home Hospital. The hospital phased out its school of nursing in 1955 because costs had become prohibitive, it was short staffed, and it was difficult to recruit nurses. Across the country, hospitals were cancelling their diploma programs, and the responsibility for educating nurses shifted to universities. Lawshe and his staff explored the need for an associate degree in nursing at Purdue.[5] Across the country, the nursing profession was a sleeping giant that was beginning to move and awaken.

In November 1960, Purdue President Frederick L. Hovde received a letter from the Indiana State Medical Association regarding its resolution to encourage colleges and universities in Indiana to consider the development of schools of nursing.[6] As a land-grant university with the mission to recognize the needs of Indiana's people, Purdue responded.

On October 18, 1961, Lawshe presented a proposal to establish an associate degree nursing education curriculum to the University Extension Council. The request was approved, and a Community Advisory Committee on Nursing Education was appointed, chaired by Lawshe. Among others, committee members included Dr. Loyal William "Bill" Combs, director of the Purdue Student Hospital and later spouse of Sally Combs, director of Public Relations for Women's Athletics; and Registered Nurse Isabelle Diehl, a graduate of Johns Hopkins University and faculty member of the School of Home Economics who taught

Professor of Nursing Helen Johnson in 1964 with the other faculty of the then new "Division of Applied Technology." *Right to left*: Charles Hutton, Gilbert Rainey, Charles Lawshe, James Maris, Denver Sams. Courtesy Purdue Archives and Special Collections.

nursing subjects and served as a nurse for the Purdue Nursery School. Diehl was also a professor in Child Development and Family Life.[7]

When Johnson made a trip to Purdue for her son's college orientation, she investigated the rumor that the university wanted to start a nursing program. Her impressive resume, savvy leadership style, and energetic spirit impressed Lawshe, who hired her almost on the spot. He had advertised far and wide for the position and received nearly thirty applications, but none had been acceptable for various reasons. Lawshe said, "It was a mighty lucky day for Purdue. We wanted to start a nursing program, but we hadn't been able to find anyone who could build it from the ground up as well as run it. We were close to giving up the idea. She was manna from heaven."[8]

Johnson was described as a "down-to-earth optimist." Over the next twenty years, she would be the force behind the development and growth of nursing education. Johnson seemed to enjoy obstacles. She met them head on with her upbeat attitude, often while wearing high-heeled shoes. Johnson saw the school through its infancy and growing pains, and its success today is testimony to her steely determination and foresight.

Johnson came to Purdue in 1962 as the sole nursing faculty member in the Department of Technology with her office in the Purdue Memorial Union. In one year, Johnson obtained funding, hired faculty, arranged clinical experiences in hospitals and other local health care agencies, developed a curriculum, and secured state approval.

Johnson obtained funding through a W. K. Kellogg Foundation grant to provide educational instruction for new faculty members, many of whom had never taught in an associate degree program. The grant also made it possible for Johnson's idea to bring nurses to Purdue from the United States and Canada to attend summer seminars and learn how to develop and teach their own associate degree programs.[9]

As part of the planning, Johnson visited the Purdue Speech and Hearing Clinic and the Purdue Nursery School in the Department of Child Development and Family Life with the impetus to integrate these resources in the teaching of patient care and offer meaningful clinical experiences for students.[10]

Purdue's two-year associate degree in nursing program opened as a pilot project in September 1963 with four faculty members, thirty students, one classroom, and three faculty offices on the third floor of what became the Purdue Student Health Center. If the pilot were successful, it would continue. Each succeeding year one additional nursing program was to open on Purdue's regional campuses: Fort Wayne, Calumet, Michigan City, and Indianapolis.[11] The following year, the School of Technology (now Purdue Polytechnic) was created, and Lawshe was named acting dean. The nursing program became a department in the new school.

Johnson kept her unwavering eye on the prize and the nursing program was a success. Students referred to the ever-busy, ever-smiling Johnson as *the* Florence Nightingale of their era.

She attracted first-class faculty, and students enjoyed the advantages of a large university's cultural and social opportunities. Some thought that the program would exist as its own separate entity outside of the traditional parameters of university art and athletic scenes. To that Johnson said, "Why should nursing students be deprived of the college atmosphere of football games, concerts, dances, and plays?"[12]

Johnson and the nursing program received an open-arms reception from both the university and the community. She was invited to speak before numerous organizations, including local hospitals, the chamber of commerce, and the medical association. She drew people into her vision with her forceful, yet tactful and personable style. She carried an aura of unstoppable pluck. Johnson said, "As a philosophy of life, I don't believe that you should ever give up. Vision requires the power of conscious imagination, going beyond the obvious, and putting to work unusual discernment and foresight."

Johnson's success may be attributed partly to her emphasis on self-actualization for each student and faculty member (and, thus, her own). She wrote, "In order for self-actualization to be learned, appreciated, and practiced by students in relation to clients, it must first be practiced by faculty in relation to students and in relation to each other. Therefore, helping both students and faculty to realize their fullest potential is one of the department's constant goals."[13]

A University News Service story described Johnson: "She accomplishes her goals without flim-flam or flummery and you soon learn that Mrs. Johnson, a fiftyish widow who heads the Department of Nursing in Purdue's School of Technology, is a no-nonsense person not given to verbal calisthenics or other forms of word wasting."[14]

For her stunning accomplishment in creating the nursing program at lightning speed and her dedicated service to the nursing profession and the health of Indiana citizens, in 1963 Johnson received the highest honor bestowed by the governor of Indiana, the Sagamore of the Wabash.

Purdue's first student nurses donned traditional starched white dresses and a crisp white cap designed to resemble the hat worn by the university's athletic mascot, Purdue Pete. At the time, Pete's hat resembled a small box perched atop his head.[15] The nurse's cap was adorned with black and gold ribbons. A nurse's cap once symbolized that the wearer had graduated from nursing school, and each school had a cap design that was uniquely theirs, ceremoniously bestowed upon graduation.[16]

By the mid-1970s, Purdue nurses had a new cap design and no longer wore the boxy Purdue Pete–inspired version. Students were granted permission to use the Purdue University seal in the design of a new pin that secured black and gold velvet ribbons to the cap.[17] The cap tradition ended in the 1980s, but the tradition of special nursing pins presented at graduation continues.

In June 1965, the first class of seventeen nursing students graduated from Purdue University with associate degrees in applied science. They were then qualified to take the state licensing examination to become registered nurses. Academic attrition had narrowed the initial thirty students to seventeen. Johnson's first graduating class scored the highest on the state examinations of any institution in the state.[18]

The following December, the nursing program received national accreditation from the National League for Nursing (NLN). The Purdue program was the first in Indiana, and one of only five in the United States, with national accreditation, and the accreditation was retroactive to cover the first graduating class. Normally, accreditation of nursing schools was not received until a program had been established for four to five years. Dean Lawshe said, "Early accreditation of the Purdue program attests to the leadership of Professor Johnson and the extremely high quality faculty which she has recruited."[19]

By 1966, all five of Purdue's campuses in Indiana had more than three hundred students enrolled. A grant from the United States Public Health Service (USPHS) of $75,000 made it possible for the course "Introduction to Nursing" to be produced on videotape and used at all campuses.[20] This was a grand venture back in the day when producing a video was a major undertaking only for professionals and home videos were virtually unheard of.

In June 1967, the first men graduated from the nursing program, one at the West Lafayette campus and the other at the Fort Wayne location. Johnson believed that nursing as a profession would be better off if it had more men in it.[21]

Competition for the Purdue program was stiff. Only one of every five students who applied were admitted, thus the quality of each graduate was first rate.[22] Johnson worked many twelve-hour days. She said, "We had to move to maintain the university's standards of excellence. Sometimes our growth was so rapid it was almost painful to keep up with it."[23]

Johnson was awarded the 1968 Indiana Nurse of the Year award during the Indiana League of Nursing's convention. It was the second to be bestowed by Allstate Foundation. As a recipient of the title, Johnson was to name a nursing school whose student would receive the Allstate student scholarship.[24] Of course, she chose Purdue.

An Upper Division Baccalaureate Degree Program for registered nurses began at Purdue's Calumet and West Lafayette campuses in September 1970 with another grant from the W. K. Kellogg Foundation. The new degree was established to give nurses "career mobility" by preparing them for leadership and management roles. By design, the associate degree curriculum was self-contained; it was not designed to be the first two years of a bachelor's degree. While other majors in the School of Technology were designed to be the two-plus-two career ladder curriculum, nursing was not. The two-year associate degree program and the four-year baccalaureate program were never interconnected.[25] In April 1975, the upper division baccalaureate program received accreditation from the NLN.

Word reached Johnson that some nurses' groups were grumbling about her lack of a doctoral degree, so in 1975 at the age of sixty, she earned her doctorate in higher education administration from Indiana University. She wrote her thesis on the history of Purdue's nursing education programs. She said, "Although we were considered a 'new' nursing program around the country, I wanted Purdue to be seen as a leader in nursing education. A doctorate is essential for someone who heads a department or school, especially at Purdue. I also knew then that I wanted the School to have a master's degree program someday. To do that, you need faculty with doctoral degrees."[26]

Johnson never stopped striving. Lawshe said, "I believe her chief characteristic is tenacity. She was not willing at any time to take 'no' for an answer from the [Purdue] president on down, when it came to the growth and development of the nursing program."[27] Next on the horizon—Johnson wanted a building dedicated solely to nursing.

HELEN R. JOHNSON HALL OF NURSING

Nursing classrooms and offices were scattered throughout campus. In March 1968, offices for the nursing faculty moved from the Purdue Student Health Center to South Campus Courts, small, barracks-like structures on Harrison Street that have since been torn down. Johnson's office had bright pink carpet and paintings of birds on the walls, as she was an avid nature lover.

During the recession of the 1970s, Purdue and other state-supported institutions were cutting back on construction and, instead, prolonging the life of old structures. Yet, Helen Johnson miraculously obtained a $1.3 million federal grant from the United States Public Health Service (USPHS) approved in 1974 to help build the Nursing and Allied Health Sciences Building—today named the Helen R. Johnson Hall of Nursing.[28]

Johnson always stressed that the faculty obtained the grant, as stipulated by the USPHS. The faculty were required to prepare the application and make the request. Johnson said, "When we had visits from United States Public Health Service, they visited with the faculty to ask them what their needs were and if they were being met in terms of facilities and resources."[29]

Yet, it had been Johnson who never stopped asking the administration for a new building. She said, "Every year we talked about it and the need for it. At one time I did visit with the president.... Hovde was then president of the university. We talked about the need to construct a building and that we could go to the United States Health Service and have perhaps two-thirds of the building paid for. He said, 'No, the program was not going to grow that much, and you can't put the application in.' Regretfully, he said that. I felt bad about that, but I didn't give it up."[30]

In 1972 after Hovde retired and Arthur G. Hansen was president of Purdue, a provost encouraged Johnson to apply for a grant to construct a nursing building. It would be Johnson's crowning achievement.

Johnson used her knowledge gained as a member of the review committee for the National Institutes of Health's construction of a nurse training facility to design and plan Purdue's nursing building. It had the latest offerings, such as a simulated hospital with mannequins where students could practice skills. Videotape equipment made it possible to record, play back, and critique nursing procedures. There were six classrooms, including one in a tiered, horseshoe seating design to allow unobstructed views of demonstrations. There was a television production area with a control room for a technician that in 1987 became the "Hook Telecommunications Studio" developed through a gift to the School of Pharmacy and Pharmaceutical Sciences from the Hook family in honor of August F. "Bud" Hook, a 1929 pharmacy graduate.[31] The top floor had an attractive reading room and corner lounge.[32]

The pride and joy of the building was the Learning Resource Center, fully equipped with more than a dozen multimedia study carrels. A newspaper story reported on the revolutionary concept decades before the age of the internet, stating, "Nursing students receive assignments, pick out the appropriate tape, put it in an audio-visual receiver, and, in the privacy of their own carrel, listened to and view the instruction."[33]

Construction of the new building began in 1975, north of Hovde Hall of Administration. The flat-roofed structure was made of Purdue's traditional red bricks but had the design twist of what is called the Brutalist style of architecture popular then. The name is derived from the French term for *béton brut*, or "raw concrete."

Brutalist buildings look strong, solid, and imposing; the new nursing building followed suit.[34] The exterior of the building was a juxtaposition of what was happening on the interior—students learning to be knowledgeable and compassionate caregivers. The nursing building was like Johnson herself—a strong fortress with a brilliant, nurturing heart.

The nursing building was dedicated on October 2, 1977, and even though there was room to admit about one hundred more students than in previous years, the program still fell short of accommodating all of the applicants.[35] That year, Johnson earned Purdue's Helen Schleman Gold Medallion Award for extraordinary service in the promotion and advancement of women students.

Johnson hired Colleen DeTurk to teach health assessment. DeTurk taught for twenty-five years before retiring. She was an advocate for male nursing students. Her son, Phil, was a Purdue graduate in aviation technology who decided to switch to nursing after he cared for his daughter when she died. "After that he said he didn't want to take care of machines anymore," DeTurk said. "He wanted to take care of people."[36]

Upon retirement in 2003, DeTurk contributed seed money to start a "men in nursing" project. She envisioned a male nursing student organization, recruitment programs, and funding to send representatives to national male student nursing association conferences. She said, "I've always enjoyed male nursing students. There is a certain self-confidence about them, an attitude of self-empowerment, a feeling that they are on the road to success. I've always said that if we had more men in the nursing profession, it would be a different profession. There would be higher salaries, for starters."[37]

The Department of Nursing grew to become the largest department in the School of Technology with 417 students enrolled by fall 1976.[38] Faculty at all campuses signed a petition advocating for a School of Nursing because they did not want the department transferred to another existing Purdue school. It had become increasingly difficult for Johnson to hire qualified faculty because professors wanted to teach at an institution where nursing was more recognized in the institution's structure. In its evaluations, the National League of Nursing had been critical about how nursing fit into the Purdue organizational chart. Dean of the School of Technology George McNelly was in full support of nursing becoming its own school and wrote a letter in April 1977 championing the idea to Felix Haas, executive vice president and provost and husband of Professor of Electrical Engineering Violet Haas.[39]

The Purdue University Board of Trustees approved the change in status from the Department of Nursing to the School of Nursing effective July 1, 1979, yet it was not a separate school with its own dean. Dean of the School of Pharmacy Varro E. Tyler was appointed dean of the School of Pharmacy, Nursing, and Health Sciences. Helen Johnson retired as head the following year, yet continued to teach nursing classes. Johnson never stopped believing that the School of Nursing needed to be an independent school with its own dean.[40]

In 1990, the nursing faculty led by Professor Emerita of Nursing Eoto R. Stokes wrote letters to Purdue President Steven C. Beering endorsing the renaming of the Nursing and Allied Health Sciences Building to the Helen R.

Dr. Helen Johnson, *left*, and Dr. LaNelle Geddes at the dedication of the renaming of the Nursing Building as Johnson School of Nursing Building in 1991. Courtesy Purdue Archives and Special Collections.

Johnson Hall of Nursing. Letters of support were also written by Charles Lawshe and George McNelly. McNelly wrote, "I cannot think of any building on the campus which comes as close to being the result of one individual's efforts as the Nursing Building." (Albeit, McNelly probably did not know the history of Matthews Hall.)

The naming ceremony took place on April 20, 1991, and Helen R. Johnson, age seventy-six, attended. At the podium, President Beering said, "Helen Johnson is one of Purdue's heroic figures."[41]

Ten years after the "house that Helen built" was named in her honor, Johnson passed away. A few months before her death, she had a visit from RuthAnn Smolen, one of her 1969 graduates. Smolen said:

> We talked about nursing; the common bond we shared from the very beginning. She shared with me that her health was fragile, but mostly, she asked about me. Her interest was always on us, her students. . . . I remember thinking, as we visited, how she had worked with incredible, unbelievable patience to educate us to practice nursing with integrity, common sense, persistence, and to care for our patients with the energy of a marathon runner! I am still running the marathon that Dr. Johnson wanted me to run. She believed in me.[42]

18

HOME ECONOMICS REORDERED FOR THE TIMES

EVA L. GOBLE, UNFLAPPABLE EXTENSION AGENT WHO BECAME DEAN

When Eva Lenore Goble, age thirty-one, interviewed for the position of Purdue extension agent in 1941, she was asked by State Leader of Home Demonstration Lella Reed Gaddis, "What makes you think you can do this job?" Goble replied, "I have never failed yet."

Goble's empowered statement earned her the extension agent position on the spot and gave her courage to try new endeavors throughout her long life of 107 years. More than half of those years were devoted to Purdue with a fierce loyalty to both Agricultural Extension and the School of Home Economics. Goble succeeded Gladys E. Vail in 1967 as dean of the School of Home Economics. When she was appointed, Goble was an alumna who had already been a longtime university staff member.

Goble grew up on a farm in Southern Clay County, Indiana, with an older brother and two younger siblings she helped tend. Her father ran a hardware store. Goble described that part of the state as having clay wrapped in soil and coal, which meant not very good soil for farming, but great soil for mining.

Early on, Goble's backbone and confidence were molded by the Girl Scouts of America, which was founded in 1912, two years after Goble was born. There was no troop established in her small community, so Goble gathered her group of childhood friends, asked their fourth grade teacher to be their leader, and started her own. Beginning at a young age, Goble organized women into supportive groups who got things done, and she would continue this effort her entire life. When she wrote about her journey decades later, she titled it, "A Lifetime of Mentoring and Being Mentored!"[1]

When the Depression hit in 1929, Goble, age nineteen, had to drop out of Indiana State Teachers College (today's Indiana State University), return home, and look for a job to help her family financially. Her family still had their farm, but her father had to close his hardware store because the mines shut down and there were no miners to frequent the store. This is when Goble first experienced a taste of job discrimination because she was female. She said, "The post office had a young boy delivering special delivery letters. I knew his family was moving, so I went to see the postmaster and asked for the special delivery letter job. The postmaster told me that it would not be proper for a girl to deliver the mail!"[2]

Goble found a job in a lamp factory in Anderson, Indiana, where she worked for twenty cents an hour until the factory closed; then she worked in a Hammond, Indiana, department store. With money she saved and $350 her father gave her after cashing out his life insurance policy, Goble returned to college and obtained a two-year teaching license. She then taught in the county school and attended college in the summers, working toward her four-year teaching license while living with her grandmother.[3]

Decades later in her retirement community apartment not far from the Purdue campus, Goble still displayed a black-and-white photo of the children she taught in the one-room schoolhouse. "I learned as much from them as they did from me," she said. In 2003 when she was ninety-three, Goble reunited with three of those early students. "We got caught up on everyone and what they are doing these days," she said. "These students looked almost as old as I! In their own ways, they were also my mentors."[4]

After Goble obtained her degree in home economics at Indiana State Teachers College in 1941, she became a Vigo County extension agent hired by Purdue's Lella Gaddis. Two years later, she became a home management specialist at Purdue and worked as a graduate assistant in the Agricultural Experiment Station researching agricultural economics and time and motion studies. "I was interested in time and motion studies because farm women needed help," Goble explained. "They had too much to do."

Goble was probably the only student to obtain a graduate degree in home economics in the School of Engineering. Dean of the Graduate School Ernest Young became her hero when Dean Mary Matthews would not accept her into a graduate program. Young was a father of daughters, one with a disability. He had a soft spot for helping women fulfill their potential. Purdue's Young Graduate House is named in his honor. Matthews claimed that Goble did not have enough science to qualify to be a graduate student in home economics. Goble said:

> I thought, oh well, if I can't, I can't. I'll do something else. So I talked to Dean Young. He said, "Oh, for Pete's sake, you can take any course you want. As long as you know how to do it." He said, "Engineers are looking for students right now in production engineering. Why don't you go over and get in engineering?" Well, I thought it wouldn't be bad—having an engineering degree. So I went over there and got a time and motion study, which is the same thing you do in home economics. I got a BS degree in Home Economics, but I did it in engineering. They were trying to break down these barriers [between schools], so I went to the right guy.[5]

Goble traveled Indiana giving talks to home economics clubs during World War II. She discussed work planning and her time and motion study, the specialty of Purdue Engineering Professor Lillian Gilbreth. In her talks, Goble said, "Every motion must count, for workers in the field, the home, or the factory today. We want to produce the most for the work we do."[6]

Goble also gave a talk titled "Psychology in Every Day Living," speaking to club leaders assembled in a county courthouse. She told the women in their hats and Sunday dresses that developing personality depends on how earnestly we work. "Honesty to one's self is the keynote to happiness."[7]

During this time, Goble lived in the grand home of Colonel Howard Ayers Sr. and his wife, Sarah, at the corner of State and South Ninth Streets in Lafayette and helped with their three children while Ayers was in Japan rebuilding the country's power industry. Each day, Goble caught the city bus on the corner in front of the house to go to campus.[8] Ayers was a Purdue graduate in mechanical and electrical engineering who was a member of General Douglas MacArthur's staff in Manila during World War II. He remained with MacArthur during the occupation of Japan.[9] Goble remained in contact with the

Ayers family throughout her life, outliving the entire family except for the Ayers daughter, Patricia.

In 1947, Goble succeeded her boss and mentor Lella Gaddis as the state leader of home demonstration agents in Cooperative Extension. She was responsible for home demonstration agents in fifty-six counties who served nearly fifty thousand women in home economics clubs around the state.[10] Goble held that position until 1958, then served as the assistant director of the Cooperative Extension Service and was fondly referred to as "Miss Director."

When Goble received a grant from the Ford Foundation to continue graduate study for a year, she obtain her PhD in adult education from the University of Chicago in 1964 at the age of fifty-four. Goble never stopped learning. When she was ninety-six, she said, "I think everybody ought to try something hard every year. If you don't try something hard to reach, it's too easy to lay back in an easy chair."[11] Goble received an honorary doctor of letters degree from Purdue in 1999 when she was eighty-nine.

Goble's null hypothesis question for her University of Chicago PhD thesis was, "Why aren't women joining home economics clubs?" She theorized that either they were afraid to be educated, their families opposed educated women, or they couldn't afford education. She found none of her hypotheses to be true. The reasons women were not joining home economics clubs were that the women had small children and no child care, plus they had no transportation. The women feared that their families would think they were neglecting their children if they attended a club meeting. The problem was solved for the most part by offering a room for children to play at club meetings.[12]

Goble was part of the team of Purdue home economics and agriculture extension staff who traveled to Vicosa, Brazil, in 1952 to establish a School of Home Economics and agricultural extension service at the Rural University of Minas Gerais (UREMG). In July 1953, she sent a letter from South America to be read at a chicken dinner for the Washington Township Ladies' Club held on a member's spacious lawn.

In her letter, Goble painted a picture of the ordinary farmer's life in Vicosa. A bamboo mud hut was his dwelling with a dirt floor and crude furniture. There were no radios, telephones, electricity, or paved roads, which made it difficult to attend church or school. There was nothing but the drudgery of existence, day in and day out. Conditions seemed worse than those our pioneer parents experienced. After Goble's letter was read, the Home Economics Club meeting was adjourned following the reading of the month's motto, "Ain't God Good to Indiana?"[13]

Before Lella Gaddis retired as state leader of home demonstration, she proposed the idea that a women's cooperative house be established to assist women majoring in home economics at Purdue. Eva Goble saw the idea through to fruition, and the "Live at Home and Learn House" was born through donations from home economics clubs in Indiana. By donating $1 each, the women raised more than $30,000 from 1948 until 1952 and loaned the money to the Purdue Research Foundation to renovate a house at 322 Waldron Street. Dean of the School of Home Economics Mary Matthews lived up the street at 629 Waldron.

The cooperative house officially opened in fall 1954, and a few years later, members named the house "Twin Pines" as a symbol of cooperation. Two pine trees were planted outside. Twin Pines Cooperative House still operates today and welcomes women in all majors. Lella Gaddis, who spawned the idea for the co-op, was made honorary president of the organization.[14]

In 1965, Goble received a Superior Service award from the US Department of Agriculture in a ceremony on the grounds of the Washington Monument. She had been a US Department of Agriculture official serving on the executive committees of the National 4-H Foundation in Washington, DC and the National Association of Administrators of Home Economics. Goble was cited for "efficient leadership at state and national levels in development of programs to strengthen and enrich family living during changing times." She was referred to as one of the nation's widely known home economics leaders. By this time, there were 65,000 home economics club members in more than 3,000 clubs in Indiana.[15]

During Goble's tenure, undergraduate enrollment in the School of Home Economics doubled, and the faculty undertook a major revision of the curriculum reflecting the needs of society.[16] Goble was dean at the cusp of a great metamorphosis of women's roles and the school. Goble said, "We're hurting ourselves if we don't develop the talents of both men and women in the respective careers they choose."[17] The school strove to publicize that men, too, majored in disciplines under the home economics umbrella. By fall 1973, there was an undergraduate enrollment of 71 men and nearly 1,500 women, compared to 1963 when there were 44 men.[18]

On November 29, 1969, the *Journal and Courier* ran a two-page feature titled "Home Economics School Invaded by Male." A photo of sophomore James R. "Rick" Spurgeon, with his long sideburns and clean-cut looks, showed him standing in front of the Home Economics Administration Building. Spurgeon majored in interior design and minored in equipment and family housing. He was the only male student in his home economics classes. It appeared that Spurgeon experienced what many women in predominately male majors experienced—isolation and the feeling that one needed to work harder than one's counterparts to succeed. Spurgeon said, "I was put in the front seat in a class of 75 girls.... It seems like I have to work twice as hard ... because I'm afraid some girl will pop up with something better."[19]

Spurgeon designed a new logo for the School of Home Economics in an art class. Dean Goble liked it. Spurgeon said, "The instructor thought it was terrible. I took it to the dean of home economics, and [she] decided to use it on the cover of the summer school catalog." The logo depicted the letters "p," "h," and "e"—symbolizing "Purdue Home Economics"—arranged to resemble a house. Spurgeon's design became the official seal of the school. Spurgeon was the first male student to be elected to the Home Economics Council, which worked as a liaison between the students and faculty. He was also art editor for the *Purdue Engineering Magazine* (PEM) and had designed the cover of the November 1969 issue featuring "Women in Engineering."

Home economics extension moved to the School of Home Economics from the School of Agriculture in 1967, the year Goble became dean, and she fostered the transition. Of the significant task, Goble said, "The extension specialists felt it was for the good of the school to have all home economists in one place so the interaction among them would be useful. I believe this effort strengthened the school as well as improved the knowledge of the specialists."[20]

The move of home economics extension from agriculture departments to home economics departments was a national trend. The transfer made sense because the country had changed. Farming had been the backbone of America, but by the late 1960s, consumerism was taking hold. The role of the home demonstration agent changed to help women with business issues, stress, balancing work and family, and so much more beyond preserving food and stretching leftovers to aid the war effort. Today, extension agents are called "educators." In 2010, Goble, age one hundred, witnessed the establishment of Purdue's College of Health and Human Sciences. She said, "Today, it's about health. It makes sense. It's the future."[21]

Since she was a little girl who started the first Girl Scout troop in her small town, Goble had understood the importance of change. When she retired in 1972 after twenty-nine years of serving the university, Goble described Purdue as "a social institution which should be reordered to fit the times."[22] No truer words were said. During the late 1970s, home economics would ride the winds of change, albeit with a bit of turbulence.

MARY ROSE HYLAND, NATIONAL SANDWICH CONTEST AND THE INTERNATIONAL DINNER SERIES

Assistant Professor of Institutional Management Mary Rose Hyland and her class were responsible for preparing nearly 150 sandwiches when Purdue's Department of Institutional Management (read of its founding in chapter 3) was selected to judge the eleventh annual National Sandwich Idea Contest. The contest was held from November 1965 to February 1966 to offer new recipes to the nation's consumers while publicizing "quantity food service" as a source of creative food ideas.

The contest sponsors were the National Restaurant Association (NRA) in cooperation with the Wheat Flour Institute, American Dairy Association, Poultry and Egg National Board, and National Live Stock and Meat Board.[23]

Restaurant and quantity food service workers from across the United States sent Hyland about 1,400 original sandwich recipe ideas that were narrowed down to 144 for taste-testing. The contest was judged by staff and faculty from across campus who selected the twenty best recipes that were then announced at the NRA Convention in Chicago. From Purdue's twenty, a panel of national food editors and restaurateurs picked the grand champion sandwich and three runners-up.

The Sandwich Coronation Party took place at Tavern-on-the-Green in New York's Central Park. Portland, Oregon, chef Clyde Allison was named Sandwich King, and his sandwich, "Dutch Diplomat," was deemed grand champion for National Sandwich Month in August. Allison's sandwich was a grilled triple-decker of turkey, coleslaw, Swiss cheese, and baked ham on caraway rye bread. His winning sandwich was reminiscent of the very first grand champion eleven years prior, the Reuben. Allison won an all-expenses-paid, two-week trip for two anywhere in the world, plus $500. He said he took his inspiration for the Dutch Diplomat from a popular cold plate served in the Montgomery Ward department store restaurant-cafeteria he managed in Portland.[24]

While Hyland had a hand in the National Sandwich Idea Contest, perhaps her greatest contribution to the university was the International Seven Restaurant in the Oval Room of what was then the Home Economics Administration Building (now Stone Hall). She opened the restaurant in 1967 as part of the advanced food service course she taught. Before coming to Purdue in 1964, Hyland had been director of food service at Stanford University's Student Union

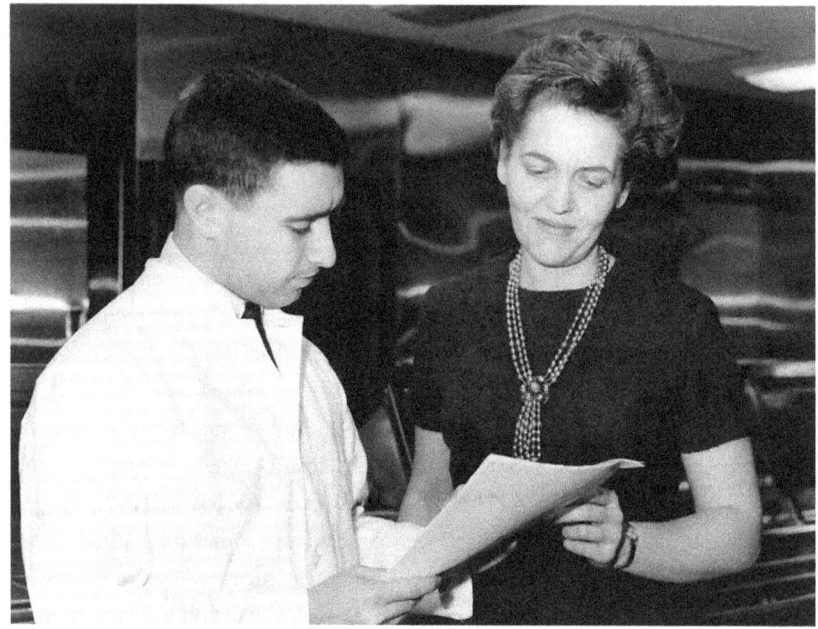

Assistant Professor of Institutional Management Mary Rose Hyland, *right*, handled the National Sandwich Idea Contest in 1965–1966 with her students making nearly 150 sandwiches for judging at Purdue. Courtesy Mary Louise Foster.

Building, taught Marquette University student nurses, and served as institutional home economist for Kraft Foods.[25]

The International Dinner Series had originated in 1958, prior to Hyland's arrival, with just two dinners offered each semester. Hyland decided to change the approach. She set up the International Seven Restaurant to operate as a laboratory of learning. Students planned twelve consecutive Thursday evening meals open to the public to gain practical experience as managers. They designed each meal and decor to transport guests to a different country. Students were given a manager's portfolio with a food requisition order form, a laundry report, a food consumption sheet, a daily report of business, and a profit and loss statement. At the time, food service was the fourth largest industry in the United States.[26]

During the first semester of the International Seven Restaurant, students hosted a Polish meal, turning the Oval Room into the "Warsaw Cellar"; a Russian dinner featured a gold Russian samovar, a metal urn to make tea on loan from former Head of the Department of Institutional Management Edith

Gamble; and the final feast for the semester served a crowd of more than one hundred with an Indianapolis 500 theme titled "Back Home."[27]

At the turn of the next decade, students renamed the restaurant Club 70. Guests who attended at least five meals received a booklet containing the recipes served that semester.[28] In 1974, the restaurant was renamed the American Tradition Restaurant and featured culinary discoveries from around the United States, rather than from other countries. Menus and prices were announced prior to each dinner in Purdue publications and on WBAA radio.[29]

Hyland was president of the Indiana Dietetics Association and received the 1966 Educator of the Year Award from the Purdue chapter of the Food Service Executive Association.[30] She was named an extension specialist in institutional management the following year when Home Economics Extension moved from Purdue's Agricultural Department to the School of Home Economics. Hyland then split her time between teaching and working as an extension agent with food service management personnel throughout Indiana.

At the 1966 Indiana Homemakers conference at Purdue, Hyland spoke on the latest trends, such as self-serve restaurants, similar to "smorgasbords," pre-prepared foods, and electronic and automated equipment. Smorgasbords or buffet-style service combated two restaurant challenges of the time: the labor shortage and patrons' wait time for a meal.

Hyland talked of revolutionary drive-in restaurants with computerized food service where a limited menu of foods could be cooked, wrapped, served, and billed without being touched by human hands.[31] Society was moving faster and the food industry adapted. Many of Hyland's predictions of technological advances in food service have come to pass.

She spoke of microwaves, although she did not use the term. She said that electronic ovens were an example of one type of new equipment and would be used extensively in the future. "Instamatic infra-red ovens cook refrigerated foods in four to ten minutes," she explained.[32]

The theme for the 1968 Homemakers Conference at Purdue was "Looking Toward the Year 2000." Hyland presented her talk, "Breaking Food Service Barriers." If Hyland had had a crystal ball back then, she would have seen that in 2000 her department would be renamed Restaurant, Hotel, Institutional, and Tourism Management (RHIT) and the PhD program would begin that year.

A new class was launched by Hyland in 1971 in which students planned a party for one hundred guests to be served in a private home or event venue. Staff and faculty used the students in the class to cater events when entertaining personal friends after games or during the holidays. The course included the making of creative hors d'oeuvres, garnishes, and flambés. "Hospitality feeding" had become a big part of the food service industry, and by this time 70 percent of the students majoring in institutional management were men.[33]

However, Institutional Management was not all theme dinners and parties; it was also about serving the health care industry. Hyland attended the 1971 White House Conference on Aging where a discussion placed food service in health care facilities on the shoulders of leaders in institutional management. Health care was experiencing tremendous growth and change in the 1970s as one of the nation's largest industries. Some hotel chains were becoming involved in health care, such as the Holiday Inn–owned Medicenters located around the country.[34]

Long-range planning was conducted for the Department of Institutional Management. Hand-in-hand with long-range planning came the need for a name change. A list of thirty two different names were first suggested, and those names were narrowed down to five. After nearly fifty years, faculty voted to change the name to Restaurant, Hotel, and Institutional Management (RHI) in fall 1974.

While planning was in the works, Hyland took a two-year sabbatical to tour venues on two continents and interview international students and faculty about their teaching methods in culinary endeavors and tourism. She traveled to Hawaii, Canada, London, Geneva, Berne, Stockholm, The Hague in the Netherlands, a few eastern states, and more. She toured hotels, restaurants, university food services, nursing homes, food manufacturing and distribution companies. Hyland took courses in tourism, cuisine, and service at the International Institute of Glion in Switzerland. As both a student and a tourist, Hyland gained insight into tourism as a global industry—its social implications, economic benefits, and growth potential.[35]

Hyland said, "Restaurant management as a science is now taught at many universities as it is at Purdue. And now I'm happy to say we have background and material to teach a course in international tourism."[36] Hyland returned to Purdue poised to energize the department as it took a giant leap into its future with its new name and invigorated mission to bring global tourism into the curriculum.

Mary "Edith" Gamble's development of the first courses for women in Institutional Management in 1917, which became the Department of Institutional Management she headed for thirty years, was now primed for a metamorphosis she would never have imagined. Today, graduates of Purdue's White Lodging–J. W. Marriott, Jr. School of Hospitality and Tourism Management (HTM) stand on Gamble's shoulders and have Hyland to thank for laying the foundation to learn about global tourism.

FLORA L. WILLIAMS, FINANCIAL COUNSELING AND MIRACLES

Flora Leona Rouch Williams led her life in the seat of spirituality, and she exemplified how ordinary people can do extraordinary things. She made her mark as an international expert in financial counseling, a full professor, researcher, author, ordained minister, and, most remarkably, as a pianist who continued to play after losing her hand in an accident.

Williams was a professor in Purdue's Department of Consumer Science and Retailing, later named Consumer Science. However, she started at Purdue in 1969 as an assistant professor in the Department of Home Management and Family Economics in the School of Home Economics[37] after teaching home economics in public schools.

Originally from Bremen, Indiana, she had been valedictorian of her 1955 high school class in Lakeville. She became an accomplished pianist and earned a bachelor's degree in music and education at Manchester College in North Manchester, before earning a Purdue master's in vocational home economics and a doctorate in family economics and resource management in 1964 and 1969, respectively.[38] Her husband, Leiw, taught at West Lafayette High School, and they had three children.

Williams devoted much of her career to instructing professionals and counselors to teach people to live within their means. She helped build the foundation for Purdue's acclaimed Financial Counseling and Planning program in the School of Home Economics. In 1974, Williams organized a "Consumer Day on Campus" for the public with authorities from five consumer protection agencies leading a panel discussion.[39]

Williams founded Purdue's Financial Advising Clinic in 1975, offering free financial counseling for people in the community. Senior students in the financial counseling and planning class acted as clinic advisors. They were required to serve clients from low, middle, and high socioeconomic classes by completing a financial plan complete with investments, funding for college, retirement planning, and estate distribution. The clinic ceased operation when Williams retired in 2000.[40]

In 1976, the School of Home Economics was renamed the School of Consumer and Family Sciences, which aligned with Williams's courses and work. She initiated a bachelor's degree program in financial counseling and planning in 1978. She developed financial counseling as a profession at Purdue, and the university's Financial Counseling and Planning program was ranked by Wealth

Management.com as one of the top twenty colleges for financial planning.[41] Through the mid 1980s, she organized intensive summer sessions on financial counseling with participants from the United States, Canada, and Australia.[42]

Williams served in court cases, such as wrongful death suits where a person's financial worth had to be determined. She was intrigued with research on how families interact about money; how, through counseling, people's attitudes about money can be deprogrammed; and how to improve a family's quality of life when their income is decreasing. She also focused on government programs affecting people, poverty issues, and household expenditures. She spoke to unemployed workers throughout Indiana when there were factory closures or layoffs.

Williams taught at the University of California at Davis; Jia Tong University in Shanghai, China; and was part of Purdue's Brazil Project, teaching at the Viscosa Federal University. She trained counselors from all over the world, presented papers in many countries, and was on boards of directors for international associations and societies. Like so many other women who supported other women through actions and programs, Williams received Purdue's Helen B. Schleman Gold Medallion Award.

Williams's successful career was devoted to financial counseling and planning until one fateful day in 1999 that changed her life. On June 28, in the jungles of Mexico, Williams, age sixty-two, was in an accident in a tourist van that took her right hand and part of her right arm. "The fact that I'm alive today took three or four miracles," she said in an interview.[43]

Williams and her husband were on vacation riding in a van to see Mayan ruins when a tire blew out and the van slid down an embankment and crashed into boulders. Williams's hand was cut off by a large rock. She could have bled to death.

However, miracles saved her: Five of the other passengers were on vacation after having just graduated from medical school. They jumped into action, stopping the blood flow in Williams's arm and calling one of their Harvard professors to obtain the name of a plastic surgeon in Mexico. Passengers flagged down passersby for help. One had ice to pack Williams's severed hand to potentially reattach it (later determined impossible), and another had a knife to cut her out of her seatbelt.

"Immediately upon impact, I started singing praise songs," Williams recalled. "I had heard that when you are in distress, you should sing praise songs and keep talking to people."

Her singing kept her from going into shock. Before Williams was removed from the wreckage, she told her rescuers that her career as a pianist was over, but her singing career had just begun.[44]

Because she was diabetic and susceptible to infection, doctors decided to amputate Williams's arm below the elbow. Five days later she was back in Lafayette where she underwent more surgeries. Her son brought her classical sheet music for one-handed piano players. "Even in the hospital, I started practicing one hour a day," Williams said. "The important thing is I concentrated on what I could do and not what I couldn't do."

Williams returned to work at Purdue the following fall semester, working from home. When she attended her first faculty meeting after the accident, she talked about her faith and the miraculous way her life was spared.[45] Colleagues said she was always upbeat and positive.

Williams said, "I was to learn ... 'to work smarter, not harder.' I was fortunate that I had taught these principles of work simplification for years in a college course."[46] She painted the nails of her prosthetic hand with polish and wore big glitzy rings on both hands as she mastered new ways to dress, eat, and write. She continued to play piano and organ at Lafayette Church of the Brethren. Williams learned to type on the computer almost as fast with one hand as she did with two. She said, "I was forced to learn quickly while on medical leave because deadlines for research reports still had to be met."

In 1999, the year of her accident, Williams was named a distinguished fellow by the Association for Financial Counseling and Planning Education of which she had been a former president. She retired from Purdue two years later. At a farewell reception she was presented with a Sagamore of the Wabash, Indiana's highest award. By this time, Williams had written nineteen books and numerous articles on family economics, credit, and financial counseling.

She shifted focus in retirement and earned a master of divinity degree from Bethany Theological Seminary, becoming an ordained minister. She wrote a book titled *Hand in Hand with God: Witnessing on the Way*, chronicling how her accident in Mexico led her to a life of ministry and service.[47] Later, Williams combined spirituality with monetary instruction in her book *The Shepherd's Guide Through the Valley of Debt and Financial Change: A Comprehensive Manual for Financial Management, Counseling, and Spiritual Guidance*, updated in 2019 when she was eighty-two. Williams passed away on September 3, 2021.

19

COMFORTING THE AFFLICTED AND AFFLICTING THE COMFORTABLE

HELEN BASS WILLIAMS, LET IT FLY

When Helen Bass Williams was a little girl, she had the opportunity to fly in an airplane over Dewmaine, Illinois, the African American coal mining community where she lived. It was the early 1900s and flight was new and magical. Up among the clouds, Williams decided then and there that she wanted her life to always feel as it did in that moment, to "let it fly."[1]

Throughout her days, Williams voiced that phrase for a variety of both good and bad happenings, such as when she was beaten, gassed, and jailed marching for civil rights in Mississippi and when she singlehandedly brought more Black students to Purdue University, spurring a revolution of attitude change between the races on campus. Williams put her three fingers to her heart, threw them out toward the heavens, and said, "Let it fly."

Born Helen Laurene Kelly in 1916, Williams was hired as a faculty member at Purdue in 1968, the year Martin Luther King Jr. and Bobby Kennedy were assassinated. She was Purdue's first Black female faculty member as an assistant professor of French but spent most of her time as a counselor to Black students in the School of Humanities, Social Science, and Education (HSSE), later named College of Liberal Arts.

Williams was recruited to Purdue by Professor Mary Endres (Fyfe) whom she had met while working on a project at Tougaloo College. Endres was a pioneering educator who helped create one of the first consolidated school districts in Illinois, and she is the namesake for Mary Endres Elementary School in Woodstock. Endres founded the Department of Elementary Education at Purdue.[2]

Williams helped African American and Latino students learn to "let it fly" as they were up against so much at Purdue, unprepared academically and culturally to succeed at the mostly white campus that struggled with racial tension during the post–Martin Luther King era. She was a large woman of extraordinary character with a little girl's voice that may have fooled some until they witnessed her unabashed strength and courage to fight for and advise the Black students she nurtured with an iron hand.

Her skin tone was light and she was often discriminated against within the Black community for both her smarts and the fact that at times she unwittingly passed as white. In turn, she was also discriminated against by the white community when they discovered she was Black. Despite it all, she was customarily charming with a childlike sense of humor in one moment and a sophisticated demeanor in another.[3] Both roles helped her deal with authority and racists.

Williams came to campus at age fifty-two on the heels of striving for civil rights as the executive director of Mississippi Action for Progress (MAP), where she was responsible for Head Start programs in twenty-five counties, garnering vast experience in standing up to bigotry, poverty, and lack of health care and education for people of color. Williams had been in the freedom trenches, kneeling in prayer in the streets of Selma, Alabama, with Martin Luther King as police dogs snapped behind their heads.[4]

Her first visit to campus occurred the year before she was hired when she was invited to be a speaker for the Old Masters Program in November 1967. Old Masters is an event that brings eminent personalities from across the country to Purdue to share their ideas and experiences with the student body. A newspaper article about her talk stated, "A Mississippi Negro educator was given a standing ovation when she appealed for 'love and social intelligence' between the races at an opening Old Masters program." She told the students serving as hosts, "I hope you will have a tomorrow that is populated with human beings."[5]

The story continued: "After hearing German-born Karl Brandt, a Stanford University research fellow, say 'Persons born in this country can't appraise what it means to immigrants,' Mrs. Williams said wryly, 'In Mississippi, I sometimes have an urge to come to America, too.' But she added, 'Some real American things are beginning to happen there.'"⁶

Williams had been married twice, first in 1934 to Jewell Bass, a physician she assisted in treating patients. While they were married, she earned a teaching certificate from Southern Illinois Normal at Carbondale in 1937 and a bachelor of arts from Southern Illinois University, majoring in French and elementary education, in 1942. Williams taught elementary school and became a principal in Dewmaine.

Her husband battled cancer for the last eight years of their marriage and died in 1949. The following year, without enough funds to become a doctor, she compromised and earned a master's degree in public health from North Carolina College at Durham. She married Leroy A. H. Williams in 1957, and they divorced in July 1968, the year Williams came to Purdue. However, divorce documents in her papers preserved in Purdue Archives state that Williams left her husband in 1961 for Jackson, Mississippi (presumably for her job), and he stayed in South Carolina, claiming in the divorce proceedings that she had abandoned him. Also in Williams's preserved papers is the couple's marriage certificate—torn in half.

Prior to leaving for Mississippi, Williams worked at the South Carolina Tuberculosis Association before joining the faculty at Benedict College, a historically Black institution. While at Benedict, she served on the board of directors of the Highlander Folk School (today the Highlander Research and Education Center), a powerful social justice hub established in Tennessee by Myles Horton, who believed that oppressed people were more powerful together. It was a training ground for civil rights leaders during the 1960s, and it profoundly influenced Williams's life. She said Highlander was where she felt platonic love for the first time, helping her to bloom and learn to love in return.

Williams courageously helped connect students with voter registration workshops and grassroots political protests incubating at Highlander. She drove students on backroads from Benedict to Highlander, a 250-mile trip, knowing that if they were found out, they risked arrest, student expulsions, and the likely loss of her job. Williams sat on the Highlander board with prominent activists, including Rosa Parks and Septima Clark.⁷

At Highlander, Williams learned strategies to deal with authority figures, what she called "tiddling." In other words, she used charm, humor, and her great intellect to thwart racial tension and injustice. And she loved to do it. For example, she used "tiddling" on a police officer by having fun with him. Her ingenuity could overcome blind power, putting an authority figure in a situation to think as an individual rather than as a member of a group or mob.[8]

In 1964, Williams earned a master's degree in French from Southern Illinois and then taught at Tougaloo College near Jackson, Mississippi, taking the position to support her activism.[9] She recalled, "I was working for a college president who resented his faculty's involvement with civil rights—the governor had threatened to cut off student stipends."[10]

Along with marching, Helen quietly volunteered, registering Blacks to vote and sitting in local post offices to help them fill out Social Security forms. She opened her home to Black students and activists who needed meals and accommodations.

After her research showed the highest maternity/infant death rate for Blacks in the country was in Mississippi, Williams established well-baby clinics in rural areas "where babies slipped through your hands, slimy with impetigo."[11] Williams said she accomplished some of her civil rights feats because she was "mad as hell" and a plain old "meanie."[12]

Next, when Williams became the executive director of MAP, she learned how to work with a white, male board of directors, witnessed the Klan's power to drive a prominent liberal family from the state, and provided research for Bobby Kennedy's commission of inquiry on southern Black needs.[13]

During the beginning of Head Start, Williams bravely "borrowed" a typewriter, ledgers, and bolts of green satin from a local Ku Klux Klan warehouse that were intended to adorn the Klansmen. A few days later, the Head Start adult sewing class had created green satin pinafores for the Head Start children.[14]

Williams brought her arsenal of in-the-trenches experiences and "mad as hell" spirit to Purdue when she became the first Black female faculty member and student coordinator, but only, as she said, "after the president [Frederick Hovde] and I had agreed that I would not be a collaborationist."[15] She sat on a committee headed by Hovde to bring more minority students and faculty to Purdue. Despite being called "Aunt Jemima" by some Blacks, she recalled that she "became hell-bent on students making up their minds to either be a success in the system or to get out."[16]

She rented a large house from the Purdue Research Foundation at 241 S. Grant and opened it to students who needed a place to stay. Students, faculty, and staff helped paint and repair the house, which became a gathering place. Williams liked to cook and always had something on the stove that could feed twenty people from what she called her "cooking vessels." A steady stream of students sat around her home with her protective "Mama Dog" lying at her feet as she told stories, imparting wisdom with her poetic lilt.

During a Purdue student housing shortage in 1976, Williams wrote to local friends stating that she had thirteen students sleeping on the floor of her house. She said, "Well, I might have to call you again since the requests are beginning to exceed the space available. Our President Hansen has issued a request that all housing sources be told to the Dean of Students Office. If anyone wants blacks [*sic*], call me."

Williams helped students pay their rent and find part-time jobs, sometimes spending her entire paycheck to help them. She also sought help from faculty and administrators. Robert Ringel, vice president for Academic Affairs, said that Williams walked into his office and asked, "How much money do you have in your pockets?" After he rummaged for a few dollars, she scoffed, "Ah, you can do better than that." She worked her way around campus until she collected enough money for a needy student.[17]

Never afraid to speak out, in an interview in *The Exponent*, Williams said, "America has never committed itself to the education of Blacks and neither has Purdue University." She may have been referring to the fact that she was tasked with bringing more Black students to campus, but administrators did not provide funds to serve them to make their experience successful.

By 1972, Williams had gathered data on the characteristics of Purdue's Black and Latino students, and she and Assistant Dean of the School of Humanities, Social Science and Education Earl B. Notestine created a "Reading Proposal." They wrote, "We and the university are currently immoral in our failure to confront and to eliminate what we feel to be the chief reason for Black student failure: the inability to read."[18] They asked for funds to create a diagnostic clinic with a supervisor, teaching assistants, textbooks, and more, ending their proposal with: "Unless they can read, Black students will continue to fail."[19]

Williams witnessed how students "with non-white, functionally deprived educational backgrounds . . . find Purdue an alien environment in which their chances for success, already low, are further diminished by their own social and psychological reactions to the university. . . . Educationally this population reflects the quality of the societies from which they come: the slums and ethnic ghettos of Gary, Hammond, East Chicago and Indianapolis, and the deprived rural hinterland of southern Indiana."[20]

Black and Latino students received little encouragement from their families and professors. Their relatives had little experience with higher education and

Helen Bass Williams, *right*, was a civil rights activist who knelt in the streets of Selma, Alabama, with Dr. Martin Luther King. She became the first Black female faculty member at Purdue in 1968. Williams was a counselor and advocate for Black and Latino students, opening her home to those in need. Courtesy Purdue Archives and Special Collections.

needed their children home to help earn a living. Latinos are taught to respect their elders, yet Williams cited an example of a professor complaining, "If he says 'Ma'am' once more, I will ask him to drop the course."

The "Reading Proposal" and the grant that resulted led to the opening of Purdue's Learning Center in room 116 of the Recitation Building (Helen B. Schleman Hall) in 1972, designed to help any student[21] who entered college ill-prepared, particularly those who needed help in English. A Reading Clinic was also offered. Students of all races worked one-on-one with tutors, faculty, graduate students, and laypeople, who served on a volunteer basis because the center was working on a shoestring budget.[22] Furniture was hand-me-down from a fraternity that was going to throw it out and books were donated by professors.

In a letter to a young, Black faculty member, Williams expressed why she wanted the center. She wrote, "The one and only thing which I wanted to achieve was a Learning Center of sufficient scope to enable the black [sic] and other minority students from Indiana to be able to understand Purdue's many imponderables and to be less afraid."[23]

In her personal notes, Williams listed questions asked by Black students that she labeled "Anxiety Indicators":

- How does one achieve a positive self-image when told to not be passive, yet, lives in a society which rewards passivity and punishes aggression?
- How to develop a less anxious approach to the academic experience?
- How can I say what I mean?
- I get so angry, I choke up. How can I keep from getting mad?[24]

In 1976, Williams still longed to have a Reading Course to help the many Black students who arrived on campus unable to read. She wrote candidly to friends about her experiences:

> So many of these students don't know how to read, write or articulate. They tell me that they want to be lawyers, doctors, Indian Chiefs. As I register them, . . . I am highly aware of the psychedelic panorama of their previous existence—high rent, high killing, high drugs. One young man told me that he simply had to stay here this summer because he couldn't take the drunkenness of his street. Many parents in Gary have called me asking if they can come work for me and live with me until they find jobs! . . . Their voices start so hopeful over the phone and end despairingly as I tell them that I cannot. . . .

> A straightforward inclusion of blacks [sic] would have to include means of teaching what they never had an opportunity to learn. Yet we still don't have a Reading Course.[25]

Williams also helped create what is now known as Purdue's African American Studies program where students researched and recorded the life, history, and culture of African ancestry and worked to develop pride in Black heritage. She helped establish what is now the Black Cultural Center. In 1975, she served on the first executive board of what became the Black Caucus of Faculty and Staff, and she was an advisor for Harambee, a Black student organization. "Harambee" is Kenya's official motto, meaning "all pull together" to place the group before the individual.[26] Also in 1975, Williams was honored with the Helen B. Schleman Gold Medallion Award for her work with advancing Black students and faculty.

Williams retired from Purdue in 1978 and returned to Southern Illinois to care for her ill mother. There, she continued her work building communities, fighting for the poor and elderly, tutoring students, and giving her time and money.

Williams died in 1991 at age seventy-five in the former mining camp of Colp, Illinois, near where she first flew in an airplane as a young girl. Her former colleague Purdue Professor of Communication Leon Trachtman gave a eulogy at her "obsequies" held in Carbondale. Trachtman understood the most vile acts of intolerance as he was an American prisoner of war who was sent to the Berga concentration camp in Germany during World War II because he was Jewish.[27] He said:

> Her life was spent comforting the afflicted and afflicting the comfortable. That was the Helen Bass [Williams] I knew and loved. She came to us in a time of troubles. The universities of our country were just beginning to understand some of their sins of omission and commission toward the minority youth of our country. And she was not bashful about telling us what to do to expiate these sins.
>
> But at the same time, she knew that some of the youngsters she counseled had set for themselves a course doomed to end in failure. And she was not bashful about telling them what they had to do to make a proper place for themselves in this society....
>
> In her special and inimitable way, she sparked a quiet revolution at Purdue.... Helen Bass Williams was, almost singlehandedly, responsible for a fundamental change in attitude at Purdue.[28]

In 1993 on the eve of the birthday of Martin Luther King Jr., the university announced the establishment of the Helen Bass Williams Scholarship created by Purdue's Black Cultural Center. The scholarship was the first at the university to honor the achievements of an African American woman. It would be awarded annually to a deserving African American student from Indiana entering Purdue.[29] Even in death, Williams would continue to uplift the lives of Black students.

In 2023, still going strong after fifty years, the Learning Center, now in Wiley Residence Hall, was renamed the Helen Bass Williams Academic Success Center. Also that year, Purdue's College of Liberal Arts unveiled an official portrait of Williams, thought to be the first commissioned of a Black female faculty member. Painted by local artist Stacy Bogan, the piece titled *To Love and to Learn* was installed on the first floor of Stanley Coulter Hall where Williams had been an assistant professor of French.

As a child, Williams spent her last pennies on an airplane ride, and when she realized she couldn't afford to fly again, she looked for another way to ascend. "I've always thought that I could pull something out of my heart and send it flying out there," she said. "And that God would want it."[30]

Williams elevated the world with her gift for seeing others. Her mentor, Myles Horton, said, "With one eye she saw people as they were and with the other how they could be."[31]

20
HELEN SCHLEMAN FIGHTS FOR FEMALE FACULTY

HAND THAT ROCKS THE CRADLE ROCKS THE EQUITY BOAT

Through the 1960s and in retirement in the 1980s, Dean of Women Emeritus Helen B. Schleman was a salary watchdog for female faculty at Purdue. She asked her friend John Hicks, executive assistant to Purdue President Arthur Hansen, for the "black book."

The black book was a computer-generated listing of all Purdue salaries, and Schleman used it to investigate the wages of female faculty compared to that of male faculty. This was a time before the Access to Public Records Act (APRA) was in place, and people were not yet allowed to openly access government documents. Today, several of Schleman's hand-scrawled tables of statistics on salaries and faculty positions of women compared to that of men are housed with her papers in Purdue University Archives and Special Collections.[1]

Cindy Metzler, the president of the Association of Women Students (AWS), presented a speech to the Purdue Women's Club in 1970 entitled "The Status of Women at Purdue University." She used Schleman's data in her presentation, and her speech set off a string of unexpected events that began slowly to turn the tide of discrimination for female faculty and staff at Purdue. Metzler wrote:

 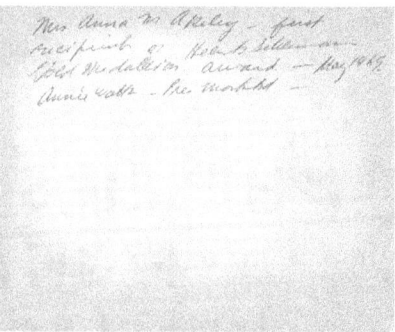

Dean of Women Emeritus Helen B. Schleman stands with Professor Anna Akeley and student Annie Watts, president of Mortar Board, holding the Schleman gold medallion. In 1969, Akeley was the second woman, after Schleman herself, to receive Purdue's Helen B. Schleman Gold Medallion Award established upon Schleman's retirement as dean of women (1947–1968). Still today, it annually honors a female faculty member or administrator who encourages women in academic and professional areas within the university. Courtesy Purdue University Archives and Special Collections.

During the 1969–1970 academic year, there were 141 male instructors and 131 female instructors employed by the university. At the rank of assistant professor, the next highest level, the figures change a little; there were 516 male assistant professors and 83 female assistant professors. Quite a change. Over one-third of these women are in the Department of Physical Education for Women, the Department of Nursing, and the School of Home Economics.

As associate professors there were 460 men and 30 women; again one-third of these women are in the fields of Home Economics, Physical Education for Women, and Nursing. Moving along to those who have attained the rank of full professor, there are 455 men and a grand total of 13 women. There are 55 heads of departments with the rank of professor; six of the department heads are women.[2]

The six women serving as heads were in Clothing and Textiles, Equipment and Family Housing, Home Management and Family Economics, Institutional Management, Physical Education for Women, and Nursing Technology. The School of Home Economics was the only school at Purdue with a woman serving as dean. That was Eva Goble. The only women holding associate dean positions were also in home economics.

"One can only wonder," Metzler wrote, "what has happened to the women on the faculty from the time they were instructors to the time a very few become professors. Since most of the faculty is recruited into the various departments by the department itself, it would appear, and can be substantiated, that women are not recruited with very much vigor."[3]

Metzler pointed out that women were not in professional areas in as great a number as were men, but "perhaps there are very real reasons for this situation. If women go through their entire undergraduate career never coming into contact with successful women, as many of them do, how are they to realize that it is possible for them to rise to the positions they see men holding all around them in a university? To make matters even more difficult, too often the hiring criteria for females is much more stringent than for a comparable male."[4]

Metzler also reported that in nearly all cases the female professor's salary was less than that for a comparable male. Metzler said that according to national surveys the median salary for women on a university teaching staff was about $1,000 less than the salary for males.[5]

Next, a bold move by a young woman furthered publicity of the inequality. A graduate student who was a women's liberation proponent obtained a copy of Metzler's speech and sent it to the Women's Equity Action League (WEAL), founded in Cleveland, Ohio, in 1968 to promote economic equality for women by focusing on educational, legal, and tax issues that impacted women. The organization is best known for its initiatives to reduce sexism in American colleges and universities. Among WEAL national advisory board members was Indiana Senator Birch E. Bayh,[6] who would author the landmark Title IX legislation in the Higher Education Act of 1972, a law guaranteeing women full educational opportunities.

After receiving a copy of Metzler's speech, WEAL filed a complaint with the Department of Health, Education, and Welfare (HEW), charging Purdue University with sex discrimination. A sex discrimination suit also had been filed against the University of Maryland and the University of Michigan that year.[7]

The university was buzzing with rumors of the eye-opening exposé, so John Hicks, who was also Purdue's Equal Opportunity Employment Officer, invited Dean of Women Beverley Stone to meet with fellow deans and vice presidents in November 1970 to discuss the situation.

Hicks publicly claimed that Purdue did not discriminate against females, saying, "We love women." And "In areas of Purdue specialty—engineering, agriculture, pharmacy, technology, veterinary science—particularly in these areas, there are very few women PhD holders anywhere in the country. I think you would expect Purdue to have fewer women proportionately than there are total women PhD recipients."[8]

Once Stone met with the group, the Office of the Dean of Women urged Hicks to create a Committee on the Status of Women, which President Hansen did in May 1971, naming Stone as chair. The committee was comprised of fifteen female members of Purdue's faculty and administration. Schleman handed her salary and ranking tabulations to Stone for use in her committee's findings.[9] The history-making committee members who would gather data were:

> Mary Zeedyk—Administrative Assistant to John Hicks as Employment Officer
> Katie Markee—Associate Professor of Library Science
> Virginia Ferris—Assistant Dean of the Purdue Graduate School, Associate Professor, Department of Entomology
> Mary Endres—Associate Professor/Founder Department of Elementary Education (who brought Helen Bass Williams to Purdue)
> Helen Clark—Professor Department of Foods and Nutrition
> Donita Stobaugh—Assistant Director of the Placement Office
> Betty Suddarth—Admissions Research, later first female Registrar at Purdue
> Jo-Ann Price—Professor of Physical Education for Women
> Vivian Johnson—Professor Department of Physics
> Betty Arnsman—Director Women's Residence Halls, until 1969
> Ann Larowe—Professor of Nursing
> Marcia Brown—Purdue Human Resources
> Eva Goble—Dean of the School of Home Economics
> Sandra Hutchins—Assistant Professor Electrical Engineering
> Betty Staaks—Administrative Assistant to Mary Fuqua, Associate Dean of Home Economics extension[10]

The committee gave an interim report in spring 1972 showing that in most departments throughout the university, except those traditionally staffed by females, it was evident that qualified women were plentiful for academic posts, but they were not being recruited. John Hicks then publicly admitted that up to that point, there had not been a determined effort to recruit women for academic positions at Purdue. "However," he said, "we feel our present intent and desire to recruit women is an honest and good one."[11]

That year, Stone gave a talk to the Purdue Women's Club, explaining the function and timeline of her Committee on the Status of Women. She began with a quote from *Children's Letters to God* by Stuart Hample and Eric Marshall:

Dear God,

Are boys better than girls? I know you are one, but please try and be fair.

Love,
Sylvia[12]

WOMEN'S CAUCUS ESTABLISHED

The Purdue Women's Caucus was established in spring 1972 with the main mission to ensure that the percentage of women on the academic staff was in direct proportion to the percentage of available candidates and to seek equitable pay for females at the university. The caucus encouraged qualified women to rise to high positions in the university hierarchy as positions opened and advocated for the availability of day care centers.[13] Members were female faculty, staff, graduate students, and some community members, along with a few males.[14]

By September 1972 a report was sent to President Hansen stating that in the previous year no female professor or administrator at Purdue made an annual salary comparable to the average salary of the 263 male professors at Purdue. The following month, Hansen spoke to about two hundred people at a Women's Caucus gathering. *The Purdue Exponent* reported that he answered questions "on Purdue's alleged discrimination against women and concluded, 'I just didn't know some of these problems existed'" and that his "consciousness has been raised quite a bit." The story continued:

> Discussing one criterion often used on promoting faculty members on the academic-administrative ladder, Hansen noted that "The amount of time spent in administrative tasks is often used to measure a person's deserving of a promotion. One problem in this university is that many women haven't

had administrative experience because they've been barred from having those positions."[15]

Hansen said, "Letters must be sent to the deans and department chairmen to get the plans for adding women implemented. I'm not going to say 'Please have more women on the faculty'; I'm asking them to recruit them as soon as possible."[16]

Hansen ducked many inquiries, saying he did not have the facts readily available. When asked if the then current search for a new humanities dean included any women candidates, he admitted, "Frankly, there were no women included on the search committee list," but added he would look into the matter.

A bit off topic, but relevant to the pervasive chilly climate for females on campus, Hansen was asked about Professor Al Wright's alleged practice of forcing female band members to bleach their hair blond when the bands traveled abroad. Again, Hansen declined to comment "because I just wasn't aware of this."[17]

TIAA-CREF LANDMARK CASE FOR FEMALE FACULTY AND STAFF

By 1973, Dean of Women Emeritus Helen Schleman had moved on from monitoring salaries to monitoring retirement benefits for Purdue's female faculty and administrators.

A committee of the Purdue Women's Caucus filed a charge of discrimination against Teachers Insurance and Annuity Association–College Retirement Equities Fund (TIAA-CREF) and Purdue University. TIAA-CREF is the retirement plan founded by philanthropist Andrew Carnegie.

The committee members were Helen Johnson, professor of Nursing and head of the School of Nursing; Kathleen Johnston, retired head of the Department of Housing, Equipment and Environmental Design in the School of Home Economics; Dorothy Mennen, associate professor of Theater Arts and chair of the Purdue University Senate; Helen B. Schleman, retired Dean of Women; and Carol J. Widule, professor of Physical Education.[18]

The caucus claimed that women were paid lower pension benefits than men, not just at Purdue, but in all workplaces, even though equal contributions were made to the pension program. The complaint said, "We feel that the decision to use sex as the sole criterion for differentiation of payments than to include other factors ... is ... discriminatory."[19]

TIAA claimed that because women in the general population lived longer, female faculty should receive lower periodic benefits. However, the only variable that TIAA used in determining benefits was gender, ignoring the different life expectancies, for instance, of smokers and nonsmokers, blacks and whites, and those with hazardous jobs. The difference in benefits was substantial; retired female faculty members received about 15 percent less than men with similar service at Purdue. In one case, the discrepancy amounted to $90 per month.[20]

Five years later, the Equal Employment Opportunity Commission (EEOC) announced a decision on the complaint made by the Purdue Women's Caucus, saying, "The use of sex-segregated actuarial tables to determine unequal employment benefits violates Title VII."[21] Title VII of the Civil Rights Act of 1964 protects individuals against employment discrimination on the basis of race and color, as well as national origin, sex, and religion. TIAA and Purdue were found to be discriminating against female retirees. The EEOC urged all parties to negotiate. The Purdue Women's Caucus agreed. TIAA and Purdue refused.

Representatives from the Purdue Women's Caucus and the American Association of University Professors wrote President Arthur Hansen a letter, which read: "We would welcome the opportunity to meet with you or your representative to discuss the case and explain the position of the AAUP (American Association of University Professors) and the Purdue Women's Caucus on the matter. Given Purdue's commitment to affirmative action under guidelines from HEW (Department of Health, Education, and Welfare), it seems to us that the University would want to go on record as supporting the rights of women employees to equal retirement benefits."[22]

In return, Hansen wrote, "I appreciate your letter of February 19 and the statement of your 'equal in-equal out' retirement benefits from TIAA-CREF. The position of the University currently is to await the outcome of several Department of Justice lawsuits pending against TIAA and various universities. This issue is fraught with complexity, as readings of the appellate courts to date have clearly indicated. Without a clear signal from the courts I think the University is not in a position to decree on what is 'fair.'"[23]

TIAA had announced that it would begin to use unisex insurance tables on July 1, 1980, but would only pay equal benefits from contributions made after that date. Schleman wrote in a memorandum: "What does this mean? Women will not receive benefits equal to men of the same age and service until 2020 when a woman who begins employment at age thirty in 1980 retires. Surely this is not the equality envisioned in Title VII of the Civil Rights Act of 1964. Forty years is too long to wait!"[24]

Schleman was seventy-eight when she decided enough was enough. She had been fighting for women's rights since she stepped on Purdue soil in 1933 as a graduate student in psychology and education. It had been nearly fifty years, and she was still willing to stand up for what was right, no matter the cost.

In 1980, a committee of Purdue women filed a class action suit in US District Court on behalf of the Women's Caucus alleging that Purdue and its retirement programs violated the Civil Rights Act of 1964. The suit demanded full equalization of benefits, plus back pay to past female retirees. Schleman was quoted in an *Exponent* story about the suit: "Women have traditionally been at the bottom of the pay scale. Unequal retirement benefit scales add up to a sizeable disadvantage. After all, retirement pay isn't a gift. It is earned. It's only a form of delayed compensation."[25]

The judgment was handed down on March 27, 1987, and each member of the class with an annuity issued prior to March 24, 1972, was awarded an equal division of a $20,000 payment. TIAA and CREF also were ordered to match annuity benefits for those women in the class action suit issued from that date to May 1, 1980. Expenses and attorneys' fees were to be paid by Purdue University, TIAA, and CREF.[26]

As a result of the seven-year lawsuit, Purdue was ordered not to contribute to any employee retirement benefit plans unless the benefits derived were calculated without regard to gender. Purdue women won the battle for equalization of benefits, plus back pay to past female retirees. It was a landmark victory for all females who worked at Purdue University. A formidable force of women made it happen through the leadership of the unrelenting Helen B. Schleman.

Looking back, Betty M. Nelson, who was hired by Schleman as an assistant dean of women in 1967 and rose in the ranks to become dean of students in 1987, said:

> I have always believed the TIAA-CREF lawsuit was one of the most significant initiatives in Helen's long and extremely valuable life. The success of that lawsuit not only had financial impact on the women who were directly involved at that time but has impact on every administrative or faculty woman who is part of a Purdue retirement plan since that date. The conditions related to that decision required equity from any retirement plan going forward.

Every woman benefits. Every woman's family benefits. Every woman should be made aware someone stood up to the biggest and most powerful retirement entity in the country—to the most powerful university administrators in the country—to assure women would have fair payout of their retirement plan. It is easy to forget a legal battle was fought so that women in the educational community could retire with dignity and security. Helen B. Schleman led that charge![27]

21

THE 1970s AND THE WOMEN'S LIBERATION MOVEMENT

NORMA H. COMPTON, THE LAST AND THE FIRST

Dean Eva L. Goble retired on April 1, 1973, and Norma Haynes Compton, age forty-eight, was appointed the next and, ultimately, the final dean of Purdue's School of Home Economics. Like Goble, she was the only female academic dean on campus. Compton would cultivate renewal in nearly every nook and cranny of the school, including its name. She became the first dean of the School of Consumer and Family Sciences (CFS).

Much as Mary Matthews and Virginia Meredith struggled to change attitudes to bring home economics to campus in the early twentieth century, Compton broke barriers to bring a rebirth to the discipline that was the "new" home economics during the women's rights movement of the 1970s. It was a transformative time for women and the workplace and, thus, also for men, and Compton and her faculty strove to rebrand home economics from its unfair and erroneous stigma of a "stitch and stir" field to one with a family-home-community emphasis.

A native of Washington, DC, Compton received an AB (Liberal Arts) degree in psychology at George Washington University in 1950. She spent a year as a researcher for Julius Garfinckel & Company, a nine-story department store.[1]

Norma Haynes Compton (*seated*), dean of the School of Home Economics that became the School of Consumer and Family Sciences, with her predecessors. *Left to right*: Beulah V. Gillaspie, Eva L. Goble, and Gladys Vail in the 1970s. Courtesy Purdue Archives and Special Collections.

Compton earned a master's in clothing and textiles at the University of Maryland and became the head of the clothing and textiles department at Utah State University. While there, she also directed the Institute for Research on Man and His Personal Environment. Her doctorate from Maryland was in human development, and she conducted postdoctoral study at the University of Iowa in 1964. She came to Purdue from Auburn University where she had been dean of the School of Home Economics.[2]

Tall and lean, Compton was the picture of energy as she began her deanship. Two months after she arrived, she gave the keynote address to open the annual Homemakers Conference on campus. She spoke of numerous social changes and talked of advances in genetics, overpopulation, new ideas about sexuality, new forms in group living, women's liberation, and the understanding that home and family play an important role in early childhood education. She predicted that in the future the division of labor would be unlikely to be based upon sex. She said, "Rather, individual couples will have to decide who is going to perform which tasks within the household."[3]

Compton addressed "singleness." She said that being unmarried would no longer be a stigma, and women would have the choice of whether to remain single or enter into a legal marriage contract or a trial marriage; have only a career or marriage plus career; or be a full-time homemaker. Couples were beginning to live together without a marriage license, and Compton alluded to this trend. She said, "These arrangements ... are not really new, but what is new in our time is that some people are advocating that society recognize all living arrangements, not as something to be ashamed of, but as part of the richness of human experience."[4]

The following February, Compton discussed her book *Foundations of Home Economics Research: A Human Ecology Approach* at the university's Books and Coffee Series in the ballroom of the Purdue Memorial Union. She acknowledged that some sociologists and psychoanalysts believed that "the [traditional] family is dead except for the first two years of child raising" or "near the point of complete extinction," yet she, on the other hand, considered the family "the giant shock absorber of society, the one stable point in an increasingly uncertain environment, an anchor against the turbulence of change."[5]

Three months later, Compton's husband, William Randall Compton Sr., passed away at the age of seventy-one. One of her "shock absorbers" was gone. William was a former professor of law at George Washington University and had taught sociology at Utah State University. He had been a colonel and former deputy general counsel for the US Army. He retired in 1963 with a physical disability.[6]

During Compton's first five years as dean of the School of Home Economics change was the name of the game. In fact, when Head of the Department of Foods and Nutrition R. Paul Abernathy asked her if he could proceed with an idea or initiative, Compton's response was always, "Why haven't you already done it?"[7]

TRANSFORMATIVE NAME CHANGE

Self-study leads to change for people and institutions. In 1975, the faculty of Purdue's School of Home Economics conducted an identity study, and on July 1, 1976, a new name was adopted: the School of Consumer and Family Sciences (CFS).

Dean Norma Compton said, "Our subject matter is both commonplace and of great social concern, for the kind of physical home environments in which people live, the ways they eat, spend their money and raise their children determine not only individual and family well-being but the welfare and stability of society as well."⁸

The name change brought some backlash from alumni, faculty, and students. Others took to the name with open arms. Many alumni felt their major had suddenly evaporated with the swipe of a pen. As the School of Home Economics celebrated its fiftieth anniversary, Compton was at the helm forging a transformation while receiving both good and bad feedback. A thick skin was in order.

Reasons for the name change were numerous. Compton wrote, "Meeting the challenges of change is a major responsibility of institutions of higher education." The school was responding to society's changes in career opportunities by updating courses, and the new name better identified the nature of the school's programs. Compton said that the former name carried the image of "cooking and sewing" and also deterred young men from entering the program.⁹ Sadly, it appeared that people forgot or never knew that home economics was based on science and research. Some of the most groundbreaking investigation in nutrition had taken place and were taking place in the School of Home Economics.

The school's highest enrollments at this time were in retailing; restaurant, hotel, and institutional management; dietetics; housing; and nursery-kindergarten teaching. It was difficult for students in these fields to interpret a degree in home economics to potential employers "because of the homemaking connotation associated with the words."¹⁰

Universities across the United States were changing the name of their School of Home Economics. Compton explained that there was a need for a new emphasis and direction that spoke directly to the pressing problems of society, particularly as they related to families. Students needed to be prepared for new, emerging roles in the country. Administrators, faculty, staff, students, and alumni were all involved in the name change decision.

Compton was bold in explaining the sensitive nature of why the name was changed. She wrote, "Because of a public stereotyping, our students and faculty were looked down upon and forced to defend the name and their curricula.... [The] stereotype might have been a past barrier in receiving outside grant funds as well as inadequate budget appropriations from the university."¹¹

For the thousands of alumni (mostly women) with Home Economics degrees, the stereotyping Compton addressed continues even today. Some alumni and faculty feared the name change would cause further confusion in a search for identity. They pointedly asked, "Which male dominated professions have changed their names to attract women students?"¹²

The name change adversely affected some women's donations to Purdue. An alumna said, "I wish to give my money where it will benefit the profession. Until Purdue puts home economics back in the curriculum, I will be donating that money elsewhere."[13]

There had been a long tradition of women not giving monetary gifts to the school. When money was given by a couple, most often the donation went to the school where the husband graduated. The reasons were manyfold, but more than likely in the first half of the twentieth century, the man was the "breadwinner" of the family, and thus he decided where the money would be spent.

Compton said people had fewer preconceived ideas of the meaning of the words "Consumer and Family Sciences," and so graduates had a chance to explain the thrusts of the programs, which were professionally oriented and adapted to business structures. She said, "We hoped to gain credibility with granting agencies and across campus. It was not feasible to change the image [cooking/sewing] as long as the name of Home Economics was retained. We hoped to attract a greater variety of students, especially men."[14]

Christine Ladisch, who was a Purdue graduate student at the time of the name change and would become the inaugural dean of the College of Health and Human Sciences in 2010, said, "I recall that there was considerable debate about the name Consumer and Family Sciences (CFS), as opposed to Family and Consumer Sciences (FCS). Purdue was an outlier in choosing CFS. Other schools chose 'Human Ecology.' This lack of consistency in naming of these schools across the country was something that plagued universities until yet another round of name changes occurred to include 'health' in the 2010s."[15]

In 2018, Ladisch also said, "I was a junior professor when Norma was dean. Norma was brave. I was a little afraid of her. She was the one that said to a field of study, 'You're behind the times, you've got to change your name.' And the punishment she took. The name change was political within the field. I can't imagine what she must have faced. Because when I speak to alums there is a group that I still encounter who when they talk about the change to the College of Health and Human Sciences, they reflect all the way back, wishing it were still Home Economics."[16]

It appears that "perception was everything" when it came to the term "home economics," essentially two words that impact every human who desires a stable home on a foundation of viable economics. Yet when paired, the individual words "home" and "economics" had long lost their individual meanings in people's psyches.

The words "home economics" no longer appeared in any job titles, except for those of home economics teachers.[17] Purdue's CFS continued to train home economics teachers and home economics extension agents, and there was still a "home economics education" major. However, student enrollment and job opportunities in these programs were becoming proportionately smaller.

Under Compton's lead, the school burst forth with what she termed "an experience in renewal." Within her first five years as dean, all administrative personnel—associate deans, assistant deans, and department heads—were newly appointed. The school was reorganized from six academic departments to four—Child Development and Family Studies; Consumer Sciences and Retailing; Foods and Nutrition; and Restaurant, Hotel, and Institutional Management.

New names were created for the buildings housing the school. In 1976, the Home Economics Building was renamed Matthews Hall after the school's first dean, Mary L. Matthews. A cement slab was placed over the words "Home Economics" engraved on the face of the building. The Home Economics Administration Building was renamed Stone Hall after Winthrop E. Stone, with the reasoning that he was president when home economics was established at the university (even though he was slow to establish home economics at Purdue in comparison to the quicker actions of other universities).

Compton believed that each department should offer knowledge beyond textbooks, so she hired faculty with industry experience. One of the goals of CFS was to be highly interdisciplinary in nature as it focused on the consumer and society.

The Oval Room in Stone Hall was renamed the John Purdue Room (now in Marriott Hall). The dining room that functioned as a learning laboratory was remodeled with new plaid carpeting, new furniture, softer lighting, the addition of "stereo background music," and photos from Purdue's Special Collections (which later became the university archives) reproduced and framed to display on the walls.[18] The Spruce Room was also redecorated and renamed the RHI Cafeteria.

During Compton's first five years as dean, the percentage of men on staff increased, there was an increase in enrollment of male students, an administrative position for the sole purpose of public relations and fundraising was added, a new logo was adopted, and more.

These changes were sculpted during a time of inflation in the United States that led to fewer state legislative appropriations and federal subsidies. National concerns became the school's concerns as the energy crisis stimulated research in the area of energy use and conservation related to home equipment. Family and Consumer Law was a new course taught for the first time via videotape in

1974.[19] Extension programs concentrated on the increase in the number of women working outside the home, dual-career marriages, changing roles of family members, child abuse, and nutrition and health.

During the 1970s and into the 1980s, Compton served on the board of directors of Armour & Company meat packing in Phoenix, Arizona, and the National Advertising Review Board of New York City. In the summer of 1980, Compton was on sabbatical in Washington, DC to work with Esther Peterson, special assistant to the president for consumer affairs (who had visited Purdue's School of Home Economics in the 1960s), to implement the Consumers Executive Order.[20] Compton also served on the White House Commission on Home Economics of the National Association of State Universities and Land-Grant Colleges.[21]

After the name change, enrollment steadily increased as programs met the needs of society. The school attracted well-qualified faculty and funding for research increased. Compton wrote, "Seldom do we hear comments about 'cooking and sewing' except from someone trying to be 'funny.'"[22]

Inaugural Dean of the School of Home Economics Mary Matthews and Purdue Trustee Virginia Meredith—trailblazers who saw home economics as a science—may have turned a bit in their graves at Compton's "cooking and sewing" statement. However, Matthews and Meredith shared a kindred creative administrative spirit with Compton. All three left a brave Purdue legacy of change in the face of opposition. In 1978, Compton wrote:

> These past five years have been "an experience in renewal" not only for the School but for me as an administrator. I have found Purdue an environment of confidence and support where I can work toward the fulfillment of myself as an administrator. Administration for me is not presiding at faculty meetings to count the votes, handing out across-the-board raises or serving as a figure head.
>
> For me, administration is a creative endeavor.... Much as a parent endures the pain and hardship of the birth of children and then reaps the pride of their growth and development and some assurance of post existence, so an administrator gives birth to ideas and influences the development of programs, faculty and students and thereby leaves a legacy for future generations. The challenge of administration is great.[23]

22

KRANNERT TRAILBLAZERS

CHARLENE SULLIVAN, KRANNERT'S FIRST FEMALE PROFESSOR OF FINANCE

Charlene Sullivan believed in the "magic of corporate finance."[1] Many people may not describe corporate finance as magical, but to Sullivan, who always thought accounting was "really good for women,"[2] finance is logical, it builds, and "the whole story fits nicely together."[3]

The same can be said for Sullivan's personal and professional story. Because she broke both of her legs when she was an undergraduate, she ended up taking accounting. Sullivan spent forty-four years as a finance professor at Purdue's Krannert School of Management (renamed the Mitch Daniels School of Business in 2023) and was associate dean of undergraduate programs beginning in 2011. She came to campus in 1971 by way of small-town Flaherty, Kentucky, where she grew up on a farm as one of eight children raised by her father after her mother died in childbirth with her tenth pregnancy.

With her deep voice, wide grin, and no-nonsense attitude, Sullivan called her college education a "charity dog story." "I went to college in 1967. Daddy said, 'You're all going to college.' And I always thought that was to get us to think beyond staying in our little town. In those days, not many people went to college. So, it was a real stretch goal."[4]

Sullivan's two older sisters chose medical fields, so she chose the same, majoring in physical therapy at the University of Kentucky as she worked her way through college. It was a science-intense, math-centric program. She was dating the man who would become her first husband, and they were in a car accident. "I ended up with two full-length casts on my legs, and I was bound and determined to return to school because we were always afraid that somehow we would get stuck and our education would get interrupted," Sullivan said.

She decided to change majors because she didn't think she could manage attending lab courses with her leg casts. "I had always been a seamstress and enjoyed that," Sullivan recalled. "So I went into home economics [retailing], and I was getting a degree in my hobby. There were a lot of business courses in that plan of study that weren't in physical therapy. I got to take an accounting course and an econ course."

After graduation in 1971, Sullivan's husband, a business major, was recruited by Purdue's business office. Not wanting the weekend and evening hours that retailing required, Sullivan found a position in the educational placement office. "Somebody from Krannert came to our office in about 1973 and said, 'We've got a new master of science and management [MSM] degree program and the world wants women and minorities in business.'" Sullivan enrolled.

Up to that point, Krannert had only offered a master of science and industrial administration (MSIA), a degree specifically for people who were scientists and engineers. Sullivan finished her MSM degree in 1975. "I cannot recall having a single female faculty member in the MSM program,"[5] she said. Her finance professor, David Kidwell, suggested that she go for a PhD in finance and accounting, and she received her doctorate in 1978, then immediately joined the Krannert faculty. She was the only woman teaching finance and one of a handful of female professors in Krannert. "Many academic people say, 'You know, there was this one person,'" Sullivan said. "Dave Kidwell was my person. He encouraged me."

Sullivan's passion for academia bloomed during her doctoral studies. "I got the opportunity to teach and really fell in love with the students," she said. "I figured out that everyone needed to understand the principles of finance, regardless of what they thought they were going to be when they grew up. I had a lot of enthusiasm for what I was teaching and tried to light the same fire in the students."[6]

In 1977, she won an award for her teaching as a graduate instructor for MGMT 310, Introduction to Financial Management. Even as she was about to retire in 2021, Sullivan still received emails from former students who said that surviving MGMT 310 was one of the greatest accomplishments of their academic lives and one of the most valuable, as they used those principles daily or still had the textbook.

Once Sullivan became part of Krannert, programs geared toward women became hers. She always thought accounting was good for women because they could obtain their CPA, take time out, have children, stay at home for a while, and they would still be a CPA when they wanted to rejoin the workforce.

Her first faculty appointment was as a research associate in Purdue's Credit Research Center (CRC), which at the time was the only research center based in an academic setting that focused on consumer and mortgage credit. Professor Robert Johnson, CRC's founding director, was another of Sullivan's mentors. "The research we were doing was unique; it was unbiased academic research that was used to craft public policy,"[7] Sullivan said. They used the research to testify before state and federal legislative bodies; they presented it to managers of financial institutions; and they were called on frequently to explain their work to the media and lawyers.

"My first quote I ever had in the *Wall Street Journal* related to a column about developments in consumer credit markets," Sullivan recalled. As a credit expert in the late 1970s, Sullivan was a trailblazer and role model as a female authority in finance. Just a few years before in 1974, women were first allowed to apply for and own a credit card in their name.[8] Without credit in their own name, women were unable to build their own credit profiles, and their credit score was dependent upon the financial choices made by their male spouses.

In 1990, Sullivan was elected to the board of the Federal Reserve Bank of Chicago and served for six years, the only woman member. "My election resulted from the knowledge that we had in CRC about consumer credit and its deregulation,"[9] she said.

Sullivan was also called upon by newspapers for quotes about consumer shopping on credit during the holiday season, in a time when credit cards were new. Over the years, she was interviewed regarding bankruptcy, interest rates, the housing market, inflation, and Indiana's economic forecast. She was on the radio in the 1990s through the Purdue Radio Newsline, and she published several articles, books, book chapters, monographs, and working papers related to credit research.

Sullivan was a rigorous teacher. "In those days, we ran the case method in our master's program," she recalled. "So every class was intense and people got cold called [called on in class]. If you didn't say anything, you would *not* get an A. If you were a quiet person and didn't participate, you were going to get a B."

Dr. Charlene Sullivan received her doctorate at Purdue in 1978 and immediately joined the faculty of the Krannert School of Management (renamed the Mitch Daniels School of Business in 2023). She was the only woman teaching finance and one of a handful of female professors in Krannert. Courtesy Purdue University Archives and Special Collections.

Many students, particularly if they were unprepared, were scared to come to class because they feared the cold call, but they showed up. Sullivan asked her students, "What do you think it's like in business? Do you think you're never going to get cold called by your boss?"[10]

She also told her students that no matter what career they chose, they would use finance—everywhere and all the time as a fundamental language. A former student working in business approached Sullivan at an alumni conference and said she took Sullivan's course twice because she flunked the first time. She looked at Sullivan and said, "You changed my life."

"We took teaching very seriously, and so those people remember us. We took great pride in it; finance was tough. But students knew there was something at the other end. It wasn't just busywork. The smart ones would realize, *Oh. If I get this, if I do well in this, if I can speak this language, I could be a CEO someday.*"[11]

Sullivan sees that her teaching style is not prevalent today. "It's so different now because the kids, and this is not a bad thing, are encouraged by all of us to get involved outside of the classroom," she explained. "Back in those old days, we didn't know what anybody was doing outside of the classroom. We just wanted to make sure what they did in the classroom was changing the way their brains were working and changing the way they were thinking about what they wanted to be. Now I think we're more likely to know students on the basis of their involvement outside of the classroom, and the opportunities for that are so rich."[12]

Sullivan was elected chair of the Purdue University Senate an unprecedented three years in a row during President Steven Beering's tenure. As chair of the University Senate representing faculty from all over campus, she was required to attend every board of trustees meeting and make presentations. "Getting faculty involved in the governance at the university level can be challenging," she said. "Participating in discussions about such issues as student success and retention at the Senate level gave me an understanding of the importance of merging the interest of the individual schools and colleges with those of the university as a whole."[13]

She cochaired the committee for developing an academic strategic plan for the university, and in 1996 for that service Beering presented Sullivan with the Order of the Griffin, one of Purdue's highest honors given to those whose commitment and service to the university go well beyond the call of duty and whose strength and vision have greatly benefited the institution.

Sullivan was involved with Purdue's Technical Assistance Program, which provides businesses in Indiana with free consulting services and Krannert graduate and undergraduate students with opportunities to address real-world business problems. She also worked for the gaming industry in Indiana for fifteen years, evaluating the license applications for riverboat gambling when it was new to the state.

Sullivan attributes her career in finance to the fact that when she first majored in physical therapy as an undergraduate, she was required to take calculus. A mother of one daughter, her work ethic was grounded in her upbringing without a mother and played a role in her parenting and teaching style, never expecting anything from her daughter or students that she would not expect of herself. "We had to be tough," she said of her childhood with her nine siblings. "We had to do a lot of raising of ourselves. You came home, changed your clothes, and got on the tractor to work the farm or in the garden. So we learned how to work."[14]

When she became the associate dean of the undergraduate program, she helped add majors and develop programs that would attract high-caliber students. "I always said I don't want more students, I want more *better* students,"[15]

Sullivan explained. During this time the Larsen Leaders Academy and the Brock-Wilson Center for Women in Management launched. In recognition of her service, Krannert created the Dr. Charlene Sullivan Transformative Impact Award for faculty, staff, and students in 2021.

Sullivan retired with a diversified portfolio of accomplishments. "So many faculty describe themselves as an inch wide and eighteen miles deep," she said, lightheartedly. "Well, I was eighteen miles wide and an inch deep."[16]

When she retired, people around campus asked, "How are we going to get along without you? You're part of the bricks." To which Sullivan replied, "After forty-four years, I really do feel like I'm part of the bricks."[17]

CAROLYN Y. WOO, FROM HONG KONG TO PURDUE—A FORCE FOR GOOD

Carolyn Yauyan Woo arrived at Purdue as a freshman from Hong Kong in the fall of 1972, the height of hippie culture and the Vietnam antiwar protests, "in the equivalent of my Catholic school uniform," she recalled.[18] Her feeling of displacement was not new. It was a family legacy that had been a theme of her formative years in China. Yet, soon her academic drive would soothe her loneliness and provide a sense of belonging and worth.

Woo would become an influential Purdue professor of strategic management in 1981 and ten years later Krannert's second woman and first woman from Asia to earn tenure.[19] She made full professor in thirteen years, led Krannert's MBA program, then at age forty was made associate executive vice president of academic affairs.

In 1997, Woo left Purdue to become the dean of the University of Notre Dame's College of Business. In 2011 she began serving as CEO for Catholic Relief Services (CRS), becoming a world leader embracing ethics, peace, compassion, and rebuilding of communities. When Woo retired from CRS, she would contribute this experience to Purdue University in her role as the President's Distinguished Fellow for Global Development. In 2013, *Foreign Policy* named Woo one of the 500 most powerful people on the planet and one of only thirty-three in the category of "a force for good."[20]

But first she would earn her degrees at lightning speed while finding solace and connection at St. Thomas Aquinas Catholic Center near campus. Born in Hong Kong in 1954, the fifth of six children, the fourth of four daughters, Woo was educated from first through twelfth grades by American missionary nuns, the Maryknoll Sisters.

She heard of Purdue only by happenstance when she helped her sister staple documents at her office. "The choice of college was settled when I met an economics professor at Trans World Airlines [TWA], where my sister Helen worked," Woo recalled. "He was on leave from Purdue University, and he told me it was a comprehensive university, and that meant anyone who went there could study anything she wanted! The fact that I had no idea where West Lafayette, or even Indiana was, or whether Purdue was even a good school, did not matter. Knowing one person from there made it real. I applied and was accepted. I would never run into that professor again."[21]

The economics professor was Muzaffer M. ErSelcuk, who left Purdue in 1969 and became director of marketing and development for TWA.[22]

Woo, age eighteen, had enough funds for just one year of study, so she signed up for twenty-one credit hours and buckled down while living at Meredith Hall. The following year she received a scholarship and kept going, earning in seven years her bachelor's in economics (1975), master's in industrial administration (1976), and doctoral degree in strategic management (1979). "I never quite slept," she said of her steady march to her PhD. "I'd brush my teeth, put on my nightgown, and go back to studying until my head collapsed on the table."[23]

When Woo applied to Purdue from Hong Kong she knew little about American universities, except that she wanted to go to one. "I had seen a lot of television programs featuring Americans," she recalled. "I thought that was just a lot of wonderful attitudes and full of adventures. So, I wanted to come to the US. My father was against it."

Woo's father had wanted a son when she was born. His two sons came later. Her father had been a purchased child, bought by a middle-class family from a poor one at a young age and educated in the western part of China. "It was an investment," Woo said of her father's move from one set of parents to another. "But it was also charity because children [were] starving to death."[24] Woo grew up in an environment of extensive refugee resettlement from China to Hong Kong. Her parents had similarly left everything behind in China when the Communist Revolution took hold.

Woo's father wanted her and her three sisters to finish high school, settle down, and stay close to the family in Hong Kong. From an early age, Woo desired much more. She had been taught by American nuns who had a different vision for girls. "They really believed that girls can do whatever they wanted to do, which is unusual in a Chinese culture,"[25] Woo said. Her high school years gave her the courage to go into new situations. "Some of my formative experiences [occurred] when my teachers organized debate teams, and they had us debating English-speaking boys.[26] We were educated to have our thoughts, our voice, and to use both for a more just society."[27]

She was also greatly influenced by her nanny, who instilled a strong sense of discipline and the willingness to work hard. She was a perfectionist in all she did. "Her instruction—'Don't play until you finish your work'—is forever chiseled into my brain,"[28] Woo said.

Woo was the only one of her parents' four daughters to attend college. She remembered vividly the prediction she made about her future while riding in the car with her father when she was in third grade. "I told him that one day I would be a professor with a doctorate. I have no idea where that came from. Perhaps my father was reading one of his favorite magazines and mentioned with admiration some accomplished scholar with a PhD. I just automatically declared that, of course, this is what I would become."[29]

Her father was distressed when Woo was leaving for America. "I had the first adult conversation with my father when I asked him to treat me as a Chinese son, give me my freedom, and in turn I would support my parents as my brothers were expected to," she said. "I would honor the family name of Woo."[30]

Woo's research on strategic management looked at how organizations succeed, particularly in light of the fact that the environment changes and what worked well yesterday may not work tomorrow. "My specific research focused on small competitors," Woo explained. "We know that large competitors, particularly market leaders, tend to have a lot of clout and be more profitable, so I was curious about the smaller competitors. How do they survive because in every market there could only be one market leader, whereas there were many market followers. My research was about how these small, low market share businesses flourished. What were their strategies?"

One year after Woo arrived on campus, she met her future husband, David Bartkus, at St. Thomas Aquinas Center. He was working on his master's in engineering. They married in 1979, the year Woo received her PhD. Their first of two sons was born in 1984 just as Woo was embarking on the last leg of her bid for tenure. The timing of the birth went against the advice she gave her female students to have their children at the same time they are preparing their doctoral thesis, if possible, and not when they are on the tenure clock.[31]

In 1990, after Woo was a full professor for about four months, Robert Ringel, executive vice president of academic affairs (EVPAA), interviewed her to become an associate executive vice president. "I had no idea what a full professor did and definitely had no idea what the provost office did," she recalled. Woo successfully figured it all out. She had come a long way from the young woman who arrived at Purdue from Hong Kong wearing the equivalent of a Catholic school uniform and having predicted in third grade that she would one day be a professor with a doctorate.

23

RATS HELP BETTER BABIES' LIVES

AVANELLE KIRKSEY, CAPTIVATED BY VITAMIN B-6

After only a few days on the job at Purdue in 1960, Arkansas native Avanelle "Nell" Kirksey was invited into the office of Head of the Department of Foods and Nutrition Gladys Vail and asked a loaded question: "Have you considered what your life's work in research will be?"

It was a sobering query for Kirksey, age thirty-three, who had just completed a doctoral program in nutrition at Pennsylvania State University where she had been awarded a General Foods Fellowship. Years later Kirksey recalled, "I felt hardly prepared for decisions for the day let alone making a lifetime decision about research."

Yet, Kirksey took on Vail's challenge of determining her life's work. After several days of intense reading in the library and "very, very serious thinking," Kirksey announced to Vail that her focus would be vitamin B-6 in early development.[1]

Days earlier, the elegant and gracious "southern lady" had arrived on the James Whitcomb Riley train at the Lafayette Depot where Vail waited to transport her to campus.[2] Kirksey arrived with an Arkansas accent that would stay with her for the more than thirty years she would work for Purdue, and Vail would become her mentor and friend.

"I was fascinated by the history of vitamin B-6," Kirksey said, "because at that time its role in human nutrition was largely unknown."[3] It turned out to be a prodigious decision that would lead to monumental discoveries. Kirksey became internationally known through her work to safeguard the well-being of infants and pregnant and lactating women, while addressing malnutrition globally. Her research was one of thousands of groundbreaking examples throughout the country proving home economics to be more than "stitch and stir" classes.

Kirksey had thought she would become a physician like her father or a nutritionist. She said, "I got into the field of nutrition and liked it, and things just sort of happened."[4] Kirksey's major professor at Penn State was the famed trailblazing professor of nutrition, Ruth Pike, who launched Kirksey into her career. As a graduate student in Pike's lab, Kirksey studied the detriment of salt restriction in pregnant women. The Ruth Pike Lectureship Series and Award at Penn State was designed to expose nutrition students to the brightest young stars that make significant contributions to the field of nutrition. Today, Purdue's Avanelle Kirksey Lecture Series at Purdue emulates the Pike Series.

KIRKSEY'S B-6 RESEARCH WITH RATS

Avanelle Kirksey and her students used the rat as an experimental model for much of their research on vitamin B-6 with interest in its role in early development, particularly early postnatal development. They manipulated the diet of rats during pregnancy and lactation and observed deviations from normal in the tissues of both the mother and the offspring.

First discovered in the late 1950s, vitamin B-6 is essential for the functioning of the central nervous system.[5] Kirksey's work was principally funded by Purdue's Agricultural Experiment Station, a standard source of support for nutrition researchers in a land-grant university until the 1970s.[6]

Consistently, Kirksey and her graduate students found that the offspring of mother rats deficient in vitamin B-6 showed signs of impairment, such as uncoordinated muscular movements, sharp cries, convulsions, and death. The research team questioned whether they were seeing only vitamin B-6 deficiency or also nutritional deficiencies. Hence, they needed to study milk composition in mother rats.

To study milk composition they needed a milk collecting machine. A graduate student invented a milk collector from simple laboratory equipment, and

Kirksey and her scientists embarked on a series of lactation studies with rats. A rat pup's brain is less than half the size of a dime, and the section the team examined was about the size of a pinhead. They photographed these sections with an electron microscope and discovered a strong association between the diet fed the mother and certain components in the brain of her young.[7]

During Kirksey's early years at Purdue her young nephew and nieces were fascinated by the white rats used in her research. "I always suspected that their delight in visiting their 'Aunt Nell' sprang more from their desire to visit the rat lab than to visit me," Kirksey said. "Their preoccupation with the rats, however, had some unexpected fringe benefits for me—a prized rat collection."[8]

Kirksey's nephew and nieces gave her rat-themed birthday and Christmas gifts. Her rat collection included rodents made from Tiffany silver, Boehm porcelain, and Steuben crystal. She owned a Mickey Mouse telephone, and rats were the theme for Kirksey's lab Christmas tree. Before students and staff left campus for holiday break, each were invited to choose a rat ornament as a memento.

Susie Sciscoe Craig, a student, painted a rock depicting the likeness of her lab rat she had named "AK-AK" and gave it to Kirksey (even though Kirksey had always directed students not to name their rats because they would be euthanized). The name was a play on Kirksey's initials and the sound one might make if a rat were underfoot. After Kirksey retired from Purdue, the "AK-AK" rock resided on her living room coffee table.

Decades later, Sciscoe Craig said, "While I only had one class with Nell, for six years she was my confidant, mentor, and wonderful friend.... I always hoped AK-AK would be a reminder of my respect, love, and affection for her, my adventures on campus, and her close connection with students through the decades at Purdue."[9]

Kirksey and rats went way back. Her graduate study was on the effects of different levels of dietary sodium on pregnancy, and she used rats in her research. In a speech she gave when she accepted the Alumni Recognition Award from the College of Human Development at Penn State, Kirksey talked about her rats without actually saying the word "rat."

She said, "Among the memories of my graduate student days ... was my first introduction to this experimental animal. I remember being forewarned that this animal would easily sense any of my fears of it, but I don't remember how I was to rid myself of fear. I was given other important information about this animal—how to pick it up and how to hold it. These were important first lessons. Seriously, I've made good use of these over the years and passed them on to countless graduate students who chose to use this animal in research."[10]

Kirksey had a two-page rat manifesto titled, "What are some important points to be considered in the handling and care of rats?" Two of her tips were, "The gentle loving care you give a rat will bring better results in our experiment because of love," and "Don't take a long time in handling because they can become irritable."[11]

After several years of experimentations with rats, graduate student Kerstin West convinced Kirksey that human subjects could be studied. Beginning in 1976, they investigated vitamin B-6 relationships in human lactation and confirmed what had been found in the animal studies: Low intake of the vitamin by the mother led to a low level of the vitamin in her milk. Her infant displayed symptoms of vitamin B-6 inadequacy, including periodic convulsive seizures.[12] In 1986, Purdue's Department of Foods and Nutrition was one of only two US laboratories in which researchers studied the vitamin B-6 content of breast milk.[13]

Vitamin B-6 is water soluble. It is not stockpiled in the body. Daily excesses are eliminated through the kidneys. Therefore, a steady supply in the diet is essential. At the time there was a widespread belief that a deficiency of vitamin B-6 was unlikely in humans. Yet, when Kirksey examined a person's seemingly adequate diet, she found it could be low in B-6. Plus, a growing list of more than forty drugs were known to interfere with the vitamin.[14] The combination of low dietary intake and drug usage could result in B-6 deficiency.

Babies born to mothers deficient in B-6 were found to have lower Apgar scores—a test to assess the newborn's physical status. With an estimated 30 percent of all pregnant women showing some degree of B-6 deficiency, Kirksey's work was invaluable for improving and safeguarding the lives of babies.[15]

Kirksey and her mentor, Purdue Professor Helen E. Clark, both presented papers at the seventh International Congress on Nutrition in Hamburg, Germany, in August 1966.[16] Throughout her career, Kirksey would make presentations to international audiences about her research on the B-6 role in prenatal development.

She also studied the effect of long-term use of oral contraceptives on B-6 levels and found that years of use prior to a woman expecting led to poor vitamin B-6 nutrition when she was pregnant and lactating. The inadequacy manifested in infants who showed signs of shrill cries, tremors, and convulsions similar to what Kirksey had seen in rat pups. The condition was quickly alleviated by supplementing the nursing mother or the infant with B-6. This groundbreaking research was picked up by the Associated Press and published nationwide by the news media.

Levels of estrogen in early forms of oral contraceptives may have caused the vitamin decrease in women in the early tests. It was determined that well-nourished women using the newer forms of oral contraceptives in the mid-eighties would have no trouble providing enough B-6 to their breast-fed infants.[17] Kirksey also studied the nutritional needs and the role of B-6 in preterm infants during a time that preemie babies were just beginning to get attention because not many of those babies had previously survived.

In February 1979, *American Baby* magazine ran an article on Kirksey's research on vitamin B-6 and its importance to brain development.[18] The research was also published that year in the *American Journal of Clinical Nutrition* and the *Federation of American Societies for Experimental Biology*. Every time an article was published about her work, a stream of letters poured into Kirksey's office from pregnant women interested in B-6 vitamins and prenatal development. Kirksey was swamped as she tried to respond to each letter.

Kirksey and her students also investigated the far-reaching consequences of deficiencies of vitamin B-6 during early infancy on the developing brain and spinal cord. A baby's brain grows more during the first six months than at any other time. The research was vital as in 1978 the American Academy of Pediatrics had recommended that human milk be used as the sole source of nutrients for infants during the first four to six months of life, a critical period for the development of the central nervous system.[19] Infant formula is prepared to reflect as closely as possible the nutrient content of human milk. The good news was that Kirksey found B-6 content in human milk increased rapidly when a mother took vitamin supplements.

The American Home Economics Association (now the American Association of Family and Consumer Sciences) honored Kirksey with the Borden Award for Research in Infant and Child Nutrition in 1980. In her acceptance speech Kirksey remembered the scientists who blazed a trail for her. She said:

> The more than forty recipients of this award have been an inspiration to many of us. Each of these scientists believed that home economics is a particularly fertile area in which to conduct research and that foods and nutrition research needs the outlook which home economics can best provide. Special tribute is paid to three former recipients whose encouragement, guidance and support have been invaluable: My respected former colleagues, Dr. Helen Clark and Dr. Gladys Vail, Professors Emeritus of Purdue University and to Dr. Ruth Pike, Professor Emeritus of Pennsylvania State University, my major professor, who first introduced me to some of the joys of research.[20]

In October 1982, Kirksey was invited by the Recommended Dietary Allowance Committee of the National Academy of Sciences to present her findings,

From 1960 and into the 1990s, Dr. Avanelle "Nell" Kirksey became internationally known through her research on Vitamin B-6 and worked to safeguard the well-being of infants and pregnant and lactating women, while addressing malnutrition globally. Courtesy Purdue University Archives and Special Collections.

which indicated that lactating women required approximately 10 mg vitamin B-6 per day if their infants were to meet the minimum requirement of the American Academy of Pediatrics.[21] This board sets the nutritional recommended daily requirements for good health in the United States. Kirksey said that presenting her research on the vitamin B-6 needs of lactating women and infants was a high point of her work.[22] She was considered the foremost authority on vitamin B-6 at the time, and she helped lead the academy to new national guidelines.

In a 1982 speech to alumni about her research, Kirksey said, "Now to the nation, we are dependent upon new discoveries and able people. I'm addressing policy makers when I say a dollar of [nutrition] prevention can avoid many dollars of cure."[23]

KIRKSEY'S RESEARCH IN EGYPT

One of Dr. Avanelle Kirksey's greatest research challenges occurred when she was principal investigator in a United States Agency for International Development–funded nutrition project in Egypt beginning in 1982. The problem regarding malnutrition in Egypt was not that numerous people died, but rather, that they didn't really live. They did not have enough to eat to function as productive human beings.

During the Carter administration, friendship between the United States and Egypt was strengthened and many programs were funded to assist the Egyptians in improving their lives. Title XII of the US Foreign Assistance Act was legislated in 1975, and the Collaborative Research Support Programs (CRSPs) were created in response.

The focus of Title XII was to bolster the role of land-grant and other US universities in creating sustainable agriculture and helping develop countries produce adequate food, fuel, and shelter materials. Purdue was one of seven US universities selected to participate. Similar nutrition projects were also carried out in Kenya and Mexico.

The project was called "Nutrition Intake and Human Function" with the underlying hypotheses that malnutrition affects human capacities and behavior and, thus, inhibits societal development. Data collected, the first of its kind, would provide a basis for policy formation to provide aid.

"The estimate of marginally malnourished is manyfold greater than hunger," Kirksey said. "There is a difference between hunger and marginal malnutrition." Hunger is much more acute than marginal malnutrition. Marginal malnutrition is a gradual starvation, which is not obvious. There are no visible signs such as bloated stomachs or emaciation.[24]

Kirksey coordinated the Human Nutritional Research Project and was senior scientist for the reproduction/lactation area studying the effect of malnutrition on women's ability to produce nutritious milk. About two hundred households were selected for study. She spent about four months of every year in Egypt until the study ended in 1987.

Kirksey elected to study the village of Kalama, located near a canal that ultimately connected to the Nile River near Cairo. In the village's typical four-room adobe house, one room would often be for the family's water buffalo. Purdue colleagues collaborated with Egyptian scientists at the Nutrition Institute in Cairo. Kirksey said:

> This study was a logistical nightmare to plan for several reasons. The pace of life in Egypt is much slower than we are accustomed to. The village was distant from the Nutrition Institute in Cairo, meaning that we had to transport workers each day to the site. Equipment was often unavailable or, if available, difficult to service, and the support staff in Egypt did not always understand the research standards we sought to attain. Faced with such seemingly overwhelming difficulties, we did as many Egyptians do—we visited the Pyramids and Sphinx at Giza for inspiration.
>
> Looking at these monumental feats of engineering and construction completed over 4000 years ago, we came to the conclusion that if the ancient Egyptians could construct the pyramids, then surely we could solve our twentieth century nutrition research problems.
>
> We did overcome the problems. This project successfully led us to several important observations on the effects of marginal malnutrition on human function as well as strengthening the nutrition research capability in Egypt. It also changed our laboratory focus at Purdue to computers and our students became more international.[25]

There were cultural challenges that came into play. Kirksey said that the United States's reliance on paperwork as part of a research program, particularly at that time, was a stark contrast to Egypt's almost total absence of paperwork. In Egypt, a person's word was his honor and that resulted in very few written records.[26] Villagers' deeply held superstitions had to be taken into account. Most feared the "evil eye," and mothers did not allow strangers to undress their children or view them naked. Since infant weight without clothes was needed for data collecting, village mothers agreed to provide the information themselves by learning to weigh their children on digital scales.[27]

A former graduate student of Kirksey's, Nancy Reiter Meyer, became the field coordinator for the study in January 1984 after she received her master's degree in foods and nutrition. She traveled to Egypt accompanied by Kirksey, who showed her the sights and culture of the country. In a letter addressed to "Nell" upon Kirksey's retirement in 1994, Meyer wrote:

When I took your class on vitamins as a graduate student at Purdue, I never imagined your capacity for fun or your determination when shopping, but being with you in Cairo opened my eyes.

On my first weekend in Egypt, you took me riding (camel riding, that is) at the pyramids and then to the bazaar for bargaining and shopping. Although everyone said not to eat food from the street vendors, we both did and suffered no ill effects. Didn't those fūl sandwiches taste wonderful?[28]

One of the groundbreaking contributions of the Egyptian study was the finding that even small amounts of animal foods in the diet improved development and cognitive function. Kirksey's work established the knowledge that eating the right foods while pregnant and nursing is one of the most important things a mother can do for her child and is related to infant behavior and intellectual growth. Millions of infants in developed and developing countries have been the benefactors of Kirksey's work.[29]

Kirksey's office on the ground floor of Stone Hall was strewn with books. *A Handbook of Vitamins* sat next to *A Guide to Egypt*. The walls were covered with pictures, rugs, and vases, all gifts from international students. She wore exquisite jewelry from her world travels. However, perhaps she most enjoyed showing visitors her two large photo collages of babies. One collage represented a few of the hundreds of infants she worked with locally over the years. The other was a collection of photos of dark-skinned babies she worked with in Egypt.

Indonesia was Kirksey's destination from 1987 to 1992 when she became program facilitator for a World Bank project to develop nutrition graduate and research programs in higher education systems there. She visited community nutrition projects in the mountain regions where tea and clove trees were abundant.

Kirksey had a sense of humor when it came to the global nature of her research and teaching. She said, "Sometimes when we've met in the lab to discuss our data, it seems like everyone is from a different country. It's like the U.N., and I may be the only American. We have a lot of laughs, but we also learn a lot from each other by asking, 'How do you go about this in your country?'"[30]

Kirksey's graduate courses were rigorous and sometimes riotous. When a class she taught fell on Halloween, a human "gorilla" appeared and carried her out of the classroom as wide-eyed students laughed with uneasy shock.

In 1984, Kirksey became the second woman in Purdue history to be named a distinguished professor when she was honored with the title of Meredith Distinguished Professor of Foods and Nutrition.[31] The first woman at Purdue to be named a distinguished professor in any field had been Kirksey's colleague

Helen E. Clark. A distinguished professor is an outstandingly original, creative, and productive individual whose achievements in scholarship or research have been internationally recognized.

The American Institute of Nutrition (AIN) honored Kirksey with the 1994 Lederle Award in Human Nutrition, made possible by Lederle Laboratories, for her studies of nutrition and infant development. She was also selected as a 1994 Fellow of the American Institute of Nutrition for her contribution to the field of nutrition and her twenty-year involvement with the institute, having been nominated by Helen Clark, herself an AIN Fellow.

The annual Avanelle Kirksey Award and Lecture Series was established at Purdue to honor Kirksey after her retirement. She often returned to Purdue from Arkansas for these lectures. She received an honorary doctorate from Purdue in 1997 and was inducted into the Purdue Department of Foods and Nutrition Hall of Fame in 2007.

In a retirement speech, Kirksey spoke of Purdue alumnus and astronaut Neil Armstrong's steps upon the moon's surface, rendering both personal and universal his famous words, "One small step for [a] man, one giant leap for mankind." Kirksey said, "We take our own 'giant steps,' perhaps not on the moon.... When I set foot on the Purdue campus in 1961, that was a giant step towards my career path: my first academic position at a world class Big Ten university, one with the reputation of attracting stellar students and having farsighted administrators. I remember how excited I felt!"[32]

In 1996, four years after her Egypt research ended, Kirksey gave a lecture on her experience and said:

> As I look back on the Egypt project, I recall what an adventure it was. We were faced with poverty, illiteracy, illness, and deprivation.... Marginal malnutrition was all around us, but we felt an incredible sense of community spirit in the village. By the end of the project the physicians and dietitians and social workers were networking with each other and with the leaders to exchange ideas to improve village life.
>
> So as I ride off into the sunset on my camel, I have a strong feeling of hope that, armed with the knowledge gained from our project, the politicians, physicians, dietitians, and social workers will continue to work with village leaders to better the life and so improve the productivity of the people of Egypt.[33]

Kirksey passed away in her native Arkansas in 2016 at the age of ninety.

24
DIETS AND SKELETONS

OLIVIA BENNETT WOOD, DIETETICS AND DETERMINATION

Olivia Bennett Wood embraced new opportunities as they appeared, and each venture became the underpinning for each new chapter in her fruitful career in dietetics. Wood was twenty-seven when she came to Purdue in 1973 and built Purdue's outstanding dietetics program, becoming director in 1976. About 70 percent of the students in the Department of Foods and Nutrition majored in dietetics.

Wood grew up in the small tourist town of Bryson City, North Carolina, the gateway to Great Smoky Mountains National Park. Her father served nine terms as mayor of Bryson City, where he lived his entire life, and her mother was a registered nurse. They owned and operated Bennett's Motor Court, a small motel. Wood emulated her parents' deep commitment to their town by serving and immersing herself in professional associations and Purdue committees.[1]

She majored in home economics at the University of North Carolina at Greensboro, graduating in 1969. She chose foods and nutrition as her major after she had been a waitress in a restaurant in Bryson City. Looking back, Wood said, "I absolutely loved being a waitress. Now remember, most of these people [customers] were staying in our motel two doors up the street, and I really knew them."

Wood went to Duke University Medical Center for her dietetics internship and worked there for an additional year as a dietitian for women with eating difficulties during the last stages of cancer and for children with cystic fibrosis. Her

Duke clinical experience provided valuable background when she later taught dietetics at Purdue.

When she heard she could obtained full funding through the US Public Health Service to earn a master's degree in public health at the University of North Carolina at Chapel Hill, she thought, *why not earn a master's?* There was a dire need for public health nutritionists across the country. Her public health traineeship was in Washington, DC, the summer of the Watergate scandal. The contacts she made while there with people in the USDA and in what was then Health, Education, and Welfare, now Health and Human Services, were invaluable when she later developed a course in public health nutrition at Purdue.[2]

The summer Wood interned in Washington, the Women, Infants, and Children's Nutrition Program (WIC) was initiated there on a trial basis. WIC is a supplemental food program created to improve the health of pregnant mothers, infants, and children in a response to the concern over malnutrition among the poverty-stricken.

Wood worked in WIC clinics housed on the bottom floors of apartment complexes for the poor. These clinics were the prototypes for the WIC clinics that opened nationwide and continue today. WIC was legislated as a permanent program in 1975.[3]

"The buildings the clinics were in were awful," Wood said. "They were in high-rise buildings, and there might have been a murder there the night before. But the clinic people were protected. We had our parking lot. The people who lived in the neighborhood were so happy to have the services that they guarded our cars. It was eye opening to learn how people live in public housing. The whole internship was a great experience."[4]

After she earned her master's in 1972, Wood was asked to fill in for one year teaching foods and nutrition at Meredith College in Raleigh, North Carolina. She had never taught before but quickly learned she loved it. "I spent every weekend trying to get ahead on lesson plans for the next week," Wood said.[5] That one year of learn-as-you-go teaching would launch her to become a prolific, award-winning instructor at Purdue.

At the end of her one-year term as a teacher, Wood saw an ad for a registered dietitian to teach the Coordinated Program in Dietetics at Purdue. The ad did not mention that the candidate was required to have a PhD. Later, she would learn that bit of information was inadvertently omitted from the ad. Had it been included, Wood would not have applied and made her mark on Purdue. "Purdue was interested in somebody with recent clinical experience with at least a

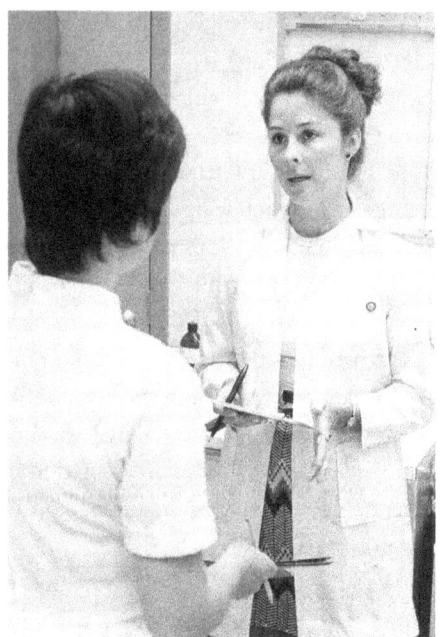

Professor of Dietetics Olivia Wood, *right*, with a student in the 1970s. Courtesy Olivia Wood.

master's," she said decades later. "I would not have applied if the ad had stated they preferred a person with a PhD."⁶

Wood was interviewed by newly appointed Dean of Home Economics Norma Compton in May 1973 and began working in July, becoming the first person Compton hired at Purdue. The university made it clear that people without a PhD were not customarily hired to teach, and that Wood should not expect her position as an instructor to lead to tenure.⁷ Elwood Reber was the head of the Department of Foods and Nutrition and his wife was a registered dietitian. The couple took Wood out to dinner and showed her the campus when she visited for her interview. "It was a beautiful campus," Wood recalled. "I flew in over fields being plowed, and I'd never seen anything like it. I'd never been anywhere where it was flat."⁸

Students in the Purdue Dietetics Program graduated in four years, worked in an internship during the fifth year, and then became registered dietitians. Across the United States, there were more students graduating in dietetics than there were available internships, most of which were at medical centers only accepting ten to twelve interns. There was a need for more internship opportunities. Wood led the initiative to develop Purdue's Coordinated Program in

Dietetics, a new national dietetics educational program that integrated clinical experiences with coursework in the junior and senior years of the undergraduate program.[9]

Wood developed new courses and revised others so both the didactic and coordinated programs could be offered at Purdue. A Didactic Program in Dietetics (DPD) refers to an academic program designed to meet the knowledge requirements for dietetics practice. In both programs a student graduates with a bachelor's degree. The difference is that in a Didactic Program there are four years of coursework. The Purdue Residence Halls offered administrative food service experiences and local hospitals provided the clinical and community nutrition practices. Purdue continues to offer both the Didactic and Coordinated Programs in Dietetics.[10]

Wood's network of colleagues from her Washington, DC, WIC traineeship and her professional associations helped her to successfully place students in internships and obtain jobs across the country. The percentage of Purdue students who obtained internships was 95 to 100 percent most years, where many programs around the country had a 50 to 60 percent placement. Eventually, 80 percent placement was required for accreditation.[11]

Wood received the highest dietitian honor awarded by the Indiana Dietetic Association in 1985, and she served two terms on the board of directors of the American Dietetic Association, receiving the Medallion Award for her service. She was on the Indiana Governor's Task Force on the Elderly and served three terms on the Governor's Council of Physical Fitness and Sport Medicine created by Governor Otis Bowen, a physician. The twenty-member council created a booklet for Indiana citizens listing where the most credible health and fitness facilities were located in Indiana.

As director of Purdue's Didactic Program in Dietetics, Wood led the charge for the university's program to be accredited by the American Dietetic Association in the mid-1980s.[12] The Purdue program was one of the first programs in the United States to receive accreditation, becoming a model for other dietetic programs. She eventually became a site reviewer for the Commission on Accreditation for Dietetics Education.

With her extensive professional association experience, deep knowledge of accreditation gained while leading Purdue's program through the process, and her success in placing students in clinical settings, Wood was sought after to give presentations throughout the United States about how a dietetic program could become accredited.

Looking back on her lecture tour, Wood said, "Purdue has an outstanding dietetic program in every way, yet the biggest part of the success was the perception that if Purdue's program director is out teaching everybody else and doing site visits, then Purdue's program must be phenomenal. I was in the golden years of all that."[13]

Wood was as much a counselor as she was a teacher. She gave words of encouragement but also guided students with the raw truth when necessary. Her courses were rigorous and students felt triumphant when they passed an "Olivia test." "My door was always open to students," she said. "I think you have to have a great presence in the classroom and be teaching the right things and be fair, but you also have to be a mentor and be able to open doors for students."[14]

Wood's love of teaching was reflected in the awards she received. Students voted to honor her with the Mary Matthews Outstanding Undergraduate Teaching Award an unprecedented four times. "I was such a different animal because I taught the most courses in the department," she said. "I advised the most students. When you work with seniors and their lives depend on getting a dietetic internship, because to them their life is over if they don't get the internship, it's very emotional, and you really get close to them. I saw my students every day. I think they saw me as a person. I didn't have biological children, so they were almost my children."[15]

Wood was inducted into the inaugural class of Purdue University's Book of Great Teachers in 1999. The Book of Great Teachers bears the names of Purdue's faculty who have devoted their lives to excellence in teaching and scholarship. They are chosen by their students and their peers as Purdue's finest educators. Each person inducted is listed on a bronze-and-walnut plaque in the Purdue Memorial Union.

Wood was also an inaugural member of Purdue's Teaching Academy. The Teaching Academy brings together the best teaching faculty at Purdue selected by their peers to create a collective voice for teaching and learning on campus. She helped conduct workshops for faculty on such topics as making a syllabus, something she had to learn herself her first year she taught in North Carolina.

Through the Teaching Academy, Wood became acquainted with faculty in Pharmacy and Nursing and together they developed, on a volunteer basis, the first interdisciplinary course for students to gain experience working in teams with people from different disciplines. A team of five students from pharmacy, nursing, health promotions and fitness, and dietetics worked on case studies and made presentations. Wood said, "It was enormous fun, and it was a nice scholarly approach because we published what we did in professional journals. We also presented the concept at our own professional meetings.... The other dietetic professors around the country couldn't believe we would give our own time to do that [teach an extra class], but we were that committed."[16]

Wood became known as the "theme queen" because of her flamboyant seasonal and holiday sweaters and jewelry. When she retired in 2007, her retirement luncheon included an auction of her memorabilia and signature holiday clothing to benefit the newly created Olivia Bennett Wood Scholarship. The one-of-a-kind retirement event raised nearly $4,000. Wood turned the tables on those who gathered to honor her thirty-four years at Purdue. As comedian Bob Hope's theme song played in the background, she and her family walked to each table and handed each colleague and friend a yellow rose tied with a black ribbon inscribed, "Thanks for the memories."[17] In 2010 Wood was inducted into the Department of Nutrition Science Hall of Fame.

MARY L. MATTHEWS CLUB CREATES A PORTRAIT

After retirement, Olivia Bennett Wood became active in the Mary L. Matthews Club. The club of about twenty women was made up of alumni, former faculty, and staff from units that are now part of the College of Health and Human Sciences, but mostly from the home economics field. It began in 1952 to honor the retirement of Dean of the School of Home Economics Emeritus Mary Matthews. Still today, club members meet monthly to hear a guest speaker and enjoy refreshments while keeping ties to their roots in home economics and one another.

In 2012 when Olivia Wood was president of the organization, the club became aware that there was no portrait of Mary Matthews in Matthews Hall. There was a portrait displayed of Lella Gaddis, Matthews's peer and first stated leader of home demonstration, but no portrait of the woman who founded the School of Home Economics and was the building's namesake.

Wood led the initiative to gather donations and have a portrait created. The Purdue Women's Club teamed with the Mary L. Matthews Club on the project. Matthews was president of the Purdue Women's Club in 1930 and active in the organization during her career. The portrait of Mary L. Matthews with an inscribed plaque was dedicated in Matthews Hall on October 26, 2012.[18]

Members of the Mary Matthews Club and the Purdue Women's Club attended the unveiling of the portrait. Those present included Patty Jischke, Purdue

University's former first lady and then president of the Purdue Women's Club; Dean of the School of Home Economics Emeritus Eva Goble, age 102, a member of the Mary Matthews Club who worked with Matthews; and then Dean of the College of Health and Human Sciences Christine Ladisch. The two deans represented the past and the present during the historic event made possible through the vision of Olivia Bennett Wood.

CONNIE M. WEAVER, STRONG BONES

Connie M. Weaver's philosophy was, "If you're going to give time and effort to do something, why not be a leader instead of a follower? Be part of a solution." Weaver's mantra served her well as a groundbreaking scientist striving to improve the health of humanity, particularly that of girls and women.

Weaver distinguished herself internationally with her research on calcium and the ingenious manner in which it was conducted. She invented the idea of "Camp Calcium" as a way to study the bones of adolescent girls. Camp Calcium was fun for the girls who participated while providing valuable research discoveries.

With eleven Camp Calciums held between 1990 and 2010, Weaver and her research team established the calcium requirements for adolescents for North America and many countries around the globe. Weaver became one of the most well-known nutrition researchers focused on adolescents in the world and was inducted into the prestigious National Academy of Medicine.[19]

The outdoorsy Weaver grew up in Oregon participating in 4-H where she honed her science skills. From the third grade, Weaver knew she wanted to be a scientist. She said, "I really loved science, and so that was a comfort area that I was familiar with—food science and nutrition. My education and career naturally evolved from that."

Weaver's trajectory advanced as she became a Distinguished Professor and Head of the Department of Foods and Nutrition at Purdue in 2000 with appointments as a member to the Food and Drug Administration (FDA) Science Advisory board and the National Institutes of Health (NIH) Advisory Committee on Research on Women's Health. The list of her accolades, awards, appointments, and elected professional positions is as impressive as her stamina and resilience. Weaver led the effort to change the department name from Foods and Nutrition to Nutrition Science.

Weaver received two degrees from Oregon State University and married during the Vietnam War. Immediately after a honeymoon, Weaver's husband, a member of the US Navy, left for two tours of duty. The couple scarcely lived together during the first three years of their marriage. Meanwhile, Weaver earned a master of science in food science and human nutrition from Oregon State and a PhD in food science and human nutrition from Florida State University.

Holding minors in chemistry and plant physiology, Weaver said, "I liked all branches of science, so rather than pick one, biology or physics, for instance, I chose an applied type science—food science and nutrition—where, interestingly, one can use all of those sciences."[20]

Weaver came to Purdue as an assistant professor in 1978. In the early years she established her laboratory and conducted research on selenium, not recognized as an essential trace mineral until 1990; the link between magnesium, hypertension, and calcium; fat substitutes; and iron deficiencies in women who exercise without a balanced diet. She was also an outstanding teacher who mentored her students with a delightful sense of humor. After eight years, Weaver was honored with Purdue's Amoco Foundation Undergraduate Teaching Award, later renamed the Murphy Award.

Weaver collaborated extensively with faculty across campus, particularly members of the College of Agriculture. One of her strong suits was her knack for bringing researchers together, not seeing walls or silos between areas at Purdue, only opportunities for synergy.

Weaver never let setbacks faze her determination. Paul Abernathy, former head of the Department of Foods and Nutrition, said, "Connie was very energetic. She could make connections better than anybody I had ever seen before. She reminded me of a kid who is running and falls down. She just gets up, goes on, and doesn't think about it."[21]

Also in those early years of establishing her career as a professor and researcher, Weaver had three sons in two years—a child born in 1979 and twins born a year later. Weaver was a role model for colleagues and students as she combined an internationally acclaimed science profession with parenting.

The year 1991 was pivotal as Weaver was propelled into leadership at Purdue, and her research on calcium ignited through National Institutes of Health grants. Yet she came close to leaving Purdue at that time because she received an offer to become the head of the Department of Food Science at Oregon State. Had she taken the Oregon position, Weaver would have returned to her home state.

Dr. Connie Weaver's groundbreaking data from her innovative Camp Calcium determined the amount of calcium adolescents need to achieve maximum bone growth and spurred a revision in the Recommended Dietary Allowances produced by the National Academy of Sciences (NAS) and used by the Food and Drug Administration. Courtesy Purdue University Archives and Special Collections.

"When I prepared for the job interview at Oregon State," she said, "I started thinking about what a department head could do and what I'd like to see done in our [Purdue's] department."

Weaver had acquired her first two NIH grants to fund what would become her famed Camp Calcium right when Paul Abernathy stepped away as head of the Department of Foods and Nutrition, and she was offered his position. The two life-changing opportunities, the research grants and the headship, swayed Weaver to stay at Purdue. Regarding managing research while a department head, Weaver said, "I can't imagine it any other way. You lose your own identity if you don't do the research, but [a] few people do manage to juggle. Many days felt like a marathon, but I was extremely happy."[22]

For more than three decades, Weaver juggled her position as a department head with her scientific career that blazed like wildfire with discoveries to benefit people across the globe. She was one of the few active department heads in the National Academy of Medicine.

There were two new heads appointed in the School of Consumer and Family Sciences in March 1991, Weaver and Professor Douglas R. Powell who was named head of the Department of Child Development and Family Studies. An article in the *Journal and Courier* announced the appointments of Weaver and Powell and included their annual salaries, setting off a firestorm of reactions. Powell had come to Purdue in 1984. The newspaper indicated that his annual salary as department head would be $80,000. Weaver's annual salary as department head would be $69,000.[23]

"The *Journal and Courier* story is how I learned of the large salary differential," Weaver said. "All weekend, everywhere I went—post office, church, store—everyone had read the story and asked what I was going to do about it and expressed concern that a male and female would be treated so differently."

When Weaver came into her office the following Monday, she found several copies of the article placed on her desk by colleagues. She called Purdue's Office of Equal Opportunity and Affirmative Action and made an appointment. Then, with a copy of the newspaper article in hand, Weaver visited her boss, Dean of the School of Consumer and Family Sciences Donald Felker. Weaver said:

> When I put the article on his desk, he said that he had received enough copies to wallpaper his office. He asked what I wanted him to do about it. I said that I didn't know, but that if he didn't do something, I had appointments with the Office of Equal Opportunity and Affirmative Action later in the week. He asked if I wanted him to take money from the salaries of my department in order to give me a higher salary. I said no, but if my faculty thought I was so poor at negotiating my own salary, how would they have any confidence in me negotiating anything on their behalf as head.[24]

Felker told Weaver he would speak to Executive Vice President Robert Ringel and get back to her. That afternoon, Felker called her for an appointment in his office. "I walked in and he put a blank sheet of paper in front of me and asked me to write down what I wanted for a salary," Weaver recalled. "I wrote down a number halfway between what was listed in the paper for my salary and Powell's salary. I told him that I appreciated his offer to negotiate, and I wanted to show him that I was able to compromise."[25]

The first thing Weaver did when she was appointed head was plan a faculty retreat at Indiana's Turkey Run State Park. She created working groups to prepare a "wish list" of topics to cover. During the retreat a five-year plan for the Department of Foods and Nutrition was created that came to fruition in less than two years. Weaver said, "The faculty were so excited to be unleashed and empowered."[26] This planning led to the creation of the Interdepartmental Graduate Nutrition Program and a new major that combined nutrition and fitness.

Weaver's inaugural Camp Calcium occurred in the summer of 1990. Fourteen teenage girls spent six week at Purdue enjoying fitness and educational activities. The girls took calcium supplements; received bone scans; gave blood, perspiration, urine, and stool samples; and were paid for their participation and time. Weaver and her team compared adolescent girls and young adult women, ages nineteen to thirty, to see how they might differ in the ways their bodies handled calcium intake. They studied the effects of calcium on female bones in an effort to make strides in preventing osteoporosis, a crippling bone disease that targets women more often than men.

No other study like Camp Calcium had ever been conducted in the United States.[27] A metabolic balance study in kids had been conducted in the department before Weaver came to Purdue paving the way for the concept. Weaver created the model for running a controlled feeding study as a summer camp and employed innovative techniques with calcium isotope tracers to measure bone metabolism. The successful model of running the living space (a vacant sorority house or residence hall) and planning activities for the camp participants around the research continued for twenty years.

Looking back, Weaver said, "In the 1980s people were beginning to understand there was a potential link between diet and bone health. It was a new idea that what you ate as a child could affect your bone health when you were older, and I wanted to measure that impact. But how could I? It wasn't feasible for teenagers to eat at home and collect samples on their own, but we could control this in a fun camp format."[28]

Participants learned about nutrition and health to potentially better their eating and exercise habits throughout their lives. Weaver told the girls, "Picture what you want to look like in seventy years. Do you want to be jogging or in a wheelchair?"[29]

The camp model allowed for control of what the girls ate and the collection of their excreta. The girls were continually supervised by camp counselors to ensure that they did not jeopardize the study by eating or drinking food not part of the calcium-rich regimen. Camp Calcium studies eventually included adolescent boys.

Olivia Wood was a collaborative investigator as the metabolic dietician for Camp Calcium. Highly organized, Wood weighed all the food to a tenth of a gram and tagged it. Wood said, "I loved being involved with Camp Calcium. I handled the kitchen. I always tell people, 'I handled the input. I didn't have to deal with the output.' It was a stinky situation, which was a problem because there was a cafeteria in the building [Stone Hall]."[30]

Weaver and her team found that even when the body utilizes calcium most efficiently, it retains only about a quarter of the calcium it takes in. The rest is lost through excrement. They also determined that calcium absorption is highest in women when they hit puberty, and that level of absorption declines steadily as a woman gets older.[31] Nearly every bodily function uses calcium, including muscle contraction and nerve impulses. "If you don't get enough from your diet, it'll rob your bones," Weaver said.[32]

Most Americans were not consuming nearly the amount of calcium necessary to maintain healthy bones late in life. Often, the result was osteoporosis, a thinning of the bones, which would lead to fractures and humped backs. There was no treatment to reverse the disease, so prevention was paramount. In addition to dietary studies, Weaver also researched the connection between exercise and strong bones. Bones must undergo mechanical stress to retain calcium.[33] At the time, Weaver said, "The increase in osteoporosis is becoming alarming. It now costs the nation about $13.8 billion annually in health-care expense."[34]

In the summer of 1997, the first Camp Calcium for Black adolescent girls took place to determine if there were differences in calcium retention between the races. On average, Black women had a higher peak bone density and were less likely to suffer from osteoporosis. Weaver proved that Black people use calcium more effectively for bone-building, with the result that most Black people have 12 percent more bone mass than white people by adulthood.[35]

Later, Weaver conducted an investigation to determine if salt intake canceled calcium's benefits. She and her team found significant clues as to why white people and Black people have different rates of hypertension and osteoporosis. Findings proved that salt is processed differently in the races, but too much salt in the diet reduces bone density in both races. Because teenagers often eat a large amount of salty fast food and not enough calcium, they can experience a double jeopardy with their health.[36]

Weaver's groundbreaking Camp Calcium data determined the amount of calcium adolescents need to achieve maximum bone growth and spurred a revision in the Recommended Dietary Allowances produced by the National Academy of Sciences (NAS) and used by the Food and Drug Administration. The new guidelines made headlines around the country.[37] The Institute of Medicine, a branch of the NAS, put forth guidelines for calcium consumption according to age group and for the first time recommended an upper limit for intake of the essential mineral.[38]

Previous guidelines took calcium requirements for adults and extrapolated the numbers to come up with guidelines for adolescents. Weaver's landmark findings determined that approach to be woefully inadequate because bone growth occurred nearly exclusively during adolescence or during the years following the onset of puberty for women.[39] She also debunked the myth that dietary calcium increases the risk of kidney stones.

The findings from Camp Calcium were reported in professional journals and mainstream media with quotes from Weaver in newspapers across the country including the *New York Times*, *Los Angeles Times*, and *USA Today*. Weaver was invited to speak at universities and professional associations across the globe.

In 2000, Weaver became director of the Botanical Center for Age-Related Diseases at Purdue with collaboration from University of Alabama Birmingham. The National Institutes of Health invested $7.8 million for the center. NIH reviewers said they were attracted to the Purdue proposal for the center because it was "creative and innovative," combining world-class expertise and technology.

The center's interdisciplinary team of twenty-seven researchers examined plants touted to prevent age-related diseases including osteoporosis, cancer, cardiovascular disease, and loss of cognitive function. Weaver tested soy products for their ability to replace estrogen and protect against bone loss in postmenopausal women. Compounds in green tea were tested for the ability to inhibit tumor growth. One of the center's goals was to learn more about the safety and effectiveness of dietary supplements. Weaver said, "Marketers of these products face less regulatory oversight than required for food additives and drugs. The problem is compounded by the fact that the burden of proof rests on the shoulders of the Food and Drug Administration, not the manufacturers. Our mission is also to communicate our findings with the public and the medical community and to train students, postdoctoral fellows, faculty, and industry scientists about this field of research."[40]

The Botanical Center was the second NIH center based at Purdue, the first being the Center for Cancer Research. It was one of only four in the United States funded by NIH for the study of dietary supplements.

President George W. Bush appointed Weaver to the Dietary Guidelines Advisory Committee in 2003 to revise the nation's dietary standards. The guidelines are revised every five years to ensure they are up to date with the most recent scientific and medical knowledge. Government feeding programs, such as school lunches, and industry nutrition labels must comply with the guidelines.[41] Weaver said, "The translation of it is bigger than most of the things we can do in the world. We can create a publication, and that does some good. But when [standards are] translated into laws, it is pretty exciting."[42]

Weaver became one of the top NIH grantees in the country. She made history in 2006 when she was the first woman in more than a half century to win the Excellence in Research Award given to the scientist who is deemed "the best of the best" by Purdue's chapter of Sigma Xi Scientific Research Society. The first Excellence in Research award was presented at Purdue in 1950. At a lecture detailing the major findings of her work over the previous two decades, Weaver said, "Calcium was so interesting that I've stuck with it for a long time. Bones are strong enough to support our body but light enough to allow mobility, which is quite an accomplishment."[43]

Purdue partnered with the Indiana University School of Medicine in 2008 to create the Indiana Clinical and Translational Sciences Institute (CTSI) through a $25 million grant from the National Institutes of Health. It was the first collaboration between Purdue and Indiana University to take place in the history of the two institutions.[44] Weaver was named deputy director of the institute for the Purdue campus. The institute was a statewide laboratory that helped medical and health researchers take their discoveries into the marketplace and also into the minds of doctors, nurses, and other medical workers.

A researcher could approach CTSI with a new drug or new technique for treating an illness, and a team would work with that researcher to move the discovery through government regulations, clinical trials, and other requirements in which scientists usually have little expertise. One of the goals of CTSI was to eliminate the "valley of death" where a basic science discovery, such as a drug, could linger due to outside regulations and requirements. CTSI helped the investigator move through the protocols and put the discovery into practice more quickly.

Weaver said, "It's one-stop shopping. They say 'Here, we'll hold your hand through the process and give you the tools you need.'[45] If you just have an idea, not even any measurements yet, we can connect you to experts in regulatory or intellectual property, or help get approval with an animal study or for human studies, and connect you with partners at Indiana University School of Medicine."[46] During this time, the university built a world-class clinical research center to support work in nutrition and for the CTSI.

The role of diet in preventing breast cancer all over the world became Weaver's topic of research in fall 2010. Weaver was part of an international team of public health scientists from the United States, France, Japan, Ghana, Uruguay, Lebanon, and Canada led by Purdue. The goal was to have enough diversity in diet and genetic data to help answer why breast cancer incidence is low in some countries and high in others.[47]

When Camp Calcium celebrated its twentieth and final year, Weaver's research focused on calcium and fiber for Mexican Americans with seventy participants, the largest group to that date. To celebrate the anniversary, a reunion of past participants and graduate students was held at Columbian Park in Lafayette.[48]

Looking back, Weaver said, "Imagine running a slumber party for fifty kids, even one night, and you are exhausted in the end. Imagine doing it all summer. I had no idea it would be a twenty year or longer adventure. But everyone was captivated. There were almost no data on kids in a controlled feeding study. Even twenty years later it is still impressing people. I am surprised it is still unique. We created a template, and I've trained a lot of people who could be doing it. But it is partly the campus. This campus was tolerant and willing to let it happen and help for two decades."[49]

In 2010, Weaver reached a pinnacle of her career when she was elected a member of the National Academy of Medicine, formerly Institute of Medicine, the health arm of the National Academy of Sciences that helps shape public health policy for the United States. She was the first female Purdue faculty member and the second person in Purdue's history to be elected to the academy, the first being Dr. Steven C. Beering, president of Purdue from 1983 to 2000, who had also been a practicing physician.

Regarding the esteemed position, Weaver said, "We have a lot of work to do to promote nutritional health as our nation struggles with an obesity epidemic and our largest ever aging adult population."[50] She also said, "It is a lifelong dream to have this achievement in my career. This is the highest honor in my field."

Weaver's alma mater, Oregon State, presented her with the Linus Pauling Prize for Health Research in 2011 that included a $25,000 prize, which Weaver put toward her dream of creating the Women's Global Health Institute (WGHI), the country's only center focused on women's preventive health designed to change the way women's health is addressed. She was the first graduate of Oregon State to receive the award.[51]

Former Purdue University trustee and alumna Susan Bulkeley Butler donated funds for the startup. Director of Purdue's Oncological Sciences Center Li Yuan Bermel took on the added role as managing director of the WGHI, which would focus on bone health, women's cancers, and neurodegenerative diseases such as dementia, Alzheimer's, and Parkinson's, along with wellness.

"We want cutting-edge discoveries for preventing health problems," Weaver said. "Prevention is sort of a new idea. The typical model is diagnose the disease after you have the disorder and try to treat it. So it takes almost a nonmedical school campus to think about prevention.[52] This is the start of a dream occurring at the right time and right place. President [France] Córdova made health visible at Purdue through creation of our new College of Health and Human Sciences [established in 2010]."[53]

Also in 2012, Weaver received the most significant research award bestowed by Purdue, the Herbert Newby McCoy Award. She was nominated by her colleagues and selected by faculty representatives and Purdue President France A. Córdova. Richard Buckius, Purdue's vice president for research, said, "Professor Weaver's findings have transformed the way the nation thinks about the value of calcium consumption, and especially its importance in establishing bone health in young girls that will last their lifetime."[54]

That same year, Weaver was awarded the Purdue University Spirit of the Land Grant Mission Award for her discoveries and their societal impact. The award is presented annually to a Purdue faculty member in the Colleges of Agriculture, Health and Human Sciences or Veterinary Medicine whose work exemplifies the university's land-grant mission of discovery, engagement, and learning.

Not to be stopped in her lifelong quest to study optimal bone health, in 2014 Weaver and an interdisciplinary team of researchers received nearly $4 million from the National Institutes of Health for the "Berries and Bone" project—research to learn if blueberries are helpful to counter menopause-induced and age-related bone loss.[55] Announcement of the study made headlines and was featured in *USA Today*.

The Department of Nutrition Science celebrated its 110th anniversary in May 2016. It had begun in the School of Science with dietetics and nutrition as an original course in 1905. Purdue offered the first dietetics major in Indiana. The Department of Foods and Nutrition, now Nutrition Science, had been part of

Home Economics since the school was created in 1926, and melded into the newly created College of Health and Human Sciences in 2010.

To kick off the anniversary gala, the newly renovated Nutrition and Exercise Clinical Research Center in Stone Hall was dedicated. The center had been a twenty-five-year dream of Weaver's. It allowed faculty to expand their research to better understand how the quality of one's diet influences chronic disease prevention and weight management and to study the intersection of nutrition and exercise. The center's futuristic-looking BodPod helped researchers evaluate body composition by measuring fat and lean body mass.[56]

The center's metabolic research kitchen made a big impact. Previously, when researchers conducted feeding studies, which ran seven days a week, food would be prepared for the weekend on Friday, but by Sunday some of the food would be moldy due to the faulty refrigeration system. Human subjects would drop out of the study if they thought the food was not of good quality. New freezers prevented that problem.[57]

Dr. Connie M. Weaver retired as Distinguished Professor Emerita after more than twenty-five years as head of Purdue's Department of Nutrition Science in December 2016. To her successor, Michele Forman, Weaver offered this advice: "The best of leaders are servant-hearted. If you find joy in helping others and find ways to say 'yes,' more than 'no,' then everyone is happier."[58] Today she is a Distinguished Research Professor at San Diego State University.

Weaver continued to focus on diet with relation to bone and heart health. Weaver said, "The career path I have chosen is very motivating and stimulating. With research comes discovery—the highest stimulant I know."[59]

25

THE WORLD NEEDS EDUCATED WOMEN

LANELLE E. GEDDES, STUNNING MIND AND COUNTENANCE

LaNelle E. Nerger Geddes was an urban legend in her own time. Impeccably dressed in fine suits, stunning pearls, and sometimes a swath of fur, the head of the Purdue School of Nursing looked as brilliant as her mind. Geddes was a sparkling scholar with a refined presence to which students and colleagues gravitated.

Geddes started her day at 2:30 a.m. By 4 a.m., she was at her office. At about 5:30 a.m., she took a brisk walk around campus. By midday, "not a hair out of place," she taught the class that every Purdue nursing student of Geddes's day remembers—pathophysiology.[1]

Geddes served as head of Purdue's School of Nursing from 1980 to 1991. She had served as assistant head for five years prior. When Purdue Nursing founder and head Dr. Helen Johnson retired in 1980, Geddes succeeded her.

Geddes was born on September 15, 1935, in Houston, where she was raised. She graduated from the University of Texas. With a Texas-sized smile, she said, "In those days, it was thought that a woman didn't need much education. But I had ambition. I've always liked to learn, and I've always been competitive.[2] I knew that I wanted to get an academic degree in nursing.... I wasn't sure about what I would do with my career, but I knew I would be much better off starting from a baccalaureate degree."[3]

Geddes's desire for a bachelor's degree would serve her well at Purdue where her legacy includes her tenacious work to institute a four-year baccalaureate program in nursing. Most of her undergraduate nursing courses at the University of Texas were taught by physicians.

Geddes's only sibling, a brother two years her junior, died at age eighteen when he was a freshman at the University of Texas and Geddes was a junior. Carl Nerger Jr. fell from a truck while assisting in cleaning a dormitory.[4] Perhaps Geddes's drive was fueled by the fact she became her parents' only living child.

Rumors circulated that the lanky Geddes was once crowned Miss Texas. She said, "No, that's not true. That's part of that urban legend. I did model, mostly to gain a presence, to know how to conduct myself and hold myself in front of an audience."

After graduating with her bachelor's degree in nursing in 1957, Geddes worked for the Houston public school system as a school nurse and in the summers for the Texas Medical Center. The school system only hired nurses with bachelor's degrees, so Geddes was in an exclusive group, as back then all one needed to be a nurse was to have a nursing license. Geddes said, "Very few nurses then had college degrees; they [the school system] paid their nurses the same salary as their teachers with master's."

Geddes enrolled in a physiology workshop at Baylor College of Medicine taught by Leslie A. Geddes, a Scotsman who would become her husband and establish Purdue's Biomedical Engineering program. The couple married and honeymooned in Japan, teaching a course in physiology to the Japanese Air Defense Corps.[5]

Leslie Geddes would eventually have more than thirty US patents in his name. He invented a regenerative tissue graft, a pacemaker that automatically increases a person's heart rate during exercise, and a portable electrocardiograph. LaNelle and Leslie Geddes became Purdue's unassuming power couple; each exuded humility and grace and were revered by their students and colleagues.

Geddes said, "After I married, . . . I went back to the University of Houston. This was maybe a year after Sputnik was launched and orbited the earth. The US was saying we are not training enough scientists, and so they instituted what was called the National Defense Education Act [NDEA], and it was to encourage more people to get education in the sciences."[6] The NDEA program fully funded Geddes's graduate education.

As an undergraduate she had taken what she called "ghetto courses" in anatomy, physiology, and chemistry—science courses specifically for nurses, which were "ghettos" or inferior because they didn't count as prerequisites for further education. Geddes spent two years retaking courses that she needed to pursue a master's degree and matriculated into a program in biophysics.[7]

When it was time for her to decide on a topic for her master's thesis, her academic advisor said she had done so well on her coursework that she did not have to write a thesis, and she could immediately start her PhD research. Geddes was the first and only female graduate student studying biophysics at the University of Houston. "It wasn't easy being a female interested in scholarly research and academia back then," Geddes recalled. "I always felt I had to prove myself."[8]

Geddes obtained her PhD in biophysical sciences in 1970. She never forgot the summer day she took her dissertation to the acting dean for his signature. He signed it and said, "The last thing this world needs is another overeducated woman."

"I remember thinking, *What a stupid thing to say*," Geddes recalled. "But I wasn't surprised."[9]

She then went to Baylor College of Medicine with a Public Health Service postdoctoral fellowship in cardiovascular physiology. After her postdoc, she began teaching half time in the Department of Physiology at the Baylor College of Medicine and half time at the Texas Women's University College of Nursing. The medical field of pathophysiology was just beginning to be recognized. Geddes was a trailblazer for women and also for medicine.

In 1974, Geddes's husband was recruited to come to Purdue to lead the Biomedical Engineering Center, but she did not follow him. She said, "I didn't come. I stayed in Houston, because my career was just getting started, and I just needed a little more foundation."[10] A year later, Geddes, age forty, arrived on campus. She served as assistant head to Helen Johnson and developed the pathophysiology class she would teach for the next twenty-eight years.[11] Geddes was the first nursing faculty member with a PhD. At the time, Johnson was working on her doctorate.

Geddes taught pathophysiology to every Purdue nursing student and to other nursing students and health care professionals around the state of Indiana. Pathophysiology is the study of alterations in physiology that are responsible for illness, disease, or bodily dysfunction. Students called Geddes "the shepherd instructor." She explained, "I'm called 'the shepherd' because in clinical studies, I let my students try things on their own."[12]

Her visionary inclusion of pathophysiology in the nursing curriculum empowered nursing students with the tools to make better clinical judgements and

Professor of Nursing Dr. LaNelle Geddes with a student in the 1980s. Courtesy Purdue University Archives and Special Collections.

to be stronger patient advocates. Regarding her effective teaching methods, Geddes said, "Students are the university's 'customers' and they deserve a quality product for the price they pay."[13]

Geddes's larger-than-life persona came about because of her daunting pathophysiology course. "They [students] think that I give a lot of material, and it's not the kind of material they can just come to class and listen and then study the night before the test," she said. "These are bright students, and they're not used to having to dig in and learn so much material. That makes them think I'm hard and demanding. But they also say I explain the material well.... But I think they perceive me as fair and trying to help them learn."[14]

One of the adages that Geddes repeated in class was, "I don't want to look up into the face of my nurse when I am hospitalized and say, 'Are you here because your pathophysiology professor graded on a curve?'"[15]

When Geddes retired, colleague Jane Kirkpatrick wrote, "When you brought the pathophysiology class to employees at Home Hospital in the late 1970s, I had the opportunity to take the course. Being a student in your class was life-changing! I had never met a person who could consistently engage an entire class for three hours while communicating complicated material. I remember thinking 'If only I could teach like that!'"[16]

Geddes's effective and engaging teaching methods earned her the James Dwyer Outstanding Teacher Award from the School of Technology and the Amoco Foundation Teaching Award (now the Murphy Award). She was an inaugural inductee into Purdue's Book of Great Teachers and fellow in the Purdue University Teaching Academy. She was also recognized by American Men and Women of Science.

From 1996 to 2003, Geddes taught physiology to IU School of Medicine students on the Purdue campus.[17] Her research focused on cardiovascular physiology.

Geddes strove to change the perceptions of nursing. In 2007, she said, "There still are a lot of people who look down on nurses and see them as maybe a little bit better than domestics." Geddes came from a clinically sophisticated health care setting at the Texas Medical center, which was a large and prestigious medical campus; however, even there nurses were not respected for their knowledge and expertise.

"Nurses were still looked upon as giving baths, emptying bed pans, passing pills, and giving shots," she said. "Nursing throughout the county was a sleeping giant that was beginning to move and wake up. So when I came here [Purdue], one of my biggest challenges was to try to bring what I call twentieth-century nursing into this community. Helen Johnson would often send me out to tackle these things, and I'd often be a lamb in pack of wolves."[18]

As an assistant head of nursing, one of Geddes's first assignments was to explain and defend the department's position on the revolutionary idea of teaching nursing students to chart subjective and medical information. She said:

> Certain physicians at one of our local hospitals were incensed that nurses would be charting subjective information.... A hospital policy was enacted that required that the faculty read and cosign all student charting to be sure no such offensive materials found their way into the chart.
>
> There was also consternation that nurses would chart observations related to such "medical matters" as breath sounds, heart sounds, and other physiological findings. More than one contentious meeting was held with representatives of the hospital and physicians with me as the point person for nursing. It was an interesting induction to the community but one that prepared me for what would come several years later.[19]

What came several years later was the criticism of the curriculum design for the new bachelor's degree. In 1978, Helen Johnson appointed Geddes to chair a committee to investigate offering a baccalaureate program in nursing at Purdue. At the time, only the two-year associate's degree was offered. Geddes said, "We looked at it very carefully for about two years.... We decided we [had] to square it with the Commission for Higher Education. Well, they were not very amenable to having 'uppity' nurses who had baccalaureate degrees or master's degrees. And the hospital did not want to have only nurses with baccalaureate degrees available for their staff. They thought they'd have to pay them more. It turned out they didn't pay them more. But the nurses wanted their baccalaureate degrees."

A lightbulb went on over Geddes's head, and she realized that the Commission for Higher Education only needed to approve *new* degree programs. They had no jurisdiction over curriculum, and Purdue already had permission to grant a baccalaureate degree in nursing. The baccalaureate curriculum was simply modified to accommodate incoming freshmen, and in 1982 the first freshman was admitted to a four-year bachelor's program in nursing.[20] The associate degree in nursing would no longer be offered.

Geddes considered the establishment of the bachelor's degree as the basic nursing program at Purdue the highlight of her career. The committee she chaired for the program was unswerving in the opinion that students should begin to develop a nursing identity from their arrival on campus, and so they designed a curriculum that offered nursing courses in the first semester. In 1994, she wrote:

> We were criticized by certain nursing "leaders" for the curriculum design, but we believed in what we were doing and stuck with our dreams, although not without some retaliation. But the loudest critics of the change to a baccalaureate program were hospital administrators. I can't tell you the hours I spent answering their questions and explaining our rationale to them.
>
> Threats galore were hurled, but once the change was a "done deal," I heard very little. I particularly remember a meeting of the professional organization of hospital administrators.... I was invited to be a "guest" and listen to their concerns about our switch from an associate to a baccalaureate degree basic program. I felt like that brave dissident in Tiananmen Square facing down a tank as all of them regaled me with their dissatisfaction. I listened politely and explained as best I could, but here we are today still carrying out the intent of the faculty that was put forward in 1978.[21]

In 1978 Geddes confronted her own health challenge. "I was forty-three when I had breast cancer," she said years later. "I had no family history of it. It took me a long time to even go to the doctor about the lump I had found. I knew a little too much: that 90 percent of lumps are benign, that I had low risk. I let it go, really, too long.... I've never had a recurrence. I volunteer for Reach to Recovery, but unless I'm asked, I don't talk about it much."

Reach for Recovery is an American Cancer Society program where breast cancer survivors help others cope with their breast cancer experience.[22] Geddes's personality and scholarly knowledge made her the perfect volunteer. A woman whom Geddes visited wrote on a comment card: "Such a neat lady who visited me! Would like to have taken her home—she was so comforting."[23]

When Geddes became head in 1980, nursing had just transitioned from a department in the School of Technology to a School of Nursing. Geddes was at the helm to nurture the new status. Geddes wrote, "One of those things was a fledgling development program seeking help from alumni and friends to further the programs in the school. From a discretionary fund of about $2,000 that first year there was over $150,000 available for enriching programs and activities when I left office in 1991.[24]

"I was most pleased with the growth in our alumnae support," Geddes said. "Nursing always has had one of the highest percentages of alumnae donors among all of the Purdue schools. This enthusiastic giving really helps us remain competitive, and our state-of-the-art Learning Resources Center [LRC] became the envy of many of our colleagues."[25]

The Fuld Institute for Technology in Nursing Education (FITNE) selected Purdue's School of Nursing as one of forty-six across the nation to become interactive video demonstration centers for nursing education in 1988. The school received two interactive video systems and a program on IV therapy for use in the Learning Resources Center.[26] An article in *Nursing Educators* touted the then new method in teaching as a "Giant Leap into the Future" and claimed "hardly a nurse educator has seen an interactive video program and not been captivated by its possibilities for nursing education."[27] Well before the advent of the internet, students learned how to respond to life-threatening situations on a personal computer connected to a videodisc player.

The new Helene Fuld Critical Care Unit in the Learning Resources Center in Johnson Hall opened in 1989 and gave nursing students the opportunity to practice on complex equipment in the campus laboratory before using it in a hospital.[28]

Geddes was instrumental in creating, implementing, and teaching the Nursing Freshman Scholar program that began in 1987. Each year, several incoming freshmen received this merit-based scholarship and participate in a seminar class. They were also paired with faculty members to assist with research. Geddes and her colleagues worked diligently to establish a scholarly face for nursing as more and more nurses sought graduate degrees.

Nurses began to take on new leadership roles and work more autonomously. An advanced practice RN or nurse practitioner saw patients without a physician present and could prescribe medication. Instead of only caring for the sick, nurses were increasingly involved in preventing illnesses by teaching about healthy lifestyles. Nurse-managed clinics emerged, and Purdue was on the forefront emulating the university's land-grant mission of service to Hoosiers by providing much-needed health care in rural towns in Indiana.

In fall 1989, Purdue received 279 applications to the School of Nursing and one hundred could be accepted. That was a 30 percent increase from the previous year. Geddes said, "All of the forces directed toward putting nursing in a more positive light, painting it as an attractive career choice with higher salaries are bearing fruit."[29]

The School of Nursing experienced a severe faculty shortage by 1990. Because of the vacancies and the nature of the nursing profession, which required much one-on-one instruction, each nursing faculty member taught twenty credit hours of courses per semester. That was more than double the number of credit hours taught by the average Purdue professor. Each faculty member also conducted research in addition to teaching.[30]

"This is a very, very highly publicized shortage that's really begun to be of crisis proportion," Geddes said. "I don't think a nurse will ever want for a job. This is the worst shortage we've seen."[31]

An idiosyncrasy that added to Geddes's mystique among her students was the fact that during a semester she strategically wore a different outfit to each class. She explained, "I realized that the students noticed what I wore to class. So I decided to use that as a hook to keep them interested. I take a little piece of paper and put it over the clothes hanger and leave it there for the semester so I know what I have worn to class already. I've maintained the same dress size over the years, so I have clothes I've had for twenty years, and I can still wear them. That's why I have several closets."[32]

She also explained her teaching philosophy. "As I did more and more teaching, it dawned on me that in order to be a good teacher you have to entertain, whether it's what you wear or what you say. You have to look like you're enjoying it, and you have to have a presence for it. The more I taught, the more that developed."³³

Students took notice of her professionalism and presence, and several said they wanted to "grow up to be her" or dress like her. Jean Gilbert Putnam, who received her BSN in 1985, said, "I recall thinking: 'This is what a true professional businesswoman should be like.' She was classy, yet personable.... She was very articulate. I was in awe of her!"³⁴

Geddes decided to return to what she loved most—full-time teaching—in 1991. Jo A. Brooks became head of the School of Nursing. Geddes retired as a professor emeritus in 2003. She still had an office and mentored students, new faculty, and young nurses and continued to arrive on campus in the predawn hours for her daily walk through Purdue's underground tunnels.

When asked about the future of nursing in 2007, Geddes said, "So much of what nurses do is foster healthy lifestyles, and lifestyle changes. Hospitals and the high technology are what we see, and that's the high price stuff. A lot can be done at a much different level and nurses are good at that. Nurses like to sit down and teach. They have been taught to interact, to cooperate with the patients. Nurses are more likely to sit down, eye to eye, and talk about things. And that has been a big change through my many years in nursing."

LaNelle Geddes died in 2016 at the age of eighty-one. She was once told that people held her in high esteem, to which she replied, "Who can ask for more in life than to have conducted yourself in a way, consistently, that people will hold you in high esteem? That, to me, is a real measure of success."

JO A. BROOKS, PUBLIC HEALTH NURSE, FOUNDER TIPPECANOE COUNTY COMMUNITY HEALTH CLINIC

Jo A. Brooks was one of the first graduates of Purdue's associate degree nursing program in 1965 while a single mother of twins. "I would pull my twin daughters down University Street in a wagon to the Humpty Dumpty Daycare Center before heading to class," she said. Brooks would go on to champion public health programs at Purdue.

During a speech at Brooks's 1965 senior recognition ceremony, Helen R. Johnson, then head of the School of Nursing, expressed her dream that one of her first graduates would someday head the school. That dream became a reality when

Brooks was named head in 1992. "We graduates chuckled among ourselves at the time," Brooks recalled, "not knowing what a prophet [Helen] would turn out to be. Helen was a pioneer in nursing education. I felt like I was carrying her legacy forward."

Brooks grew up in nearby Attica, Indiana, where her father owned a Shell service station and was a night supervisor at Harrison Steel Castings Company. She was the son her father never had; she had her own toolbox and helped him put a roof on their house. It took Brooks a few tries to finish her nursing degree as she was a rebel. She said, "Back then, the bed had to be made just so, but I was always creative." She quit school, worked in several hospitals, married, had twin girls, divorced, and returned to Purdue to complete her associate's degree.

After snooping in her high school scholastic records as a teenager, Brooks learned how smart she really was and it was her kick in the pants. "I discovered I had something to live up to," she said. "When I worked for my high school principal. I was in the guidance office and just for fun took a peek at my I.Q. test score. Call it a self-fulfilling prophecy, but I figured I had better start doing something with myself after that."[35]

Brooks worked at a county hospital while earning her bachelor's degree one course at a time at Indiana University. She liked to get to know people and assist them, no matter who they were. In the early years of her career, the "town drunk" came to the hospital where she was working. "No one else wanted to take care of him," she said. "He was mean but he needed help, and he let me help him. For years after that, he would send me a lace handkerchief in a card every Christmas. That's how I knew he finally died—the handkerchiefs stopped coming."[36]

She worked several years for the Bureau of Public Health and earned a master's degree in public health nursing from the University of Michigan in 1972. That year, Helen Johnson recruited her to return to Purdue as a public health instructor. "I had my life as a public health nurse all planned out," Brooks said. "But Helen was a lady who wouldn't take no for an answer."

After Brooks returned as an instructor, she became aware that students needed experience in performing routine health assessment tests. So she and a group of volunteer nurses started a health referral center in a church basement, which eventually grew into the Tippecanoe County Community Health Clinic where nursing students gained clinical public health nursing experience. Later it became Riggs Community Health Center with three locations in Lafayette and one in Lebanon, Indiana.

When there was interest in RNs learning to do physical exams, Brooks created a two-week health assessment course and advertised free physicals for Purdue faculty and staff. "By noon on the first day, 150 people had called for appointments," Brooks said. "We had to run all around campus and tear the posters down since we were not prepared to handle any more."

Today, patients are familiar with visiting a nurse practitioner who can provide excellent, affordable primary care. This was not the case when in December 1980, Brooks and Mary Lou Holle were awarded a $250,000 grant from the United States Public Health Service to establish a Nursing Center for Family Health (NCFH) as a learning laboratory for nursing students. A storage room on the lower level of Johnson Hall of Nursing was remodeled to create examination rooms and office space, and the NCFH opened in 1981, giving students experience in health screenings, education, and counseling as they served Purdue students, faculty and staff.[37]

"We see people with health questions who haven't seen a doctor for years," Brooks said. "Our center is [a] very comfortable, nonthreatening place. We find many of our clients, even those who have a regular doctor, tell us things they may not tell their doctor."[38] Brooks advocated for nurse-managed clinics because of their focus on treating the whole person and the whole family. As one of the first nurse-managed clinics at a school of nursing, the NCFH served as a national model. Later, the NCFH was located in Lyles-Porter Hall.

Before coming to Purdue, Holle had been director of nursing services at Memorial Hospital in Logansport, Indiana. Holle, an avid mystery reader, found that doctors were often spotlighted as amateur detectives in novels, while few nurses were featured. After retirement, Holle wrote a novel titled *Conundrum*, which placed fictitious head nurse Amber Brooks into a web of lies, deceit, and intrigue after an elderly woman is murdered in the hospital chapel. Holle drew on her years of experience in nursing to depict a realistic medical setting with the main character named after her colleague Jo Brooks.[39]

Brooks was named Indiana Nurse of the Year by the Indiana League of Nursing in 1986. The award honors outstanding nurses in the state who make noteworthy personal contributions to their profession and community. She was cited for her work on the creation and development of the Women's Health Awareness Month sponsored by the Association for Women Students and the School of Nursing.[40]

During her career, Brooks was recognized with the Dwyer Award for Outstanding Undergraduate Teacher in the School of Technology, the Woman

Faculty Award from the Association of Women Students, the Council on the Status of Women's Violet Haas Award for contributions to women at Purdue, and the Indiana Rural Health Volunteer Award for Central Indiana.[41]

When LaNelle Geddes stepped away from the headship in 1991, Brooks became head of Nursing. Brooks was also associate dean of the Schools of Pharmacy, Nursing, and Health Sciences. Among the school's goals was to increase research by recruiting faculty with doctorates and to appoint a director of research.

"This move toward scholarly activities reflected the maturation level of the nursing program as well as the entire nursing profession," Brooks said. "LaNelle had succeeded in making our baccalaureate program top-notch. Now we needed to refine our curriculum to position the School as a leader in nursing education in the rapidly approaching twenty-first century."[42]

Brooks's tenure as head of nursing was challenging because of the rapid changes in health care, both political and technological. Brooks and the faculty predicted that community-based programs would become more prevalent and the demand for nurses with advanced degrees would increase. She worked to secure funds to provide computers to faculty and students.

In 1995, Brooks launched the Family Health Clinic of Carroll County in a 500-square-foot space on the Delphi, Indiana, courthouse square. It was a joint effort between the School of Nursing and St. Elizabeth Medical Center in Lafayette. "At that time, residents of surrounding rural counties had no local access to health care, so they were using the Lafayette hospital emergency rooms at an overwhelming rate," Brooks said. "The community really needed a clinic."

A satellite Family Health Clinic opened in the small town of Monon, Indiana, in 2006. Many of the patients of the clinic were the "working poor," who had jobs but lacked health insurance and had little money and no transportation.[43]

The Delphi clinic grew substantially from its humble beginnings on the courthouse square, and in 2008 a $2.5 million, 12,500-square-foot facility was built in Carroll County. John Walling, then president of North Central Health Services, the new structure's funding agency, asked Brooks if it was all right to name the building after her. Brooks recalled, "I was speechless, if you can believe that."[44] The Brooks Center was a hub for health care and social services from five of Carroll County's human service organizations.

The School of Nursing partnered with the nonprofit North Central Nursing Clinics organization to open two community health clinics in Burlington and Wolcott in 2016. The clinics provided training opportunities for Nursing students as well as Purdue College of Pharmacy Fellows and interns.[45]

Dr. Jo A. Brooks was one of the first graduates of Purdue's associate degree nursing program in 1965 while a single mother of twins. She became head of Purdue Nursing and founder of the Tippecanoe County Community Health Clinic in Lafayette. Courtesy Purdue University Archives and Special Collections.

Brooks had always wanted to travel to Russia ever since she read *Anna Karenina* as a young girl, and later, after she saw the movie *Dr. Zhivago*. Her dream came true in 1997 when she joined a group of nurse executives for a Citizens Ambassador Trip to Russia and Romania. "I met the most amazing group of nurses who are trying to move nursing from the 1950s to the 1990s," Brooks said. "And they want to avoid the mistakes we in the West made. They are doing an incredible job under the most trying conditions, but the one thing I noticed in all of them was their caring."[46]

In 2002, Brooks was honored with the Sagamore of the Wabash award, the highest honor the governor of Indiana can bestow. It is a personal tribute to those who have rendered a distinguished service to the state. The term "Sagamore" was used by Indigenous people to describe a great man among the tribe to whom the chief would look for wisdom and advice. Brooks was a great woman to whom students, colleagues, and patients in Indiana looked for nursing and leadership wisdom. A woman who would help anyone in need, working for the good of public health.[47] Brooks died on February 22, 2023, in West Lafayette at the age of eighty-seven.

26
STRIDES FOR MINORITIES AND COMMUNITY

CLARA E. BELL, FOUNDER OF MINORITY STUDENTS IN NURSING

Clara E. Bell forged a personal footpath that developed her empathy for the complexities that faced Purdue's Black students and her Black colleagues. She shined a spotlight on the distinct needs of minority nursing students, minority faculty, and what became Purdue's Division of Diversity and Inclusion.

Born February 9, 1934, in Terre Haute, Indiana, Bell was the first African American student to attend St. Anthony Hospital School of Nursing there. In 1995, Bell recalled, "When I first went to St. Anthony's on a scholarship, I wasn't permitted to live with the other students. After six months, they voted and decided that I could live with them. A lot has changed since then, but discrimination in health care and other professions is still there. It just usually is covert, or hidden, now because prejudiced people are afraid of being looked down upon by their colleagues or of being sued."[1]

Bell earned her bachelor's degree in nursing from Indiana State University and her master's and doctoral degrees at Indiana University School of Education.[2] A diabetic, Bell's doctoral dissertation was on diabetic-patient teaching.

She was active in the Indiana State Diabetes Association and the American Diabetes Association, winning their top service awards.³

Bell joined the Purdue nursing faculty in 1981, and four years later she was named Purdue's director of continuing education in nursing. Prior to arriving on campus, Bell had been director of continuing education in nursing at Indiana University–Kokomo. She lived in Logansport where her first husband, Gregory, was a dentist at the Logansport State Hospital. The couple and their three children lived in a cottage on the Longcliff grounds. Many called the psychiatric hospital "Longcliff," referring to the long bluff where the campus was perched.⁴ When he was a student at Indiana University, Gregory had been a 1956 Olympic long jump gold medalist.⁵ While Clara was known by students and colleagues as "Dr. Bell," she married Charles L. Session in 1990 and took on his surname.

In 1984, Bell led the charge to form the Minority Students in Nursing organization, the precursor to the Diversity in Nursing Association at Purdue. Four students attended the first meeting facilitated by Bell and Eleanor Stephan, academic advisor for the School of Nursing. Afterward, the two wrote a summary of the meeting titled, "Black Nursing Students Articulate Their Needs." They penned:

> Numbers are insignificant when one speaks of one's personal experience. This is true in the personal experience of black nursing students at Purdue University. There are six in the bachelor of science nursing program, a program which numbers 400 students. How insignificant a number, yet how important each personal experience is to each one of the six as compared with the majority.
>
> The isolation of the black student was brought to light when it was learned individually that these students were unaware of other black students in the program, nor did they know Dr. Clara Bell, a black professor in the school of Nursing.⁶

The first meeting of the Black nursing students "sparkled with enthusiasm and camaraderie. It was an occasion long overdue."⁷ The students shared their experiences, discussing academic needs and how they could help one another to succeed. They felt isolated and wanted to help newly admitted Black students who might have felt the same. The four Black nursing students realized that they represented potential leaders of their race and shared a desire to survive in their chosen career in spite of any odds. They wanted to meet with Black professionals

In 1984, Professor of Nursing Dr. Clara Bell, shown here in 1992, led the charge to form the Minority Students in Nursing organization, the precursor to the Diversity in Nursing Association at Purdue. Courtesy Purdue University Archives and Special Collections.

on campus and ask questions, such as, "How did you do it? How did you cope in a white, middle-class environment? What advice can you give me?"[8]

On May 3, 1985, the Minority Student Nurses' Association (MSNA) adopted a constitution and by-laws and became an official Purdue student organization. Any female nursing student who was nonwhite was considered a minority for this group. The MSNA became active in the Greater Lafayette community through service projects to help the Minority Health Coalition of Tippecanoe County, of which Bell was a board member, and the Battered Women's Shelter. By 2000, the MSNA had thirteen members.[9]

Bell also helped Black faculty members by forming the Minority Faculty Fellows program in 1988 to encourage and support Purdue's administration in hiring minority professors. The program brought minority faculty to campus for eight weeks during the summer to teach and conduct research so they could get to know the university and provide campus awareness of diverse cultures.[10] The Minority Faculty Fellows program was the forerunner of the Office of Diversity and Multicultural Affairs established in 1993.[11]

Regarding the office, Bell said, "The covertness of prejudice does still exist in the academic setting. That's why it is important to have an office like this. It keeps faculty, staff, and students aware that Purdue promotes integration and equality."

Bell also supported Black faculty nationally by cochairing the National Congress of Black Faculty Council on Research and Education and was a charter member of the Association of Black Nursing Faculty in Higher Education. She served as a cabinet member on the Human Rights Committee of the American Nurses Association.

Soon after her retirement from Purdue, Bell passed away in her home in Terre Haute on March 3, 1996, at age sixty-two. That year, the Purdue University Black Caucus of Faculty and Staff honored Bell by instituting the annual Clara E. Bell Academic Achievement Award to the senior in nursing or health sciences with the highest grade point average. In 2013, she was posthumously awarded the Title IX Distinguished Service Award for her contributions to gender equity in education.

The year prior to her passing, Bell said, "Purdue has no problems recruiting minority faculty and students, but does have problems with retaining and promoting them. The answer is to promote a climate conducive for them to want to remain there. That's what minorities have here at the School of Nursing—a friendly, warm environment."[12]

JANE KIRKPATRICK, BRINGING ENGINEERING INTO NURSING

When Jane Kirkpatrick was a student at West Lafayette High School in the early 1970s, a friend urged her to become a candy striper at St. Elizabeth Hospital in Lafayette. Candy stripers were typically teenage girls who wore red-striped pinafores as they volunteered in hospitals. Kirkpatrick's candy striper experience sparked her career trajectory. In 2009 she would become head of Purdue's School of Nursing, doubling its size, launching a PhD program, and envisioning a new building.[13]

Kirkpatrick started as a nursing student in fall 1972 when Helen R. Johnson was head. The program was a "two plus two" offering. After two years, a student earned an associate degree and could take the state licensing exam to become a registered nurse. A student had to reapply to be accepted into the upper division. As a registered nurse, Kirkpatrick worked in the obstetrics department at St. Elizabeth Hospital while earning her bachelor's degree.

After graduation, Kirkpatrick worked for several years at Home Hospital in Lafayette; first in the neonatal intensive care unit and later in the education department orienting new nurses and providing staff development in maternal child health. She shared an office with a woman who became her mentor. "She said to me, 'You should teach at Purdue,'" Kirkpatrick recalled. "When somebody sees something in you, they plant a seed and nurture it."

At the suggestion of her mentor, Kirkpatrick set up a meeting with Helen Johnson who told her she needed a master's degree to teach. Johnson's office was in the then new nursing building, which would later be named after her and where Kirkpatrick would work years later.

Purdue did not yet offer a graduate-level degree, so Kirkpatrick attended Indiana University at the then Indiana University Purdue University at Indianapolis (IUPUI) campus and majored in perinatal nursing with a minor in nursing education. She conducted her student teaching at Purdue.

After earning her master's in 1981, Kirkpatrick was hired by LaNelle Geddes, the second woman to head Purdue's School of Nursing. Geddes taught her pathophysiology course to nurses working at Home Hospital, where Kirkpatrick first met Geddes. "I remember sitting in her class just mesmerized," Kirkpatrick said. "She was the most amazing educator. She took a concept that was complicated and made it make sense to all of us. I dreamed of being able to teach like LaNelle. She was my role model and mentor for teaching when I was hired at Purdue. Over the years we had many early morning conversations about how to help our students learn."

During her career, Kirkpatrick received the LaNelle Geddes Excellence in Teaching Award multiple times.[14] She was also inducted into Purdue's Book of Great Teachers and served as chair of Purdue's Teaching Academy.

Kirkpatrick taught maternal-newborn nursing and searched for the best way to teach students how to perform physical exams on newborns. Live demonstrations during clinicals were not time efficient or consistent, so Kirkpatrick worked with Purdue's Center for Instructional Services to create a video to teach the head-to-toe assessment of a newborn.

Her Physical Assessment of the Newborn program won an American Journal of Nursing honorable mention. By the mid-1990s, Kirkpatrick had taken several instructional design and computer technology classes and obtained some funding to redesign the program and create a duet of videos. Thousands of copies were sold worldwide. Yet, Kirkpatrick was not satisfied because students needed interaction.

In the early 2000s, Kirkpatrick worked with a graphic designer with the School of Pharmacy to develop a "virtual baby" to provide a way for students

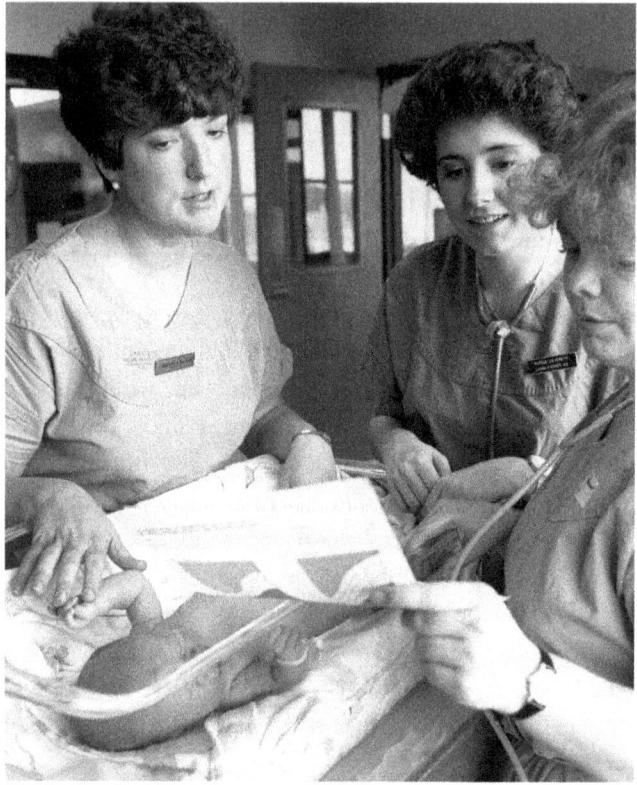

Dr. Jane Kirkpatrick, shown here on the left in 1988, taught newborn nursing and created a groundbreaking video to teach the assessment of a newborn. She became head of Purdue's School of Nursing, doubling its size, launching a PhD program, and envisioning a new building, which would become the Nursing and Pharmacy Education Building. Courtesy Purdue University Archives and Special Collections.

to learn and practice APGAR assessments. This interactive software was partnered with Kirkpatrick's Gestational Age program, which taught students how to assess a baby's growth and development in the womb between conception and birth. Students could self-quiz, practice scoring, and receive feedback using the computer-based program, a strategy that was pioneering for the time. The CD-ROM garnered Kirkpatrick the 2002 Purdue University Award for Excellence in Distance Learning.

Kirkpatrick continued to analyze her innovation as part of her doctoral research. She tracked how students used the CD-ROM to determine which design features were used most and how it influenced their learning.[15] Kirkpatrick received her PhD in education with an emphasis in instructional design and educational technology in 2007 and the following year received the Outstanding Dissertation Award for Nursing Education from the Midwestern Nursing Research Society. Her findings were disseminated at an international conference and in nursing literature.

In the early 2000s, Kirkpatrick served as the content expert for the instructional design of a multimedia, interactive program on physiology related to labor and delivery. She collaborated with Linda Caputi from the College of DuPage in Glen Ellyn, Illinois. The series was called PhysWhiz, a play on the word "physiology." PhysWhiz II: Labor and Delivery received both a national and international award from Sigma Theta Tau, International, the nursing honorary society.[16]

Following a national search, in 2009 Kirkpatrick was named head of Purdue's School of Nursing and associate dean in the College of Pharmacy, Nursing, and Health Sciences. The following year, the freshman nursing class had the highest SAT scores of any major at Purdue, and the next year, the school received a record 1,100 applications.[17]

Around this time, the US health care system was undergoing rapid change. Groundbreaking publications pointed to key skills that nurses needed to move the profession forward to promote the health of the nation. Kirkpatrick led faculty through strategic planning for the future of nursing, including a major curricular revision of the undergraduate program.

Quality improvement and safety outcomes became paramount in health care. Employers wanted nurses with a fundamental understanding of systems, quality, and safety. In 2011, Kirkpatrick hired Sara McComb, an engineer, to hold a joint faculty appointment between Nursing and the School of Industrial Engineering.[18] She conducted research on team communication, cognition, and collaboration on interactions, such as that between physicians and nurses.[19]

McComb also taught Lean Six Sigma principles to students seeking a doctor of nursing practice (DNP) degree. Customarily thought of as a method for the business and industrial world, the Lean Six Sigma method aims to reduce waste with the goal of quality control. By paying careful attention to how waste affects production processes (and vice versa), leaders can take significant strides toward optimizing their operations. McComb's teachings spanned the breadth of situations nurses encounter, such as improving efficiency of a hospital discharge process, defining problems with appointment scheduling, or evaluating a nurse's daily processes for efficiency and productivity.

Many of Purdue's Nursing faculty had not received formal training in quality improvement techniques, so Kirkpatrick sponsored a core of ten professors to complete Yellow Belt Lean training, the most complete certification package available to help understand and apply the fundamentals of the Lean Six Sigma methodology. Faculty and graduate students published numerous articles on how Purdue adapted engineering principles to a nurse's role. This all led to the school's recognition as a National League for Nursing Center of Excellence.

In 2014, Purdue's School of Nursing celebrated its fiftieth anniversary. Lyles-Porter Hall opened that year at the corner of Harrison and University streets, and the Nursing Center for Family Health relocated there from Johnson Hall. The practice clinics of Nursing, Speech Language Hearing Sciences, Psychology, IU Medicine, Health and Kinesiology, Nutrition Science, and Psychological Science were now gathered under one roof. Students learned to work together as a team with the same patient across disciplines.[20]

Under Kirkpatrick's leadership, the School of Nursing became a part of the Indiana Center for Nursing (ICN), an organization that strives to ensure the state generates highly qualified nurses to meet the health care needs of Indiana's people. Kirkpatrick was on the inaugural ICN Board of Directors and served as president.[21]

In 2016, only 1 percent of all nurses held a PhD, and the demand for nursing scientists, executives, and faculty outpaced the supply.[22] A growing faculty shortage spawned the 2017 launching of Purdue's doctor of philosophy in nursing degree, the second PhD program in nursing in Indiana. The program helped meet the national goal to double the number of nurses who hold a doctorate by 2020.

Against the backdrop of a statewide nursing shortage and a pool of qualified applicants that were annually turned away, Kirkpatrick and the faculty made a proposal to then Purdue President Mitch Daniels to double the size of the undergraduate program from about 100 students per year to 200 by 2017.[23] The project was funded, given the green light, and in 2019 the school was on its way to an enrollment of 1,000 scholars.[24]

During Kirkpatrick's tenure, a new health clinic was established in Wolcott, Indiana, and the Family Health Clinic of Monon celebrated the opening of a new building. The School of Nursing also responded to the local community's need for mental health care. The Mental Healthcare Forum of Tippecanoe County approached Kirkpatrick and asked if the school would open a program for psychiatric mental health nurse practitioners. Today, the Psychiatric Mental Health Nurse Practitioners curriculum offers multiple tracks.

Before Kirkpatrick retired in 2018, she worked on a plan for a new Nursing building that would be shared by the College of Pharmacy.[25] Her foresight would come to fruition in the Nursing and Pharmacy Education Building at the corner of Mitch Daniels Boulevard and Russell Street.

Kirkpatrick's journey was monumental for herself and for Purdue. She metamorphosed from a hospital candy striper and walking campus as an undergraduate, to becoming a department head and innovative researcher. She increased enrollment and launched the PhD program. Kirkpatrick strengthened Nursing's foundation, priming it to better lives within the ever-shifting health care landscape.

27
HISTORIC TREKS IN SPEECH AND HEARING

RACHEL E. STARK, EXPEDITION IN BABY SOUNDS

Sixty years after mountaineer and former Purdue Latin Professor Annie Smith Peck climbed to the summit of the Matterhorn in the Swiss Alps in 1895, Dr. Rachel Elizabeth "Betty" Stark was a member of the first women's Himalayan climbing expedition. Later, she moved mountains in the scientific understanding of a baby's babbling as a Purdue researcher. The Scottish-born Stark came to Purdue in 1987 to become head of the Department of Audiology and Speech Sciences. She arrived with a portfolio of experiences as impressively woven as a tartan plaid.

Born September 17, 1923, Stark earned degrees from Jordanhill College of Education of Glasgow, Glasgow's School of Speech Therapy, and the Royal Academy of Music of London. She was a speech therapist in the public school system and worked for a hospital in Scotland before coming to the United States in 1962 to pursue graduate studies. She arrived in America shortly after she climbed the Himalayas.

In spring 1955, Stark, age thirty-one, was a member of the first team of women to climb the Himalayas in Nepal. Monica Jackson, Evelyn Camrass, and Rachel Elizabeth Stark, all mountaineers from the UK, climbed a range of wild and unexplored crests perched on the border between Nepal and Tibet and made the

Dr. Rachel "Betty" Stark (*center*), shown here in 1955 with Monica Jackson (*left*) and Evelyn Camrass (*right*), were the first team of women to climb the Himalayas in Nepal. Later, as a researcher, Stark determined for the first time that a baby's sounds are an important precursor to language and created the first coding system for describing babies' sounds. Courtesy Ladies Scottish Climbing Club.

first ascent of a twenty-two-thousand-foot peak. They named the peak Gyalgen after Mingma Gyalgen, their lead Sherpa.[1]

The climb took a little more than two months. The women encountered storms, forest fires, drunken Sherpas, and problems of finding privacy on a glacier. Stark and Jackson wrote of the women's expedition in a 1956 book published in Britain titled *Tents in the Clouds*.[2]

Stark first met Dr. Max Steer, founder of what is today Purdue's Department of Speech, Language, and Hearing Sciences, at a meeting in London. "I told him of my interest in going to the states," she said, "but that I didn't think this was feasible for me. He said, 'Nonsense. You can get a graduate assistantship.'"

Stark never forgot what Steer said as she earned a master's degree from Northwestern University, then returned to Scotland to begin a new career. She soon realized that opportunities were much greater in the United States, so she headed back to earn a PhD in communication disorders at the University of Oklahoma Medical Center in 1965.[3]

With her doctorate in hand, Stark became a research scientist and professor in the Department of Neurology at the Johns Hopkins School of Medicine with a joint appointment in the Department of Psychiatry. Later, she became director of the Divisions of Communication Sciences and Disorders at the John F. Kennedy Institute for Handicapped Children of Baltimore where she became internationally known for her pioneering research on how infants learn to talk.

She worked with visual displays of speech to teach deaf children and used a device invented at Bell Telephone that produced a visual pattern on a screen when one spoke into a microphone. "I wasn't enthusiastic about the device," she recalled. "But to my surprise, the display worked with deaf children, and for quite a while I worked with school-age deaf youngsters and then very young ones."

Stark believed that if she was going to teach speech, it was important to find out how babies begin to talk; however, she discovered that it was an arduous undertaking. She said:

> There was no information on this [how babies talk], and when I began to work on it, I learned this was probably because the research is enormously difficult. Sound patterns in infants are different from that of adults because the vocal tract of a baby, that is, from the larynx—or voice box—to the lips, is similar to the nonhuman primate.
>
> A newborn infant's tongue is huge compared with the inside of its mouth. A baby has not enough control for talking either. What happens is that the voice box moves downward with growth and the bones of the face make the mouth bigger. The process takes about 4½ years or even a little longer and changes the fastest in the first year of life.[4]

Before Stark's research, it was thought that a baby's babbling was unrelated to language development. But Stark determined that a baby's sounds are an important precursor to language. She created the first coding system for describing sounds that babies make, their transition from sounds to babbling and then to first words.[5] She discovered that some sounds, notably the consonants, occurred in "quantum leaps" at certain intervals, while others, such as the vowels, developed along a steady, gradual curve.[6]

Stark was named head of Purdue's Department of Audiology and Speech Sciences in 1987 and brought with her a seven-year research grant, the prestigious Javits Neuro-Science Award from the National Institutes of Health. In those seven years, she procured more than $2,500,000 in external funding and singlehandedly elevated the Department of Audiology and Speech Sciences to a higher level.[7]

"My research project is concerned with children with various types of language impairments," she said. "They are within the normal range in intelligence but cannot express themselves and sometimes cannot understand what's said to them. These children have low self-esteem and a great deal of difficulty educationally, emotionally, and socially. The causes are not well understood. I'm going to be investigating some patterns of impairment hoping to understand why they are in this situation."

When she was interviewed about her new position from her office stacked with boxes in the basement of Heavilon Hall (demolished in 2024), Stark said that she identified two very challenging areas in the department: space and funding. "In our field and across the country, there's been a falling off in number of students applying," she said. "That's primarily because AUS is a woman's field [particularly in speech pathology], and a lot more opportunities have recently opened up for women in other fields."[8]

Stark trained doctoral students and postdoctoral researchers to work with severely hearing-impaired, deaf children and adolescents beginning in 1989 through a grant by the US Department of Education's Office of Special Education and Rehabilitative Services. Stark said, "Many [deaf] children communicate by means of sign language, but for those who are not children of deaf parents, and thus don't become native signers, there is disagreement about what form of sign language they should be taught."

The project enabled Purdue students to become familiar with new technology available for training speech production. At the time, many hearing-impaired children did not speak well enough to be understood, and few learned to read beyond the fifth-grade level.[9] Students worked with specialists at the Indiana School for the Deaf, the Indiana University Medical Center, the Center for Childhood Deafness of the Boys Town Institute in Nebraska, and the program for hearing-impaired children in Purdue's Department of Audiology and Speech Sciences.

During Stark's headship, the Department of Audiology and Speech Sciences received a grant from Psi Iota Xi sorority to produce a live, interactive television series on speech, language, and hearing disorders. Psi Iota Xi is a national philanthropic organization that assists the communicatively impaired. In a time before the internet, the series was telecast throughout Indiana to twenty-six viewing sites, including hospitals and universities, equipped with talk-back units, enabling viewers to interact with presenters.[10]

Stark retired in 1994 and was named professor emeritus. In 2000, *Tents in the Clouds* was published for the first time in the United States, nearly half a century after it was originally published in Britain. Stark passed away the following year at age seventy-six.

After their historic mountain trek, Stark and her co-author wrote, "The days of strenuous endeavor we spent on the high ridges, glaciers and snowfields of the Jugal ... will remain forever in our memories as not only the happiest, but also, strangely enough, the most serene and peaceful days of our lives."[11]

MACALYNE FRISTOE AND HER REVOLUTIONARY ARTICULATION TEST

After Barbara Solomon heard the renowned Macalyne Watkins Fristoe speak at a convention of the New York State Speech-Language-Hearing Association in 1978, she approached the tall, dark-haired Fristoe and began what became a life-changing conversation. "You don't know me," Solomon said. "But I saw there is a position open at Purdue University as clinic coordinator, and I'm thinking of applying."[12] At the time, Solomon was the speech-language coordinator at Syracuse University.

Fristoe was the graduate program director in Purdue's Audiology and Speech Sciences Department. For nearly half of her twenty-year tenure at Purdue, her office was in the decrepit ground floor of Heavilon Hall (torn down in 2024). "Tell me about yourself," Fristoe said to the young Solomon. After the two professors, about twenty years apart in age, chatted, Fristoe encouraged Solomon to apply for the position of clinic coordinator for the Purdue Speech Clinic.

In the 1960s, Fristoe had worked with Professor Ronald Goldman at Vanderbilt University on research that would place her as a legend in her own time in the speech-language-hearing world with her creation of the Goldman-Fristoe Test of Articulation (GFTA). Fristoe conducted extensive research and created a filmstrip in the early years of the work, using her natural artistic talents to draw by hand images that appealed to children. The GFTA is a test that checks how well a child can say different speech sounds. It helps speech therapists determine if a child has trouble with certain sounds and needs extra help. The GFTA continues to be the most popular tool to examine a child's ability to pronounce different speech sounds and diagnose disorders that can inhibit a child's articulation and intelligibility.

"Macalyne was an amazing researcher, and the Goldman-Fristoe Test of Articulation is the number one articulation speech-sound test in our profession," Solomon said years later. "She has three editions, and it has been translated into Spanish. A number of people have researched the test and said how absolutely phenomenal it is. But the story was that she did most of the work to develop the test. In those days women wound up taking a second seat, so to speak. So when the test was developed, although it should have probably been referred to as the Fristoe-Goldman Test, it wound up being the Goldman-Fristoe."[13]

Born March 14, 1931, in Nashville, Tennessee, Fristoe received her bachelor's degree, cum laude, from Vanderbilt University in 1953 and then earned her master's and PhD degrees there. She served on the faculty of Vanderbilt's Departments of Psychology and Audiology and Speech as a speech pathologist. Later, she worked at the University of Alabama-Birmingham as director of the language intervention center and assistant professor of bio communication.[14] During this time, she conducted most of the research for the test for which Professor Ronald Goldman took top billing.[15]

Fristoe recalled, "I took the position at Birmingham because I had just ended a very difficult marriage, and jobs were sparse at that time, plus I had two young kids to raise. Luckily I ended up with a project that was very helpful to the field of communication disorders and helped me to be highly regarded, leading to publications and invitations to give talks at many locations all over the United States, which brought glory to the Birmingham program and led to my being called to Purdue to be the speech clinic director."

The GFTA was initially created as the Film Strip Articulation Test in the mid-1960s when Fristoe was coordinator of Speech Pathology Services at the Bill Wilkerson Hearing and Speech Center at Vanderbilt. Goldman was assistant professor of Speech Pathology there.

In 1969 the GFTA was published as a notebook-sized kit that could be opened and displayed on a table like an easel. In the beginning, Fristoe hand drew the thirty-five pictures, first in black and white and later in color, depicting objects familiar to children—a chair, girl, boy, pear, and a carnival, for example—for children to verbally identify and reveal their articulation capabilities.[16] She continued to update the test with the most recent GFTA-3 published in 2015 when she was eighty-four.[17] Today, the GFTA is administered on portable electronic devices.

When investigation for the GFTA began as a filmstrip in the mid-1960s, Fristoe gave talks about her research at meetings of the American Speech and Hearing Association, describing the advantages:

> We have found that this test takes significantly less time to provide the same amount of information that is obtained from a longer test, . . . and we also were able to obtain significantly more spontaneous speech samples using the Film Strip Test. Our research has shown that the high interest value stimulated by this test, plus its relatively short period of administration enables the examiner to get much more information about the articulatory skills of immature, retarded,[18] and brain damaged as well as normal children. For the first time, we have been able to complete an articulation inventory on some children who would not attend to any other type of articulation test. By testing more than one speech sound per word the examiner is able to test all speech sounds in a period of time comparable to that usually taken by screening tests of articulation.[19]

The Film Strip Articulation Test was distributed by the Vanderbilt Bill Wilkerson Hearing and Speech Center as a kit with fifty scoring sheets for $5.00.[20] The rear projection filmstrip viewer was selected as the best type of equipment for administering the test because it was quiet and portable.[21] Later, Fristoe created a slideshow, and her own son appeared in the photos she took to use for the test. Years later, her granddaughters would be test takers for updates of the GFTA.

Of the various methods available for assessing young children, the "picture test" appeared to be the most advantageous because the tester could obtain a spontaneous response that was more likely to resemble conversational speech sounds. Seventy-two total sounds could be tested.[22]

At the time, the Hejna Developmental Articulation Test was in popular use by clinicians, and Fristoe and Goldman determined the Film Strip Articulation Test was superior regarding time necessary to administer and the number of desired, spontaneous responses produced. Nearly all of the children tested preferred the filmstrip method. It worked particularly well for those with cerebral palsy or cognitive challenges. Clinicians found that hyperactivity was reduced and attention span increased with the filmstrip test.[23]

In the 1960s, Dr. Macalyne Fristoe, shown here in the 1970s, conducted research that placed her as a legend in her own time in the speech-language-hearing world with her creation of the Goldman-Fristoe Test of Articulation (GFTA) still used today. Courtesy Andrew Fristoe.

At age thirty-six and a single mother of two sons ages three and six (Andrew, the younger, being the original GFTA test taker), Fristoe decided to devote full time to earning a master's degree in psychology. She had known she wanted to be a psychologist since she was twelve. Fristoe said, "I could have stayed where I was forever, but I felt I had more capability than I was using."[24] She combined her background in speech and psychology in her work at Purdue beginning in 1976, specializing in language disorders, studying alternative communication systems for the mentally and physically handicapped.

Also that year, Fristoe received the Women in Research Award from the Kennedy Institute, Johns Hopkins University.[25] In the spring, she participated on a panel with three other female scientists for a program titled "Women in Research" sponsored by the Kennedy Institute for Handicapped Children at the Maryland Academy of Sciences in Baltimore. The moderator was famed feminist Gloria Steinem, cofounder and then editor of *Ms.* Magazine. A newspaper story about the program quoted Fristoe, who said, "I always thought there was something wrong with me that I was just not getting treated seriously. I finally saw that what was the matter was that I was female."[26]

Dr. Macalyne Fristoe, shown here in 1988, did most of the research at Vanderbilt University to create the renowned Goldman-Fristoe Test of Articulation (GFTA) still used today. However, Professor Ronald Goldman received top billing in the naming of the test. Courtesy Purdue University Archives and Special Collections.

Fristoe retired from Purdue as professor emerita in 1996. In November 2016 at their annual convention in Philadelphia, the American Speech-Language-Hearing Association bestowed on Fristoe, age eighty-five, the organization's highest distinction, the Honors of the Association Award for lifetime achievement. Colleagues and young professionals in the speech, language, and hearing sciences gathered around Fristoe as if she were a rock star, the legend who had developed the Goldman-Fristoe Test of Articulation.[27] There to fete her former colleague and friend who had encouraged her to apply for a Purdue position two decades earlier was Barbara Solomon.

Looking back on her career, Fristoe said, "I specialized in developing communication systems for persons of all ages who were unable to speak, whether they were autistic, cerebral palsied, alaryngeal or due to other causes, and I loved the opportunities that I had, and our clients, and the students we had who came from all over the world."

BARBARA SOLOMON, GIVING PEOPLE THEIR VOICE

When Barbara Solomon first met Macalyne Fristoe and inquired about a Purdue position in 1978, Solomon was the speech-language coordinator at Syracuse

University. A native of New York City who grew up in Brooklyn, Solomon met people who smoked and consequently had various voice-related medical problems.

She knew what she wanted to study immediately upon taking an introductory undergraduate course at City College of New York where she obtained her bachelor's and master's degrees. "Once I took coursework in speech-language pathology, I knew that voice disorders would be what I wanted to specialize in, and the whole area of medical speech-language pathology was intriguing," Solomon said.[28]

Solomon, age twenty-nine, flew into the Purdue University Airport in a small plane to be interviewed for the position of speech clinic coordinator. The diminutive aircraft and Midwest landing strip were a bit of cultural shock for the New Yorker. Bernd Weinberg, who was head of the department then named Audiology and Speech Sciences (AUS), picked Solomon up and took her to lunch. Bernd's research area was voice disorders and laryngectomies or oral, head, and neck cancers. Solomon said, "On a napkin he drew for me the latest device that had been developed in 1978. It was a prosthesis for people who have laryngectomies, and turns out, that became one of my specializations."[29]

For more than forty years, the Brooklyn-bred Solomon served Purdue, her graduate students, and countless number of children and adults with voice disorders. She and her husband, Bruce Solomon, a professor in Purdue's Department of Statistics, raised two sons who are both Purdue graduates. She worked with eight different department heads. "One of the reasons we moved to the Midwest was the tradition and reputation of the university," Solomon said. "There are people all over the world who have voice disorders, and Purdue's name is well recognized throughout the US and worldwide."[30]

The comical Doug Noll, who served as department head for a time, became Solomon's mentor. Their offices in Heavilon Hall were neighboring, and they often walked to the Memorial Union for coffee. "The partition between our offices was about six feet tall," Solomon recalled. "Every time Doug walked by, he would look in. I'd be meeting with a student, and he would make some kind of face at me. It took so much for me not to respond."

Noll had his serious side, and he gave Solomon advice, yet, best of all, he listened. "He suggested that I look at national-level volunteer work, and I became involved in the American Speech-Language-Hearing Association [ASHA] and the Indiana Speech-Language-Hearing Association [ISHA] for about thirty years," Solomon said. "I don't think I would have done that had it not been for him. I was selected as a Fellow of the ASHA and received Honors of the ISHA.

Doug was this incredible mentor who encouraged me to do more, to give back to the profession. He was such a kind, caring person. He would always stand beside you."[31]

Solomon was also a close friend with her colleague Robert Ringel who in 1970 became head of the Department of Audiology and Speech Sciences and later became the dean of the School of Humanities, Social Science and Education and eventually executive vice president for Academic Affairs. "Bob and I worked very closely together," Solomon said. "He was from Brooklyn, as I am, and we shared the same area of specialization. We taught the voice course together and talked on a regular basis throughout our careers." Ringel's final research work before he died in 2006 was to help develop regeneration of laryngeal tissue to repair the vocal folds that showed early signs of success in animals.[32]

Solomon became director of what was then called the M. D. Steer Speech-Language Clinic in 1989 and stepped down twenty years later to help coordinate and develop the medical speech language pathology program. In 2018 Solomon said, "Today our students receive state of the art training with other medical professionals at Lafayette Otolaryngology Associates, IU Health Arnett Hospital, and others. One of the most spectacular programs we have is the swallowing services we provide to patients. We go to the hospital and conduct swallow studies. Students evaluate patients with specialized equipment that can visualize the swallow from beginning to end and determine if a person has a swallowing problem."[33]

Solomon and her graduate students worked on and off campus to provide services, seeing five to ten patients per week. They worked with those who had voice and swallowing challenges, primarily adults with Parkinson's disease and head and neck cancer. Elite athletes who had respiratory problems while competing had vocal cord dysfunction. Solomon worked closely with the athletic trainers in the Department of Health and Kinesiology and local ear, nose, and throat physicians to provide respiratory therapy.

Other patients had vocal nodules from vocal misuse (screaming too much) or had spasmodic dysphonia, a neurological disorder that causes the voice muscles to experience sudden involuntary movements or spasms, making a person's speech difficult to understand. Solomon also helped transgender individuals who were transitioning from male to female or female to male and wanted a voice consistent with their gender. She worked with the Counseling and Psychological Services (CAPS) program at Purdue to help transgendered people who sought services there.[34]

Beginning in 1978 and for more than forty years, Dr. Barbara Solomon, shown here in 1994, helped countless number of children and adults with voice disorders. Solomon was also the director of Purdue's M. D. Steer Speech-Language Clinic for twenty years. Courtesy Purdue University Archives and Special Collections.

Solomon retired from Purdue in 2020. Looking back, she said, "I was very lucky to work in a department that is so creative and innovative. The quality of our students is amazing. I could not have done what I do without the students challenging me and asking questions, coming up with new ideas, and providing the best kind of care for our patients."[35]

28

FORGING NEW FIELDS OF STUDY

As the twentieth century saw more and more women faculty in STEM at Purdue, two women worked to make strides in developing the emerging field of rhetoric and composition in the English Department. Muriel Harris founded the now world-famous Writing Lab at Purdue in 1975, and Janice Lauer came to Purdue in 1981 to develop a doctoral program in the field of rhetoric and composition. Both women were strong advocates for the study of writing and how such study could improve the writing skills of Purdue students.

Rhetoric and composition is the field of study that is focused on how writing can persuade others. While it is often connected to university-level first-year writing instruction, rhetoric and composition is also closely connected to technical and professional writing, upper-level writing classes, and second language instruction. What unites all of them is that writing can serve as a foundational communicative medium for sharing information and persuading others. Muriel Harris and Janice Lauer both shared this belief in writing as an influential medium for making change in the world.

The field emerged in the mid-twentieth century with the 1949 founding of the Conference on College Composition and Communication (CCCC), an offshoot of the National Council of Teachers of English.[1] The conference primarily focused on the ins and outs of first-year writing instruction but also advocated for the need for research in this area. For many years, the conference and the resulting journal, *College Composition and Communication*, focused on very practical strategies and approaches to the teaching of writing. Luminaries in the field such as Lauer in the 1970s ushered in research on rhetoric and the teaching of writing, and Harris pushed the field outward toward other ways that faculty could engage with students about writing.

MURIEL HARRIS

Muriel "Mickey" Harris came to Purdue in the 1970s with her husband, Samuel, who had accepted an offer to join the faculty in Physics. Harris had followed him as he pursued a postdoc at Columbia University and embarked on her own journey there to earn a PhD in English Renaissance literature. Like many women at the time, Harris again followed her husband to Purdue when he was hired as an assistant professor. She explains, "I had to do a dissertation in absentia when we came here. For the first couple of years, when we had little kids, I wanted to stay home and be with them. And when our little one hit kindergarten, I went over to see what I could do at Purdue."[2]

Harris had no prior experience teaching. She had graduate fellowships at the University of Illinois and then at Columbia, so her first introduction to teaching writing was at Purdue. "I never taught writing," she recalled in 2024. "I didn't know how to talk to each writer. I couldn't believe that they all needed the same thing. The department at that time had an assistant director, who was in charge of assigning the classes graduate students and adjuncts would teach. He handed me a textbook and said, 'Your mailbox is over there. Go.' And that was my introduction to teaching writing."[3]

Around the mid-1970s, there were rumblings at Purdue about the need for tutoring students in writing. *Time* magazine and other outlets had published articles claiming that "Johnny can't write!" Amid this public outcry, the English Department decided to offer tutorials on writing, originally staffed by a graduate student. Harris volunteered to help out, thinking, *Okay, I could sit in there and help because our son, the younger one, was old enough to go to kindergarten.*[4]

Harris and the grad student sat in a room on the fourth floor of Heavilon Hall (torn down in 2024), but no one came and nothing happened. The grad student and Harris wrote a proposal to start a tutoring center more integrated into the department. Members of the English Department agreed to try more tutoring and offered a space for writing in the building for a year on an experimental

Dr. Muriel Harris taught writing at Purdue beginning in the 1970s and humbly began what would become the Online Writing Lab (OWL), today a renowned resource on writing used by people around the world. Courtesy Purdue University Archives and Special Collections.

basis. Harris volunteered to run the tutoring space that would eventually become the Writing Lab.

Starting a new venture like the Writing Lab was challenging. What would it be like? Who would staff it? Who would come and why? During the summer, Harris was joined by two graduate students who had volunteered to help. Harris said that together they spent the summer of 1975 contemplating these quandaries: "What is the writing lab? What is the writing center? What do we do? Should it be one-to-one? How long should sessions be? What do we talk about? The larger question was what is our role in the interaction?"[5] They developed a plan for the writing lab. Harris explained, "We never expected to be paid during our summer of planning, and we weren't. But for the fall semester 1975, they gave us a room, which had been a grad student office, 226 in Heavilon, and . . . we were given two cubicles and a couple of tables and began to advertise it."[6]

But what to call this new venture? Harris's experience with her husband, a scientist, gave her some perspective. She looked around Purdue and noticed that all of the centers were *research* centers. At that time, she explained, there were fifty to seventy centers for research on various topics. "I was comfortable with the scientists [I knew] through my husband," she recalled. "The labs at Purdue were places where kids came in and broke glass tubes or slides or were having difficulties following the instructions, and asked for help from grad students who were usually in charge, and said, 'How do I do this?' It was a place for people to talk and try out and go back and do it again, guided by someone trained to assist, who could offer feedback and suggestions, and explain when the student needed added information. So I called it the Writing Lab, and we got our space. As the field of writing center studies evolved, the preferred term became 'writing center,' but we kept our original name."[7]

They soon discovered that one-to-one tutoring was not enough; they needed resources that students could take with them after their sessions. Harris said, "We should have handouts, because students love when you give them a piece of paper and they've got something to carry away." She and the two graduate students began to generate handouts on the common problems they were encountering in student writing: "How do you explain how a paragraph works? How do you suggest strategies for a good introduction? How do you offer suggestions for how to think about audience? We just sat around drumming up things that needed help and spent time writing handouts."[8] Over time, the three worked to refine the handouts based on what worked and what didn't work with students.

While the in-person Writing Lab became an important resource for Purdue, most people came to know it through the online version: The Online Writing Lab (OWL) essentially started from the exigencies of student life. "We couldn't stay open on the weekends because the building had no security," she said. "Since a good chunk of students write their papers on Sunday night to turn in on Monday, we didn't know what to do to make all those handouts accessible."[9]

After finding a way to get the handouts online through email—the only way available at that time—the OWL was born. Later, Dave Taylor, who had followed his girlfriend to Purdue, wandered into the lab. According to Harris, he was a techie who came from Hewlett-Packard where he had developed the widely used text-based ELM email program in 1986. (The name ELM originated from the phrase electronic mail.)

Taylor walked into the Writing Lab and asked Harris if she could hire him for anything. She said, "We have this one lone computer, but we don't know how to use it very well, and we've got all these handouts available only as email." Taylor replied, "Well, we could put all the handouts online though a browser." Taylor came in when web browsers first became available, and he said he could get the handouts on a website. The handouts had been shared via email and Gopher, an early internet directory program, but not on a static website. Taylor helped put the handouts into a web browser and the OWL was reborn as a website in 1994.[10]

The OWL became well known, but not from use by Purdue students, as many of them did not yet have computers or did not use email. Thus, Purdue students largely ignored the OWL, and the hits that the website received came from outside of Purdue. Soon, popular publications like *PC Magazine* and others started giving the OWL awards, but today Harris downplays those accolades, saying they were largely overhyped. As the OWL grew, so did demands on the technology. Harris was nervous.

The OWL was getting so much internet traffic that it needed more server space, but she didn't know where to go to help fund more servers. One day, she ran into the dean of Liberal Arts, English professor Margaret Rowe. Harris explained the situation to Dean Rowe, who gave her the funds she needed, replying: "I don't know what you're doing, but I believe in you."[11] If anyone is to be thanked for the OWL, Harris says, it's Margaret Rowe who provided the funding they needed to meet the demand.

Harris retired in 2003 and downplays her role in the success of the Writing Lab. She believes that she "happened to be at the right place at the right time where she learned that the one-to-one interaction with writers is an integral part of helping writers develop their writing skills. That two-person conversation is so powerfully effective because it can be tailored to fit the unique needs and goals of each unique writer."

Like her colleague Janice Lauer, Harris helped to create an entire field of studies for writing centers. When she first started the Writing Lab, there were very few like it at other universities. At one of her first conferences where she presented on the Writing Lab, she and the other panel participants expected one or two audience members, but the room overflowed with people lined up in the hallway to hear about what was happening at Purdue.

Out of that session came the Writing Lab listserv, WCenter (hosted by Texas Tech University), where writing center directors could share information, and Harris initiated the first journal in the field of writing center scholarship, *WLN: A Journal of Writing Center Scholarship* (https://wac.colostate.edu/wln). The journal is a hub for scholarship on writing centers and is now available to all on the WAC Clearinghouse website as one of the Clearinghouse's collection of open access books and journals in the field of rhetoric and composition.

JANICE LAUER

Unlike Muriel Harris who "fell into" writing center work, Janice Lauer used her drive and ambition to help create the field we now know as rhetoric and composition. Janice Marie Lauer was born in Detroit, Michigan, on November 18, 1932, and adopted by Vincent and Viola Lauer. Lauer was always quick and clear to say she was adopted, making it part of her personal identity. She grew up with a great love of her father.

Lauer entered the order of Servants of the Immaculate Heart of Mary (IHM), a Catholic religious community, and became Sister Janice Marie Lauer. She attended, then later taught, at Marygrove College. She went to Saint Louis University for her master's degree where she studied with Father Walter J. Ong, Society of Jesus, who was a scholar of rhetoric. Lauer obtained her EdD at the University of Michigan. Because there was no field of rhetoric and composition proper at the time, she created her own plan of study, working with her committee to write a dissertation on rhetorical invention. She credits her father for instilling in her a love of rhetoric, ending the acknowledgment of her dissertation with: "I owe my long standing appreciation for rhetoric to my father, Vincent Lauer, whose writing, like his life, was always a source of delight and admiration" (p. iv). Her sisters in the IHM order helped type and edit her dissertation.[12]

After her dissertation defense in 1968, Lauer taught at the University of Detroit, where she developed a long-running National Endowment for the Humanities (NEH) summer seminar in rhetoric beginning in 1976, inviting famous scholars to teach this emerging field called Rhetoric and Composition to new scholars who came to learn. She developed the seminar based on the need for education in rhetoric for those in the Midwest who could not travel to study the field. She explained:

> I got a phone call from Barbara Hamilton, who taught at Oakland University in Michigan, and I was at the University of Detroit. And she said she wanted to study rhetoric, and she wanted to go to USC where Ross Winterowd was starting the first rhetoric program. And Ross was a friend of mine. So anyway, she said she couldn't because of ... raising her family. So I said I would look into it. And I thought, "What is there in the Midwest for people to learn about rhetoric?" Which was nothing. So I got the idea of having a rhetoric seminar in the summer that would [provide] graduate credit [with] faculty [who] were beginning to do good research in rhetoric ... to teach, and I asked Ross Winterowd to direct with me.[13]

The university approved the idea of students in the seminar earning credit and started advertising the NEH summer seminar. "Ross and I wondered if we would have anybody," Lauer recalled, "especially in Detroit for two weeks, and we had sixty-one people."[14] Many foundational scholars in the field attended Lauer's NEH summer seminars, including Victor Vitanza, Sharon Crowley, and others who would quickly become leaders in the field. Likewise, Lauer invited scholars such as Walter Ong, Richard Young, Ross Winterowd, and others to teach in the summer seminar. She left the IHM order during her time at the University of Detroit.

In 1980, Purdue hired Lauer away from the University of Detroit to develop a graduate program in Rhetoric and Composition. As she acknowledged, "Starting a program is no small task."[15] She hit the ground running, developing a series of five core courses and starting to recruit graduate students, first from within the department and then nationwide. Until this point, the department had been completely centered on the study of literature. Lauer developed a curriculum grounded in history and methodology, which drew from other fields and was unheard of at the time. She developed a yearlong mentoring course for new teaching assistants in which she carefully instructed them in the art of rhetoric. When alumni are asked why there was no official graduate course in rhetorical theory, they explain that there was no need because Lauer taught it to them during her mentoring course that trained new graduate students how to teach writing.

As Lauer built the program, she brought in faculty who would become well-known scholars in the field: James A. Berlin, Patricia Sullivan, Irwin Weiser, Shirley Rose, Thomas Rickert, and more. Patricia Sullivan would take over directing the graduate program from Lauer when she retired in 2002. Lauer also brought the NEH summer seminar in rhetoric to West Lafayette, where it was offered until 1989.

In 1993, Lauer conceived of and founded the Doctoral Consortium of Programs in Rhetoric and Composition, hoping for a community of faculty who were also directing doctoral programs and with whom she could discuss the issues involved in graduate education. The importance of the consortium cannot be underestimated; as part of its work, the group developed a category for rhetoric and composition in the Dissertation Abstracts International (DAI) and had rhetoric and composition programs represented in the National Center for Educational Statistics, in the Survey of Earned Doctorates, and on the National Research Council's Emerging Field list.[16] Lauer retired as the Reece McGee Distinguished Professor of English at Purdue University in 2003 after directing fifty-seven dissertations.

One of Lauer's pedagogical hallmarks in the graduate program was the "WO" or Writing Opportunity prompts. She assigned these prompts to be written in

In 1980, Purdue hired Dr. Janice Lauer away from the University of Detroit to develop a graduate program in Rhetoric and Composition. She founded the Doctoral Consortium of Programs in Rhetoric and Composition in 1993. Courtesy Purdue University Archives and Special Collections.

class, on the spot, as a way to quiz graduate students on their knowledge. Students, of course, saw them as "woes" to be endured, but they really taught students how to understand the emerging field. Janice would often ask them to write on how a particular scholar would respond to another scholar who was a polar opposite, or how Ann Bertoff,[17] with whom she herself had several famous scholarly exchanges in journals, would respond to her. "How would Lauer respond to . . ." was one of the prompts she offered.

During her career, Lauer received many accolades, including the 1998 CCCC Exemplar Award, the highest award in the field of Rhetoric and Composition. She wrote two textbooks, coedited the composition entries to *The Encyclopedia of English Studies and Language Arts*, and published on invention, persuasive writing, classical rhetoric, and composition studies as a discipline. She chaired the College Section of the National Council of Teachers of English (NCTE) and served on the executive committees of CCCC, the MLA Group on the History and Theory of Rhetoric, and the Rhetoric Society of America.[18] She also served as a founding member of the Rhetoric Society of America.[19]

In her personal life, Lauer was married to David Hutton in 1984 until his untimely death of a brain tumor in 1999. She was known affectionately by her step-grandchildren as "Gran-Jan." In 2010, she married John Rice and together they enjoyed extensive traveling until they were no longer able because of their health. Lauer died on April 7, 2021, in West Lafayette, Indiana.[20]

Perhaps most influential to her life's work was Lauer's commitment to her Catholic faith. She was a member of St. Thomas Aquinas, the Catholic Center at Purdue where she attended Mass on a daily basis. She often offered "special intentions" during daily Mass that were in response to a happening in her department at Purdue. She was committed to the Aquinas Educational Foundation, an organization affiliated with St. Thomas Aquinas that promoted the rich intellectual tradition of the Catholic faith. After retiring, Lauer revived the foundation from dormancy and served as its president for several years. She brought several famous Catholic speakers to Purdue.

Mickey Harris and Janice Lauer knew one another but were opposite sides of a coin. Harris's work was perceived as very practical and hands on, whereas Lauer's work came across as much more theoretical. In actuality, both were creating theories of writing but from different vantage points. One of Harris's recollections bears this out: "Janice, Patty Harkin, Peg Finders, and I formed a little writing group, and we would sort of clear our papers with each other, just as a weight. And I thought if I could share some of the stuff I was writing with Janice, she might begin to understand what we do. I remember her comment about one paper. She said, 'Oh, it's much too pedagogical. It's not theoretical enough.' At that time, I was getting feedback from NCTE to whom I had sent off my book about conferencing, *Teaching One-to-One* [NCTE, 1986], and they wrote back, saying it's too theoretical. You need a lot more pedagogy up front."[21]

This memory points to an important observation: Women founders of programs at Purdue, like Harris and Lauer, were able to succeed because they could combine the practical and the theoretical. They could provide applied opportunities while also developing sophisticated theories for what they were doing. In short, Harris and Lauer were helping to build fields of study from the inside out.

29

FASHION DESIGN, HISTORIC COSTUMES, AND THE PURDUE TARTAN

NANCY STRICKLER, TAILORING THE PROGRAM

On the second floor of Matthews Hall, dress forms, tall and small, torsos in cream mounted on rolling stands, had for decades modeled the fashions created by students in the Apparel Design and Technology Program (ADT). When not in use, dozens of dress forms created a silent, artful arrangement in the laboratories where, since the first home economics classes were held there in the 1920s, students had put pen to paper to design apparel.

For nearly one hundred years, students made patterns, cut fabric on wide tables, threaded bobbins in the industrial sewing machines, and stitched fabric to fulfill dreams of becoming fashion designers. The dress forms held the stories of students making it big in the fashion industry and of professors like Nancy Strickler, the instructor who encouraged innovative thinking.

Nancy Strickler was the woman behind the dress forms, so to speak, from 1992 until she retired in May 2016. Strickler obtained her Purdue undergraduate degree in 1973 and her master's in 1977, both in Consumer and Family Sciences Education (today called Family and Consumer Sciences Education or FACS).

Her students went on to work for major fashion labels in New York, design costumes in California, establish careers at nationwide clothing retailers, or launch their own fashion lines.

Strickler began her career in Purdue's ADT program as clinical associate professor in what was the Department of Consumer Sciences and Retailing as a lecturer and was named a continuing lecturer in 1999. Her courses were lab-based as she taught varying levels of apparel design.[1] Strickler said, "We provide students with hands-on experience of apparel pattern engineering, computer-aided design, computer-aided manufacturing, and textile science. The students [were] able to develop and produce an apparel product line from concept to consumer."[2]

She also taught the history of fashion where she pulled out historical, intricately tailored garments from a climate-controlled closet to teach students about construction techniques from different time periods. Most of the historical fashions that Strickler coddled with great care were donated to the department by prominent Purdue alumni and administrators, such as the 1927 collection from Ophelia Fowler Duhme and the designer garments donated by Caroline Risk of Kirby Risk Corporation founded in Lafayette, Indiana. Risk's wedding dress was from the now defunct Steven's Department Store in Chicago. She was married at the 1933 Chicago World's Fair where she was a member of the fair's Queen's Court.[3] Colorful hats that had belonged to her friend Priscilla Hovde, wife of Purdue President Frederick Hovde, were also part of the historic costume collection.

Strickler led a number of study trips to New York City and international fashion study tours in Italy and Paris. In the summer of 2000, Strickler participated in a two-week JCPenney Professor Internship program. The program was held annually to provide academic partners a working knowledge of the current retail industry and JCPenney, specifically. She spent one week at JCPenney in Tippecanoe Mall in Lafayette, where, coincidentally, she had assisted in the store's opening in 1974. There, Strickler focused on merchandising techniques, human resource programs, technology, and store culture. She spent the following week at the JCPenney home office in Plano, Texas, where she met with senior executives and participated in a series of seminars about brand management, buying, catalog strategies, international sourcing, marketing, internet commerce, and more.[4]

When she joined the Purdue faculty in 1992, an informal fashion show had been held sporadically in the auditorium of Matthews Hall with students modeling apparel they had designed and sewn. By the time she retired, the Purdue fashion show was a spectacular annual spring event held in such venues as

Mackey Arena or the France A. Córdova Recreational Sports Center. Strickler fostered students in organizing the first fashion show in 2000 in the Purdue Memorial Union.[5] In 2008, two shows were held in Ross-Ade Pavilion attracting more than 1,300 people.[6]

Development and implementation for the show was a year-long process handled entirely by students to showcase their capstone collections they had worked on throughout the year. It was a crash course in planning, budgeting, coordination, communication, and leadership. Strickler guided the students through the process. "I try to stay out of it until we have a disaster," Strickler said in jest. "But those are the fun times, too, because I can see them figuring things out for themselves. They learn from it."[7]

Proceeds from ticket sales went to scholarships. Alumna Ann Day, co-owner of Day Furs and Luxury Outerwear in Carmel, Indiana, established an Excellence in Construction Award she presented each year during the show.[8] Students were not allowed to model their own creations. They were required to work with models so they could learn how to fit a garment to the body. "The fashion show gives students actual experience of putting on a show, from the business aspect of it to design, selecting music and staging, show order, even promotion," Strickler said. "But the biggest advantage for students is that it's a big self-esteem booster."[9]

In spring 2012, Purdue's Department of Consumer Science invited Consumer Science and Retailing students to participate in a competition to design a symbolic tartan inspired by the history and official colors of Purdue University. Strickler was one of the contest coordinators, and Christine Ladisch, then dean of the College of Health and Human Sciences, was one of the eight judges. Tartan refers to a pattern of interlocking stripes running in both the warp and weft (horizontal and vertical) of the cloth.[10]

Out of eleven entries, three were chosen for an online competition. The winning tartan was designed by Krizia Phillips, a senior majoring in apparel design and technology. Her approach was to create a tartan that combined traditional Purdue with a modern style. She said, "I incorporated the classic Purdue 'old gold' into a vivacious pattern to emphasize the spirit of Purdue."

Phillips incorporated symbolism regarding the history and legacies of Purdue in her design. The eighteen-count dark grey yarn represented the number of NCAA team sports offered at Purdue. The yarn count for the black was twenty-two to represent the number of astronauts educated at the university at the time. As a member of a sorority, Phillips made the gold yarn count to be

Two unidentified students model in the 2018 Purdue Fashion Show spearheaded by Professor Nancy Strickler. It gave students in apparel design the experience to plan, budget, and coordinate the event to showcase their capstone apparel creations. In 2008, two shows were held in Ross-Ade Pavilion attracting more than 1,300 people. Courtesy Nancy Strickler.

forty-eight to represent the number of fraternity chapters on campus. Finally, the white yarn was a twelve count to signify the year 1912 when the song "Hail Purdue" was written by alumnus James Morrison and set to music by Edward Wotawa who graduated that year.[11]

Phillips's winning tartan was verified and reviewed for originality by the Tartan Registry in Edinburgh, Scotland. The Purdue tartan was made into a scarf, key fob, pocket square, bow tie, and a necktie produced and sold online by Collegiate Tartan Apparel. Funds raised are used for scholarships for students in the Department of Consumer Science.[12]

When the College of Health and Human Sciences formed in 2010, the Department of Consumer Sciences and Retailing was renamed Consumer Science and merged into the new college. Four years later, administrators announced that the apparel and design technology major would be discontinued. Apparel design and technology became an undergraduate concentration within the retail management major rather than its own major.

The last ADT graduating class held its fashion show in April 2018. By then Nancy Strickler had retired. "I felt a great sense of pride to see how they pulled it together, knowing I wasn't involved," Strickler said. To honor Strickler, an award recognizing a fashion design student who demonstrated strong academic skills, leadership, and community service was named in her honor.

30
FAMILY FIRST

CHERYL ALTINKEMER, ANN HANCOOK, AND THE FELKER LEADERSHIP CONFERENCE FOR WOMEN AND PHILANTHROPY

Donald W. Felker became the first male dean of Purdue's School of Consumer and Family Sciences (CFS) in 1987. "Don was one of the rare people who conducted his work life and his family life in the same manner," said Cheryl Painter Altinkemer, then director of development and alumni relations in CFS. "Family always came first, so as an employee, I knew I could go to him for counsel, flexibility, and understanding when my personal life needed guidance. Knowing I had that type of support motivated me to give more in my job."[1] Later, Altinkemer became the senior associate vice president for international advancement at Purdue Research Foundation.

A native of Bower Hill, Pennsylvania, Felker and Purdue President Steven C. Beering were classmates in the prestigious Allderdice High School. Concerned that too few female faculty received mentoring to reach top administrative posts, Felker appointed a committee to select a female faculty member each year to attend a program at Bryn Mawr, a women's liberal arts college in Pennsylvania that trained women who wanted to move into higher education administration. Dr. April Mason, associate professor of foods and nutrition, received the first Bryn Mawr fellowship supported by the Donald W. and Evelyn H. Felker Endowment Fund Don established to honor his wife.[2] Later, Mason became provost and senior vice president at Kansas State University.

"What impressed me the most about the dean was his concern about women," Altinkemer said. "When he came to Purdue, the administrative group of the School only had two females. Today [1992], that number has increased to five out of nine administrators, nearly total gender equality."[3]

After Donald Felker passed away in 1992, Cheryl Painter Altinkemer, then director of development and alumni relations in the School of Consumer and Family Sciences (CFS) and Ann Hancook, associate dean for extension in CFS, wanted to honor and pay tribute to his mentorship and support of women in leadership. Felker had nurtured both Altinkemer and Hancook in their professional evolutions. So together, they planned the Felker Leadership Conference for women and philanthropy.[4]

The women interviewed department faculty to explore CFS's research on children, families, nutrition, family economics, and more. Then they brought 100 women alumni to campus to discuss societal issues and how CFS's groundbreaking research contributed to solutions to those issues.

"We went around the room with this famous question," Altinkemer recalled. "'If you had one million dollars, and knowing that Purdue and the School of Consumer and Family Sciences could solve these problems, how would you give the money?'"[5]

Lorene McCormick Burkhart, a 1956 alumna of the School of Home Economics (later CFS), sat in the audience soaking in every word. Burkhart was an entrepreneur and author who formed Burkhart Network to develop books for children and adults.

Burkhart remembered, "It was a fascinating idea because, first of all, I had never been in a meeting of all women where anyone ever suggested that there might be one million dollars available somewhere in that group of women. That was pretty flattering.... I had been giving a lot of thought to how I might be financially involved at Purdue. That really sparked my interest to start thinking about exactly how I wanted to be involved. Out of that came my thought [that] it would be a great idea to give one million dollars to something that has to do with families."[6]

During morning break, Burkhart announced to Altinkemer that she would give one million dollars to establish the Center for Families at Purdue. It was a historic moment for women and the university. There was no other entity in the United States like Purdue's Center for Families.[7]

After Burkhart made her initial large gift to establish the Center for Families, she encouraged her fellow alumni to make pledges by creating the Center for

Families Advocates. Burkhart said, "What I loved about going out and meeting with women and getting them excited about being advocates was telling them about how it feels when you realized that all of the things that we've learned to do our whole lives in our families can now be a much bigger story."[8]

"Funding the Center for Families was the foundation of everything we do," Altinkemer said. "I felt a sense of pride that we put it out there, front and center, that research on families was really what our university should be doing in order to make all other [initiatives] happen. We hear about astronauts all the time, so to put families into the university conversation was really special."[9]

The year before the Center for Families was established, Ann Hancook passed away after battling cancer. She had served Purdue's Cooperative Extension Service for twenty-three years and set the stage for the creation of the center. Yet, she did not live to see it to fruition. Many alumni gave memorial gifts to the center in Hancook's name.[10]

SUSAN KONTOS AND THE CENTER FOR FAMILIES

Susan Kontos, who had joined the Purdue faculty in 1985, was named founding director of the Center for Families in April 1994. Originally from California, Kontos received her doctorate from Iowa State University in 1980. She had served on faculties at the University of Northern Colorado and Penn State before arriving on campus. Ann Hancook, Susan Kontos, Lorene Burkhart, and Cheryl Altinkemer are considered the founding mothers of the Center for Families, which celebrated its thirtieth anniversary in 2024.[11] Each year, faculty can apply for the Kontos, Hancook, and Burkhart faculty fellowship to pursue research projects.

Kontos was one of the first researchers to take a serious look at informal family child care. Douglas Powell, who chaired the search committee that recruited Kontos from Penn State, said, "It was a form of child care that did not get anyone's attention back then. Susan wrote a wonderful monograph, *Family Day Care: Out of the Shadows into the Limelight*, on the quality of family child care by neighbors and relatives."[12]

Kontos wrote a 1992 monograph that was backed by the National Association for the Education of Young Children (NAEYC). At that time, Kontos was the associate editor and her Purdue colleague Douglas Powell was the editor of the NAEYC scholarly journal *Early Childhood Research Quarterly*.[13]

Kontos was an international authority as a top-notch researcher who investigated young children's development through the lens of their early education and care. She was committed to the well-being of children who had traditionally been disadvantaged or underrepresented. As director of Project Neighborcare from 1984 to 1993, Kontos developed systems for family caregivers to receive training with a focus on supporting care for children with special needs, particularly those with physical disabilities.

Kontos received the Hoosier Early Childhood Lifetime Achievement Award from the Indiana Association for the Education of Young Children. In 2002, Kontos codirected the first Purdue summer study abroad program specifically designed for Human Development and Family Studies held in Glasgow, Scotland.[14]

The Center for Families fulfilled Purdue's land-grant mission through research, teaching, and outreach, and it continues to be a concrete reminder that families, in all their diverse forms, are the foundation of society. In 1994, Kontos wrote:

> I envision the work of the Center to focus on improving the service families and children receive as well as the polices that influence their lives. Although the needs of all Hoosier families are of paramount importance, the special needs of families who are poor or otherwise at risk should be given priority.
>
> As director of the Center for Families, it would be my goal that Indiana state legislators would become quite familiar with the work of the Center through regular updates on the needs of Hoosier families and the impact of state and federal policies on them. A second goal would be to stimulate new and creative thinking about maximizing the well-being of all Hoosier families and to disseminate that thinking to academic colleagues as well as practitioners. Finally, a third goal would be to improve the training of professionals working with families and children.[15]

Nearly all of Kontos's visionary goals for the center were realized. The first project funded at the center was "It's My Child, Too," a parenting curriculum directed by Kontos and Powell aimed at young, unwed fathers. Five years later, the program had been instituted by schools, community centers, and detention centers in more than twenty states. It attracted the attention of judges and prosecutors. Some court systems sent young fathers to the program because they were delinquent in paying child support.[16]

Through the Hoosier Family Policy Summit, the center published the *Hoosier Family Policy Source Book* in 1994, the first in a series of resource materials summarizing Indiana demographic data and population projections through 2030. It provided population statistics that focused on the family and the economy.[17]

The year the Center for Families was founded, Kontos was diagnosed with cancer. Her daughter was five. For nine years Kontos, a single mother, valiantly struggled with her cancer as she strove to develop the center to its full potential. Kontos passed away on September 12, 2003, at age fifty-three, as the Center for Families prepared to celebrate its tenth year. The center's anniversary theme was "Sustaining Families, Supporting Children, Securing the Future," words that also described the career and legacy of Susan Kontos.

SHELLEY MACDERMID WADSWORTH SUCCEEDS KONTOS

Shelley MacDermid Wadsworth was named the second director of Purdue's Center for Families in 1996. Later, she became the founding codirector of a nationally groundbreaking initiative of the center, the Military Family Research Institute (MFRI).

From the time she was a young girl growing up in Canada, MacDermid Wadsworth had worked with children. "Children, families, and education were part of everything I did from the time that I was ten years old," MacDermid Wadsworth said. Her mother was a nurse who worked nights, and her father was a tradesman who became an entrepreneur. MacDermid Wadsworth's upbringing instilled a foundation of how running a small business and shift work affects workers and their families. She went on to study the meshing of those experiences.

MacDermid Wadsworth double-majored in family studies and child studies as an undergraduate at the University of Guelph in Ontario. There was no PhD program in family studies offered in Canada at the time, so she looked to the United States for a university where she could complete her graduate work. She earned an MBA, master's degree, and PhD in human development and family studies from Pennsylvania State University.

After she was awarded her doctorate in 1989, MacDermid Wadsworth was hired at Purdue as assistant professor of Child Development and Family Studies. In 1995, she was promoted to chair of the graduate program, and the following year Kontos stepped down for health reasons as director of the Center for

Dr. Shelley MacDermid Wadsworth succeeded Dr. Susan Kontos as director of the Center for Families, School of Consumer and Family Sciences in 1996. Later, she became the founding co-director of a nationally groundbreaking initiative of the center, the Military Family Research Institute (MFRI). Courtesy Purdue University Archives and Special Collections.

Families, and MacDermid Wadsworth was selected as her successor. Looking back on Kontos's work, MacDermid Wadsworth said:

> Susan was a big personality. She was quick to laugh, she was blunt, which I very much enjoyed. She was passionate about children and families. She did a lot of work around Indiana and worked really well with people both on and off campus. She was a good researcher, a good writer, believed in rigor but also believed in trying to do work that was meaningful and useful away from campus. I still miss her a lot.
>
> She gathered rigorously controlled data in messy, chaotic environments full of young children. It is a really ... difficult problem, but that was where she felt she needed to be. She was not alone. People who share that conviction run through the fabric of this department.[18]

The founders of the center wanted families to be a highly visible focus at Purdue, alongside the engineering, agricultural, and other concentrations that were already prominent. Most of all, they wanted governmental decision makers whose actions deeply affect families in our society to be more guided by the scientific evidence discovered by researchers at Purdue and elsewhere. MacDermid Wadsworth took the founders' dreams and expanded upon them.[19]

She said, "We try to shrink the distance between researchers and educators, human service professionals, employers, and policymakers using the logic that if those people could do their jobs in ways that are more tightly connected to cutting-edge science about children and families, they would do a better job for families."

Kontos and MacDermid Wadsworth edited a monograph titled *For the Greater Good: Contributions of the School of Consumer and Family Sciences at Purdue University to Family Well-Being* to commemorate the fifth anniversary of the Center for Families in 1999. Kontos designed and initiated the volume as one of the center's first projects. Contributors were then current and former faculty of the School of Consumer and Family Sciences. Kontos titled her chapter "A Star Is Born: The Origins of the Center for Families at Purdue University."[20]

Each year in November the Center for Families leads a consortium of ten organizations in hosting a Family Impact Seminar for Indiana's state lawmakers. It is the center's major annual work that addresses the policymaker audience. The seminar focuses on a single, family-centered topic with nonpartisan presentations by leading researchers and experts. The objective is to present unbiased information on current issues affecting families. The seminar educates Indiana state legislators about the latest scientific evidence related to policies they are debating, and the topic of each seminar is selected by legislators themselves.[21]

Often, information presented at the seminar informs legislation that positively affects families. Examples include passage of a bill establishing full-day kindergarten and a bill regulating family child care. A seminar on middle school violence and safety led to legislation requiring that a school safety specialist establish procedures on discipline, safety, crime, violence, and bullying.[22]

The ethos of being connected to the real world has always been a theme in the Department of Human Development and Family Studies. MacDermid Wadsworth explained:

> It's not enough just to do good research, but if you can figure out a way to do research that is respectful of practice and is informed by practice, that is really good. We want practitioners to be using research in their work, but we also want researchers to be doing research that's informed by practice. I'm not a practitioner. I don't tell practitioners how to do their job, but I want my research to be useful to them, and I want to really understand the world

where they live. Some marvelous innovation that you create for early childhood teachers or for caseworkers and social services, for example, is no good if they are unable to put it into practice.[23]

A family policy internship was created where graduate students learn about policymaking. "It's been a really nice launching pad for students," MacDermid Wadsworth said. "One of the things that's lovely about it is that it focuses on state policy. There's so much that happens in the state, rather than the federal level, and each state is very different." Thanks to endowment funding provided by Betty Krejci, a former assistant director for policy in the Center for Families, the policy internship comes with the Levien scholarship, created to honor her parents' commitment to education.

In 2015, the center became home to the Family Impact Institute, relocated from the University of Wisconsin where it was the headquarters for a network of twenty states also conducting Family Impact Seminars.

The Kanter Award for Excellence is given annually to researchers who publish findings on groundbreaking research and promote greater understanding of relationships between work conditions and family life. This is the center's major work that targets employers. Questions have been analyzed such as: "Is there a motherhood penalty in workplaces?" "What are the sources of earning inequality?" and "Are there gender differences in free time?"

Named for Rosabeth Moss Kanter, known for her influential work-and-family contributions in the 1970s, the award is a partnership of the Center for Families and the Center for Work and Family at Boston College. Since 2006, the award effort has been supported by significant funding from the Alliance of Work-Life Progress, the major national organization of work-life professionals,[24] and from corporate members of the National Workforce Roundtable, who are responsible for shaping policies, practices, and programs in the largest and most recognizable companies in the world that affect millions of employees. The tight connection between the award effort and the practitioner community helps to increase the "on the ground" impact of scientific evidence.

MILITARY FAMILY RESEARCH INSTITUTE

In 1999, MacDermid Wadsworth, Howard Weiss, then head of the Department of Psychological Sciences, and Stephen Green, then a faculty member in the

Krannert Graduate School of Management, wrote a proposal for an $8 million federal grant from the Department of Defense (DoD), and much to their surprise, given their lack of military experience, they received the funding and the Military Family Research Institute (MFRI) was born.

Under an agreement with the Office of Military Community and Family Policy in the Department of Defense, the MFRI was created within the Center for Families and MacDermid Wadsworth and Weiss became co-directors. They functioned as a research arm of the Office of Military Community and Family Policy in the Office of the Secretary of Defense. This initiative put the scientific, policy, and engagement expertise of the Center for Families to work on behalf of the families who volunteer to serve in our nation's armed forces.

"The MFRI was a giant leap, because I had never thought much about doing military work," MacDermid Wadsworth said. "Then I became aware that the US military has an enormous family support infrastructure. The US military runs the largest child care system in the world. They have family support centers on every installation that are staffed by social workers, therapists, and others whose job it is to try to help families, often young families, deal with the challenges associated with military service."

In its early years, MFRI conducted several novel and impactful projects. One series of longitudinal studies of National Guard families was among the first to examine processes of reintegration in the year following a combat deployment, which generated one of MFRI's most-cited research articles. Another documented the experiences of service members as fathers, revealing ways that families work to maintain strong connections with children during deployments.

MFRI research also informed DoD decisions about how best to assist military parents in gaining access to high-quality care for their young children while parents are working. MFRI helped multiple DoD partners to evaluate programs aimed at supporting families and children coping with deployments.[25]

MFRI expanded its mission in 2007 with a significant grant from Lilly Endowment Inc. "By that time we were on the cusp of the surge, when a force of over 100,000 service members would be maintained in the Middle East," MacDermid Wadsworth said. "The National Guard in Indiana had been deployed in large numbers. At one point, the Army National Guard in Indiana had deployed more service members than any Army National Guard in any state."

MFRI quickly responded to the urgent need for support. Through the Heroes Tree initiative, local libraries in more than seventy counties partnered with

MFRI to educate community members about how to support military families. This effort eventually spread to thirty states and nine countries.

With support from the National Military Family Association, MFRI created the first Operation Purple camp for Indiana children with a parent in the reserves. This was the first such camp hosted in Indiana and the only one held on a university campus. MFRI also partnered with Sesame Workshop to evaluate a series of multimedia tools designed to help military children cope with a parent's multiple deployments or the return of a parent from combat with an injury.

In 2008, the first International Research Symposium on Military Families was organized by MFRI; at this writing, the series has produced five books with over fifty thousand downloads of chapters or books.

MacDermid Wadsworth was invited to the White House in 2009 to witness the presidential signing of the National Defense Authorization Act, which included provisions expanding the Family and Medical Leave Act that were based in part on MFRI's work. In 2011 former First Lady Michelle Obama and then Second Lady Dr. Jill Biden, who would become first lady in 2021, created Joining Forces, an initiative calling Americans to rally around service members, veterans, and their families to ensure they have the tools they need to succeed throughout their lives.[26] Prior to the launch of Joining Forces, MacDermid Wadsworth was involved in multiple discussions with Obama's and Biden's staff, and she visited the White House for several meetings.

"They had reached out, and we had several conversations about what they could do, what they should do, how they should frame it, how it should be organized," MacDermid Wadsworth said. "The first time I went to the White House for a meeting with the two of them (Michelle Obama and Jill Biden) and people from several major family-serving organizations, I represented the only university that was included."

She had high praise for how Obama and Biden organized Joining Forces:

> I thought it was such a smart effort because Mrs. Obama and Dr. Biden did such a nice job of acknowledging but never trivializing the military experience. I felt like that was due to their homework and how hard they listened—and of course, Dr. Biden is a military mom.
>
> People tend to think that all military members and veterans are either heroes or broken. It's so easy to get the narrative wrong, because if you are trying to

get people to pay attention to their issues, it tempts you to focus on the negative. The most serious danger is that you could convince service members, veterans, and their families who are not broken that they are.

In 2011, Bill and Sally Hanley Hall was built adjacent to Fowler Memorial House located at Martin Jischke Drive and State Street (now Mitch Daniels Boulevard). The buildings are connected by a skybridge. Bill and Sally Hanley donated $3 million toward the building. A grant from the Lilly Endowment Inc. helped to create a permanent area in the building for MFRI, formerly located in a rented space away from campus.

Bill and Sally Hanley Hall allowed four groups that were previously separate to come together under one roof. They are the Department of Human Development and Families Studies, Military Family Research Institute, Purdue Center on Aging and the Life Course, and Ben and Maxine Miller Child Development Laboratory School. The Center for Families was already housed in Fowler Memorial House.

Today, MFRI is the leading institute focusing on military family issues in the United States. It conducts research on issues that affect military and veteran families and works to shape polices, programs, and practices that improve their well-being. It addresses a variety of needs through grants, educational materials, engagement programs, training workshops, and public policy work. The impact of MFRI is far-reaching, bringing change to systems.

MFRI and its partners began Star Behavioral Health Providers (SBHP) in 2011 to train community-based behavioral health practitioners to be better prepared to help address the unique psychological challenges service members, veterans, and their families face. When military-connected people seek care, they can receive it from someone who understands their experiences. SBHP has won multiple awards, including recognition from the Association of Public and Land Grant Universities, the Washington Center, and the Army National Guard.

"Sometimes therapists misunderstand where military people are coming from," said MacDermid Wadsworth. "They may think they should protect service members from the military. Well, if you are a service member who has sworn an oath, and you're the eighth generation in your family who has served, that may not be how you see it. A therapist has to be ready to join the client where he or she is."

MFRI is a resource for congressional officials. Several federal policies have been influenced by MFRI's work. In 2018, MacDermid Wadsworth was appointed to serve on a National Academies of Sciences, Engineering and Medicine committee focusing on military families' well-being. It was her third time to serve on a National Academies of Sciences panel.[27]

MacDermid Wadsworth was named one of the Top Ten extraordinary contributors to the field of work and family research in a study conducted by researchers at Brigham Young University. She is a fellow of the National Council on Family Relations and a recipient of the Work Life Legacy Award from the Families and Work Institute and Purdue's Violet Haas Award for Leadership on behalf of women. In 2012, she received the Morrill Award from Purdue in recognition of outstanding career achievements that have had an impact on society.[28]

MacDermid Wadsworth wants MFRI's work to help military families for generations to come. "We are building knowledge for future conflicts," she said. "We hope those conflicts never come, but recent history suggests they will."

31
RISING THROUGH THE RANKS AND CREATING A NEW COLLEGE

CHRISTINE M. SCHMITZ LADISCH—INAUGURAL DEAN OF COLLEGE OF HEALTH AND HUMAN SCIENCES

Of any woman in Purdue's history, Christine M. Schmitz Ladisch is the only one to have transitioned from master's student to faculty member to vice provost to a groundbreaking inaugural dean creating a new college—Health and Human Sciences (HHS). All while in her spare time decompressing by wielding a tennis racket on the court—her "salvation."

For decades, Ladisch was a leading figure at Purdue who enjoyed having the influence and ability, particularly when she was an associate dean and then vice provost, to find ways to "get something done" for those who don't have the authority, access, or experience to achieve a change on their own. One of her proudest accomplishments as vice provost was to, with the support of her mentor, Provost Sally Mason, create and manage a system for extending the tenure clock for new parents.

When she became dean, Ladisch used her skills in spades to rally her leadership team to go where few universities have trod—bringing nine academic units from three different colleges across campus together under the umbrella of one newly formed college. Other universities watched and wondered how she and Purdue did it.

Born the oldest of three daughters in Terre Haute, Indiana, on June 10, 1951, Ladisch lived a chunk of her childhood in Louisiana and went to first grade in Canada because her family moved often as her father, a chemical engineer, assisted with the startup of chemical plants. However, Terre Haute was home base, and she graduated from high school there.

Ladisch's mother was a nurse. "Which I find so special," Ladisch said. "Because nursing is part of the College of Health and Human Sciences. When I was child, she volunteered giving vaccinations or helping with other medical needs. She always kept her nursing registration active. I joke that the day my youngest sister started school, she went back to work. She was very dedicated."[1]

Ladisch grew up in a traditional 1950s–1960s environment. "I wanted to be either a teacher or a nurse," she recalled. "It wasn't a world where we were encouraged to be engineers or scientists, or maybe I would have grabbed that brass ring. But, I recall playacting as the teacher and giving assignments, but then, eventually, I ended up being the principal. Maybe there was some leadership progression even then, thinking about careers. I had only seen male principals, though. At that age, I didn't think that a female principal existed."[2]

In 1973 Ladisch received her undergraduate degree in education from Indiana State University. "I did student teaching, and that was the experience that said, 'No, Chris, this is not what you want to do.' It was less about teaching, unfortunately, and more about all the other stuff associated with the job, such as being a proctor at the football game events on Fridays. The wonderful thing that came out of that experience was that I learned about myself. I could teach; I enjoyed that role. It took some time to figure out that there was college teaching as a profession. That's where the fire got lit."[3]

She came to Purdue and earned her master's degree in textile science in 1975. Her first assignment was to teach a textiles lab. "This was when everything started lining up, because my first supervising teacher at Purdue was Mary Alice Nebold," Ladisch recalled. During her Purdue career, Nebold was a professor in the department of clothing and textiles, an academic counselor, director of student services, and the assistant dean for undergraduate education in the School of Consumer and Family Sciences (CFS, formerly Home Economics and later one of the three colleges to realign and form HHS).

"Mary Alice was an amazing mentor and trailblazing woman in a professional field dedicated to students," Ladisch said. "I have not met anybody so singularly and unselfishly dedicated to students. She was my first encounter with that level of dedication and professionalism."[4]

Midway through the time she was obtaining her master's degree, Ladisch met her future husband, Mike, described as a "tall, serious Philadelphian."[5] It happened on a Saturday night in the cafeteria at Grad West, now Hawkins Hall. "I was at one end of the long cafeteria table with my hallmates, and he was at the other end of that table with his chemical engineering hallmates. Dinner ended, and he came up to me and said, 'Hi, I'm Mike Ladisch. I couldn't help but hear you talking about your research.' What a line, right?"

Mike said that it sound like their research had commonalities. "Very engineer-like, but there was something so endearing about it," Ladisch recalled. The two sat down and discussed their research for a couple of hours. "There was chemical connections between what he was doing and what I was doing," Ladisch said, not recognizing the romantic pun. "A couple of hours into this conversation, suddenly he says, 'Well, excuse me, but I have homework I have to go do.'"

Ladisch went to her room for the night and set her hair in rollers. At about 11 p.m. she heard a knock at the door. "I'm in the big hair curlers, so I wouldn't open the door," Ladisch said.

"Who is it?" she asked from inside.

"This is Mike. Remember me from earlier? I finished my homework and thought you might want to go out?"

"It was just precious," Ladisch remembered nearly forty-five years later. "Of course there was no way I was going to open the door. I said, 'Not tonight, but if you'll come back tomorrow, I'd love to go out.' And he came back the next day, and that's the story."[6] They were married the following year and lived in Married Student Housing, later named Purdue Villages, located south of State Street near Martin Jischke Drive (razed in 2022).

The Ladischs both worked toward earning their doctorate degrees and collaborated with a team of researchers who originated part of the process/solvent to efficiently and economically convert cellulose-rich material such as cornstalks, paper, and waste wood into alcohol and other chemicals. Ladisch had been working with cellulose in textiles. The solvent made it possible to replace the petroleum base in many substances, such as plastics, synthetic rubber, industrial chemicals, and gasoline, with elements derived from renewable plant sources.[7] Ladisch worked with the engineers as the one who knew polymers and fibers, particularly the kind of fiber that had a chemistry significant to the research. "I was just in seventh heaven working on my science with all these engineers," Ladisch recalled.[8]

After the couple received their PhDs they were both hired as Purdue faculty members with Mike in Agricultural Engineering (today Agricultural and Biological Engineering) and Chris in CFS.

Donald W. Felker became the first male dean of CFS in 1987, and he believed and lived the maxim "family first," exuding a caring approach to administration. Ladisch became the mother of a son and daughter in the 1980s. "There were people who were game-changers for me, and Don was one," Ladisch said. "During an era when I was working toward tenure and having children, I reached a point where I felt like I couldn't do it all. I felt overwhelmed by everything. Family, career, working toward tenure, so I actually came to a point where I was going to step out for a while. If that meant that the rules of Purdue were such that I literally had to give up my position, we were at that point."[9]

Ladisch approached her department head about her idea of "stepping away" for a short time. At that juncture there was no such thing as "stop-the-clock" tenure. The department head said he didn't know what was possible, but he would ask Felker. Within a couple of hours, the department head called Ladisch.

"I was terrified," Ladisch recalled. "But what I heard back was that Don's reaction was, 'Chris is somebody we want to keep. We will find a way to do this.' It was an example of a leader having the power, the influence, and the ability to find ways for people, and to get something done." In years to come, Ladisch would remember Felker's example of leadership and exemplify it.

In 1992 as an associate professor of consumer sciences and retailing, Ladisch received the Mary L. Matthews Award for Undergraduate Teaching. From 1993 to 1996 she was associate dean for academic affairs in CFS. "That is where I learned the power and the joy of having an administrative role that could make a difference for someone else," she said. Today, faculty have Ladisch and her encouraging advisor, former Provost Sally Mason, to thank for tenured track flexibility that did not exist when she had her children and nearly quit because the stress of juggling parenting and professorship became too much.

"The role of associate dean is critical to a college. In many ways you're the worker bee in the dean's office," Ladisch said. "These are the people who get the job done. As dean, I can talk about a new initiative or task that must be done in the college, but, honestly, the people that get that work done are the associate deans. When that was my role, I absolutely loved it. I found my joy. As associated dean, you are the middle person with a task that has to be done, and you're the person with the resources, capacity, or access to get it done. You're the person that makes it possible, and I just loved that role."

Dr. Christine Ladisch earned her masters (1975) and PhD (1978) in textile science at Purdue. She rose in the ranks, becoming a professor of consumer sciences and retailing, the associate dean of the School of Consumer and Family Sciences, department head, associate provost, vice provost of academic affairs, and in 2010 the inaugural dean of the newly created College of Health and Human Sciences. Courtesy Purdue University Archives and Special Collections.

Ladisch admits that the associate dean role is one where someone else is on the stage and their work is sometimes silent. They have to trust that others understand what they have done and the value of it.

Her next role was department head, sometimes described as the most difficult job on campus. "When you become department head, you are the front line for human resources issues, and I don't know that you can ever be fully prepared for that," Ladisch admitted. "One day I was associate dean. The next day I was department head, and it was like a switch flipped. I had human resources issues on my desk the very first day. However, while it may be the most difficult job on campus, in many ways the job prepares you for the next level of administrative jobs."

Her next big leap was becoming an associate provost followed by being named vice provost for academic affairs. As vice provost, Ladisch was able to help design and manage a system for tenured track flexibility that did not exist when she had her children and nearly quit because the stress of juggling parenting and professorship became too much.

"I loved my position as vice provost, but it's hard for me to separate out completely how much I loved the work and how much I loved my boss, Sally Mason," Ladisch said.

Sally K. Mason became the first female provost at Purdue in 2001. Mason made a difference in Ladisch's career. "Anyone who has a boss they want to emulate who is a mentor like Sally Mason is pretty lucky," Ladisch said. "She was an accomplished scientist, a zoology major as an undergraduate and a biology major as a graduate student at Purdue. She was extremely clear to the people who worked for her as to what she wanted. She was creative, firm, and she didn't let the guys push her around. I got to witness that a lot. And believe me, when you get to watch that in action, you learn how to lead effectively, and it's a gift to watch."

As vice provost, Ladisch got to know the campus working with many of the departments in problem solving and it prepared her for becoming dean. In 2010, Ladisch was hired for a two-year term as the inaugural dean of HHS, bringing together the departments (some renamed) of Health and Kinesiology; Psychological Sciences; Speech, Language, and Hearing Sciences; Human Development and Family Studies; Nutrition Science; Consumer Science; as well as the schools of Hospitality and Tourism Management; Nursing; and Health Sciences. HHS absorbed the College of Consumer and Family Sciences, the School of Nursing, and the School of Health Sciences.

Previously, these nine units had been spread across three different colleges. Now together they would spawn a synergy. The college would facilitate faculty collaborations and interdisciplinary studies for students, while elevating Purdue's commitment to the health and well-being of society.

The notion of the college emerged from faculty town hall discussions with then Provost Randy Woodson about how the administration could support the numerous faculty members in health-related fields scattered across campus in various departments who wanted to find each other and work together. CFS as a college of four departments had accomplished a great deal, but there were thoughts that they had perhaps hit a ceiling. Dean Dennis Savaiano had encouraged conversations about what was next for CFS.

Research concluded that there were few similar colleges at other universities, and those that were close to the Purdue idea carried different names. "Probably the closest was at Oregon State," Ladisch recalled. "They had created their college eight years before and had many of the same departments that HHS would have. We studied Oregon, but beyond that there was not a lot to compare, so in many ways we built HHS from scratch."

Part of the success story in forming HHS is that Purdue's initiative has been copied. "I joked, but it's true. I literally could have made a living as a consultant after we built the college and it began to have an identity as other universities looked at similar ideas. I had so many phone calls with provosts' offices."

Other universities liked the idea but would hit a wall on the "how." How did Purdue do it? "The notion of merging departments, of realigning departments—the human factors—are so complicated," Ladisch said. "That's where they would stall."

Looking back, along with the euphoria and the excitement about leading the new college, Ladisch's first thought after becoming inaugural dean was, "How am I going to keep all this together?" She and her leadership team set to work to create a sense of identity for faculty, staff, students, and alumni. Many aspects had not been thought through in advance or had been underestimated by the university.

One example was that the college's first budget was built with "an efficiency model in mind"—the treasurer's words. Then six months after the college was formed, Purdue announced a budget cut of 6 percent across the board. "You can imagine when we all just started, and we're hit with a budget cut, departments naturally say, 'We didn't join this college to be worse off,'" Ladisch recalled. "It is an example of the unexpected tensions that came out in the early years. We had to make some pretty difficult decisions."

The other challenge was to bring together different cultures. "No department is like another, and most don't know each other," Ladisch said. "With the approval of the Board of Trustees, the college began on July 1, 2010, and nine departments came together. It's like saying to nine people moving into a house, 'Today you're a family. I hope y'all love each other.'"

The most critical difference in departments was their various cultures of promotion and tenure, aspects near and dear to faculty because it is their future. Thus, the HHS leadership team held a culture retreat to talk about promotion and tenure with department heads. "It was the most amazing afternoon spent together because it was respectful, it was challenging, it was informative," Ladisch said. "We learned what each department valued in a faculty member when they're considering promotion and tenure."

At the end of the retreat it was agreed that for the first few years, promotion and tenure would be with respect to the culture that that department brought to the system, rather than immediately being evaluated with a new set of standards brought on by the college formation.

Ladisch also brought cohesion to the new college with her idea to talk to potential new faculty members when they were interviewing for a job. "I deduced that a way to get to know departments better would be to talk to those interviewing for faculty positions," Ladisch explained. "Plus, the future of our college hinged on who we hire." She met for about thirty minutes with each faculty candidate. Little did she realize the volume of people she was committing to, yet the time spent was a good investment in getting know the departments with the added value of when a person was hired, Ladisch already knew them and had a touchpoint of connection.[10]

When HHS was formed it was described as Purdue's "full new initiative," an anomaly in the history of Purdue, a university known for slow change. "If you think about Purdue," Ladisch said, "in the past, Purdue did not reorganize itself much at all. We're a big, sandy, slow-moving ship."

As such a groundbreaking, monumental change was made, one of the biggest lessons learned was the power of communication. People who knew Ladisch said she was accessible, genuine, and knew how to work a room. These attributes were invaluable as she spoke to alumni who graduated from different departments from three different colleges with no allegiance to the new college. "We chose early to communicate to these alums that we were a new college, that their former programs were assimilated into this new college, that we cared about that, that we honored the history, that we embraced them as alums of this new college," Ladisch said.

She was on the road a lot talking to alumni groups and came to fondly divide the audience into three categories. "One group, and fortunately, it was the smallest, was the group that really didn't want change to occur, and I represented change," Ladisch said. "Sometimes, and this seems a little harsh, I could feel them look at me and think, *I don't like what you represent.* So I worked very hard to talk with this group and explain why we were doing what we were doing. And sometimes I would see the posture relax as they head about it. I would start to see heads nod, and some people were won over by the story. And sometimes, as I matured into the role, I just accepted that I had to move on." Her experience with this group was akin to what she observed as a junior professor when Dean Norma Compton faced kickback when the School of Home Economics was renamed the School of Consumer and Family Sciences in 1976.

The second and largest of the groups was a bit doubtful but open to understanding. They said, "Tell me more. I need to learn more." Ladisch was transparent and she had a good story to tell about the future filled with excitement and opportunities. Her words resonated, and most members of that group came on board once they heard her speak. The third group, and it was small, was the cluster that knew some sort of change was needed, even if they did not know what that change should be, and said, "Well, it's about time."

After a national search, in 2013 Ladisch was named dean (no longer *inaugural* dean). When it was announced, Ladisch said, "It's a special day for me. It's a whole lot of emotion.... I'm humbled by the opportunity. Our work was to build the college. Now, in a sense, the real work begins. The foundation is laid.... Now we get onto the very important business of being strategic. That's the real job."[11]

Under her guidance, HHS celebrated the opening of Lyles-Porter Hall and a $2 million National Institutes of Health grant to bring a clinical MRI to campus for health and life sciences research.[12] She also led the college's fundraising effort, which exceeded its $77 million goal for "Ever True: The Campaign for Purdue" one year ahead of schedule.[13] It was Purdue's largest fundraising campaign in its history to that point to propel initiatives forward.[14]

In 2017, the Butler Center for Leadership Excellence awarded Ladisch the Violet Haas Award for the professional advancement of women, and the following year, the Distinguished Woman Scholars Award. She completed her term, stepped out of her role as dean in 2018, and returned to a faculty position as dean emerita and professor of public health in the new Department of Public Health. The department began under her leadership as a graduate program in the college just prior to the COVID-19 pandemic that called for the vital need for more people in the public health workforce. Ladisch co-chaired the Ideas Festival that was the centerpiece of the university's sesquicentennial celebration in 2018–2019. She received the Excellence in Undergraduate Teaching Award in 2022 and retired in 2024.

In recognition of her service as dean, the Christine M. Ladisch Faculty Leadership Award was established to recognize women faculty who have excelled in leadership and support those aspiring to even greater responsibilities. The awardee must be a female faculty member in the College of Health and Human Sciences who has taken significant leadership roles within her department, college, the university, or the nation.

Of Ladisch's legacy, former Provost Jay Akridge stated, "As I have said on a number of occasions, it is one thing to run a college, it is something else entirely to build one."

POSTSCRIPT

The life stories of the women profiled here are inspiring as they demonstrate the resilience, dedication, and courage needed to succeed at Purdue University, especially in the face of many diverse forms of discrimination over the last 150 years. We can learn a lot of lessons from these women: to not take "no" as the final answer; to keep asking questions and keep pushing for change; to come up with creative solutions to problems; and to support other women as they climb to the top.

Lest we think that these stories signal the end of Purdue's female founders, consider these facts. As of fall 2024, the latest data available, 31 percent of tenured and tenure track faculty are women, and of those women, only twenty-six, or .01 percent, identify as African American.[1] Of the ten academic deans at Purdue, only one is a woman.[2] And among our students, 41 percent are female and 59 percent are male. Purdue still has a long way to go to achieve parity among men and women at the student, faculty, and administrative levels. We still need many more women to serve as female founders.

There is still much work to be done to include women's experiences in all arenas and to inspire female students to greatness. Many of the women in this volume started out as Purdue undergraduates and became higher education faculty because someone believed in them and made space at the table. We hope that the stories here will continue to encourage Purdue to support women in all their educational pursuits.

NOTES

EPIGRAPHS

Note to first epigraph: Katey Watson Oral History Interview with Mary O'Hara, August 16, 2019, Purdue University Archives and Special Collections.

Note to second epigraph: Kat Eschner, "Three Things to Know about Pants-Wearing Mountaineer Annie Smith Peck," Smithsonian Magazine, October 19, 2017, https://www.smithsonianmag.com/smart-news/three-things-know-about-pants-wearing-mountaineer-annie-smith-peck-180965297/.

INTRODUCTION

1. K. Crenshaw, "Mapping the Margins: Intersectionality, Identity Politics, and Violence Against Women of Color," *Stanford Law Review* 43, no. 6 (1991): 1241–99.

CHAPTER 1

1. John Norberg, *Ever True: 150 Years of Giant Leaps at Purdue University* (Purdue University Press, 2019), 37.
2. Annual Register of Purdue University 1876–77, UA175i003, UA175, Collection of Purdue University Course Catalogs, Purdue University Archives and Special Collections.
3. "Our Roots," Antioch University, accessed July 23, 2021, https://www.antioch.edu/about/history/.
4. Robert W. Topping, *A Century and Beyond: The History of Purdue University* (Purdue University Press, 1988), 88–89.
5. Jacob Piatt Dunn, *Greater Indianapolis* (Lewis Publishing, 1910), 108.
6. Dorothy A. Nicholson, "Indiana State Capitol Architectural Illustrations, CA. 1831, 1834," Indiana Historical Society, November 2010, https://indianahistory.org/wp-content/uploads/indiana-state-capitol-illustrations.pdf.
7. Dunn, *Greater Indianapolis*.
8. "Sarah Oren Haynes Dead," *The Indianapolis News*, April 25, 1907, 18.
9. "Passed Away. Death of Hon. Lycurgus Dalton, Postmaster of the House," *The South Bend Tribune*, March 25, 1895, 2.

10. Robert W. Topping, *A Century and Beyond: The History of Purdue University* (Purdue University Press, 1988), 88–89.
11. "Pilalethean Literary Society, Purdue University Archives and Special Collections," accessed August 6, 2021, https://archives.lib.purdue.edu/agents/corporate_entities/447.
12. Topping, *A Century and Beyond*.
13. Angie Klink, *Divided Paths, Common Ground* (Purdue University Press, 2011), 108.
14. Topping, *A Century and Beyond*, 89.
15. Annual Report of the Treasurer of the Board of Trustees of Purdue University, UA35i002, UA165, Purdue University Annual Reports collection, Purdue University Archives and Special Collections.
16. "Annie Smith Peck Record-Breaking Mountaineer," *American Masters*, UNLADYLIKE2020, accessed July 26, 2021, https://www.pbs.org/wnet/americanmasters/annie-smith-peck-record-breaking-mountaineer-myztdj/14637/.
17. Edward H. Clarke, *Sex in Education, or A Fair Chance for the Girls* (James R. Osgood, 1873), 18.
18. Hannah Kimberley, *A Woman's Place Is at the Top* (St. Martin's Press, 2017), 41–42.
19. Russell A. Potter, "Annie Smith Peck," accessed July 27, 2021, https://w3.ric.edu/faculty/rpotter/smithpeck.html.
20. Kimberley, *A Woman's Place Is at the Top*, 48–58.
21. Kimberley, *A Woman's Place Is at the Top*, 58–59.
22. Kimberley, *A Woman's Place Is at the Top*, 59.
23. "Annie Smith Peck," *American Masters*.
24. "Annie Smith Peck," *American Masters*.
25. "The Annual Dinner," *The Purdue Exponent*, January 4, 1907, 1, 3.
26. Potter, "Annie Smith Peck."
27. Brook Sutton, "Climber Annie Smith Peck Shocked the World—By Wearing Pants," June 17, 2021, accessed July 27, 2021, https://www.adventure-journal.com/2021/06/historical-badass-annie-smith-peck/.
28. Robert Messenger, "Go Type It on the Mountain: Pecking Away on a Blick at 18,000 feet," ozTypewriter, November 27, 2015, accessed July 28, 2021, https://oztypewriter.blogspot.com/2015/11/go-type-it-on-mountain-pecking-away-on.html.
29. "Annie Smith Peck," *American Masters*.
30. "Miss Annie Peck Appears Tonight in Purdue Course," *The Purdue Exponent*, January 23, 1913, 1, 3.
31. Pete KJ, "Annie Smith Peck," *Base Camp Denver*, December 20, 2018, https://denver.basecampguides.com/2018/12/20/annie-smith-peck/.

32. Benjamin Pollard, "Annie Smith Peck: The Brown Student Who Should Have Been, but Never Was," *The Brown Daily Herald*, March 18, 2021, accessed July 28, 2021, https://www.browndailyherald.com/2021/03/18/annie-smith-peck-the-brown-student-that-should-have-been-but-never-.was/#:~:text='Remarkable'%20life%2C%20career%20of,to%20University%2C%20rejected%20in%201874&text=When%20Annie%20Smith%20Peck%20submitted,response%20from%20President%20Ezekiel%20Robinson.
33. "Ewing, Emma P. (Emma Pike) (1838–)/Purdue University Libraries," August 13, 2009, accessed August 23, 2018, http://www.lib.purdue.edu/archon/?p=creators/creator&id=193.
34. Rabelais Fine Books on Food & Drink, accessed July 26, 2021, https://www.rabelaisbooks.com/pages/books/6957/mrs-emma-p-ewing-emma-pike-ewing/soups-and-soup-making-cookery-manuals-no-.
35. Purdue University School of Domestic Economy Brochure, 1887–1888, Box 1, Folder 1, UA 15, College of Health and Human Sciences Records, Purdue University Archives and Special Collections.
36. Emma P. Ewing Papers, 1888–1892, Finding Aid Biographical Note, Purdue University Libraries, Archives and Special Collections.
37. Finding Aid Biographical Note, Emma P. Ewing Papers, 1888–1892, 5.
38. The History and Development of the Department of Restaurant, Hotel, and Institutional Management, Purdue University, Box 1, Folder 2, UA 15, College of Health and Human Sciences Records, Purdue University Archives and Special Collections 4.
39. Finding Aid Biographical Note, Emma P. Ewing Papers, 1888–1892.
40. Laura Anne Fry to Ross C. Purdy, April 15, 1940, Art Club Collection, Box 1, Folder 1, Tippecanoe County Historical Association, Lafayette, IN.
41. Fry to Purdy, April 15, 1940.
42. "Rookwood Pottery, Maria Longworth Storer," YouTube video, 4:44, November 8, 2019, https://www.youtube.com/watch?v=4kAft6MwjWk.
43. Fry to Purdy, April 15, 1940.
44. Kenneth E. Smith, "Laura Anne Fry: Originator of Atomizing Process for Application of Underglaze Color," *Bulletin of the American Ceramic Society—Ceramic History* 17, no. 9 (September 1938): 370.
45. Herbert Peck, *The Book of Rookwood Pottery* (Crown, 1968), 37.
46. Nancy Owen, "Marketing Rookwood Pottery: Culture and Consumption, 1883–1913," *Studies in the Decorative Arts* 4, no. 2 (1997): 2–21, accessed August 3, 2021, http://www.jstor.org/stable/40662580.

47. Smith, "Laura Anne Fry," 371.
48. Fry to Purdy, April 15, 1940.
49. Hannah E. Spector, "Ladies' Hall Rejuvenated," *Exponent*, October 24, 1922. 1
50. "Serves on Committee," *The Purdue Exponent*, December 17, 1914.
51. "Purdue Graduate Has Art Exhibit," *Journal and Courier*, July 11, 1934, 3.
52. Marybelle Halstead Clark, "Miss Laura Anne Fry and the Art Club," May 4, 1983, Art Club Collection, Tippecanoe County Historical Association, Box 1, Folder 1.
53. Lillian W. Toth, *Lafayette Art Association History 1909–1968* (Lafayette Art Association, 1969), 1.
54. *Debris* Yearbook (1913), *Debris* Yearbook Collection, Archives and Special Collections, Purdue University, West Lafayette, IN. Purdue University, https://earchives.lib.purdue.edu/digital/collection/debris/id/26288.
55. "The University Service Flag," *1919 Debris*, 12.
56. Anne DeCamp, *From Calling Cards to Computer Printouts* (Purdue Women's Club, 1978), 10, 11.
57. Fry to Purdy, April 15, 1940.
58. "Miss Helen Golden Quits," *The Indianapolis News*, March 31, 1920, 21.
59. H. B. Knoll, *The Story of Purdue Engineering* (Purdue University Studies, 1963), 172.
60. "Josephine Golden Claimed by Death," *Journal and Courier*, October 19, 1935, 4.
61. "Frank McGrath on Faculty at Purdue," *Journal and Courier*, March 31, 1920, 6.
62. Purdue Board of Trustees minutes, June 3, 1890, Purdue University Libraries, Archives and Special Collections.
63. "Helen Golden Is Called by Death," *Journal and Courier*, November 6, 1935, 2.
64. "About GPI," Glass Packing Institute, accessed August 6, 2021, https://www.gpi.org/about-us.
65. George B. Cummins, *J. C. Arthur and the First Twenty-Five Years of the Botany Department*, 1942, 2, Purdue Libraries, Archives and Special Collections, https://earchives.lib.purdue.edu/digital/collection/ua9/id/630/rec/42.
66. Andrew F. Smith, *Pure Ketchup: A History of America's National Condiment, with Recipes* (University of South Carolina Press, 1996), 80.
67. Elizabeth Gardner, "Purdue Celebrates 'Father of the FDA,' Indiana's Harvey Wiley, at the State Fair," August 14, 2006, accessed January 19, 2023, https://www.purdue.edu/uns/html3month/2006/060814.Fair.Wiley.html.
68. Smith, *Pure Ketchup*, 82.
69. Katherine Golden Bitting Resume, "Katherine E. Golden Bitting," MSF 39, Katherine E. Golden Bitting Folder 1, "Article/Vita/Bibliographies 1909," Purdue University Archives and Special Collections Communal Collections 16.

70. "Bitting, K. G. (Katherine Golden), 1869–1937," Purdue University Archives and Special Collections, accessed January 19, 2023, https://archives.lib.purdue.edu/agents/people/760.
71. "National Library Gets Books of Katherine Golden Bitting," *Journal and Courier*, April 3, 1940, 4.

CHAPTER 2

1. Angie Klink, *Divided Paths, Common Ground* (Purdue University Press, 2011), 8–9.
2. Frederick Whitford, Andrew G. Martin, and Phyllis Mattheis, *The Queen of American Agriculture* (Purdue University Press, 2008), 52.
3. Klink, *Divided Paths*, 10–12.
4. Whitford et al., *The Queen of American Agriculture*, 226.
5. Klink, *Divided Paths*, 109–10.
6. Klink, *Divided Paths*.
7. "Miss Potter Joins Purdue Faculty as Prof.," *Journal and Courier*, February 21, 1968.
8. Klink, *Divided Paths*, 14.
9. Whitford et al., *The Queen of American Agriculture*, 220.
10. Whitford et al., *The Queen of American Agriculture*, 14–15.
11. Whitford et al., *The Queen of American Agriculture*.
12. The Department of Household Economics Brochure, 1906, Box 1, Folder 1, UA 15, College of Health and Human Sciences records, Purdue University Archives and Special Collections, 1–10.
13. Department of Household Economics Brochure, 1906, Box 1, Folder 1, 11.
14. Purdue University School of Science Department of Household Economics Brochure signed, "The Registrar," undated, Box 1, Folder 1, UA 15, College of Health and Human Sciences Records, Purdue University Archives and Special Collections.
15. Department of Household Economics Brochure, 1906, Box 1, Folder 1, 12.
16. Department of Household Economics Brochure, 1906, Box 1, Folder 1.
17. "The Science of Right Living," accessed February 5, 2018, https://innovators.vassar.edu/.
18. "Science of Right Living."
19. Klink, *Divided Paths*, 34.
20. Klink, *Divided Paths*, 4.
21. Klink, *Divided Paths*, 35.
22. Klink, *Divided Paths*, 37.

23. Klink, *Divided Paths*, 33.
24. Klink, *Divided Paths*, 32–33.
25. Klink, *Divided Paths*, 4.
26. Klink, *Divided Paths*, 64.
27. Wayne D. Rasmussen, *Taking the University to the People* (Iowa State University Press, 1989), vii.
28. Upon her retirement in 1947, Gaddis hired Goble as her successor.
29. Klink, *Divided Paths*, 233.
30. The Gaddis portrait was originally displayed in the Agriculture Administration Building alongside portraits of her colleagues; then it went missing. Klink, *Divided Paths*, 192–94.
31. Klink, *Divided Paths*, 69–70.
32. "Through the Years," *Indiana Extension Homemakers Association, Inc. 75th Anniversary 1913–1988*, 7.

CHAPTER 3

1. "Form New Courses in Home Economics," *The Purdue Exponent*, March 4, 1917, 3, www.exponent.lib.purdue.edu.
2. Memorial Resolution for Mary Edith Gamble, September 1972, Box 6, Folder 4, UA 15, College of Health and Human Sciences Records, Purdue University Archives and Special Collections.
3. Angie Klink, *Divided Paths, Common Ground* (Purdue University Press, 2011), 75.
4. "Miss Edith Gamble Conducts Dietetics Class for Nurses," *The Purdue Exponent*, April 7, 1917, 1, www.exponent.lib.purdue.edu.
5. Memorial Resolution for Mary Edith Gamble, September 1972, Box 6, Folder 4.
6. "Miss Mary Kieffer Was Hostess," *The Eugene Guard*, July 31, 1920, www.exponent.lib.purdue.edu.
7. Diane Dietz, "Architect's Pipe Dream?" *The Register-Guard*, December 12, 2016, http://projects.registerguard.com/.
8. Memorial Resolution for Mary Edith Gamble, September 1972, Box 6, Folder 4.
9. Klink, *Divided Paths*, 71.
10. Klink, *Divided Paths*, 95–102.
11. "Food Exhibit for War Conference," *The Purdue Exponent*, February 13, 1917, 1, www.exponent.lib.purdue.edu.
12. "War Substitutes Given in Bulletins," *The Purdue Exponent*, March 1, 1918, 1, www.exponent.lib.purdue.edu.

13. "Purdue to Teach Women Means of Winning This War," *The Purdue Exponent*, June 5, 1918, 1, www.exponent.lib.purdue.edu.
14. Molly Billings, "The Influenza Pandemic of 1918," February 2005, https://virus.stanford.edu/uda/.

CHAPTER 4

1. Angie Klink, *Divided Paths, Common Ground* (Purdue University Press, 2011), 111–12.
2. "Contractor Begins Digging Foundation for New Structure," *The Purdue Exponent*, October 28, 1921, 1, www.exponent.lib.purdue.edu.
3. Klink, *Divided Paths*, 140.
4. Klink, *Divided Paths*, 75.
5. "University Trustees to Dine in Economics Bldg.," *The Purdue Exponent*, November 3, 1922, 1, www.exponent.lib.purdue.edu.
6. "Potter to Speak at Auditorium Opening," *The Purdue Exponent*, November 8, 1922, 1, www.exponent.lib.purdue.edu.
7. "Home Ec Building Will Be Formally Opened," *The Purdue Exponent*, March 27, 1923, 1, www.exponent.lib.purdue.edu.
8. "Enrollment of Girls Largest in History," *The Purdue Exponent*, September 19, 1919, 1, www.exponent.lib.purdue.edu.
9. Klink, *Divided Paths*, 74–75.
10. "Mary Louise Foster Continues to Touch Students' Lives," *Focus on CFS*, Spring 1999, 1–2, Box 7, Item 7, UA 15, College of Health and Human Sciences Records, Purdue University Archives and Special Collections.
11. Klink, *Divided Paths*, 80–81.
12. Norma H. Compton, "1977–1978 Annual Report and Historical Summary," July 1978, Folder 1, Box 7, UA 15, College of Health and Human Sciences Records, Archives and Special Collections, Purdue University Libraries.
13. "The Practice Babies," Cornell, accessed July 29, 2021, http://practicebabies.blogspot.com/p/cornell.html.
14. NPR Staff, "'Practice Babies': An Outdated Practice, Rediscovered," *All Things Considered*, WBAA, January 6, 2011, accessed July 29, 2021, https://www.npr.org/2011/01/06/132708047/practice-babies-an-outdated-practice-discovered.
15. Klink, *Divided Paths*, 78–79.
16. "New Addition Made to Home Economics Course," *The Purdue Exponent*, October 20, 1922, 1, www.exponent.lib.purdue.edu.

17. John Georgeoff and Kathleen Pearl Brewer, "The History and Development of the Department of Restaurant, Hotel, and Institutional Management, Purdue University" (research paper, Education 500 B, 1986), 5, Folder 2, UA 15, College of Health and Human Sciences Records, Purdue University Archives and Special Collections.
18. Faculty of the School of Home Economics, "Memorial Resolution for Dean Emeritus Mary Lockwood Matthews" (Purdue University, June 18, 1968), 1.
19. Purdue Recipe File artifact, Box 1, Vault 16I2, Purdue University Archives and Special Collections.
20. "Purdue Recipe File," *Purdue Home Economics News*, May 1930, Box 1, ASC Vault 17A4, College of Health and Human Sciences Records, Addition 3, Purdue University Archives and Special Collections.

CHAPTER 5

1. "History of A.C.A.C.W.," MSA 273, Murphy Family Papers, Folder 4, Purdue University Archives and Special Collections.
2. "History of A.C.A.C.W.," MSA 273, Murphy Family Papers, Folder 4.
3. Read more about Winthrop Stone's death and the heroic survival of his wife, Margaret, in Angie Klink, *Divided Paths, Common Ground* (Purdue University Press, 2011), 112–15.
4. Catherine Cottrell, "Fifty Years of Physical Education for Women," *50th Anniversary Newsletter*, May 1975, 1, Purdue University Health and Kinesiology Archives.
5. Cottrell, "Fifty Years of Physical Education for Women."
6. Cottrell, "Fifty Years of Physical Education for Women."
7. Cottrell, "Fifty Years of Physical Education for Women."
8. Cottrell, "Fifty Years of Physical Education for Women," 2.
9. Chas. Wingate Reed memo to Rosemary Murphy, October 30, 1925, Murphy Family Papers, MSA 273, Folder 1, Purdue University Archives and Special Collections.
10. Cottrell, "Fifty Years of Physical Education for Women," 2.
11. Cottrell, "Fifty Years of Physical Education for Women," 2.
12. Sally Watlington, email message to author, January 5, 2018.
13. Cottrell, "Fifty Years of Physical Education for Women," 3.
14. Erika Janik, "Vintage Wisconsin: Summer Camp Taught Girls Survival Skills," Wisconsin Public Radio, accessed March 4, 2018, https://www.wpr.org/vintage-wisconsin-summer-camp-taught-girls-survival-skills.
15. "Mrs. Meredith, Famed Hoosier Leader, Is Dead," *Journal and Courier*, December 10, 1936.
16. "Meredith Rites Are Impressive," *Journal and Courier*, December 12, 1936.

17. *Virginia C. Meredith, A Trustee of Purdue University 1921–1936*, Memorial Booklet, Box 1, ASC Vault 17A4, College of Health and Human Sciences, Addition 3, Purdue University Archives and Special Collections.
18. "Forest Dedicated to Mrs. Meredith," *Indianapolis Star*, May 28, 1938, 6, www.newspapers.com.
19. Catherine Cottrell, "A New Building," *50th Anniversary Newsletter Dept. of Physical Education for Women* 9, no. 1 (May 1975): 3, Archives of Dept. Health & Kinesiology, Purdue University.
20. "Title IX and Sex Discrimination," US Department of Education, April 2015, https://www2.ed.gov/about/offices/list/ocr/docs/tix_dis.Fhtml.

CHAPTER 6

1. Angie Klink, *Divided Paths, Common Ground* (Purdue University Press, 2011), 169.
2. "Baby Boilermakers Enrolled in Purdue's Nursery School," *Journal and Courier*, February 7, 1934, 3, www.newspapers.com.
3. Rebecca Staples New and Moncrieff Cochran, "Read, Katherine (1904–991)," *Early Childhood Education: O–Z* (Greenwood Publishing Group, 2007), 687–88, https://books.google.com.
4. Klink, *Divided Paths*, 170–71.
5. Helen Dawson Miller, "Alumni Letters," *Focus on CFS,* Fall 1998, page 7, Archives, College of Health and Human Sciences, Purdue University.
6. Joan McShane, "Child Lab Marks Twin Milestones," *Journal and Courier*, September 25, 1996, 12, www.newspapers.com.
7. Klink, *Divided Paths*, 172.
8. Joseph H. Tiffin interview by Robert B. Eckles, June 22, 1970, MSO2i044_01_tiffin, MSO 2, Purdue Office of Publications Oral History Program collection, Purdue University Archives and Special Collections Research Center, Purdue University Libraries.
9. "Nursery School Will Open Soon," *Journal and Courier,* September 11, 1931, 8, www.newspapers.com.
10. Ron Grossman, "Long Before Google, There Was the Encyclopedia," *Chicago Tribune*, December, 7, 2017, accessed April 20, 2018, http://www.chicagotribune.com/news/opinion/commentary/ct-perspec-flash-encyclopedia-world-book-britannica-1210-20171205-story.html.
11. "Education 1929–1941," Encyclopedia.com, accessed April 20, 2018, https://www.encyclopedia.com/education/news-and-education-magazines/education-1929-1941.

12. Sonya Michel, "The History of Child Care in the U.S.," Social Welfare History Project, Virginia Commonwealth University, accessed February 4, 2019, https://socialwelfare.library.vcu.edu/programs/child-care-the-american-history/.
13. "Teachers Start Training Course," *Journal and Courier*, January 26, 1934, 7, www.newspapers.com.
14. "Dr. O'Shea Chosen Committee Leader," *Journal and Courier*, December 7, 1934, 8, www.newspapers.com.
15. "Dr. Harriet O'Shea Is Chosen National School Consultant," *Journal and Courier*, April 11, 1936, 4, www.newspapers.com.
16. "1939: Grover Whalen," The City Reliquary, accessed April 20, 2018, http://www.cityreliquary.org/1939-grover-whalen/.
17. Thomas G. Plante, *Contemporary Clinical Psychology* (John Wiley & Sons, 2010), 52.

CHAPTER 7

1. Kayla Gregory, "What's in a Name?," College of Liberal Arts, Purdue University, Fall 2006, https://www.cla.purdue.edu/about/history/index.html. (accessed March 24, 2018).
2. Patricia Albjerg Graham, phone discussion with the author, March 23, 2018.
3. "History of UW-Stout," Recollection Wisconsin, http://recollectionwisconsin.org/history-of-uw-stout (accessed March 30, 2018).
4. "New Staff Members," *Purdue Home Economics News*, November 25, 1929, 3, Box 1, ASC Vault 17A4, College of Health and Human Sciences Records, Addition 3, Purdue University Archives and Special Collections.
5. Patricia Albjerg Graham, phone discussion with the author, March 23, 2018.
6. "Madonna Paintings on Exhibit in Union," *Journal and Courier*, December 8, 1952, 5, www.newspapers.com.
7. Laurentza Schantz-Hansen, "Analysis of Line Within the Field of the Practical Arts," Laurentza Schantz-Hansen Papers, MSF 440, Folder 1, Purdue University Archives and Special Collections.
8. Helen Thompson Terry, "Letters," *Focus on CFS*, Spring 1997, page 6, Archives, College of Health and Human Sciences, Purdue University.
9. "Home Ec Students to Design Posters," *Exponent*, 1933.
10. "Poster Exhibit at Lafayette Gallery," *Journal and Courier*, May 1935.
11. "Omicron Nu Sponsors Foods Poster Contest," Applied Design and Art Scrapbook, Box 6, Folder 1, UA 15, College of Health and Human Sciences Records, Purdue University Archives and Special Collections.

12. "Department Head Elected to Indiana Institute Post," *Exponent*, October 25, 1933.
13. "Art Teachers in Conference at the College," *The Star Press* (Muncie, IN), February 25, 1934, 13, www.newspapers.com.
14. "Art Scholarship to Purdue Professor," *Journal and Courier*, May 7, 1936, 7, www.newspapers.com.
15. "Science School to Be Split," *Journal and Courier*, November 27, 1962, 11, www.newspapers.com.
16. "Designer Will Speak Today," March 7, 1935, Applied Design and Art Scrapbook.
17. John H. Moriarty to Laurentza Schantz-Hansen, March 9, 1956, Box 5, Folder 3, UA 15, College of Health and Human Sciences Records, Purdue University Archives and Special Collections.
18. "Venues—Eliza Fowler Hall," Hall of Music Productions, http://www.purdue.edu/hallofmusic/Venues/Fowler/Fowler.html.
19. "Gown Collection Shown at Purdue," *Journal and Courier*, January 25, 1969, 9, www.newspapers.com.
20. Virginia C. Meredith Home Economics Club, "Historical Style Show," 1952, Archives, College of Health and Human Sciences, Purdue University.
21. "Delicate Lace Collection—A Rare Gift," *Journal and Courier*, July 1, 1961, 30, www.newspapers.com.
22. "Rare Collection of Lace Items Shown at Purdue Arts Festival," *Anderson Herald*, April 22, 1966, 5, www.newspapers.com.
23. Jane Chandler, "CSR Historic Collection a Gift—A Retirement," Focus on CFS, Spring 1989, Archives, College of Health and Human Sciences, Purdue University.
24. "Seven Profs Are 'Most Appreciated,'" *Journal and Courier*, May 3, 1965, 26, www.newspapers.com.
25. "3 on Clothing, Textile Program," *Journal and Courier*, June 19, 1968, 20, www.newspapers.com.
26. Chandler, "CSR Historic Collection."

CHAPTER 8

1. George Palmer Putnam, *Soaring Wings: A Biography of Amelia Earhart* (George G. Harrap, 1940), 221.
2. Putnam, *Soaring Wings*, 222.
3. Putnam, *Soaring Wings*.
4. Putnam, *Soaring Wings*.
5. Putnam, *Soaring Wings*, 223.

6. Putnam, *Soaring Wings*.
7. Putnam, *Soaring Wings*.
8. Edward C. Elliott letter to Amelia Earhart, May 18, 1935, Purdue University Archives and Special Collections, https://earchives.lib.purdue.edu/digital/collection/epurdue/id/492/rec/28.
9. Edward C. Elliott letter to Amelia Earhart, May 18, 1935.
10. Edward C. Elliott letter to Amelia Earhart, May 18, 1935.
11. Angie Klink, *The Deans' Bible: Five Purdue Women and Their Quest for Equality* (Purdue University, 2014), 58.
12. Basem Wasef, "Amelia Earhart's 1937 Cord Is Officially an Historic Car," *Robb Report*, March 10, 2023, https://robbreport.com/motors/cars/amelia-earhart-1936-cord-1234816878/.
13. Dorothy C. Stratton letter to Edward C. Elliott, September 21, 1935, Purdue Archives, https://earchives.lib.purdue.edu/digital/collection/epurdue/id/495/rec/36.
14. "To Launch Amelia Earhart Fashions Late in Month in National Store Tieup," *Women's Wear Daily*, December 11, 1933, Earhart Scrapbook 11, Purdue University Archives and Special Collections.
15. Thaddeus Morgan, "Amelia Earhart's Other Runway: The Aviator's Forgotten Fashion Line," August 29, 2018, https://www.history.com/news/amelia-earharts-other-runway-the-aviators-forgotten-fashion-line.
16. "Amelia Earhart Plans to Return," *Journal and Courier*, April 7, 1936, 7, www.newspapers.com.
17. Putnam, *Soaring Wings*, 232.
18. Klink, *The Deans' Bible*, 65.
19. Klink, *The Deans' Bible*, 86.
20. Klink, *The Deans' Bible*.
21. Klink, *The Deans' Bible*.
22. Klink, *The Deans' Bible*, 87–88.
23. Klink, *The Deans' Bible*, 88.
24. Edward C. Elliott telegram to George Palmer Putnam, March 25, 1937, "Amelia Earhart at Purdue," Purdue Archives and Special Collections, https://earchives.lib.purdue.edu/digital/collection/epurdue/id/198/rec/34.
25. Klink, *The Deans' Bible*, 90.
26. Klink, *The Deans' Bible*.
27. Klink, *The Deans' Bible*.
28. Klink, *The Deans' Bible*.
29. Author interview with Sally Watlington, 2013.

30. Klink, *The Deans' Bible*, 89.
31. "Biography of Lillian Moller Gilbreth," Rosen Center for Advanced Computing, Purdue University, accessed February 23, 2023, https://www.rcac.purdue.edu/knowledge/gilbreth/bio.
32. Robert W. Proctor and Sung-Hee Kim, "100 Years of Human Factors/Ergonomics at Purdue University," *Ergonomics in Design* (January 2016): 31–32.
33. Actually, Gilbreth gave birth to thirteen children, and eleven survived to adulthood. Christopher Roser, "50 Years After the Death of Lillian Evelyn Gilbreth," *All About Lean*, January 2, 2022, https://www.allaboutlean.com/50-years-after-the-death-of-lillian-evelyn-gilbreth/.
34. Klink, *The Deans' Bible*, 70.
35. Gary McCormick, "Respect: Engineer Lillian Gilbreth Added Efficiency and Humanity to the Workplace," August 2, 2017, Redshift, https://www.autodesk.com/redshift/lillian-gilbreth/.
36. Andrey A. Potter, "Reminiscences of the Gilbreths," *Purdue Alumnus*, February 1972, 4.
37. Klink, *The Deans' Bible*, 70.
38. Klink, *The Deans' Bible*, 71–75.
39. Gilbreth, Lillian Moller, 1878–1972, Biographical Information, Purdue University Archives and Special Collections, accessed March 30, 2025, https://archives.lib.purdue.edu/agents/people/79?&filter_fields[]=subjects&filter_values[]=Home+economics#:~:text=Her%20work%20and%20research%20focused,died%20on%20January%202%2C%201972.
40. Klink, *The Deans' Bible*, 76.
41. Klink, *The Deans' Bible*, 78.
42. "Lillian Moller Gilbreth Trailblazer," *Engineer Girl*, accessed February 23, 2023, https://www.engineergirl.org/123474/Lillian-Moller-Gilbreth.
43. "Her Thing—Automation and the Human Spirit," *Purdue Alumnus*, February 1972, 3.
44. "Lillian Moller Gilbreth Trailblazer."

CHAPTER 9

1. Anna Mandler Frost Akeley, *The Earth Is Round: The Memoirs of Anna Mandler Frost Akeley* as told to Agnes Aronson Schenkman, 2000, 81.
2. Akeley, *The Earth Is Round*.
3. Steve Weiss and Samuel Harris, *Anna Akeley*, April 2, 2020, accessed January 26, 2023, https://www.physics.purdue.edu/about/prizes_awards/akeley.html.

4. Lori Futcher, "Four Words to Freedom," *Life Care Leader*, Summer/Autumn 2003, 16, Anna Akeley Papers, Purdue University Archives and Special Collections.
5. William Laird Kleine-Ahlbrandt, *Bitter Prerequisites* (Purdue University Press, 2001), 214–15.
6. Kleine-Ahlbrandt, *Bitter Prerequisites*, 220.
7. Author interview with Ellen Fischer, January 26, 2023.
8. Roentgen-Memorial, *Wilhelm Conrad Röntgen*, Google Arts and Culture, accessed January 25, 2023, https://artsandculture.google.com/story/BQVxmHPGTRkMJQ.
9. Akeley, *The Earth Is Round*, 51.
10. Akeley, *The Earth Is Round*, 79–80.
11. Akeley, *The Earth Is Round*, 150.
12. Akeley, *The Earth Is Round*, 162.
13. Akeley, *The Earth Is Round*.
14. Weiss and Harris, *Anna Akeley*.
15. Angie Klink, *Divided Paths, Common Ground* (Purdue University Press, 2011), 196.
16. Klink, *Divided Paths*.
17. Weiss and Harris, *Anna Akeley*.
18. Kathy Matter, "One Man's Eye and Passion for Collecting Becomes the Thread of a Couple's Existence," *Journal and Courier*, May 7, 1995, 39.
19. Author interview with Sharon Theobald, January 23, 2023.
20. Matter, "One Man's Eye," 37.
21. Author interview with Sharon Theobald, January 23, 2023.
22. Author interview with Sharon Theobald, January 23, 2023.
23. Email to author from Kirstin Marie Gotway, December 6, 2024.
24. Email to author from Kirstin Marie Gotway, December 6, 2024.
25. Edith Weisskopf-Joelson, *Father, Have I Kept My Promise?* (Purdue University Press, 1988), 25–26.
26. Weisskopf-Joelson, *Father, Have I Kept My Promise?*, 28.
27. Weisskopf-Joelson, *Father, Have I Kept My Promise?*, 27.
28. James C. Naylor, "The History of Psychology at Purdue," April 1971, 8. Abbreviated version obtained via email from David Rollock, Head of Department of Psychological Sciences, Purdue University, January 16, 2018.
29. Viktor E. Frankl, *Man's Search for Meaning* (Beacon Press, 2006), 6.
30. Weisskopf-Joelson, *Father, Have I Kept My Promise?*, 33.
31. Weisskopf-Joelson, *Father, Have I Kept My Promise?*, 34.
32. Weisskopf-Joelson, *Father, Have I Kept My Promise?*, 51.
33. Weisskopf-Joelson, *Father, Have I Kept My Promise?*, 111.

34. Weisskopf-Joelson, *Father, Have I Kept My Promise?*, 115.
35. Weisskopf-Joelson, *Father, Have I Kept My Promise?*, 116.
36. Weisskopf-Joelson, *Father, Have I Kept My Promise?*, 118.
37. Weisskopf-Joelson, *Father, Have I Kept My Promise?*, 137.
38. Frankl, *Man's Search for Meaning*, 166.
39. Weisskopf-Joelson, *Father, Have I Kept My Promise?*, 152.
40. "At Strawberry Time, We Honor Professor of Jam," *Des Moines Tribune*, June 9, 1971, 40, www.newspapers.com.
41. Edith M. Sunderlin, "Some Facts Concerning the Professional Life of Gertrude Laura Sunderlin," August 1984, MSF 369, Box 2, Folder: Gertrude Sunderlin Papers, Purdue University Archives and Special Collections.
42. "Gertrude Sunderlin, 95," *Iowa City Press-Citizen*, June 21, 1990, 12, www.newspapers.com.
43. "Dr. Sunderlin Retiring; Develope," *Journal and Courier*, June 18, 1954, 11, www.newspapers.com.
44. "Recommends Master Mix for Baking," *The Noblesville Ledger*, January 19, 1949, 4, www.newspapers.com.
45. "Women Find Master-Mix Solves Baking Problems," *Muncie Evening Press*, May 3, 1949, 16, www.newspapers.com.
46. "Faded Signals," accessed April 26, 2018, http://fadedsignals.com/post/110769531280/the-national-farm-and-home-hour-ran-from-1928-to.
47. "Purdue's Master Mix Formula Can Do All Sorts of Wonders," *The Indianapolis News*, December 22, 1949, 26, www.newspapers.com.
48. "Master Mix in Quantity," *Journal and Courier*, February 2, 1952, 18, www.newspapers.com.
49. "At Strawberry Time, We Honor Professor of Jam."
50. "Ruth Siems, Creator of Stove Top Stuffing," *Journal and Courier*, November 24, 2005, 10, www.newspapers.com.
51. "Ruth Siems, Creator of Stove Top Stuffing."

CHAPTER 10

1. "Home Administration School Is Divided," *Palladium-Item*, Richmond, IN, January 12, 1946, 15, www.newspapers.com.
2. Richard K. Kerckhoff, "Traces of CDFS" (Partial History of the Dept. of Child Development and Family Studies, 1986), 11, Folder 3, Box 1, UA 15, College of Health and Human Sciences records, Archives and Special Collections, Purdue University Libraries.

3. "Nursery School Moves," *Journal and Courier*, September 19, 1959, 7, www.newspapers.com.
4. "Hoosier Weather Best, Says Nurse," *Journal and Courier*, February 27, 1945, 3, www.newspapers.com.
5. "Two-Year Nursing Program to Be Offered at Purdue," *Journal and Courier*, July 11, 1962, 14, www.newspapers.com.
6. Kerckhoff, "Traces of CDFS."
7. "Women of Distinction," *Journal and Courier*, January 24, 1959, 26, www.newspapers.com.
8. "Community Resources Fall Short of Meeting Mental Health Need," *Journal and Courier*, October 6, 1956, 3, www.newspapers.com.
9. James C. Naylor, "The History of Psychology at Purdue," April 1971, 10. Abbreviated version obtained via email from David Rollock, Head of Department of Psychological Sciences, Purdue University, January 16, 2018.
10. "Purdue Names Family Life Specialist," *Journal and Courier*, September 20, 1961, 17, www.newspapers.com.
11. Suzanne Topping, "Pleased to Read Purdue Child Care," *Journal and Courier*, June 10, 2006, 5, www.newspapers.com.
12. Jean Greives, "Professor Elaine Dolch: A CDFS Tradition," *CDFS Update*, Spring 1988, 2, emailed to author from Lisa L. Stein.
13. Elaine Dolch to Bob Lewis, interoffice memorandum, December 1, 1986, emailed to author by Lisa L. Stein.
14. Vita, Elaine T. Dolch, January 1988, emailed to author by Lisa L. Stein.
15. Vita, Elaine T. Dolch, January 1988.
16. Jane Chandler, "New Home for Purdue Child Care Program," *Focus on CFS*, Fall 1988, Archives, College of Health and Human Sciences, Purdue University.
17. Memo to CDFS Faculty, staff, and graduate students from CDL Staff, February 28, 1991, emailed to author by Lisa L. Stein.

CHAPTER 11

1. "Retiring Dean Is Praised for 41 Years' Leadership," January 22, 1952, newspaper clipping given to author by Mary Louise Foster.
2. Remarks by A. A. Potter, January 21, 1952, given to author by Mary Louise Foster.
3. "Endowment Fund Activity Report," given to author by Mary Louise Foster.
4. "Purdue Will Bestow 9 Honorary Degrees," *Journal and Courier*, May 29, 1953, 1. Given to author by Mary Louise Foster.
5. Angie Klink, *Divided Paths, Common Ground* (Purdue University Press, 2011), 227.

6. Robert W. Topping, *A Century and Beyond* (Purdue Research Foundation, 1988), 326.
7. "Here Are the Companies Whose Products Bear the Coveted Sealtest Symbol," accessed May 21, 2018, https://archive.lib.msu.edu/DMC/sliker/msuspcsbs_seal_sealtest16/msuspcsbs_seal_sealtest16.pdf.
8. "Brazil, Purdue Replant Seeds of Cooperation," *Journal and Courier*, April 15, 2010, Box 6, Folder: Clippings, 1966–2010, Collection 469, Mary Louise Foster Papers, Purdue University Archives and Special Collections.
9. "History of the Universidade Federal de Vicosa—UFV," accessed May 22, 2018, http://www.portalufv.ufv.br/portalufv/site/ingles/?area=history.
10. "Purdue in Brazil," September 29, 1964, Box 1, Folder 3, MSF 3, Eva Goble Papers, Purdue University Archives and Special Collections.
11. "Anita Dickson Obit," *Journal and Courier*, January 26, 1989, Box 6, Folder: Clippings, 1989–2009, Collection 469, Mary Louise Foster Papers, Purdue University Archives and Special Collections.
12. "Anita Dickson Obit," *Journal and Courier*, January 26, 1989.
13. Menicucci Sobrinho, "The Rural University of the State of Minas Gerais and the Rural Extension the Land Grant College System," page 1, Box 1, Folder 3, MSF 3, Eva Goble Papers, Purdue University Archives and Special Collections.
14. Anita Dickson, "Ten Years of Progress of Home Economics Work in Brazil," Box 1, Folder 3, MSF 3, Eva Goble Papers, Purdue University Archives and Special Collections.
15. "Escola Superior De Ciencias Domesticas," page 5, Box 1, Folder 3, MSF 3, Eva Goble Papers, Purdue University Archives and Special Collections.
16. Dickson, "Ten Years of Progress of Home Economics Work in Brazil," page 11, Box 1, Folder 3, MSF 3, Eva Goble Papers.
17. "Dean Gillaspie to Leave for Brazil July 2," *Journal and Courier*, June 24, 1959, 10, www.newspapers.com.
18. Frederick L. Hovde, "The Early Identification and Attainment of Contract Objectives," July 13, 1965, Box 1, Folder 3, MSF 3, Eva Goble Papers, Purdue University Archives and Special Collections.
19. "Lively Brazilians Pick Up American Techniques at Purdue," *Journal and Courier*, March 31, 1962, 24, www.newspapers.com.
20. Gladys Vail, "Letter from the Dean," *School of Home Economics Newsletter*, Spring 1966, 5, Archives, College of Health and Human Sciences, Purdue University.
21. Maria de Fatima Lopes to Family and/or Friends of Anita Dickson, March 18, 1992, page 5, Box 1, Folder 3, MSF 3, Eva Goble Papers, Purdue University Archives and Special Collections.

22. Donald W. Felker to Mary Louise Foster, May 11, 1989, Box 1, Folder: Information on Anita Dickson, 1988–1989, MSF 469, Mary Louise Foster Papers, Purdue University Archives and Special Collections.

CHAPTER 12

1. Margaret Church, Paper Written for Fortieth Reunion Yearbook, Radcliffe College, 1982, Margaret Church Papers, MSF 74, Folder 1, Purdue University Archives and Special Collections.
2. Church, Paper Written for Fortieth Reunion Yearbook.
3. Margaret Church Biographical Information, Purdue University Archives, accessed December 6, 2024, https://archives.lib.purdue.edu/agents/people/1166.
4. Church, Paper Written for Fortieth Reunion Yearbook.
5. Norm Bess, "Purdue Staff, Students Mourn Margaret Church," *The Indianapolis News*, September 3, 1982, 36.
6. Bess, "Purdue Staff, Students Mourn Margaret Church."
7. "Grants to Be Given," *Exponent*, February 9, 1970, 7.
8. "Critical Quarterly Published by Club," *Journal and Courier*, February 17, 1955, 12.
9. "Journal Reaches Milestone," *Journal and Courier*, December 13, 1975, C-4.
10. "About Modern Fiction Studies," College of Liberal Arts, accessed October 23, 2023, https://cla.purdue.edu/academic/english/publications/mfs/about/.
11. "Professional Achievement, Appointments and Elections," *Exponent*, November 26, 1975, 11.
12. Bess, "Purdue Staff, Students Mourn Margaret Church."
13. Church, Paper Written for Fortieth Reunion Yearbook.
14. Bess, "Purdue Staff, Students Mourn Margaret Church."
15. Thomas P. Adler, "Foreword," Margaret Church, *Structure and Theme: "Don Quixote" to James Joyce* (Ohio State University Press, 1983), viii.
16. Church, Paper Written for Fortieth Reunion Yearbook.
17. "Martha Chiscon: A Beacon for Women," College of Science, Purdue University, accessed January 31, 2024, https://www.purdue.edu/science/Alumni/martha_chiscon.html.
18. Keven Cullen, "'We Will Only Need Three or Four People to Replace Her,'" i, May 27, 2000, 1.
19. Lillian Price, "Mentor, Champion, Friend, Role Model, Purdue Fan, Confidante—Martha Chiscon," *Lafayette Leader*, April 23, 2004.
20. Martha Chiscon interview with Katherine Markee, Purdue University Archives and Special Collections Oral History Program, MSO1i200708038, January 22, 2008.

21. Chiscon interview with Katherine Markee.
22. Chiscon interview with Katherine Markee.
23. Chiscon interview with Katherine Markee.
24. Chiscon interview with Katherine Markee.
25. Kathe Schuckel, "Profs Have Good Chemistry," *Journal and Courier*, July 29, 1990, 19.
26. Cullen, "'We Will Only Need Three or Four People to Replace Her.'"
27. Chiscon interview with Katherine Markee.
28. "Top Chemist Cut Her Teeth on the Farm," Purdue University News Service, February 7, 1974.
29. Price, "Mentor, Champion, Friend, Role Model."
30. Chiscon interview with Katherine Markee.
31. "Title IX Distinguished Service Award Recipients," accessed February 5, 2024, https://www.purdue.edu/titleix/index.php
32. Chiscon interview with Katherine Markee.
33. Chiscon interview with Katherine Markee.
34. Chiscon interview with Katherine Markee.
35. Chiscon interview with Katherine Markee.
36. Cullen, "'We Will Only Need Three or Four People to Replace Her.'"
37. Bob Scott, "Women Honored for Endeavors," *Journal and Courier*, October 12, 2004, 9.

CHAPTER 13

1. Angie Klink, *Divided Paths, Common Ground* (Purdue University Press, 2011), 228.
2. Lotys Benning Stewart, "Purdue University Is Proud of New 'House of Tomorrow,'" *Indianapolis Star*, February 16, 1958, 60, www.newspapers.com.
3. "Tour Questions and Information About Home Economics Building Administration," Box 1, Addition 3, College of Health and Human Sciences Records, Purdue University Archives and Special Collections.
4. Richard L. Pierce, "Special Report on New Construction," *Campus Copy*, November 1957, 9, Archives of College of Health and Human Sciences, Purdue University.
5. Pierce, "Special Report on New Construction."
6. Pierce, "Special Report on New Construction," 10.
7. Gladys Vail, "Letter from the Dean," *School of Home Economics Newsletter*, Spring 1965, Archives of College of Health and Human Sciences, Purdue University.
8. Stewart, "Purdue University Is Proud of New 'House of Tomorrow,'" 76.
9. "Tour Questions."

10. "Dr. K. A. Johnston Joins Home Economics Staff," January 8 1957, UA 15, College of Health and Human Sciences Records, Purdue University Archives and Special Collections.
11. "Tour Questions."
12. "'Luscious' Food Found at Purdue Dining Rooms," *Indianapolis Star*, February 16, 1958, 72, www.newspapers.com.
13. "Fried Chicken Shortage Seen," *Indianapolis Star*, January 18, 1948, 14, www.newspapers.com.
14. "Schedule Annual Egg, Cattle Feeders' Days," *Journal and Courier*, March 30, 1957, 39, www.newspapers.com.
15. "Directory of Scientists Will Now List Women," November 23, 1971, *The New York Times*, https://www.nytimes.com/1971/11/23/archives/directory-of-scientists-will-now-list-women.html.
16. ASN History & Archives, ASN, accessed September 16, 2018, https://nutrition.org/about-asn/asn-history/.
17. "Dr. Gladys Vail Wins High Honor," *Journal and Courier*, January 9, 1959, 10, www.newspapers.com.
18. "Institute Cites Prof. Clark for Work in Nutrition Field," *Journal and Courier*, April 2, 1979, www.newspapers.com.
19. "Dr. Gladys Vail Wins High Honor," *Journal and Courier*, January 9, 1959, 10. www.newspapers.com.
20. "About Us," IFT, accessed May 31, 2018, http://www.ift.org/about-us.aspx.
21. "IFT Fellows," IFT, accessed September 16, 2018, http://www.ift.org/Community/Fellows/IFT-Fellows.aspx.
22. Chung Ja Lee, Diane F. Birt, Avanelle Kirksey, and Connie M. Weaver, "Helen E. Clark (1912–2001)," *Journal of Nutrition* 133, no. 6 (June 1, 2003): 1773, https://doi.org/10.1093/jn/133.6.1773.
23. Chung Ja Lee et al., "Helen E. Clark (1912–2001)," 1774.
24. "New Corn Described as Human Food Boon," Box 5, UA 15, College of Health and Human Sciences Records, Purdue University Archives and Special Collections.
25. "Hall of Fame, 2007 Inductees," Department of Nutrition Science, accessed May 29, 2018, http://www.purdue.edu/hhs/nutr/about/awards/hall_fame/hall_fame-2007.html.
26. "Hall of Fame, 2007 Inductees."
27. Edward W. Cotton, "A Hungry World Is Her Stage," 1968, clipping, Box 5, UA 15, College of Health and Human Sciences Records, Purdue University Archives and Special Collections.

28. Mary Schlott, "Dietary Guinea on Hog in Lysine," *Journal and Courier*, December 5, 1959, 30, www.newspapers.com.
29. "New Rice Variety Seen as Aid in the Fight on World Hunger," *Journal and Courier*, September 18, 1970, 22, www.newspapers.com.
30. "Nutrition Experiment Explained," *Journal and Courier*, September 5, 1960, 13, www.newspapers.com.
31. Cotton, "A Hungry World Is Her Stage."
32. "Pioneer: A Tribute to Helen Clark," *Foods and Nutrition*, Purdue University, Summer 2004, page 5.
33. Olivia Bennett Wood interview with author, June 1, 2018.
34. Helen E. Clark, Biographical Note, Helen E. Clark (1912–2001) Papers, 1939–1995, MS 295, Special Collections Department, Iowa State University, Ames, IA.
35. Helen E. Clark, Remarks, Borden Award, June 27, 1968, Box 4, Folder 7, HSF 502, Avanelle Kirksey Papers, Archives and Special Collections, Purdue University Libraries.
36. Mary Ruth Snyder, "Purdue Home Economics Alumni to Meet October 2," proposed article for IHEA newsletter, Archives College of Health and Human Sciences, Purdue University.
37. "Image of Home Economics Must Be Improved, Editor Says," *Journal and Courier*, September 23, 1967, Box 5, Folder 5, UA 15, College of Health and Human Sciences records, Archives and Special Collections, Purdue University Libraries.
38. "Image of Home Economics Must Be Improved."
39. Mary Ruth Snyder, "School Organization Study," *Alumni Newsletter*, Spring 1967, 2, Purdue University College of Health and Human Sciences Archives.
40. Frederick L. Hovde letter to Mary Ruth Snyder, Chairwoman, Purdue Home Economics Alumni Executive Board, April 26, 1967, Archives of College of Health and Human Sciences, Purdue University.

CHAPTER 14

1. "Remembering the Life and Legacy of Virginia Ferris," *Envision*, August 22, 2027, https://ag.purdue.edu/envision/remembering-virginia-ferris/.
2. Virginia Ferris interview with Katherine Markee and Valerie Yazza, January 16, 2007, https://collections.lib.purdue.edu/oral-history/interviews/11.
3. All Ferris quotes are taken from Virginia Ferris interview with Katherine Markee and Valerie Yazza, January 16, 2007, https://collections.lib.purdue.edu/oral-history/interviews/11.

4. "The Pregnancy Discrimination Act of 1978," US Equal Employment Opportunity Commission, accessed April 18, 2023, https://www.eeoc.gov/statutes/pregnancy-discrimination-act-1978.
5. "Roundworm Expert Compares Notes with Local Entomologists," *Journal and Courier*, March 22, 1969, 12.
6. Byron Parvis, "Praiseworthy," *Journal and Courier*, February 23, 1988, 27.
7. "Affirmative Action Polices Throughout History," American Association for Access, Equity and Diversity, accessed April 19, 2023, https://www.aaaed.org/aaaed/History_of_Affirmative_Action.asp.
8. "The Phi Beta Kappa Society," accessed April 21, 2023, https://www.pbk.org/About#:~:text=A%20Rare%20Honor,credential%20that%20has%20national%20recognition.
9. "Faculty, Staff Receive Honors," *Journal and Courier*, April 28, 1997, 12.
10. "Susan Edgell Discusses How Her Mother, Virginia Ferris, Became the First Woman Appointed to Purdue Agriculture Faculty," *This Is Purdue* podcast, July 6, 2023, https://ag.purdue.edu/news/department/entomology/2023/07/podcast-virginia-ferris.html.
11. "Susan Edgell Discusses."
12. "Faculty, Staff Receive Honors."

CHAPTER 15

1. Chuck McWilliams, "Boilermakers," *The Purdue Engineer*, February 1966, 28.
2. Leigh Karlin, "Math Provides Firm Background," *The Purdue Exponent*, March 15, 1979, 6.
3. Purdue News Service, "Women in Engineering Programs Celebrate 25th Anniversary," *Purdue News*, April 1995.
4. Judy Hensel, "Lecturer Notes Women's Profit in Engineering," *The Purdue Exponent*, January 28, 1982, 4.
5. Claire D'Amico, "Haas Remains Optimistic About Women Engineers," *Exponent*, September 27, 1974, 6.
6. Karlin, "Math Provides Firm Background."
7. "Grounded in IHM Tradition and Charisma Since 1920," Immaculata University, accessed March 7, 2023, https://www.immaculata.edu/about/mission-heritage/.
8. McWilliams, "Boilermakers."
9. "Violet B. Haas Facts for Kids," *Kiddle Encyclopedia*, accessed March 8, 2023, https://kids.kiddle.co/Violet_B._Haas#:~:text=Haas%20resided%20in%20West%20Lafayette,January%2021%2C%201986%20at%20St.

10. "Intrigued by Exotic Designs?," *The Purdue Engineer*, February 1, 1966, 24.
11. Hensel, "Lecturer Notes Women's Profit in Engineering."
12. David Ching, "Welcoming Women Engineers to Purdue," Purdue University, February 10, 2023, accessed March 9, 2023, https://stories.purdue.edu/welcoming-women-engineers-to-purdue/.
13. Karen Clem, "Laws Bar Professional Wives from Careers at Many Universities," *The Purdue Exponent*, February 1, 1973, 6.
14. D'Amico, "Haas Remains Optimistic About Women Engineers."
15. D'Amico, "Haas Remains Optimistic About Women Engineers."
16. D'Amico, "Haas Remains Optimistic About Women Engineers."
17. Karlin, "Math Provides Firm Background."
18. "History," About Purdue SWE, accessed March 8, 2023, https://www.purdueswe.org/about.
19. Karlin, "Math Provides Firm Background."
20. Ching, "Welcoming Women Engineers to Purdue."
21. Ching, "Welcoming Women Engineers to Purdue."
22. "Violet B. Haas Facts for Kids."
23. Council on the Status of Women Records, "Historical Information," Purdue University Archives and Special Collections, Accessed December 7, 2024, https://asc03p.lib.purdue.edu/repositories/2/resources/455.
24. "Council on the Status of Women at Purdue Announces Violet Haas Recognition Award," Press Release, February 11, 1991, "Violet Haas Award Committee, 1991," MSP 49 Council on the Status of Women Records, Box 6, Folder 1, Purdue University Archives and Special Collections.
25. Violet B. Haas and Carolyn C. Perrucci, *Women in Scientific and Engineering Professions* (University of Michigan Press, 1984), 12–13.
26. Haas and Perrucci, *Women in Scientific and Engineering Professions*, 235–36.
27. Katherine Markee, "Felix Haas Interview," Purdue University Libraries Archives and Special Collections, April 27, 2007, https://collections.lib.purdue.edu/oral-history/interviews/29.
28. Leah H. Jamieson, "Engineering and Social Responsibility: A View from the EPICS Program," University of California, Berkeley, July 12, 2013, https://www.youtube.com/watch?v=uEpMi_HA5zI.
29. Jamieson, "Engineering and Social Responsibility."
30. "Leah H. Jamieson 77," Princeton University, accessed April 27, 2023, https://www.princeton.edu/~alco/CTNAT/2009/jamieson.html.
31. Leah Jamieson, Armstrong Building Dedication, Purdue University, 2014, https://www.c-span.org/video/?318300-1/doug-brinkley-neil-armstrong-recordings.

32. Leah Jamieson email to author, October 31, 2024.
33. "Leah Jamieson," Women in Computer Science, accessed April 27, 2023, https://users.sdsc.edu/~jsale/CRAW/craw_bro.html.
34. Kelsey VanArsdall, "Engineering Professor Wins Grant; Plans to Put It to Good Use," *Exponent*, November 7, 2001, 1.
35. "Epics Program Snares State Volunteer Award," *Journal and Courier*, January 16, 2003, 15.
36. Kevin Cullen, "Looking for Women Mentors," *Journal and Courier*, April 15, 1998, 12.
37. Cullen, "Looking for Women Mentors."
38. Cullen, "Looking for Women Mentors."
39. "Interview with Leah Jamieson," CRA-WP, originally printed in Winter/Spring 2010 Newsletter, https://cra.org/cra-wp/interview-with-leah-jamieson/.
40. "Haas Award Presented," *Exponent*, April 25, 2000, 8.
41. Kimberley Adank, "Professor Hopes to Inspire New Engineers," *Exponent*, January 26, 2006.
42. National Academy of Engineering, *The Engineer of 2020: Visions of Engineering in the New Century* (National Academies Press, 2004), http://doi.org/10.17226/10999.
43. Mary Besterfield-Sacre, Larry J. Shuman, Harvey Wolfe, Cynthia J. Atman, Jack McGourty, Ronald L. Miller, Barbara M. Olds, and Gloria M. Rogers, "Defining the Outcomes: A Framework for EC-2000," *IEEE Transactions on Education* 43, no. 2 (2000): 100–10.
44. Leah Jamison manuscript proofing comment, October 31, 2024.
45. Tanya Brown, "New Dean Eyes Updates to Engineer," *Journal and Courier*, August 24, 2006, C3.
46. National Academy of Engineering, *Changing the Conversation: Messages for Improving Public Understanding of Engineering* (National Academies Press, 2008), https://doi.org/10.17226/12187.
47. "3 Purdue Professors Elected to Arts and Sciences Society," *Journal and Courier*, April 20, 2011, 9.
48. Purdue Engineering Communications Team, "Dreams—College of Engineering—Purdue University," June 29, 2017, 20–21.
49. Amy Raley, "Conversation with Leah Jamieson, Dean of Engineering, 2006–2017," *Engineering Impact*, Summer 2017.

CHAPTER 16

1. "Stanford Appoints Dr. Clifton," *Indianapolis Star*, October 28, 1973, 112.

2. Catherine Cottrell, "Fifty Years of Physical Education for Women," *50th Anniversary Newsletter*, May 1975, 3, Archives, Purdue University Dept. of Health and Kinesiology.
3. "Monthly Memories," *West Lafayette History Blog*, April 26, 2016, http://westlafayettememories.blogspot.com/2016/04/monthly-memories.html.
4. Ray Anne Shrader interview with Katherine Markee, February 5, 2007, POH0607022(Shrader), Purdue Office of Publications Oral History Program collection, Purdue University Archives and Special Collections Research Center, Purdue University Libraries.
5. "Physical Education for Women Takes New Turn," *Journal and Courier*, September 9, 1964, 21.
6. "Physical Education for Women Takes New Turn."
7. "Freshman Women to Study Human Movement," *Purdue Reports to Indiana Schools*, page 3, Archives, Purdue University Dept. of Health and Kinesiology.
8. Bonnie Schile from C. Widule, "Human Movement Research Laboratory," Newsletter Article—Research Laboratory, Archives, Purdue University Dept. of Health and Kinesiology.
9. Hope M. Smith, *Introduction to Human Movement* (Addison-Wesley, 1968), foreword.
10. "Women's Phys Ed Divisions Doubled," *Journal and Courier*, September 15, 1970, 51.
11. "Marguerite Clifton Is Academy Fellow," *Journal and Courier*, March 30, 1966, 16.
12. "Prof. Fellow in Physical Education Unit," *Journal and Courier*, March 12, 1970, 16.
13. Ray Anne Shrader, "The Last Decade," *50th Anniversary Newsletter*, May 1975, 3, Archives, Purdue University Dept. of Health and Kinesiology.
14. "Perceptual-Motor Symposium: A Multidisciplinary Approach to Understanding and Action," *Journal of Health, Physical Education, Recreation* 40, no. 1 (1969): 47, https://doi.org/10.1080/00221473.1969.10613891.
15. Lloyd B. Walton, "Every Little Movement and the Meaning All Its Own," *Indianapolis Star*, January 29, 1972, 54.
16. "DME: Developmental Movement Education," Description, Archives, Purdue University Dept. of Health and Kinesiology.
17. Judy Horak, "Kids, Parents, Have 'Circus' While Learning," *Journal and Courier*, May 1, 1975, 21.
18. Horak, "Kids, Parents, Have 'Circus' While Learning."
19. Horak, "Kids, Parents, Have 'Circus' While Learning."
20. Walton, "Every Little Movement and the Meaning All Its Own."
21. "Agnew Calls Addiction Excuses 'Hogwash,'" *Indianapolis Star*, March 11, 1972, 17.
22. Ron Rosenbaum, "The Great Ivy League Nude Posture Photo Scandal," *The New York Times Magazine*, 1995, https://nyti.ms/2986VpA.

23. Associated Press, "Purdue, IU Students Among Subjects in Nude Posture Photos," *Journal and Courier*, February 24, 1995, 19.
24. Associated Press, "Purdue, IU Students Among Subjects in Nude Posture Photos."
25. Betty M. Nelson, Dean of Students Emerita, Purdue University, interview by author, June 26, 2018.
26. Hannah Harper, "Did You Know?: Felix Haas Hall," *Purdue Today*, March 13, 2014, https://www.purdue.edu/newsroom/purduetoday/didyouknow/2014/Q1/did-you-know-felix-haas-hall.html.
27. "Marguerite Clifton Leads the Department in a Decade of Progress," *Newsletter Department of Physical Education for Women* 9, no. 1 (May 1975): 1, Archives, Purdue University Dept. of Health and Kinesiology.
28. "Collegiate Sports for Girls?," *Journal and Courier*, October 14, 1965, 39.
29. "Physical Education for Women Takes New Turn," *Journal and Courier*, September 9, 1964, 21.
30. History.com Staff, "Title IX Enacted," 2009, History.com, A+E Networks, accessed June 26, 2018, https://www.history.com/this-day-in-history/title-ix-enacted.
31. "The Title IX Distinguished Service Award Recipients," *Title IX*, accessed June 28, 2018, https://www.purdue.edu/titleix/45years/45years.html#Carole.
32. "Title IX Distinguished Service Award," *Title IX*, accessed December 9, 2024, https://www.purdue.edu/titleix/Title%20IX/archives/Title%20IX%20Distinguished%20Service%20Awards/50years.php#:~:text=Each%20of%20the%20Title%20IX,to%20women%20in%20higher%20education.
33. Richard C. Bell, "A History of Women in Sport Prior to Title IX," *The Sport Journal*, March 14, 2008, http://thesportjournal.org/article/a-history-of-women-in-sport-prior-to-title-ix/.
34. Jacob Houser, "Association for Intercollegiate Athletics for Women," *The 'Mad' 70s*, http://sites.jmu.edu/mad70s/2013/04/05/association-for-intercollegiate-athletics-for-women-1970-1982/.
35. Houser, "Association for Intercollegiate Athletics for Women."
36. "Coaching Future Goal for Women's Phys Ed," *Journal and Courier*, August 26, 1975, 45.
37. "What's New? Coaching Courses!," *50th Anniversary Newsletter*, May 1975, 9, Archives, Purdue University Dept. of Health and Kinesiology.
38. "Prof to Lead National Group," *Journal and Courier*, April 29, 1977, 4.
39. Jo-Ann Price Obituary, accessed April 13, 2023, https://www.legacy.com/us/obituaries/indystar/name/jo-ann-price-obituary?pid=144514131.

40. "Hansen Appoints Committees to Propose Plans for Implementation of Women's Intercollegiates," *50th Anniversary Newsletter*, May 1975, 8, Archives, Purdue University Dept. of Health and Kinesiology.
41. Rob McCurdy, "Mansfield's Carol Mertler Built Purdue's Women's Athletics from Scratch," *Mansfield News Journal*, May 3, 2014, https://www.mansfieldnewsjournal.com/story/news/2014/05/03/mansfields-carol-mertler-built-purdues-womens-athletics-from-scratch/8676249/.
42. McCurdy, "Mansfield's Carol Mertler Built Purdue's Women's Athletics from Scratch."
43. Reni Winter, "Life of 'Voice of Purdue' John DeCamp to Be Celebrated This Week," *Purdue News*, January 14, 2004, https://www.purdue.edu/uns/html3month/040114.Vruggink.memorial.html.
44. Sally Combs Elliott interview with Katherine Markee, December 4, 2006, POHO607017(Elliott), Purdue Office of Publications Oral History Program collection, Purdue University Archives and Special Collections Research Center, Purdue University Libraries.
45. "Girls Sports Head Named at Purdue," *Journal and Courier*, July 16, 1975, 1.
46. "Fall Sports Callout for Purdue Women," *Journal and Courier*, August 27, 1975, 36.
47. "Gebhardt Picked to Guide Purdue Women Cagers," *Journal and Courier*, October 2, 1975, 21.

CHAPTER 17

1. Lotys Benning Stewart, "Nurse Helen Johnson," *Indianapolis Star*, March 2, 1952, 20, Box 6, Folder 5, Purdue SON, Virginia Kelly Karnes Archives and Special Collections Research Center, Purdue University Libraries.
2. Stewart, "Nurse Helen Johnson."
3. Stewart, "Nurse Helen Johnson."
4. "Helen Johnson's Vision Lives On in Purdue School of Nursing," Purdue SON, Virginia Kelly Karnes Archives and Special Collections Research Center, Purdue University Libraries.
5. Helen R. Johnson, "History of Purdue University's Nursing Education Programs," Thesis, page 11, May 1975, Box 1, Folder 1, Purdue SON, Virginia Kelly Karnes Archives and Special Collections Research Center, Purdue University Libraries.
6. Johnson, "History of Purdue University's Nursing Education Programs," 22.
7. Johnson, "History of Purdue University's Nursing Education Programs," 24.

8. "Helen Johnson's Vision Lives On in Purdue School of Nursing," Purdue SON, Virginia Kelly Karnes Archives and Special Collections Research Center, Purdue University Libraries.
9. Johnson, "History of Purdue University's Nursing Education Programs," 45.
10. "Nursing Section, Purdue University First Annual Report to the W. K. Kellogg Foundation, June 1, 1963-June 1, 1964," Box 2, Annual Reports to Kellogg Foundation, Purdue SON, Virginia Kelly Karnes Archives and Special Collections Research Center, Purdue University Libraries.
11. Johnson, "History of Purdue University's Nursing Education Programs," 44.
12. Eleanor Crandall, "Nursing Education Dons New Cap," *Campus Copy*, Vol. 20, No. 9, page 3, May 1968, Virginia Kelly Karnes Archives and Special Collections Research Center, Purdue University Libraries.
13. Johnson, "History of Purdue University's Nursing Education Programs," 58.
14. "A Down-to-Earth Optimist," *Purdue People*, University News Service, Purdue University, No. 17, June 1968, Box 6, Folder 1, Purdue SON, Virginia Kelly Karnes Archives and Special Collections Research Center, Purdue University Libraries.
15. "Caps Patterned After Boilermaker Pete's," Purdue SON Scrapbook, Cabinet 2, Virginia Kelly Karnes Archives and Special Collections Research Center, Purdue University Libraries.
16. Emeline Rodenas, "Nurses Recall Tradition of Caps," KPC News, May 6, 2017, http://www.kpcnews.com/features/life/kpcnews/article_fc53db33-c08b-5b50-974d-909a36e26b9b.html.
17. "Nursing Program Students," photo caption, Cabinet 2, Purdue SON Scrapbooks, Virginia Kelly Karnes Archives and Special Collections Research Center, Purdue University Libraries.
18. C. H. Lawshe letter to Dr. Steven C. Beering, President, July 20, 1990, Box 1, Folder 1, Purdue SON, Virginia Kelly Karnes Archives and Special Collections Research Center, Purdue University Libraries.
19. "2-Year Nursing Program Gets National Approval," *Journal and Courier*, December 21, 1965, Cabinet 2, Purdue SON Scrapbooks, Virginia Kelly Karnes Archives and Special Collections Research Center, Purdue University Libraries.
20. "Purdue Puts Beginning Course on Video Tape," *The American Journal of Nursing*, July 1966, Cabinet 2, Purdue SON Scrapbooks, Virginia Kelly Karnes Archives and Special Collections Research Center, Purdue University Libraries.
21. "First 2 Men Nurse Grads Point at Anesthetic Field," *Journal and Courier*, June 7, 1967, 18, www.newspapers.com.

22. Dennis M. Royalty, "Purdue Nursing Director's Aim of Decade Takes Shape," *Indianapolis Star*, Cabinet 2, Purdue SON Scrapbooks, Virginia Kelly Karnes Archives and Special Collections Research Center, Purdue University Libraries.
23. "The History of Purdue Nursing 1962–1998, Part 1, The Helen Johnson Years," document emailed to author by Lynn Holland.
24. "Mrs. Johnson Wins Year's Nurse Award," Cabinet 2, Purdue SON Scrapbooks, Virginia Kelly Karnes Archives and Special Collections Research Center, Purdue University Libraries.
25. LaNelle Geddes video interview with Colleen DeTurk, The Faculty Committee for the 25th Anniversary Celebration of Nursing Education at Purdue University 1963–1988, "Remembrances," 1988, Archives of College of Health and Human Sciences, Purdue University.
26. "The History of Purdue Nursing 1962–1998, Part 1, The Helen Johnson Years."
27. Richard P. Smith, "Nursing: 'House' That Helen Built," *Perspective*, Summer 1989, Box 6, Folder 2, Purdue SON, Virginia Kelly Karnes Archives and Special Collections Research Center, Purdue University Libraries.
28. Royalty, "Purdue Nursing Director's Aim of Decade Takes Shape."
29. Helen Johnson video interview with Colleen DeTurk, The Faculty Committee for the 25th Anniversary Celebration of Nursing Education at Purdue University 1963–1988, "Remembrances," 1988, Archives of College of Health and Human Sciences, Purdue University.
30. Helen Johnson video interview with Colleen DeTurk.
31. "Television Classroom Added to Facilities in Nursing Building," *Vital Signs*, School of Nursing, Purdue University, January 1987.
32. Dedication Program, October 2, 1977, Box 5, Folder 4, Purdue SON, Virginia Kelly Karnes Archives and Special Collections Research Center, Purdue University Libraries.
33. Kevin Cullen, "Purdue's Nursing Building Officially Open," *Journal and Courier*, October 5, 1977, 3, www.newspapers.com.
34. Christopher Muscato, "Brutalist Architecture: Buildings, Architects & Style," accessed July 10, 2018, https://study.com/academy/lesson/brutalist-architecture-buildings-architects-style.html.
35. "Nursing Unit's Own Building Will Be Dedicated on Oct. 2," *Journal and Courier*, August 27, 1977, 38, www.newspapers.com.
36. "Adult/Community Health Pioneer Retires," *Purdue Nurse* (Summer 2004): 24, https://www.purdue.edu/hhs/nur/media/documents/summer2004.pdf.

37. "Adult/Community Health Pioneer Retires."
38. Memorandum to Dr. F. Haas from G. W. McNelly, April 27, 1977, Box 1, Folder 2, Purdue SON, Virginia Kelly Karnes Archives and Special Collections Research Center, Purdue University Libraries.
39. Memorandum to Dr. F. Haas from G. W. McNelly, April 27, 1977.
40. Helen Johnson video interview with Colleen DeTurk.
41. "Nursing Building Gets New Name," *Journal and Courier*, September 22, 1990, Box 5, Folder 1, Purdue SON, Virginia Kelly Karnes Archives and Special Collections Research Center, Purdue University Libraries.
42. RuthAnn Smolen email to Lynn Holland, December 4, 2001, shared with author by Holland.

CHAPTER 18

1. Eva L. Goble, "A Lifetime of Mentoring and Being Mentored!" MSF 3, Box 1, Folder 6, Eva Goble Papers, Virginia Kelly Karnes Archives and Special Collections Research Center, Purdue University Libraries.
2. Goble, "A Lifetime of Mentoring and Being Mentored!"
3. Eva L. Goble interview with Katherine Markee, January 5, 2007, http://collections.lib.purdue.edu/oralhistory/POH0607019_pt1(Goble).mp3.
4. Eva L. Goble interview with author, July 15, 2010.
5. Goble interview with author, July 15, 2010.
6. "How to Work to Be Theme of Lowell Meet," *The Times* (Munster, IN), August 2, 1944, 13, www.newspapers.com.
7. "Over 30 Leaders in Home Economics Meet in Auburn," *Garrett Clipper*, August 22, 1946, 2, www.newspapers.com.
8. Goble interview with author, July 15, 2010.
9. Col. Howard Ayers, Sr., *Find a Grave*, accessed July 13, 2018, https://www.findagrave.com/memorial/152496235/howard-ayers.
10. Angie Klink, *Divided Paths, Common Ground* (Purdue University Press, 2011), 217.
11. Goble interview with Markee, January 5, 2007.
12. Goble interview with author, July 15, 2010.
13. "Washington Twp. Ladies Hear of S. American Life," *Vidette-Messenger of Porter County* (Valparaiso, IN), July 25, 1953, 2, www.newspapers.com.
14. "New Co-Op House Visited by Leaders," *Journal and Courier*, January 12, 1954, 4, www.newspapers.com.

15. Robert Kellum, "Department Honors 2 Hoosiers," *Indianapolis Star*, May 19, 1965, 27, www.newspapers.com.
16. "Home Ec School Among U.S. Best," *Journal and Courier*, September 9, 1969, Box 5, Folder 8, UA 15, College of Health and Human Sciences records, Archives and Special Collections, Purdue University Libraries.
17. Sue Mortell, "Home Ec Offers Men Good Employment Outlook," Box 5, UA 15, College of Health and Human Sciences records, Archives and Special Collections, Purdue University Libraries.
18. Marie Stewart, "Picture of Home Economist Shows Purdue Men Studying," *Journal and Courier*, March 13, 1974, CFS Consumer and Family Sciences, Addition 3, Box 1, Vault 17C2, Virginia Kelly Karnes Archives and Special Collections Research Center, Purdue University Libraries.
19. Charlene Gierkey, "The Life of a Male in a World for Women," *Journal and Courier*, November 29, 1969, 37, www.newspapers.com.
20. Goble, "A Lifetime of Mentoring and Being Mentored!"
21. Klink, *Divided Paths*, 234.
22. "Purdue's Dean Eva Goble Retires," *Journal and Courier*, May 22, 1972, 12, www.newspapers.com.
23. "Purdue Tries Sandwiches by Hundreds," March 1966, Box 5, Folder 4, UA 15, College of Health and Human Sciences records, Purdue University Archives and Special Collections.
24. "Far Cry from Peanut Butter Jelly," *Journal Times* (Racine, WI), August 28, 1966, 35, www.newspapers.com.
25. "Dietetic Head of Indiana Purdue Prof," *Journal and Courier*, November 6, 1968, 8, www.newspapers.com.
26. Nancy Baker, "International Served by . . .," *Journal and Courier*, May 27, 1967, 32, www.newspapers.com.
27. Baker, "International Served by . . ."
28. "Students Run Restaurant," *Indianapolis Star*, May 3, 1970, 113, www.newspapers.com.
29. "Culinary 'Tour' of U.S. Offered," *Journal and Courier*, January 28, 1974, 15, www.newspapers.com.
30. "Home Ec. Professor Opens Foods Service Restaurant," *Exponent*, February 7, 1968, Box 5, Folder 6, UA 15, College of Health and Human Sciences records, Purdue University Archives and Special Collections.
31. Nancy Sinders, "Learn About Trends in Food Service," *Vidette-Messenger of Porter County*, June 16, 1966, 20, www.newspapers.com.

32. Sinders, "Learn About Trends in Food Service."
33. "Class at Purdue Explores Specialty Foods, Cuisine," *Palladium-Item* (Richmond, IN), December 26, 1971, 12, www.newspapers.com.
34. Margaret Golden McClain, "Golden Nuggets," *Logansport Press*, January 7, 1972, 8, www.newspapers.com.
35. "Europeans Dine—Americans Eat?" *The Republic* (Columbus, IN), March 23, 1973, 8, www.newspapers.com.
36. "Europeans Dine—Americans Eat?"
37. "New Staff Member," *Journal and Courier*, September 15, 1979, 14, www.newspapers.com.
38. "Rev. Dr. Flora L. Williams," Google Books, *Springing Forth: Growing Younger While Old*, accessed January 10, 2019, https://books.google.com.
39. "Workshop to Study Consumer Affairs," *Journal and Courier*, June 20, 1974, 29, www.newspapers.com.
40. Flora Williams email to author, January 31, 2019.
41. "Financial Counseling and Planning," Department of Consumer Science, Purdue University, accessed July 21, 2021, https://www.admissions.purdue.edu/majors/a-to-z/financial-counseling-and-planning.php.
42. Flora L. Williams, Vita, File given to author by Debra J. Booth, Director of Development Operations, College of Health and Human Sciences, Purdue University.
43. Kevin Cullen, "Professor/Pianist Measures What She Had, Not What She Lost," *Journal and Courier*, January 19, 2000, 1, www.newspapers.com.
44. Cullen, "Professor/Pianist Measures What She Had, Not What She Lost."
45. Cullen, "Professor/Pianist Measures What She Had, Not What She Lost."
46. Flora L. Williams, "Tragedy into Victory," 2001, File given to author by Debra J. Booth, Director of Development Operations, College of Health and Human Sciences, Purdue University.
47. "Book Briefs, 'Witnessing Book,'" *Journal and Courier*, July 27, 2006, 25, www.newspapers.com.

CHAPTER 19

1. Katey Watson Oral History Interview with Mary O'Hara, August 16, 2019, Purdue University Archives and Special Collections.
2. Mary E. Fyfe Obituary, December 25, 2005, *Chicago Tribune*, accessed April 6, 2023, https://www.chicagotribune.com/news/ct-xpm-2005-12-25-0512250173-story.html.

3. Watson, Oral History Interview with Mary O'Hara
4. Scott Kallstrom, "Helen Bass Williams: Her Soft Voice Delivered Hard Truths," *Purdue Alumnus*, November 1993, 16.
5. "'Old Master' Urges Love, Social Intelligence," *Journal and Courier*, November 7, 1967, 10.
6. "'Old Master' Urges Love, Social Intelligence."
7. Dave Bangert, "Portrait Unveiled of Helen Bass Williams, Purdue's First Black Professor," *Based in Lafayette* Substack, January 30, 2023.
8. Mary O'Hara, Journal Notes on Helen Bass Williams, Spring 1991, Mary O'Hara Papers on Helen Bass Williams, MSP 311, Box 3, Folder 1, Purdue University Archives and Special Collections.
9. Helen Bass Williams, Biographical Data for Use by "Who's Who in Mississippi," Helen Bass Papers, MSP 310, Box 4, Purdue University Archives and Special Collections.
10. Bridget Walsh, "People Can Be Taught to Love, a Profile of Helen Bass Williams," *Prairie Citizen*, July–August, 1986, 6.
11. Walsh, "People Can Be Taught to Love."
12. Walsh, "People Can Be Taught to Love."
13. Walsh, "People Can Be Taught to Love, 6–7.
14. Walsh, "People Can Be Taught to Love."
15. Walsh, "People Can Be Taught to Love, 7.
16. Walsh, "People Can Be Taught to Love."
17. Kallstrom, "Helen Bass Williams: Her Soft Voice Delivered Hard Truths," 20.
18. Helen Bass Williams, Earl B. Notestine, "Reading Proposal," 1975, Helen Bass Williams Papers, MSP 310, Series 5: Career and Activism, Subseries: Purdue University, File 3, Folder 4, Purdue University Archives and Special Collections.
19. Williams and Notestine, "Reading Proposal."
20. Helen Bass Williams, "Descriptive Data," 1973, Helen Bass Williams Papers, MSP 310, Series 5, Subseries 4, File 3: "Proposals—Purdue Minority Students," Folder 4, Purdue University Archives and Special Collections.
21. Barb Bohusz, "Tutoring at No Cost: The Learning Center," *The Purdue Exponent*, October 10, 1972, 7.
22. Earl B. Notestine, Helen Bass Williams, "A Learning Center at Purdue University," *Multi-Ethnicity in American Publishing* 1, no. 3 (Winter 1974).
23. Letter from Helen Bass Williams to Luther Williams, 1975 or 1976, Helen Bass Williams Papers, MSP 310, Box 4, Folder 7, File 6: Correspondence, Purdue University Archives and Special Collections.

24. Helen Bass Williams, "Anxiety Indicators," Helen Bass Williams Papers, Series 5: Career and Activism, Subseries: Purdue University, MSP 310, File 5: Africana Studies, Folder 6, Purdue University Archives and Special Collections.
25. Helen Bass Williams Letter to Friends, July 19, 1976, Helen Bass Williams Papers, Series 5: Career and Activism, Sub-Series 4: Purdue University, MSP 310, File 28 "Letter to Friends," Box 4, Folder 3, Purdue University Archives and Special Collections.
26. Mwende Mutuli Musau, "Harambee: The Law of Generosity That Rules Kenya," October 5, 2020, https://www.bbc.com/travel/article/20201004-harambee-the-kenyan-word-that-birthed-a-nation.
27. Bob Johnson, "Holocaust Survivors Tell Oral Histories in 'Bitter Prerequisites,'" *Purdue News*, February 16, 2001, https://www.purdue.edu/uns/html4ever/010216.ST.Ahlbrandt.book.html.
28. Leon Trachtman, Eulogy—Helen Bass Williams, Helen Bass Williams Papers, MSP 310, Box 4, Purdue University Archives and Special Collections.
29. "Purdue Launches Minority Scholarship Fund Drive," Purdue University News Service, January 14, 1993, Mary O'Hara Papers on Helen Bass Williams, MSP 311, Series 1: Personal Papers, File 3, Box 1 Folder 3, Purdue University Archives and Special Collections.
30. Walsh, "People Can Be Taught to Love," 7.
31. Kallstrom, "Helen Bass Williams: Her Soft Voice Delivered Hard Truths," 20.

CHAPTER 20

1. Angie Klink, *The Deans' Bible* (Purdue University Press, 2014), 333–34.
2. Cindy Metzler, "The Status of Women at Purdue University," 1970, MSF 466 Beverley Stone Papers, Box 10, Folder 10, Purdue University Archives and Special Collections.
3. Metzler, "The Status of Women at Purdue University."
4. Metzler, "The Status of Women at Purdue University."
5. Metzler, "The Status of Women at Purdue University."
6. Charlene Gierkey, "No Discrimination of Women in Faculty Jobs, Says Hicks," *Journal and Courier*, April 29, 1971, 11.
7. Klink, *The Deans' Bible*, 334–45.
8. Klink, *The Deans' Bible*.
9. Klink, *The Deans' Bible*, 334–35.
10. Beverley Stone, "Equal Employment Opportunity Ad Hoc Advisory Committee to Dr. John Hicks" minutes, November 1, 1971, MSF 466, Beverley Stone Papers, Box 10, Folder 10, Purdue University Archives and Special Collections.

11. Karen Clem, "Commission Report Indicates Paucity of Faculty Women," *The Purdue Exponent*, March 30, 1972, 1.
12. Beverley Stone, "Ad Hoc Advisory Committee to EEO Officer," Talk to Purdue Women's Dinner Club, November 14, 1972, MSF 466, Beverley Stone Papers, Box 10, Folder 10, Purdue University Archives and Special Collections.
13. Stone, "Ad Hoc Advisory Committee to EEO Officer."
14. Eddie Tucker, "Women's Caucus Active, 58 Strong," *The Purdue Exponent*, October 10, 1972, 6.
15. Renee Wyman, "Women's Caucus Confronts Hansen on Discrimination," *The Purdue Exponent*, October 10, 1972, 1.
16. Wyman, "Women's Caucus Confronts Hansen on Discrimination."
17. Wyman, "Women's Caucus Confronts Hansen on Discrimination."
18. Helen B. Schleman, Notes on Discrimination Lawsuit Against TIAA-CREF and Purdue University, Helen Schleman Papers, MSF 334, Box 6, Folder 12, Purdue University Libraries and Special Collections.
19. Schleman, Notes on Discrimination Lawsuit Against TIAA-CREF and Purdue University.
20. Schleman, Notes on Discrimination Lawsuit Against TIAA-CREF and Purdue University.
21. Schleman, Notes on Discrimination Lawsuit Against TIAA-CREF and Purdue University.
22. Letter from Lois N. Magner, Barbara Elsbury, and Linda Levy Peck to Arthur Hansen, February 19, 1979, Beverley Stone Papers, MSF 466, Box 10, Folder 10, Purdue University Archives and Special Collections.
23. Letter from Arthur Hansen to Lois N. Magner, Barbara Elsbury, and Linda Levy Peck, March 2, 1979, Beverley Stone Papers, MSF 466, Box 10, Folder 10, Purdue University Archives and Special Collections.
24. Schleman, Notes on Discrimination Lawsuit Against TIAA-CREF and Purdue University.
25. Kevin Cullen, "Purdue Sued over Pension Pay," *Journal and Courier*, February 5, 1980, 3.
26. Johnston, et al., v. Purdue University, et al., L80-4 (Ind. 1987).
27. Betty M. Nelson, email message to author, April 14, 2023.

CHAPTER 21

1. "Garfinckel's (Julius Garfinckel & Co.)," DC Historic Sites, accessed August 10, 2018, http://historicsites.dcpreservation.org/items/show/229?tour=1&index=10.

2. "Norma Compton Assumes Deanship of Home Economics," *Purdue Reports*, May 1973, Archives and Special Collections, Purdue University Libraries.
3. "Homemakers Told Life Style Change," *The Tribune* (Seymour, IN), June 13, 1973, 14, www.newspapers.com.
4. "Homemakers Told Life Style Change."
5. "Dean Compton to Discuss Her Book," *Journal and Courier*, February 6, 1974, 25, www.newspapers.com.
6. "Norma Compton Dean," *Journal and Courier*, August 27, 1974, 46, www.newspapers.com.
7. R. Paul Abernathy interview with author, September 18, 2018.
8. Norma Compton, "From the Dean," *CFS Newsletter*, Vol. 1, No. 1, August 1978, Archives, College of Health and Human Sciences, Purdue University.
9. Norma Compton, Summary of Consumer and Family Sciences Name Change, CFS Records, Addition 3, Archives and Special Collections, Purdue University Libraries.
10. "Name Change Noted for Home Ec School," *Journal and Courier*, August 28, 1976, 44, www.newspapers.com.
11. "Name Change Noted for Home Ec School."
12. "Name Change Noted for Home Ec School."
13. "Name Change Noted for Home Ec School."
14. "Name Change Noted for Home Ec School."
15. Christine Ladisch note to author, January 25, 2019.
16. Christine Ladisch, interview by Angie Klink, March 5, 2018.
17. Norma Compton, "Consumer and Family Sciences: New Name Updates Old School," September 1976, page 3, Folder 4, Box 6, UA 15, College of Health and Human Sciences records, Archives and Special Collections, Purdue University Libraries.
18. Compton, "Consumer and Family Sciences: New Name Updates Old School."
19. "Home Ec Careers Vary Widely," *Journal and Courier*, August 27, 1974, 46, www.newspapers.com.
20. Norma Compton, "From the Dean," *CSF Newsletter*, Vol. 3, No. 2, August 1980, Archives, College of Health and Human Sciences, Purdue University.
21. Kathleen Pearl Brewer, "The History and Development of the Department of Restaurant, Hotel, and Institutional Management Purdue University," August 6, 1986, page 12, Folder 2, Box 1, UA 15, College of Health and Human Sciences records, Archives and Special Collections, Purdue University Libraries.
22. Compton, Summary of Consumer and Family Sciences Name Change.
23. Compton, "1977–1978 Annual Report."

CHAPTER 22

1. Eric Nelson, "Fond Farewell," *Krannert Magazine* 1, no. 23 (Spring 2022).
2. Author interview with Charlene Sullivan, May 2, 2023.
3. Author interview with Charlene Sullivan.
4. Author interview with Charlene Sullivan.
5. Nelson, "Fond Farewell."
6. Nelson, "Fond Farewell."
7. Nelson, "Fond Farewell."
8. Robin Saks Frankel, "History of Women and Credit Cards: 1970s to Present," *Forbes Advisor*, December 2, 2022, https://www.forbes.com/advisor/credit-cards/when-could-women-get-credit-cards/.
9. Nelson, "Fond Farewell."
10. Author interview with Charlene Sullivan.
11. Author interview with Charlene Sullivan.
12. Author interview with Charlene Sullivan.
13. Nelson, "Fond Farewell."
14. Author interview with Charlene Sullivan.
15. Author interview with Charlene Sullivan.
16. Author interview with Charlene Sullivan.
17. Author interview with Charlene Sullivan.
18. Rafael Alvarez, "Dr. Carolyn Woo's Mission of Charity," *St. Anthony Messanger*, accessed October 31, 2023, https://www.franciscanmedia.org/st-anthony-messenger/dr-carolyn-woos-mission-of-charity/.
19. "Alums Carolyn Woo and Kenneth Tan—Forces for Good," accessed October 31, 2023, https://www.purdue.edu/aaarcc/events/heritage-2021/woo.php.
20. Alvarez, "Dr. Carolyn Woo's Mission of Charity."
21. Carolyn Y. Woo, *Working for a Better World* (Catholic Relief Services, 2015), 60.
22. Muzaffer ErSelcuk Obituary, accessed November 1, 2023, https://www.legacy.com/us/obituaries/nytimes/name/muzaffer-erselcuk-obituary?id=14208593.
23. Woo, *Working for a Better World*.
24. Woo, *Working for a Better World*.
25. Carolyn Y. Woo Oral History Interview with Katherine Markee, May 14, 2010, Purdue University Archives and Special Collections.
26. Woo Oral History Interview with Katherine Markee.
27. Carolyn Woo email, October 12, 2024.

28. Woo, *Working for a Better World*, 43.
29. Woo, *Working for a Better World*, 39.
30. Woo, *Working for a Better World*, 61.
31. Angela Townsend, "Women at Purdue Juggle Roles, Goals," *Journal and Courier*, April 17, 1995, A1.

CHAPTER 23

1. Avanelle Kirksey, "Retirement Seminar Lecture," Fall 1994, Purdue University, Folder 3, Box 11, MSF 502, Series 2, Avanelle Kirksey Papers, Purdue University Archives and Special Collections Research Center, Purdue University Libraries.
2. Avanelle Kirksey, "Friend of Purdue Award Speech," Purdue University, 1995, Folder 3, Box 11, MSF 502, Series 2, Purdue University Archives and Special Collections Research Center, Purdue University Libraries.
3. Kirksey, "Friend of Purdue Award Speech."
4. Susan Oberiander, "Prof's Second Home Is Kalama, Egypt," *Journal and Courier*, January 31, 1987, 3, www.newspapers.com.
5. Avanelle Kirksey, "Research with Vitamin B-6," Pennsylvania State University Seminar, May 6, 1977, Folder 7, box 8, MSF 502, Series 2, Avanelle Kirksey Papers, Purdue University Archives and Special Collections Research Center, Purdue University Libraries.
6. Connie M. Weaver and Bruce R. Hamaker, "Avanelle Kirksey, PhD (1926–2016)," *The Journal of Nutrition*, American Society for Nutrition, March 2, 2017, given to author by Connie M. Weaver.
7. Weaver and Hamaker, "Avanelle Kirksey, PhD (1926–2016)."
8. Kirksey, "Retirement Seminar Lecture."
9. Mary Alice Nebold email to author, June 6, 2019.
10. Avanelle Kirksey, Penn State Speech, 1985, Folder 5, Box 4, MSF 502, Series 2, Avanelle Kirksey Papers, Purdue University Archives and Special Collections Research Center, Purdue University Libraries.
11. "Important Points in Care of Rats," MSF 502, Avanelle Kirksey Papers, Purdue University Archives and Special Collections Research Center, Purdue University Libraries.
12. Avanelle Kirksey, "Nutrition Research: Personal Reflections or Looking Ahead," 1982, Speech to Alumni, page 3, Folder 11, Box 5, MSF 502, Series 2, Avanelle Kirksey Papers, Purdue University Archives and Special Collections Research Center, Purdue University Libraries.

13. "Purdue's Kirksey Studies Needs of Preterm Infants," *Journal and Courier*, September 22, 1986, 25, www.newspapers.com.
14. Kirksey, "Nutrition Research: Personal Reflections," 10.
15. "Avanelle Kirksey 1980 Borden Award Winner," *IMPACT!*, Vol. 3, No. 3, January 1981, Folder 3, Box 3, MSF 502, Series 1, Avanelle Kirksey Papers, Purdue University Archives and Special Collections Research Center, Purdue University Libraries.
16. "Prof. Helen E. Clark," *Journal and Courier*, August 6, 1966, 9, www.newspapers.com.
17. Rebecca J. Goetz, "Vitamin B6 and Oral Contraceptives," *Science News*, July 2, 1985, Folder 5, Box 3, MSF 502, Series 1, Avanelle Kirksey Papers, Purdue University Archives and Special Collections Research Center, Purdue University Libraries.
18. Douglas W. Spangler to Norma H. Compton, Inter Office Memorandum, Purdue University, December 28, 1978, Folder 5, Box 3, MSF 502, Series 1, Avanelle Kirksey Papers, Purdue University Archives and Special Collections Research Center, Purdue University Libraries.
19. Kirksey, "Nutrition Research: Personal Reflections."
20. Avanelle Kirksey, "Acceptance of the Borden Award for Nutrition Research," June 23, 1980, AHEA Annual Meeting, Dallas, Texas, Folder 2, Box 4, MSF 502, Series 1, Avanelle Kirksey Papers, Purdue University Archives and Special Collections Research Center, Purdue University Libraries.
21. Kirksey, "Nutrition Research: Personal Reflections."
22. Marty Meyer, "Nutrition Growing Research Area," *Purdue Alumnus*, December 1981, Folder 2, Box 3, MSF 502 Series 1, Avanelle Kirksey Papers, Purdue University Archives and Special Collections Research Center, Purdue University Libraries.
23. Meyer, "Nutrition Growing Research Area."
24. Dave Lim, "Purdue Studies Malnutrition," *Exponent*, October 21, 1983, 14, Folder 7, Box 3, MSF 502, Series 1, Avanelle Kirksey Papers, Purdue University Archives and Special Collections Research Center, Purdue University Libraries.
25. Kirksey, "Retirement Seminar Lecture."
26. Janet Barstow, "Scientists to Study Marginal Diets," *Purdue Alumnus*, May 1983, 9, Folder 3, Box 3, MSF 502, Series 1, Avanelle Kirksey Papers, Purdue University Archives and Special Collections Research Center, Purdue University Libraries.
27. Nancy Steel, "Researcher Probes Africa in Search of Cure," *Southwest Times Record* (Fort Smith, AK), Folder 3, Box 3, MSF 502, Series 1, Avanelle Kirksey Papers, Purdue University Archives and Special Collections Research Center, Purdue University Libraries.

28. Nancy Meyer to Avanelle Kirksey letter, November 1, 1994, Folder 13, Box 4, MSF 502, Series 2, Avanelle Kirksey Papers, Purdue University Archives and Special Collections Research Center, Purdue University Libraries.
29. Weaver and Hamaker, "Avanelle Kirksey, PhD (1926–2016)."
30. Oberiander, "Prof's Second Home Is Kalama, Egypt."
31. Frederick Whitford, Andrew G. Martin, and Phyllis Mattheis, *The Queen of American Agriculture* (Purdue University Press, 2008), 238.
32. Kirksey, "Friend of Purdue Award Speech."
33. Kirksey, "Friend of Purdue Award Speech."

CHAPTER 24

1. Oliva Bennett Wood Interview with Katherine Markee, June 10, 2013, MSO1i201213015, Purdue University Archives and Special Collections Research Center oral history, email from Stephanie Schmitz to author, May 31, 2018.
2. Olivia Bennett Wood interview with author, June 1, 2018.
3. "WIC Program Overview and History," National WIC Association, accessed September 11, 2018, https://www.nwica.org/overview-and-history.
4. Wood interview with author, June 1, 2018.
5. Wood interview with author, June 1, 2018.
6. Wood interview with author, June 1, 2018.
7. Wood interview with author, June 1, 2018.
8. Wood Interview with Markee, June 10, 2013.
9. Olivia Bennett Wood email to author, September 16, 2018.
10. Wood email to author, September 16, 2018.
11. Wood Interview with Markee, June 10, 2013.
12. Wood Interview with Markee, June 10, 2013.
13. Wood Interview with Markee, June 10, 2013.
14. Wood Interview with Markee, June 10, 2013.
15. Wood interview with author, June 1, 2018.
16. Oliva Bennett Wood Interview with Katherine Markee, August 28, 2013, MSO1i201213015, Purdue University Archives and Special Collections Research Center oral history, email from Stephanie Schmitz to author, May 31, 2018.
17. "Olivia Wood Looks Back on 34 Years," *Foods & Nutrition*, 2008, page 7, Archives College of Health and Human Sciences, Purdue University.

18. "Mary L. Matthews Portrait, Plaque Place in Matthews Hall," *PURA Newsletter* 37, no. 2 (April 2013): 1, https://www.purdue.edu/retirees/docs/PURA_2013-04newsletter.pdf.
19. Connie M. Weaver interview with author, May 31, 2018.
20. Weaver interview with author, May 31, 2018.
21. Paul Abernathy interview with author, September 18, 2018.
22. Weaver interview with author, May 31, 2018.
23. "University Trustees Appoint 3 New Department Heads," *Journal and Courier*, March 23, 1991, 9, www.newspapers.com.
24. Connie M. Weaver email to author, September 16, 2018.
25. Weaver email to author, September 16, 2018.
26. Weaver email to author, September 16, 2018.
27. Chris Schenk, "Summer Fun Includes Calcium Injections," *Exponent*, Jun 7, 1993, Folder: Clippings, Box 1, 20131104.papers, Purdue University Archives and Special Collections Research Center, Purdue University Libraries.
28. "Fun, Fitness and Dietary Recommendations," Folder: Clippings, Box 1, 20131104.1, Connie Weaver Papers, Purdue University Archives and Special Collections Research Center, Purdue University Libraries.
29. "Camp Calcium," *Chippewa Herald* (Chippewa Falls, WI), July 16, 1995, 11, www.newspapers.com.
30. Wood interview with author, June 1, 2018.
31. Angela Townsend, "Younger Is Better for Calcium," *Journal and Courier*, May 24, 1995, 13, www.newspapers.com.
32. Joe Gerrety, "Nutrition Expert Finds New Reasons to Drink Milk," *Journal and Courier*, May 18, 1992, 5, www.newspapers.com.
33. Gerrety, "Nutrition Expert Finds New Reasons to Drink Milk."
34. Paul Recer, "Report: Americans Need More Calcium," *Journal and Courier*, August 14, 1997, 5, www.newspapers.com.
35. Tanya Brown, "Honor a First for Purdue Women Educators," *Journal and Courier*, October 14, 2006, 11, www.newspapers.com.
36. Amy Patterson, "Pre-Teen Girls Take Part in Purdue Study . . .," *Journal and Courier*, July 9, 2000, 14, www.newspapers.com.
37. Steve Tally, "Female Adolescents Need Calcium During 'Window of Opportunity,'" August 1997, https://www.eurekalert.org/pub_releases/1997-08/PU-FANC-130897.php.

38. Sheryl Gay Stolberg, "Brand-New Recipe for Healthy Bones Adds More Calcium," *The New York Times*, August 14, 1997, Folder: Clippings, Box 1, 20131104.1, Connie Weaver Papers, Purdue University Archives and Special Collections Research Center, Purdue University Libraries.
39. "Weaver: Adolescents and Calcium Needs," *Inside Purdue*, August 26, 1997, 7, Folder: Clippings, Box 1, 20131104.1, Connie Weaver Papers, Purdue University Archives and Special Collections Research Center, Purdue University Libraries.
40. Jeanne V. Norberg, "Purdue Center to Lead National Research in Dietary Supplements," September 19, 2000, https://www.purdue.edu/uns/html4ever/000920.Weaver.nihcenter.html.
41. "Nutrition Expert to Help Decide Nation's Menu," September 10, 2003, 9, www.newspapers.com.
42. Eric Weddle, "Calcium Expert Receives Top Purdue Research Honor," *Journal and Courier*, May 2012, 27, B6, www.newspapers.com.
43. Tanya Brown, "Honor a First for Purdue Women Educators," *Journal and Courier*, October 14, 2006, 11, www.newspapers.com.
44. Eric Weddle, "Solid Benefits Seen in Purdue-IU Alliance," *Journal and Courier*, February 22, 2009, 23, www.newspapers.com.
45. Brian Wallheimer, "$25 Million Grant to Help Purdue Get Discoveries to Markets," *Journal and Courier*, May 30, 2008, 1, www.newspapers.com.
46. Weddle, "Solid Benefits Seen in Purdue-IU Alliance."
47. Taya Flores, "Team Researching Link Between Diet, Breast Cancer," *Journal and Courier*, October 1, 2010, 26, www.newspapers.com.
48. Maryjane Slaby, "Camp Celebrates 20 Years of Calcium Research," *Journal and Courier*, June 26, 2011, 23, www.newspapers.com.
49. Eric Weddle, "Calcium Expert Receives Top Purdue Research Honor," *Journal and Courier*, May 2012, 27, B6, www.newspapers.com.
50. Amy Patterson Neubert, "Foods and Nutrition Head Elected to Institute of Medicine," November 2010, Folder: Clippings, Box 1, 20131104.1, Connie Weaver Papers, Purdue University Archives and Special Collections Research Center, Purdue University Libraries.
51. "Weaver First OSU Alum to Receive Linus Pauling Prize," Synergies, Oregon State University, September 16, 2011, http://synergies.oregonstate.edu/2011/connie-weaver-first-osu-alum-to-receive-linus-pauling-prize/.
52. Eric Weddle, "Purdue Launches Women's Health Initiative," *Journal and Courier*, March 24, 2012, 1, www.newspapers.com.

53. "Launch of Women's Global Health Institute," June 2012, Purdue University Discovery Park, https://www.purdue.edu/discoverypark/WGHI/.
54. Amy Patterson Neubert, "Calcium Expert Honored with University's Top Research Award," Purdue University, May 22, 2012, https://www.purdue.edu/newsroom/faculty/2012/120522WeaverMcCoy.html.
55. "Miracle Berries: How Blueberries Can Improve Bone Health," October 31, 2016, Research Features, https://researchfeatures.com/2016/10/31/miracle-berries-how-blueberries-can-improve-bone-health/.
56. "110th Gala Celebration," Department of Nutrition Science program, May 6, 2016, page 4, Archives of College of Health and Human Sciences, Purdue University.
57. Meghan Holden, "'Dream' Center Revives Purdue Exercise, Nutrition," *Journal and Courier*, May 25, 2016, A3, www.newspapers.com.
58. Emily Vian, "Nutrition Head Ready to Pass On Her Legacy," *Exponent*, December 7, 2016, https://www.purdueexponent.org/campus/article_ce393761-94cb-50d2-bfb8-6c789dc938c5.html.
59. "Weaver First OSU Alum to Receive Linus Pauling Prize."

CHAPTER 25

1. "School Bids Farewell to Nursing Legend," *Purdue Nurse*, February 2004, https://www.purdue.edu/hhs/nur/media/documents/spring2004.pdf.
2. "School Bids Farewell to Nursing Legend."
3. LaNelle Geddes interview with Katherine Markee, March 6, 2007, http://earchives.lib.purdue.edu/cdm/search/searchterm/POH0607025(Geddes).
4. "Set Services," *El Paso Times*, October 17, 1955, 7, www.newspapers.com.
5. "Geddes," *Journal and Courier*, September 23, 2006, 11, www.newspapers.com.
6. Geddes interview with Markee, March 6, 2007.
7. Geddes interview with Markee, March 6, 2007.
8. "The History of Purdue Nursing Part Two: The LaNelle Geddes Years," page 7, emailed to author by Lynn Holland.
9. Sharon L. Martin, "Gender Equity," *Purdue Alumnus*, March/April 1996, LaNelle Geddes Papers, Purdue University Archives and Special Collections Research Center, Purdue University Libraries.
10. Martin, "Gender Equity."
11. "School Bids Farewell to Nursing Legend."

12. Julia Sweeney, "Professor 'Matures' Students," *Exponent*, 1993, LaNelle Geddes Papers, Purdue University Archives and Special Collections Research Center, Purdue University Libraries.
13. LaNelle E. Geddes, "What Do WE Do? Share Insights? Or 'Bestow Pearls?'" *Perspective*, Spring 1986, page 8, LaNelle Geddes Papers, Purdue University Archives and Special Collections Research Center, Purdue University Libraries.
14. "School Bids Farewell to Nursing Legend," 3.
15. "Crazy Things Professors Say," *Purdue Alumnus*, LaNelle Geddes Papers, Purdue University Archives and Special Collections Research Center, Purdue University Libraries.
16. Jane Kirkpatrick letter to LaNelle Geddes, Retirement Scrapbook, LaNelle Geddes Papers, Purdue University Archives and Special Collections Research Center, Purdue University Libraries.
17. "Dr. LaNelle E. Geddes, Obituary," *Journal and Courier*, January 28, 2016, C2, www.newspapers.com.
18. Geddes interview with Markee, March 6, 2007.
19. LaNelle Geddes, Comments to Delta Omicron Chapter Sigma Theta Tau, June 7, 1994, LaNelle Geddes Papers, Purdue University Archives and Special Collections Research Center, Purdue University Libraries.
20. Geddes interview with Markee, March 6, 2007.
21. Geddes, Comments to Sigma Theta Tau.
22. "Reach to Recovery," American Cancer Society, accessed October 8, 2018, https://www.cancer.org/treatment/support-programs-and-services/reach-to-recovery.html.
23. "Reach to Recovery Visit," Comment Card, LaNelle Geddes Papers, Purdue University Archives and Special Collections.
24. Geddes, Comments to Sigma Theta Tau.
25. "History of Purdue Nursing."
26. Memo to Nursing Faculty and Staff from Joan Lohmann, Director of Development, Purdue University School of Nursing, October 31, 1988, Purdue SON, Purdue University Archives and Special Collections.
27. "Giant Leap into the Future," *Nursing Educator*, Vol. 2, No. 7, October/November 1988, Purdue SON, Purdue University Archives and Special Collections.
28. "New Critical Care Unit Enhances Student Learning," *Vital Signs*, January 1990, Folder: Vital Signs Newsletters 1984–2000, Box 5b, Purdue SON, Purdue University Archives and Special Collections.

29. John Norberg, "More Students Apply for Nursing School," *Journal and Courier*, February 25, 1989, 83, www.newspapers.com.
30. "School of Nursing Already Hurting for Faculty," *Journal and Courier*, April 22, 1990, 11, www.newspapers.com.
31. "School of Nursing Already Hurting for Faculty."
32. "School Bids Farewell to Nursing Legend."
33. "School Bids Farewell to Nursing Legend."
34. Email from Jean Putnam to Roxanne J. Martin, December 13, 2015, LaNelle Geddes Papers, Purdue University Archives and Special Collections Research Center, Purdue University Libraries.
35. "Always a Smile: Meet Jo Brooks," *Vital Signs*, Winter 1993, Folder: Vital Signs Newsletters 1984–2000, Box 5b, Purdue SON, Purdue University Archives and Special Collections.
36. "Jo Brooks, RN, C, DNS," *Vital Signs* 7, no. 1 (Spring 2000), https://www.purdue.edu/hhs/nur/media/documents/spring2000.pdf.
37. "History of Purdue Nursing."
38. "Nursing Clinic Offers Health Services," *Purdue Today*, February 3, 1986, Purdue SON Scrapbook, Cabinet 2, Purdue University Archives and Special Collections.
39. "Former Professor Writes Nursing Novel," *Vital Signs*, Fall 1979, Folder: Vital Signs Newsletters 1976–1988, Box 5b, Purdue SON, Purdue University Archives and Special Collections.
40. "Purdue Prof Is Nurse of Year," *Journal and Courier*, September 23, 1986, Purdue SON Scrapbook, Cabinet 2, Purdue University Archives and Special Collections.
41. "The History of Purdue Nursing," *Vital Signs*, Vol. 6, No 15, Spring 1999, Purdue SON, Purdue University Archives and Special Collections.
42. "The History of Purdue Nursing," *Vital Signs*.
43. "Delta Omicron Members Active in Outreach for Medically Underserved," *KeyNotes*, Spring 2006, Purdue SON, Purdue University Archives and Special Collections.
44. Lynn Holland, "Brooks Center Honors Purdue Nurse," *Purdue Nurse*, January 2009, accessed October 11, 2018, https://www.purdue.edu/hhs/nur/media/documents/spring2009.pdf.
45. "Our History," Family Health Clinic, accessed October 7, 2018, https://www.familyhconline.com/about/.
46. Jo A. Brooks, "West Meets East: Excerpts from My Diary," *Vital Signs*, Spring 1997, page 2, Folder: Vital Signs Newsletters 1984–2000, Box 5b, Purdue SON, Purdue University Archives and Special Collections.

47. "Jo Brooks Named Sagamore of the Wabash," *Purdue Nurse*, Summer 2002, https://www.purdue.edu/hhs/nur/media/documents/summer2002.pdf.

CHAPTER 26

1. "Making a Difference for Minorities," *Vital Signs*, Winter 1995, page 7, Folder: Vital Signs Newsletters 1984–2000, Box 5b, Purdue SON, Virginia Kelly Karnes Archives and Special Collections Research Center, Purdue University Libraries.
2. "Dr. Clara Bell Session, Professor, African American Leader," *Journal and Courier*, March 5, 1996, Box 9, Minority Student Nurses Assoc. Diversity Materials, Purdue SON, Virginia Kelly Karnes Archives and Special Collections Research Center, Purdue University Libraries.
3. "Clara Bell Named Nursing Director," *Lafayette Leader*, August 5, 1985, Box 9, Minority Student Nurses Assoc. Diversity Materials, Purdue SON, Virginia Kelly Karnes Archives and Special Collections Research Center, Purdue University Libraries.
4. Mitchell Kirk, "Longstanding Longcliff: Logansport State Hospital Turns 130," *Pharos-Tribune*, June 27, 2018, http://www.pharostribune.com/news/local_news/article_8f145e0d-e0c7-5a85-855c-bd269d2c0207.html.
5. Lynn Dancey, "Dr. Bell Tells Children What Olympics Stand For," *Logansport Press*, February 10, 1972, 2, www.newspapers.com.
6. Clara Bell and Eleanor Stephan, "Black Nursing Students Articulate Their Needs," February 20, 1984, Box 9, Minority Student Nurses Assoc. Diversity Materials, Purdue SON, Virginia Kelly Karnes Archives and Special Collections Research Center, Purdue University Libraries.
7. Bell and Stephan, "Black Nursing Students Articulate Their Needs."
8. Bell and Stephan, "Black Nursing Students Articulate Their Needs."
9. "Minority Student Nurses' Association," Purpose Statement, Box 9, Minority Student Nurses Assoc. Diversity Materials, Purdue SON, Virginia Kelly Karnes Archives and Special Collections Research Center, Purdue University Libraries.
10. Kathe Schuckel, "Leaders from Black Colleges Establish Ties at Purdue," *Journal and Courier*, September 29, 1988, Purdue SON Scrapbook, Cabinet 2, Virginia Kelly Karnes Archives and Special Collections Research Center, Purdue University Libraries.
11. "Clara Bell Sessions," *Purdue Today Presenting Profiles on Title IX Service Awardees*, June 20, 2013, https://www.purdue.edu/newsroom/purduetoday/releases/2013/Q2/purdue-today-presenting-profiles-on-title-ix-service-awardees3.html.

12. "Making a Difference for Minorities," *Vital Signs*, Winter 1995, page 7, Folder: Vital Signs Newsletters 1984–2000, Box 5b, Purdue SON, Virginia Kelly Karnes Archives and Special Collections Research Center, Purdue University Libraries.
13. Jane Kirkpatrick interview with author, February 11, 2019.
14. Kirkpatrick interview with author, February 11, 2019.
15. "CD-ROM Helps Teach Newborn Assessment," *Purdue Nurse*, Summer 2002, 7.
16. "Teaching Awards," *Purdue Nurse*, Summer 2004, 29.
17. Jane Kirkpatrick, "From the Head," *Purdue Nurse*, February 2010, 2.
18. Kirkpatrick, "From the Head."
19. "School of Nursing Welcomes Joint Appointment with Engineering," *Purdue Nurse*, February 2011, 8.
20. "Transdisciplinary Collaborations," *Purdue Nurse*, Summer 2015, 14–15.
21. Kirkpatrick, "From the Head."
22. Amy Patterson Neubert, "Purdue Nursing to Double Undergraduate Enrollment and Open Ph.D. Program to Meet State's Job Demand," *Purdue University News*, November 3, 2016, https://www.purdue.edu/newsroom/releases/2016/Q4/purdue-nursing-to-double-undergraduate-enrollment-and-open-ph.d.-program-to-meet-states-job-demand.html.
23. Kirkpatrick interview with author, February 11, 2019.
24. Sarah Fentem, "In Shadow of Looming Shortage, Purdue Doubles Nursing Enrollment," WFYI Indianapolis, November 4, 2016, https://www.wfyi.org/news/articles/in-shadow-of-looming-shortage-purdue-doubles-nursing-enrollment.
25. Kirkpatrick interview with author, February 11, 2019.

CHAPTER 27

1. Monica Jackson and Elizabeth Stark, *Tents in the Clouds* (Seal Press, 2000), 13.
2. Jackson and Stark, *Tents in the Clouds*, 14.
3. "Profile of a Department Head," Box 13, Folder: "Purdue Retiree Newsletters," MSF 360, Max D. Steer Papers, Virginia Kelly Karnes Archives and Special Collections Research Center, Purdue University Libraries.
4. Josephine Novak, "Researcher Translates Baby," *The Evening Sun* (Baltimore), May 10, 1977, 21, www.newspapers.com.
5. "Dr. Rachel E. Stark, 76," Obituary, *Journal and Courier*, September 9, 2000, 8, www.newspapers.com.
6. Sheridan Lyons, "Babies' Babbling Is Seen as an Aid in Predicting Potential Speech Problems," *The Baltimore Sun*, May 6, 1984, 68, www.newspapers.com.

7. Annual Report 1994, Department of Audiology and Speech Sciences, Purdue University, page 4, given to author by Teasha McKinely, administrative assistant, Speech, Language and Hearing Sciences.
8. "Profile of a Department Head," Box 13, Folder: "Purdue Retiree Newsletters," MSF 360, Max D. Steer Papers, Virginia Kelly Karnes Archives and Special Collections Research Center, Purdue University Libraries.
9. "Purdue Initiating Training Grant," *The Times* (Munster, IN), September 27, 1989, 13, www.newspapers.com.
10. Purdue University News Release, October 25, 1990, MSF 360, Max D. Steer Papers, Virginia Kelly Karnes Archives and Special Collections Research Center, Purdue University Libraries.
11. Jackson and Stark, *Tents in the Clouds*, 13.
12. Barbara Solomon interview with author, February 5, 2019.
13. Solomon interview with author, and previously with Andrew Fristoe, 2019.
14. "Macalyne Fristoe," Prabook, accessed February 13, 2019, https://prabook.com/web/macalyne.fristoe/81081.
15. Solomon interview with author.
16. Dorothy Sherman, "Review of Goldman-Fristoe Test of Articulation," *Professional Psychology* 1 (Fall 1970): 493–94, https://psycnet.apa.org/record/2005-10329-009.
17. Barbara Solomon email to author, February 12, 2019, Subject: GFTA.
18. "Retarded" was a medical term in the late nineteenth and twentieth centuries to describe children with intellectual disabilities or retarded mental development. Today it is a derogatory term, no longer used in the medical field.
19. Macalyne Freeman (Fristoe) letter to Sarah E. Butler, May 19, 1966, Macalyne Fristoe personal files.
20. Macalyne Freeman (Fristoe) letter to Sarah E. Butler, May 19, 1966.
21. Ronald Goldman and Macalyne Fristoe, "The Film Strip Articulation Test," *Exceptional Children* (September 1966): 42, Macalyne Fristoe personal papers.
22. Goldman and Fristoe, "The Film Strip Articulation Test," 43.
23. Goldman and Fristoe, "The Film Strip Articulation Test."
24. Celia Viggo, "Lost the Thrill of Working?" *Journal and Courier*, September 21, 1980, 21.
25. Who's Who Lifetime Achievement, April 27, 2017, https://wwlifetimeachievement.com/2017/04/27/macalyne-fristoe/.
26. Randi Henderson, "Women Scientists Find Discrimination Hindering Climb," *The Baltimore Sun*, April 29, 1976, 25.
27. As told to author by Andrew Fristoe, son of Macalyne Fristoe.

28. Solomon interview with author.
29. Solomon interview with author.
30. Solomon interview with author.
31. Solomon interview with author.
32. Dan Shaw, "Devoted Professor, Dean Dies," *Journal and Courier*, accessed August 23, 2018, https://www.purdue.edu/uns/html3month/2006/060515.Ringel.story.html.
33. Solomon interview with author.
34. Solomon interview with author.
35. Solomon interview with author.

CHAPTER 28

1. https://archives.library.illinois.edu/ncte/wp-content/uploads/sites/96/2023/04/NCTE-Centennial-Exhibits-ConferenceonCollegeCompositionCommunication.pdf.
2. Muriel Harris interview with editor, December 6, 2024.
3. Harris interview with editor, December 6, 2024.
4. Harris interview with editor, December 6, 2024.
5. Harris interview with editor, December 6, 2024.
6. Harris interview with editor, December 6, 2024.
7. Harris interview with editor, December 6, 2024.
8. Harris interview with editor, December 6, 2024.
9. Harris interview with editor, December 6, 2024.
10. https://www.purdueexponent.org/campus/indiana-s-most-famous-owl/article_c0d12e3e-3675-11ef-9f9a-1b8022e9abe1.html.
11. Harris interview with editor, December 6, 2024.
12. https://www.proquest.com/openview/0476141fefc2d4a9fc3af395d6367789/.
13. RSA Oral History Narrative, page 3, Purdue Archives, https://rheteric.org/oralhistory/files/original/dc40638faf875ef629febed009351194.pdf.
14. RSA Oral History Narrative, page 4, Purdue Archives, https://rheteric.org/oralhistory/files/original/dc40638faf875ef629febed009351194.pdf.
15. RSA Oral History Narrative, page 4, Purdue Archives, https://rheteric.org/oralhistory/files/original/dc40638faf875ef629febed009351194.pdf.
16. "Dappled Discipline at Thirty: An Interview with Janice M. Lauer."
17. Elizabeth B. House and William J. House, "Problem-Solving: The Debates in Composition and Psychology," *Journal of Advanced Composition* (1987): 62–75.
18. https://ccccdoctoralconsortium.org/lauer-award/.

19. https://ishr-web.org/aws/RSA/pt/sd/news_article/363604/_PARENT/layout_details/true.
20. https://soller-baker.com/obituary/janice-lauer-rice/.
21. Harris interview with editor, December 6, 2024.

CHAPTER 29

1. "Nancy Stickler Inducted into Purdue Teaching Academy," *CSR Today*, Spring 2004, Archives, College of Health and Human Sciences, Purdue University.
2. "Designing Clothes for Today's Consumers," *Focus*, Fall 2001, 16, Box 7, UA 15, College of Health and Human Sciences records, Archives and Special Collections, Purdue University Libraries.
3. Angie Klink, *Kirby's Way* (Purdue University Press, 2012), 54–55.
4. "Summer Spent in Professional Experiences," *CSR Today*, 2000, page 4, Archives, College of Health and Human Sciences, Purdue University.
5. Kat Braz, "The Day Has Finally Arrived," *Purdue Alumnus*, Summer 2018, 56–61.
6. "Photo Album," *Focus*, Spring/Summer 2008, page 17, Archives, College of Health and Human Sciences, Purdue University.
7. "Photo Album."
8. Braz, "The Day Has Finally Arrived."
9. Braz, "The Day Has Finally Arrived."
10. "What Is a Tartan?" College of Health and Human Sciences, Purdue University, accessed January 15, 2019, https://www.purdue.edu/hhs/alumni/tartan/what-is-a-tartan.html.
11. Krizia Phillips, Purdue Tartan Plaid essay, spring 2012, accessed January 15, 2019, https://www.purdue.edu/hhs/alumni/tartan/documents/Purdue%20Tartan%20Plaid%20Essay%20by%20Winning%20Designer%20Krizia%20Phillips.pdf.
12. Judith Barra Austin, "Online Voters Pick Student's Design as Official Purdue Tartan," Purdue News, November 13, 2012, https://www.purdue.edu/newsroom/releases/2012/Q4/online-voters-pick-students-design-as-official-purdue-tartan.html.

CHAPTER 30

1. "Felker Leaves Legacy of Caring and Leadership," *Inside Purdue*, December 14, 1992, Box 6, Folder: Clippings Pertaining to Deans 1952–2008, MSF 469, Mary Louise Foster Papers, Virginia Kelly Karnes Archives and Special Collections Research Center, Purdue University Libraries.

2. "Felker Leaves Legacy of Caring and Leadership."
3. Larry Greenemeier, "Community Honors Deceased Professor," Box 6, Folder: Clippings Pertaining to Deans 1952–2008, MSF 469, Mary Louise Foster Papers, Virginia Kelly Karnes Archives and Special Collections Research Center, Purdue University Libraries.
4. "A Look Back . . . Celebrating 20 Years of the Center for Families at Purdue University," College of Health and Human Sciences at Purdue, April 30, 2015, https://www.youtube.com/watch?v=oUaa4Ow6qWI.
5. "A Look Back . . ."
6. "A Look Back . . ."
7. "Alumni Are Showing Support for the Center for Families," *Focus on CFS*, Spring 1994, page 1, Archives, College of Health and Human Sciences, Purdue University.
8. "A Look Back . . ."
9. "A Look Back . . ."
10. "Ann Hancook Memorial," Center for Families, Purdue University, accessed January 18, 2019, https://www.purdue.edu/hhs/hdfs/cff/giving/founders/hancook-memorial/.
11. Shelley MacDermid Wadsworth interview with author, December 11, 2018.
12. Douglas Powell interview with author, February 8, 2019.
13. Powell interview with author, February 8, 2019.
14. "Susan Kontos Memorial," Center for Families, Purdue University, accessed January 18, 2019, https://www.purdue.edu/hhs/hdfs/cff/giving/founders/kontos-memorial/.
15. Susan Kontos, "Thoughts About Mission, Focus, Funding," Adapted from Application Letter, January 1994, Archives, College of Health and Human Sciences, Purdue University.
16. "Center for Families Helps Fathers with Parenting Skills," *Focus*, Spring 1999, page 7, Archives, College of Health and Human Sciences, Purdue University.
17. "Families Listed by the Numbers," *Journal and Courier*, July 29, 1994, 15, www.newspapers.com.
18. MacDermid Wadsworth interview with author.
19. Shelley MacDermid Wadsworth, "Living Their Dream," *Celebrating the 20th Anniversary of the Center for Families* brochure, accessed January 21, 2019, https://www.purdue.edu/hhs/hdfs/cff/wp-content/uploads/2015/12/2015_Anniversary_Living-Their-Dream.pdf.
20. Susan Kontos and Shelley M. MacDermid, *For the Greater Good: Contributions of the School of Consumer and Family Sciences at Purdue University to Family Well-Being*, 1998, 2.

21. "Family Impact Seminars," *Families Facing Challenges* brochure, page 17, Archives, College of Health and Human Sciences, Purdue University.
22. "Family Impact Seminars."
23. MacDermid Wadsworth interview with author.
24. "Kanter Award Recognizes Key Family Research," *Families Facing Challenges* brochure, page 16, Archives, College of Health and Human Sciences, Purdue University.
25. MacDermid Wadsworth, "Living Their Dream," *Celebrating the 20th Anniversary of the Center for Families*.
26. "About Joining Forces," Joining Forces, accessed January 21, 2019, https://obamawhitehouse.archives.gov/joiningforces/about.
27. "Making a Difference in the Lives of Families," *Celebrating the 20th Anniversary of the Center for Families*.
28. "CFF Director Recognized as a Top Contributor to Work and Family Research," Center for Families, Purdue University, accessed January 22, 2019, https://www.purdue.edu/hhs/hdfs/cff/2018_cff-director-recognized-as-a-top-contributor-to-work-and-family-research/.

CHAPTER 31

1. Christine Ladisch, interview by Angie Klink, March 5, 2018.
2. Ladisch, interview by Angie Klink.
3. Ladisch, interview by Angie Klink.
4. Ladisch, interview by Angie Klink.
5. Howard Stevens, "Purdue Husband, Wife Combine Research Talents," *The Terre Haute Tribune*, December 8, 1977, 29.
6. Ladisch, interview by Angie Klink.
7. "Dinner Talk Led to Discovery," *Journal and Courier*, December 4, 1977, 26.
8. Ladisch, interview by Angie Klink.
9. Christine Ladisch interview with author, May 21, 2018.
10. Ladisch, interview by Angie Klink.
11. Mikel Livingston, "Purdue's Health Sciences College Gets Dean," *Journal and Courier*, January 10, 2013, C3.
12. Jay Akridge, "Dean Christine M. Ladisch, College of Health and Human Sciences," accessed January 22, 2024, https://www.purdue.edu/elist39/documents/2017/dean-christine-m.-ladisch,-college-of-health-and-human-sciences.php.

13. Greg McClure, "Inaugural Dean Steps Down, Feeling Pride in HHS's Strength, Confidence in Its Future," *Life 360*, https://www.purdue.edu/hhs/life360/2018-fall/ladisch-led-creation.html.
14. Steven Lincoln, "Purdue Launches Largest Fundraising Campaign in Its History," Purdue University Newsroom, October 9, 2015, https://polytechnic.purdue.edu/newsroom/purdue-launches-largest-fundraising-campaign-its-history.

POSTSCRIPT

1. https://www.purdue.edu/datadigest/.
2. https://www.purdue.edu/provost/about/directory.html.

INDEX

Page numbers in italics indicate Photos.

AAHPER. *See* American Association for Health, Physical Education and Recreation
AAUP. *See* American Association of University Professors
Abernathy, Pat, 241, 242
ABET. *See* Accreditation Board for Engineering and Technology
ACACW. *See* Athletic Conference of American College Women
Academic Affairs, 3, 194, 284
Access to Public Records Act (APRA), 199
Accreditation Board for Engineering and Technology (ABET), 153–54
Adler, Thomas P., 113
ADT. *See* Apparel Design and Technology Program
Adventure, Department of, 67–75, *71*
Affirmative Action Policy, 137–38
African Americans. *See* Blacks
African American Studies, 4, 196–97
Agency for International Development (AID), 104, 230
Agnew, Spiro T., 159–60
Agricultural and Biological Engineering, 315
Agricultural Engineering, 315

Agricultural Experiment Station, 32, 35; Clark, H., at, 125; Goble at, 177, 178–79; Home Economics Extension at, 185; at Pennsylvania State University, 122
Agricultural Extension Department: Gaddis, L., at, 33–35, *34*, 39–40; Master Mix and, 95; Meredith, V., at, 26
agriculture: Ferris, V., and, 131–41, *138*; scarcity of women professors in, 202
Agriculture, College of, 241; Purdue University Spirit of the Land Grant, 249
Agriculture, School of, 32; Department of Entomology in, 137; home economics in, 182; Hovde, F., and, 130; at Purdue-Brazil Technical Assistance Program, 104
AIAW. *See* Association for Intercollegiate Athletics for Women
AID. *See* Agency for International Development
AIN. *See* American Institute for Nutrition
Akeley, Anna Mandler "Anni," 80–88, *83*, *87*, 200
Akeley, Edward Stowe, 80–81, 83–84, 85–88
Akridge, Jay, 320
Alderman, Olivia T., 8

All-College Play Day, 51
Alliance of Work-Life Progress, 307
Allison, Clyde, 183
Altinkemer, Cheryl Painter, 300–302
Alumni Recognition Award, 226
Amelia Earhart Fund for Aeronautical Research, 73
Amelia Fashions, 70
American Academy of Arts and Sciences, 154
American Academy of Pediatrics, 228
American Academy of Physical Education, 158, 164
American Association for Health, Physical Education and Recreation (AAHPER), 158–60, 161
American Association for the Advancement of Science, 23, 124
American Association of Family and Consumer Sciences, 28
American Association of University Professors (AAUP), 205
American Association of University Women, 144
American Baby, 228
American Cancer Society, 257
American Dairy Association, 183
American Dietetic Association, 237
American Home Economics Association, 28, 57, 95, 228
American Institute for Nutrition (AIN), 124
American Journal of Clinical Nutrition, 228
American Journal of Nursing, 101
American Men of Science, 123, 125
American School of Classical Studies, 10

American Speech-Language-Hearing Association (ASHA), 283
American Tradition Restaurant, 185
American Women in Science, 147
Amoco Foundation Undergraduate Teaching Award, 241, 255
Analog Computer Handbook (Haas, V.), 145
Anchorage Tea House, 38–39
Andrews, Frederick N., 138
Annunciation (Carrington), 87
Antioch College, 6
Apparel Design and Technology Program (ADT), 295–96, 299
Applied Design, Department of, 62–64
Applied Technology, Division of, *169*
APRA. *See* Access to Public Records Act
Aquinas Educational Foundation, 294
Armstrong, Neil, 149–50, 155, 233
Arnsman, Betty, 202
art: Akeley, A., and, 80–88, *83*, *87*; ceramics, 14–20; Fry, L., and, 14–20, *19*; Rupel and, 64–66, *65*; Schantz-Hansen and, 62–64
Art, Department of, 30
Art and Design Department, 64, 122
Art Club, 18
ASHA. *See* American Speech-Language-Hearing Association
assistant provosts, 138–39
Associated Parents Nursery School, 98
Association for Financial Counseling and Planning Education, 189
Association for Intercollegiate Athletics for Women (AIAW), 162–63, 165
Association for Women in Mathematics, 147
Association for Women Students, 261, 262

Association of Women's Studies (AWS), 199–200
Athletic Affairs Committee, 118–19, 164
Athletic Conference of American College Women (ACACW), 49
Audiology and Speech Sciences (AUS), Department of: Fristoe at, 278–82, *281*, *282*; Ringel at, 284; Solomon, Barbara, at, 278, 282–85, *284*; Stark in, 274–78, *275*
Avanelle Kirksey Lecture Series, 225, 232
AWS. *See* Association of Women's Studies
Ayers, Howard, Sr., 179–80
Ayers, Patricia, 180
Ayers, Sarah, 179–80

Baker, Anna Embree, 18
Bartkus, David, 222
Barton, Clara, 167
Bass, Jewell, 192
Bayh, Birch E., 201
Baylor College, 252, 253
Beeman, Margaret, 122
Beering, Steven C., 120, 151, 175–76
Bell, Clara E., 265–68, *267*
Bell, Gregory, 266
Bellows, John, 59
Bells on Their Toes, 76
Ben and Maxine Miller Child Development Laboratory School, 55, 99
Bendix, Vincent, 72
Benedict College, 192
Berg, Mona, 86
Berlin, James A., 292
Bermel, Li Yuan, 249
Berry, Jessie Yost, 65
Berry Lace Collection, 65

Bethany Theological Seminary, 189
Better Homes and Gardens, 94
Biden, Jill, 309
Big Ten, 114, 119, 165, 233
Bilhuber, Gertrude, 49–50
Billings, Margaret, 94
Biomedical Engineering Center, 252, 253
Bitting, Arvil, 22, 23–24
Bitting, Katherine E. Golden, *21*
black book, 199
Black Cultural Center, 4, 197
Blacks (African Americans), 321; Bell, C., 265–68, *267*; Camp Calcium for, 245; in School of Nursing, 265–68, *267*; Williams, H., 3–4, 190–98, *195*
Bloye, Amy Irene, *47*, 48, 123
Boarding House, 8
Board of Trustees, 25, 42, 49, 72, 175
Bogan, Stacy, 198
Boilermakers, 1–2
Book of Great Teachers, 238, 269
Books and Coffee, 110
"Books for the Hospitalized Child" (Dolch), 101
Borden Award for Outstanding Research, 129
Borden Award for Research in Infant and Child Nutrition, 228
Botanical Center for Age-Related Diseases, 246
Boulder Conference, 60–61
Bowen, Otis, 237
Brandt, Karl, 191–92
Brazil, 104–8, 180, 188
Briarcliffe College, 89
Brock-Wilson Center for Women in Management, 220

Brooklyn College, 144
Brooks, Jo A., 259–64, *263*
Brown, Lynne Harrington, 117
Brown, Marcia, 202
Brown University, 9, 76
Brutalist architecture, 174
Bryn Mawr College, 300
Buckius, Richard, 249
Building Two, 55, 63
Burkhart, Lorene McCormick, 301
Bush, George W., 160, 247
Butler, Susan Bulkeley, 249
Butler Center for Leadership Excellence, 320

Cabeza de Tehuana (Rivera), 86
calcium, 240–50, *242*
Calvin, Henrietta, 32
Camp Calcium, 240, 242, *242*, 244–46, 248
Camrass, Evelyn, 274–75, *275*
CAPS. *See* Counseling and Psychological Services
Caputi, Linda, 271
Careers for Women, 69
Carrington, Leonora, 87
Catholic Relief Services (CRS), 3, 220
Cat on a Hot Tin Roof (Williams, T.), 111
CCCC. *See* Conference on College Composition and Communication
Center for Cancer Research, 246
Center for Families, 291–92; Kontos at, 302–6; MacDermid Wadsworth at, 304–7, *305*
Center for Instructional Services, 269
ceramics, 14–20
Cereal Society, 8
CFS. *See* Consumer and Family Sciences

Chascon, M., and, 119
Chats About Children, 99
Chautauqua Institution, 18
Cheaper by the Dozen, 76
Cheney, Laura J., 43
Chicago Training School of Cookery, 12–13
Chicago World's Fair, 18, 27, 296
child care, 99–101. *See also* Center for Families; nursery schools
Child Development and Family Studies, Department of, 100–101, 213; Cooperative Extension Service and, 99; Diehl at, 169; Johnson, H., at, 170; MacDermid Wadsworth at, 304; Martin at, 103; in School of Home Economics, 99
Child Development Laboratories, 100, 101
Children's Letters to God (Hample and Marshall), 203
Chiscon, J. Alfred "Al," 115–16, *117*, 119
Chiscon, Martha Oakley, 113–20, *117*
Chiscon Award, 120
Christie, George I., 32, 33
Christine M. Ladisch Faculty Leadership Award, 320
Church, Margaret, 109–13, *112*
Cincinnati Pottery Club, 15
City Academy, 6
civil rights, 190–98, *195*
Civil Rights Act of 1964, 205, 207
Civil Works Administration, 60
Clark, Barbara S., 118
Clark, Helen E., 53, 123–29, *126*, 202, 227
Clark, Ruby, 58
Clark, Septima, 192
Clarke, Edward H., 9

Clifton, Marguerite Ann "Mickey," 156–64, *163*
Clinton, Hillary Rodham, 132, 160
Clore Act of 1911, 32
Clothing and Textiles Department, 64–66, 200, 313
Club 70, 185
Collaborative Research Support Programs (CRSPs), 230
College Composition and Communication, 286–87
colleges within Purdue University. *See specific disciplines*
Columbia University: Church at, 110; Gamble at, 37; Gilbreth, L., at, 76; nude photos from, 160; O'Shea, H., at, 59; Schantz-Hansen at, 62
Combs, Loyal William "Bill," 166, 168
Combs Elliott, Sally Dodds, 165–66
Commission for Higher Education, 256
Commission on Accreditation for Dietetics Education, 237
Committee on the Status of Women, 202–3
Community Advisory Committee on Nursing Education, 168
Comparative Literature, 110, 111
Compton, Norma, 210–14, 238, 319
Computer Science, Department of, 161
Computer Science Women's Network, 118
Computing Research Association – Widening Participation (CRA-WP), 153
Conference on College Composition and Communication (CCCC), 286–87, 293
Conference on Women's Work and Opportunities, 70, 149

Consumer and Family Sciences (CFS), School of, 45, 187–89, 211–13; Felker at, 300–302, 315; HHS and, 317; Ladisch, C., at, 315; Nebold at, 313; Powell at, 243; Weaver at, 243
Consumer Day on Campus, 187
Consumer Sciences and Retailing, Department of, 187, 213, 295–99, *298*, 317
Consumer Sciences and Retailing Historic Collection, 66
Cook, Barb, 139
Cookery Manuals (Ewing), 14
cooking, 12–14; Gilbreth, L, and, 77–78; National Sandwich Idea Contest and, 183–86, *184*; Sunderlin and, 93–97, *96*
Cooking and Castle Building (Ewing), 12
Cooperative Extension Service, 31–34, 94, 99, 180, 302
Coordinated Program in Dietetics, 235, 236–37
Córdova, France A., 249
Cornell University: Edgell at, 140; Ferris, V., at, 133–35; practice baby at, 45–46
Cosmopolitan, 72
Coulson, Zoe, 129–30
Coulter, Lucy Post, 20
Coulter, Stanley E., 20
Council on the Status of Women, 140–41, *143*, 148–49. *See also* Violet Haas Award
Counseling and Psychological Services (CAPS), 284
COVID-19 pandemic, 40, 320
Coyle, Edward, 151
CRA-WP. *See* Computing Research Association--Widening Participation
Credit Research Center (CRC), 217

Crenshaw, Kimberlé, 4
Cross, Nancy, 166
CRS. *See* Catholic Relief Services
CRSPs. *See* Collaborative Research Support Programs
CTSI. *See* Indiana Clinical and Translational Sciences Institute
CystX, 140

DAI. *See* Dissertation Abstracts International
Dalton, Lycurgus, 6
Dance of the Dream (Kahlo), 86
Daniels, Mitch, 272
Darwinism, 9
Day, Ann, 297
Debris, 14, 22, 41
DeCamp, John, 65, 166
Decker, Leola K., 65
Department of Defense, U.S. (DoD), 308
Department of Health, Education, and Welfare, U.S. (HEW), 201, 205, 235
departments within Purdue University. *See specific disciplines*
DeTurk, Colleen, 175
DeTurk, Phil, 175
Development Movement Education (DME), 159
Dewey, Carol, 165
Dickson, Anita, 104–8, *106*
Didactic Program in Dietetics (DPD), 237
Diehl, Isabelle, 98, 168–69
Dietary Guidelines Advisory Committee, 247
dietetics: Wood and, 234–39, *236*. *See also* Nutrition

Dietz, Hank, 151
Dissertation Abstracts International (DAI), 292
Diversity in Nursing Association, 266
DME. *See* Development Movement Education
DNA, 140
Doctoral Consortium of Programs in Rhetoric and Composition, 292
DoD. *See* Department of Defense
Dolch, Elaine T., 99–101
Domestic Economy, Department of, 14, 27
Donald W. and Evelyn H. Felker Endowment Fund, 300
Douglas Aircraft Co., 145, *146*
DPD. *See* Didactic Program in Dietetics
Dr. Charlene Sullivan Transformative Impact Award, 220
Dream of the Dance (Meza), 83
Duhme, Ophelia Fowler, 64–66, 296
Duhme Hall, 65, 69
Duke University, 92–93; Church at, 110; Wood at, 234–35
Dwyer Outstanding Teacher Award: to Brooks, 261–62; to Geddes, LaNelle, 255

Earhart, Amelia, 2, 149; Department of Adventure of, 67–75, *71*; Gilbreth, L., and, 75; at playground, 57, *58*; in residence halls, 65, 69, 70–71
Earhart Residence Hall, 140–41
Early Childhood Programs (Read), 56
Early Childhood Research Quarterly, 302
The Earth is Round (Akeley, L.), 80–81
Edgell, Susan Ferris, 140, 141

Education, Department of, 59. *See also specific departments*
Education for All Handicapped Children Act of 1975, 100
EEOC. *See* Equal Employment Opportunity Commission
Egg Day, 123
Egypt, 230–33
Eisenhower, Dwight D., 78
Elaine T. Dolch Children's Library, 101
Electrical Engineering, School of, 147
Electrical Engineering Building, 50, 54
Elementary Education, Department of, 191
Elementary Home Economics (Matthews, Mary), 42
Eliza Fowler Hall, 64–65
Elliott, Edward C.: Combs, S., and, 166; Earhart and, 67–69, 70, 72, 73, 74–75; Gilbreth, L., and, 75, 78; Matthews, Mary, and, 102; Meredith, V., and, 53; O'Shea, H., and, 59; PE and, 49, 50
Emergency Food Leaflets, 40
Emergency Nursery Schools, 60
Endres, Mary, 191, 202
energy crisis, 213–14
engineering: Golden, H., and, 3, 20–22, *21*; Haas, V., and, 142–50, *143, 146*; Jamieson and, 149–55, *152*; scarcity of women professors in, 201. *See also* Women in Engineering Program; *specific types*
Engineering, College of, 153, 154
Engineering, School of, 28; Gilbreth, L., at, 78; Goble at, 179; WISP and, 118
Engineering Projects in Community Service (EPICS), 151

English, Department of, 30; Books and Coffee in, 110; Harris, M., in, 287–90, *288*; Lauer, J., at, 290–94, *293*
Entomology, Department of, 131, 136, 137, 139–40
Ephron, Nora, 160
EPICS. *See* Engineering Projects in Community Service
Equal Employment Opportunity Commission (EEOC), 205
Equal Opportunity Employment Officer, 201–2
Equipment and Family Housing, Department of, 122, 200
ErSelcuk, Muzaffer M., 221
Essentials of Nursery Education with Special Reference to Nursery Schools (O'Shea, H.), 60
Ewing, D. D., 148
Ewing, Emma Pike, 3, 12–14, *13*
Excellence in Construction Award, 297
Excellence in Research Award, 247
Excellence in Undergraduate Teaching Award, 320
"Experiments on the Spoilage of Tomato Ketchup" (Bitting, A.), 24

Fackler, Sue, 165
Faghihi, Jamal, 140
Family and Consumer Law, Department of, 213–14
Family and Medical Leave Act, 309
Family Day Care (Kontos), 302
Family Health Clinic, 262
Family Impact Institute, 307
Family Life, Department of, 97–101
Farmers' Institute Act of 1889, 26

Farmers' Institutes, 26, 27, 32
Father, Have I Kept My Promise? (Weisskopf-Joelson), 93
FDA. *See* Food and Drug Administration
Federation of American Societies for Experimental Biology, 228
Feeding Children in Group Care, 58
Felker, Donald W., 243, 300–302, 315
Ferris, John, 131, 133–36, 140
Ferris, Virginia, 2, 131–41, *138*, 202
Financial Advising Clinic, 187
Financial Counseling and Planning, 187–89
Fink, Willis C., 93
Fisher, Lillie Fry, 18
FITNE. *See* Fuld Institute for Technology in Nursing Education
Fitzsimmons, Cleo, 45, 97
Food and Drug Administration (FDA), 240, 246
Foods (Vail), 124
Foods and Nutrition, Department of, 57–58, 213; Clark, H., at, 123–29, *126*; Kirksey at, 224–33, *229*; in School of Home Economics, 249–50; Stone Hall and, 122; Vail at, 123–24, 224; Weaver at, 240–50, *242*; Wood at, 234–39, *236*
Food Science Institute, 127
Ford Foundation, 180
Forman, Michele, 250
For the Great Good (Kontos and MacDermid Wadsworth), 306
Foster, Mary Louise, *44*, 45, 57, 107
Fowler, Eliza, 64–66
Fowler, Moses, 64–66
Frankl, Viktor, 88, 91, 93
Frazier, Marian, 71

French, Department of, 30
Fristoe, Macalyne Watkins, 278–82, *281*, *282*
Fry, Henry, 17
Fry, Laura Anne, 14–20, *19*, 30
Fuld Institute for Technology in Nursing Education (FITNE), 257

Gaddis, Bertha "Kate," 33, 39–40, 239
Gaddis, Lella Reed, 33–35, *34*, 177, 178, 180, 181
Gamble, Edith, 37–39, *38*, 42, 47, 70, 103, 184–85, 186
Gastronomic Bibliography (Bitting, K.), 22, 24
Gebhardt, Deborah L., 166
Geddes, LaNelle E. Nerger, *176*, 251–59, *254*, 269
Geddes, Leslie A., 252
General Foods, 66, 96, 224
"Germination of Seeds" (Golden, E.), 22
Gestational Age program, 270
GFTA. *See* Goldman-Fristoe Test of Articulation
Gilbreth, Frank, 75–77, 78
Gilbreth, Lillian Moller, 75–79, *77*; Earhart and, 75; Goble and, 179; with Hazelton, *52*; in residence halls, 78; at Windsor Halls, 65
Gillaspie, Beulah V., 102–4, *104*, 107, 121–23
Girls Rifle Team, 51
Glass Container Association, 22, 24
The Glass Menagerie (Williams, T.), 111
Glass Packaging Institute, 22
Glendale Female College, 25
Goble, Eva L., 34, 200; on Committee on the Status of Women, 202; Mary L.

Matthews Club and, 240; at School of Home Economics, 177–82, 240
Goetz, Lucy, 94
Golden, Helen, 3, 20–22, *21*
Golden, Michael Joseph, 20–21, *21*
Goldman, Ronald, 278
Goldman-Fristoe Test of Articulation (GFTA), 278–82, *281*, *282*
Governor's Council of Physical Fitness and Sport Medicine, 237
Governor's Task Force on the Elderly, 237
Grabill, Pat, 160–61
Graduate House, 122
Graduate School: Ferris, V., and, 131, 137–38; Goble at, 179
Graham, Patricia Albjerg, 63
Great Depression, 60, 68, 70, 79, 178
Green, Stephen, 307–8
Green Revolution, 125
"Guides to Speech and Action" (Read), 57

Haas, Felix, 116, 144, 145, 161, 175
Haas, Violet Bushwick, 2, 3, 142–50, *143*, *146*
Hall, Bill, 310
Hall, Sally Hanley, 310
Hall of Music, 54
Hample, Stuart, 203
Hancock, Ann, 300–302
Hand in Hand with God (Williams, F.), 189
Handyman's Course, 70
Hansen, Arthur G., 119; Committee on the Status of Women and, 202; intercollegiate sports and, 164; Johnson, H., and, 174; Purdue Women's Caucus and, 203–4; TIAA-CREF and, 205; Williams, H., and, 194
Hansen, J. H., 59
Hanson, Dale Lester, 164
Harcoff, Lyla Marshall, 18
Harner, Ivy F., 29, 32
Harris, Muriel "Mickey," 287–90, *288*
Harris, Samuel, 287
Harvard University: nude photos from, 160; Peck and, 9; Schantz-Hansen and, 63, 64
Haynes, Wesley, 8
Hazelton, Helen W., 50–52, *52*, 70, 156–57
Head Start, 191, 193
Health and Human Sciences (HHS), College of, 3, 182, 212, 250; Ladisch, C., at, 240, 297, 312–20, *316*; Mary L. Matthews Club and, 239; Purdue University Spirit of the Land Grant Mission Award of, 249; School of Hospitality and Tourism Management in, 37
Health and Kinesiology, Department of, 284, 317
Health Sciences, School of, 317
Heavilon Hall, 277, 278, 283, 287
Helen Bass Williams Academic Success Center, 198
Helen Bass Williams Scholarship, 197–98
Helen B. Schleman Gold Medallion Award: to Akeley, A., 85, 200; to Chiscon, M., 120; to Church, 110; to Ferris, V., 139; to Haas, V., 148; to Jamieson, 153; to Johnson, H., 174; to Williams, F., 188; to Williams, H., 197
Helen B. Schleman Hall, 195
Helene Fuld Critical Care Unit, 257

Helen R. Johnson Hall of Nursing, 173–77, *176*
Hepburn, William M., 18
Herbert Newby McCoy Award, 249
HEW. *See* Department of Health, Education, and Welfare
HHS. *See* Health and Human Sciences
Hicks, John, 199, 201–3
Higher Education Act of 1972, 201. *See also* Title IX
Highlander Research and Education Center, 3, 192–93
High School Play Day, 51
Hilton, James, 93
historical costume curator, 64–66, *65*
"The History of Psychology at Purdue" (Naylor), 90–91
Hitler, Adolf, 89
Holle, Mary Lou, 261
Home Administration, Department of, 97
Home and Family Conference, 36
home economics, 14; Akeley, A., and, 85; Gaddis, L., and, 33–35, *34*; Gamble and, 37–39, *38*; Goble and, 177–82; Hyland and, 183–86, *184*; IHEA and, 35–36; Matthews, Mary, and, 30–32, *31*; Meredith and, 3, 25–30, *29*; Practice House and, 43–45, *44*; reordered for the times, 177–89; Richards and, 28, 30, 32; Williams, F., and, 187–89; in World War I, 39–40
Home Economics, Department of, 28–30; Master Mix and, 95; at School of Science, 46
Home Economics, School of, 35, 45, 46, 47; in Brazil, 104–8, 180, 188; Clothing and Textiles Department in, 64–66; Compton of, 210–14, 238, 319; Department of Applied Design in, 62–64; Department of Child Development and Family Life in, 99; Department of Foods and Nutrition in, 249–50; Diehl in, 168–69; family life and, 97–101; Financial Counseling and Planning in, 187–89; Gillaspie at, 102–4, *104*, 107, 121–23; Goble at, 177–82, 240; Hovde, F., and, 130; at Johns Hopkins University, 98; logo for, 182; Mary L. Matthews Club and, 239; Matthews, Mary, at, 97, 102–3, 181, 214, 239–40; Meredith, V., at, 26, 214; number of professors in, 200; Vail at, 129–30, 177. *See also* Consumer and Family Sciences, School of
Home Economics Administrative Building (Stone Hall), 121–23, 213; Clark, H., in, 127; Kirksey in, 232; Nutrition and Exercise Clinical Research Center in, 250
Home Economics Alumni Day, 129–30
Home Economics Building (Matthews Hall), 41–43, 57, 65, 121, 176, 213, 296
Home Economics Clubs, 36, 42, 179, 180, 181
Home Economics Conferences, 36
Home Economics Extension, 185
Home Economics Food Service, 38
Homemakers Conference, 185
Home Management and Family Economics, Department of, 28, 45, 77, 97, 187, 100
Home Management House (Practice House), 43–45, *44*, 46
"Home Nursing and Child Care," 46
Hook, August F. "Bud," 174

Hook Telecommunications Studio, 174
Hoosier Early Childhood Lifetime Achievement Award, 303
Hoosier Family Policy summit, 304
Hoosier Family Source Book, 304
Hooton, E. A., 160
Hoover, Herbert, 78, 79
Hornig, Lili, 149
Horton, Myles, 192, 198
Hospitality and Tourism Management (HTM), School of, 37, 39, 186, 317
Household Economics, Department of, 28; Gaddis, L., and, 33–35, *34*; Matthews, M., at, 30–35, 39, 40
Housing, Equipment and Environmental Design, Department of, 204
Hovde, Frederick L., 65; Combs, S., and, 166; Matthews, Mary, and, 102, 103; nursing and, 168; School of Agriculture and, 130; School of Home Economics and, 130; Stone Hall and, 121; Williams, H., and, 193
Hovde, Priscilla, 65, 296
Hovde Hall of Administration, 174
Howe, Amy L., *47*, 66
Howe, Jean, 127
HSSE. *See* Humanities, Social Science, and Education
HTM. *See* Hospitality and Tourism Management
Human Development and Family Studies, Department of, 97–101, 317
Human Ecology, 212
Humanities, School of, 64, 284
Humanities, Social Science, and Education (HSSE), School of, 109–13, *112*, 190, 194

Human Movement Research Laboratory, 157–58
Human Nutritional Research Project, 230
Hunter's Dinner, 123
Hutchins, Sandra, 202
Hutson, Edna, *58*
Hutton, Charles, *169*
Hutton, David, 293
Hyland, Mary Rose, 183–86, *184*

ICN. *See* Indiana Center for Nursing
Ideas Festival, 320
IEEE. *See* Institute of Electrical and Electronics Engineers
IFT. *See* Institute of Food Technologists
IHEA. *See* Indiana Home Economics Association
Indiana Association of Clinical Psychologists, 60
Indiana Center for Nursing (ICN), 272
Indiana Clinical and Translational Sciences Institute (CTSI), 247–48
Indiana Commission for Women, 120
Indiana Dietetics Association, 185, 237
Indiana Federation of Clubs, 53
Indiana Food Administration, 40
Indiana Heart Foundation, 168
Indiana Home Economics Association (IHEA), 35–36, 129
Indiana League of Nursing, 172, 261
Indianapolis Star, 45, 122
Indiana Speech-Language-Hearing Association (ISHA), 283
Indiana State House, 6
Indiana State Poultry Association, 123
Indiana State University: Bell, C., at, 265; Ladisch, C., at, 313

Indiana University: Bell, C., at, 265–66; CTSI and, 247–48; Geddes, LaNelle, at, 255; Johnson, H., at, 172; Kirkpatrick at, 269; Weisskopf-Joelson at, 90
Individuals with Disabilities Education Act of 1990, 100
Industrial Arts Department, 16
influenza pandemic of 1918, 40
Institute for Consumer and Family Studies, 100
Institute of Electrical and Electronics Engineers (IEEE), 153, 155
Institute of Food Technologists (IFT), 124
Institutional Management Department: Gamble at, 37–39, *38*, 184–85, 186; Hyland at, 183, 186; Stone Hall and, 122
intercollegiate sports: Combs, S., and, 165–66; Mertler and, 164–65; public relations for, 165–66; uniforms for, 297. *See also* Title IX
Interdepartmental Graduate Nutrition Program, 244
International Congress on Nutrition, 227
International Dinner Series, 184
International James Joyce Foundation, 110
International Mental Health Association, 98
International Seven Restaurant, 183–85
intersectionality, 4
Introduction to Human Movement, 157–58, 159
Iowa State University, 14; Clark, H., at, 125; College of Home Economics at, 93; Kontos at, 302
ISHA. *See* Indiana Speech-Language-Hearing Association

Jackson, Monica, 274–75, *275*, 277
James Joyce Foundation, 111
Jamieson, Leah Hope, 2, 149–55, *152*
Javits Neuro-Science Award, 277
JC Penney, 296
Jischke, Martin, 88
Jischke, Patty, 239–40
Joan of Arc Equal Suffrage League, 11
John Purdue Club, 166
John Purdue Room, 213
Johns Hopkins University: Church and, 111; Department of Neurology at, 276; Diehl at, 168–69; School of Home Economics at, 98; Stark at, 276
Johnson, Helen R. Snyder, *169*; Geddes, LaNelle, and, 253, 255, 256; Kirkpatrick and, 269; at School of Nursing, 167–76, *169*, *176*, 204, 253, 255, 256, 269
Johnson, Lyndon B., 79
Johnson, Robert, 217
Johnson, Vivian, 202
Johnson Hall, 257, 272
Jordan, Ruth, 103
Joseph, Jacques, 89
Journal and Courier, 181–82, 243
Joy, Ellen, 51–52
Joy Camps, 51–52
Joyce, James, 110, 111

Kahlo, Frida, 86
Kansas State University: Clark, H., at, 125; Mason at, 300; Vail at, 129
Kanter, Rosabeth Moss, 307
Kanter Award for Excellence, 307
Katehi, Linda P. B., 153
Kelley, Ida B., 98–99

Kennedy, Bobby, 190
Kennedy, John F., 79
Kessler, David, 139
ketchup, 22–24
Kidwell, David, 216
Kieffer, Mary S., 38
Kimberley, Hannah, 10
kinesiology, 156–58
King, George, 164, 166
King, Martin Luther, Jr., 190, 191, *195*, 197
Kirkpatrick, Jane, 254–55, 268–73, *270*
Kirksey, Avanelle "Nell," *229*; in Egypt, 230–33; vitamin B-6 and, 224–30
Knaufft, Ernest, 17
Koffler, Henry, 115–16
Kokoschka, Oskar, 82
Kontos, Susan, 302–6
Kramer, Mary Akers, 95–96
Krannert School of Management, 86, 215–21, *218*, 220–23, 308
Kruel, Lee, 100
Ku Klux Klan, 193

Ladies Hall: Department of Home Economics, 30; Department of Household Economics at, 34–35; Ewing at, 14; Fry, L., at, 17, 18; Gaddis, L., and, 34–35; Home Economics Food Service in, 38; Oren at, 8; PE in, 50; poor condition of, 41; Stone Hall and, 121–23
Ladisch, Christine M. Schmitz, 3, 212; at CFS, 315; at College of Health and Human Sciences (HHS), 240, 297, 312–20, *316*; Mary L. Matthews Club and, 240

Ladisch, Mike, 314–15
Lafayette Art Association, 18
Lafayette Art League, 18
Lake Placid Conference, 27–28
Lambert Fieldhouse, 161, 165
LaNelle Geddes Excellence in Teaching Award, 269
Lark-Horovitz, Karl, 81, 84
Larowe, Ann, 202
Larsen Leaders Academy, 220
Last Flight (Earhart), 75
Latinos, 191, 194–95, *195*, 248
Latta, William C., 26, 27, 28
Lauer, Janice, 2–3, 286–87, 290–94, *293*
Lauer, Vincent, 291
Lawshe, Charles H., 168–69, *169*, 170, 171–72, 173, 176
Lean Six Sigma, 271
Learning Center, 4, 195–96, 198
Learning Resource Center (LRC), 174, 257
Liberal Arts, College of, 190, 198; Church and, 109–13, *112*. *See also* Humanities, Social Science, and Education
"Liberty Breads," 40
library: Dolche and, 101; Oren and, 6–8
"A Lifetime of Mentoring and Being Mentored" (Goble), 178
Lilly, Josiah K., 72
Linus Pauling Prize for Health Research, 248–49
Literary Awards, 110, 111
Literature, Department of, 30. *See also* Comparative Literature
logotherapy, 88, 91, 93
Lonhuda Pottery Company, 18
Lost Horizon (Hilton), 93

Louisiana Industrial Institute, 32
LRC. *See* Learning Resource Center
Lyles-Porter Hall, 272, 320
lysine, 125–26

MacArthur, Douglas, 179
MacDermid Wadsworth, Shelley: at Center for Families, 304–11, *305*; MFRI and, 304, 307–11
Mackey Arena, 166, 297
Made, Harris, 154
Manchester College, 187
Mann, Horace, 6
Manning, Harry, 73
Man's Search for Meaning (Frankl), 88, 93
MAP. *See* Mississippi Action for Progress
Margaret Church Memorial Fund, 113
Margaret Church Modern Fiction Studies Memorial Prize, 113
Mariotte-Davies, Pauline, 30
Maris, James, *169*
Markee, Katie, 202
Marquette University, 184
Married Student Housing, 314
Marriott Hall, 213
Marshall, Eric, 203
Martin, William E., 103
Marygrove College, 291
Mary L. Matthews Award for Undergraduate Teaching, 315
Mary L. Matthews Club, 103, 239–40
Mary L. Matthews Outstanding Undergraduate Teaching Award, 103, 238
Mary L. Matthews Scholarship Fund, 103
Mason, April, 300
Mason, Sally, 312, 315–17

Massachusetts Institute of Technology (MIT): Bitting, K., at, 22; Haas, V., at, 144, 148, 149; Jamieson at, 150; Richards at, 28
Master Mix, 93–97, *96*
master of science and industrial administration (MSIA), 216
master of science and management (MSM), 216
Mathematical Sciences, Division of, 145
Matthews, Mary Lockwood, 3, 26, 27, 30–32, *31*; Earhart and, 70; Gaddis, L., and, 33–35; Gamble and, 39, Goble and, 179; Home Economics Building and, 43; at IHEA, 35–36; Meredith, V., and, 26, 27, 32, 39, 53; playground and, 57; Potter, A., and, 28; practice baby and, 45–46; Practice House and, 43–46, *44*; Purdue Nursery School and, 55; at School of Home Economics, 46, 47, 97, 102–3, 181, 214, 239–40; World War I and, 40. *See also* Mary L. Matthews
Matthews, Meredith, 25, 27
Matthews Hall (Home Economics Building), 41–43, 57, 65, 121, 176, 213, 296
Mattson, Marion, 58
Maurice G. Knoy Hall of Technology, 21
Maver, Jane, 159
McCall's Magazine, 103
McComb, Sara, 271
McKenzie, Donna Frohreich, 147–48
McNelly, George, 175, 176
McRae, Emma Montgomery, 18–19, 30
McWilliams, Chuck, 142, 144–45
M. D. Steer Speech-Language Clinic, 284, *285*
Meat Inspection Act, 22

Mechanical Engineering, School of, 77
Memorial Gymnasium, 51, 54; Department of Physical Education for Women at, 163–64; Haas, F., and, 145, 161; nude photos at, 160–61; PE in, 157, 161
Memorial Mall, 122
Memorial Union: Book of Great Teachers in, 238; Gilbreth, L., at, 78; Johnson, H., in, 169; Literary Awards Banquet at, 111; Matthews, Mary, banquet at, 102–3; PE in, 54; Schantz-Hansen and, 63; Strickler in, 297
Mennen, Dorothy, 204
mental health, 98; Kirkpatrick and, 272; PE and, 157; in World War II, 61
Meredith, Henry Clay, 25–26
Meredith, Solomon, 26
Meredith, Virginia Claypool, 3, 25–30, *29*; on Board of Trustees, 25, 49; death of, 52–53; Home Economics Building and, 43; at IHEA, 35–36; Matthews, Mary, and, 26, 27, 32, 39, 53; PE and, 49–50; at School of Home Economics, *47*, 214
Meredith Distinguished Professor, 53; to Clark, H., 128; to Kirksey, 232–33
Meredith Residence Hall, 53
Mertler, Carol S., 164–65
Mertz, Edwin T., 125
methionine, 125
Metzler, Cindy, 199–201
Meyer, Nancy Reiter, 231–32
Meza, Guillermo, 83
MFRI. *See* Military Family Research Institute
MGMT 310, 216–17
Michael Golden Laboratories, 21
Miles, Gabrielle, *58*

Military Family Research Institute (MFRI), 304, 307–11
Miller, Helen Dawson, 57
Minority Faculty Fellows, 267
Minority Student Nurses' Association (MSNA), 267
Minority Students in Nursing, 266
Mississippi Action for Progress (MAP), 191, 193
MIT. *See* Massachusetts Institute of Technology
Mitchell E. Daniels, Jr. School of Business, 215
Modern Fiction Studies, 110, 111, *112*
Morrison, Harry, 114, 118
Morrison, James, 298
Mortar Board, 110
Motion Study (Gilbreth, L, and Gilbreth, F.), 76
Mottelson, Ben R., 84
mountain climbing: by Peck, 2, 8–12; by Stark, 274–75
Movement Sciences Research and Learning Center, 161
MSIA. *See* master of science and industrial administration
MSM. *See* master of science and management
MSNA. *See* Minority Student Nurses' Association
Mundel, Marvin, 78
Murphy Award, 120

NAEYC. *See* National Association for the Education of Young Children
NAS. *See* National Academy of Sciences
National Academy of Engineering, 79, 153

National Academy of Medicine, 240, 242, 248
National Academy of Sciences (NAS), 128, 228–29, 246, 310
National Association for the Education of Young Children (NAEYC), 302
National Association of Administrators of Home Economics, 181
National Association of State Universities and Land-Grant Colleges, 214
National Christie Award, 123
National Collegiate Athletic Association (NCAA), 119, 161, 162–63, 165
National Congress of Black Faculty Council on Research and Education, 268
National Council of Teachers of English (NCTE), 293
National Defense Authorization Act, 309
National Defense Education Act (NDEA), 252
National Education Association, 60
National Endowment for the Humanities (NEH), 291–92
National Farm and Home Hour, 95
National Institutes of Health (NIH), 174; HHH and, 320; Javits Neuro-Science Award from, 277; Stark and, 277; Weaver and, 240, 241–42, 246, 247
National League for Nursing (NLN), 171–72, 175, 272
National Live Stock and Meat Board, 183
National Military Family Association, 309
National Restaurant Association (NRA), 183
National Sandwich Idea Contest, 183–86, *184*

National Science Foundation (NSF), 2; Chiscon, M., and, 115, 116–17, 118; Ferris, V., and, 134, 137, 140; Haas, V., and, 145
Naylor, James C., 90–91
NCAA. *See* National Collegiate Athletic Association
NCFH. *See* Nursing Center for Family Health
NCTE. *See* National Council of Teachers of English
NDEA. *See* National Defense Education Act
Nebold, Mary Alice, 313–14
NEH. *See* National Endowment for the Humanities
Neil Armstrong Hall of Engineering, 150
Nelson, Betty M., 206–7
nematology, 131–32, 134–36, *138*
nepotism, 135, 145
Nerger, Carl, Jr., 252
Nesbitt, Margaret, 97
Newton, Isaac, 85
New York Art Students League, 16
New York World's Fair, 60
Nightingale, Florence, 167
NIH. *See* National Institutes of Health
Nimitz Drive Cooperative Nursery School, 97, 99
Nixon, Richard M., 137–38
NLN. *See* National League for Nursing
Noll, Doug, 283–84
Noonan, Fred, 73
Norberg, Jeanne, 161
Northwestern University, 275
Notestine, Earl B., 194
Novak, Joseph D., 115

NRA. *See* National Restaurant Association
NSF. *See* National Science Foundation
nude photos, 160–61
The Nursery School (Read), 56
nursery schools: Associated Parents Nursery School, 98; Emergency Nursery Schools, 60; Nimitz Drive Cooperative Nursery School, 97, 99. *See also* Purdue Nursery School
nursing, 98; Johnson, H., and, 167–76, *169*, *176*; in School of Technology, 257; in Teaching Academy, 238–39
Nursing, Department of, 171, 175; number of professors in, 200
Nursing, School of, 98; Bell at, 265–68, *267*; Brooks at, 259–64, *263*; Geddes, LaNelle, at, 251–59, *254*, 269; HHS and, 317; Johnson, H., at, 167–76, *169*, *176*, 204, 253, 255, 256, 269; Kirkpatrick at, 268–73, *270*; woman serving as head in, 200
Nursing and Allied Health Sciences Building, 173, 175
Nursing Center for Family Health (NCFH), 261, 272
Nursing Freshman Scholar, 258
Nutrition and Exercise Clinical Research Center, 250
Nutrition Intake and Human Function, 230–33
Nutrition Science, Department of, 249–50, 317. *See also* Foods and Nutrition

Oakes, Bill, 151
Oakland Farm, 26
Obama, Michelle, 309

Office of Equal Opportunity and Affirmative Action, 243
Office of the Dean of Women, 69, 202
Oglesby, Carole, 162
Ohio State University, 164
Old Masters Program, 191
Olivia Bennett Wood Scholarship, 239
Oncological Sciences Center, 249
Ong, Walter J., 291, 292
Online Writing Lab (OWL), *288*, 289–90
oral contraceptives, 227–28
orchard, 7–8
Order of the Griffin: to Akeley, A., 88; to Sullivan, 219
Oregon State University: HHS and, 317; Weaver at, 241, 248–49
Orem, Delpha Ann Eva, 65–66
Oren, Sarah Allen, 5–8, *7*
O'Shea, Harriet Easterbrook, 58–61, *61*, 70
O'Shea, Michael Vincent, 59
osteoporosis, 245
Outstanding Dissertation Award for Nursing Education, 271
Oval Room, 122–23, 183–85, 213
OWL. *See* Online Writing Lab

PAEYC. *See* Purdue Association for the Education of Young Children
Palmer, Lisa, 86
pants: Earhart and, 2, 71; Peck and, 2, 8–9
Parent Advisory Council, 101
Parks, Rosa, 192
Partch, Laura, 46, 55–59, *56*, *58*
Parvis, Delpha Jeanette, 65–66
patents: of Fry, L., 16; of Geddes, Leslie, 252
pathophysiology, 253–54

PE. *See* physical education
Peck, Annie Smith, 2, 8–12
pectin, 95–96
PEM. *See Purdue Engineering Magazine*
Penner, Babette, 46
Pennsylvania State University: Agricultural Experiment Station at, 122; College of Human Development at, 226; Kirksey at, 225, 226; Kontos at, 302; MacDermid Wadsworth at, 304
Perrucci, Carolyn C., 148
Peterson, Esther, 214
pharmacy: scarcity of women professors in, 202; in Teaching Academy, 238–39
Pharmacy, School of, 174, 175, 269–70
Phi Beta Kappa, 132, 139
Philalethean Literary Society, 8
philanthropy, 300–302
Phillips, Krizia, 297–99
Physical Assessment of the Newborn, 269
physical education (PE): Bilhuber and, 49–50; Clifton and, 156–60, *163*; Hazelton and, 50–52, *52*; at Memorial Gymnasium, 51, 54; Meredith, V., and, 49–50, 53; nude photos for, 160–61; Title IX and, 54. *See also* intercollegiate sports
Physical Education, Health and Recreation Studies, Department of, 164
Physical Education for Women, Department of, 41, 163–64; Clifton at, 156–60; Combs, S., at, 166; Hazelton at, 49, 50, 51, 156; number of professors in, 200; woman serving as head in, 200
physics: Akeley, A., and, 80–88, *83*, *87*; Chiscon, M., and, 114–15; Harris, S., and, 287

PhysWhiz, 271
Pike, Ruth, 225
playground, 57, *58*
Potter, Andrey Abraham "A. A.," 28, 42; Gilbreth, L., and, 76–77, 78; Matthews, Mary, and, 102–3; Meredith, V., and, 53
Potter, Helen, 28, 77
pottery, 14–20
Poultry and Egg National Board, 123, 183
Powell, Douglas R., 243, 302
Practical Mechanics Department, 20
practice baby, 45–46
Practice House (Home Management House), 43–45, *44*, 46
Pregnancy Discrimination Act of 1978, 135
PRF. *See* Purdue Research Foundation
Price, Jo-Ann, 164, 202
Project Neighborcare, 303
Psychological Services, Department of, 307, 317
psychology: Kelley and, 98–99; Weisskopf-Joelson and, 88–93, *90*. *See also* mental health
Psychology, Department of, 89, 92
Public Health Association, 168
Public Health Service, 253
Purdue, John, 64
Purdue Alumni Association, 11
Purdue Association for the Education of Young Children (PAEYC), 100
Purdue Association of Women Students, 148
Purdue-Brazil Technical Assistance Program, 105–8
Purdue Child Care Program, 99–101
Purdue Committee on Women's Studies, 148

Purdue Dietetics Program, 236–37
The Purdue Engineer, 142, 144–45
Purdue Engineering Magazine (PEM), 182
Purdue Exponent, 8; Golden, E., at, 22; on Haas, V., 145–47; on Home Economics Building, 42; on Peck, 11, 12; on Purdue Women's Caucus, 203–4; on TIAA-CREF, 206; on Williams, H., 194
Purdue Galleries, 86, 87, *87*
Purdue Girls' Club, 18–19
Purdue Graduate Women's Club, 122
Purdue Hall, 7–8
Purdue Home Economics Alumni Organization, 129
Purdue Intercollegiate Athletics Hall of Fame, 165
Purdue News Service, 161, 171
Purdue Nursery School: Johnson, H., at, 170; Nesbitt at, 97; O'Shea, H., and, 58–61, *61*; Partch and, 55–59, *56*, *58*; Schantz-Hansen and, 64
Purdue Pete, 171
Purdue Polytechnic, 170
Purdue Purchasing Department, 122
Purdue Radio Newsline, 217
Purdue Recipe File, 48
Purdue Research Foundation (PRF), 72; Altinkemer at, 300–302; Purdue Child Care Program and, 100; Williams, H., and, 193–94
Purdue Speech and Hearing Clinic, 170
Purdue Sportswomen Society, 166
Purdue Student Health Center, 170, 173
Purdue Student Hospital, 166, 168
Purdue University. *See specific topics*

Purdue University Airport, 73, 283
Purdue University Award for Excellence in Distance Learning, 270
Purdue University Black Caucus of Faculty and Staff, 268
Purdue University Senate, 204
Purdue University Spirit of the Land Grant Mission Award, 249
Purdue Village Preschool, 99
Purdue Villages, 314
Purdue Women Faculty in Engineering Committee, 153
Purdue Women's Caucus, 203–4; TIAA-CREF and, 204–7
Purdue Women's Club, 20, 199–201, 203, 239–40
Purdy, Ross C., 20
Pure Food and Drug Act, 22
Putnam, George Palmer, 68, 72, 73–75
Putnam, Jean Gilbert, 259

Radcliffe College, 110, 113
Rainey, Gilbert, *169*
Rankin, Dick, 122
Reach for Recovery, 257
Read, Katherine Haskell, 56–57
Reading Clinic, 195
Reading Proposal, 194, 195
Reber, Elwood, 236
Recitation Building, 195
Recommended Dietary Allowances, of NAS, 228–29, 246
Reece McGee Distinguished Professor of English, 292
Reichard, Hugo, 110, 113
"Remarks of a Free-Floating Spirit" (Weiskopf-Joelson), 93

Reserve Officers' Training Corps (ROTC), 84
residence halls, 198; DPD and, 237; Earhart in, 65, 69, 70–71; Ferris, V., and, 140–41; Gilbreth, L., in, 78; Ladies Hall as, 8; Meredith, V., and, 53
Restaurant, Hotel, and Institutional Management (RHI), Department of, 100, 186, 213
Restaurant, Hotel, Institutional, and Tourism Management (RHIT), 185
Rhetoric and Composition, 2–3, 290–94, *293*
Rhetoric Society of America, 293
RHI. *See* Restaurant, Hotel, and Institutional Management
RHI Cafeteria, 213
RHIT. *See* Restaurant, Hotel, Institutional, and Tourism Management
Rice, John, 293–94
Richards, Ellen Swallow, 28, 30, 32
Rickert, Thomas, 292
Ringel, Robert, 120, 194; at Department of Audiology and Speech Sciences, 284; Solomon, Barbara, and, 284; Weaver and, 243; Woo and, 223
Risk, Caroline, 296
Rivera, Diego, 86
Robinson, Ezekiel G., 9
Roentgen Institute, 82
Rogers, Bruce, 18
Rookwood Pottery, 14–16
Roosevelt, Eleanor, 67–68
Roosevelt, Franklin D., 78, 110
Rose, Shirley, 292
Ross, David E., 41, 50, 72

ROTC. *See* Reserve Officers' Training Corps
Rowe, Margaret, 290
Rupel, Esther Fern, 64–66, *65*
Rural University of Minas Gerais (UREMG), 104–8, 180
Ruth Pike Lectureship Series, 225

Saint Louis University, 291
salaries, 203–4, 243
Sams, Denver, *169*
Samson, Nellie P., 18, 30
Savaiano, Dennis, 317
Sawyer, Diane, 160
SBHP. *See* Star Behavioral Health Providers
Schantz-Hansen, Laurentza, 2–3, *47*, 62–64
Schleman, Helen Blanche, 85; Combs, S., and, 166; female faculty activism by, 199–207, *200*; Ferris, V., and, 139; Gillaspie and, 103; TIAA-CREF and, 204–7. *See also* Helen B. Schleman Gold Medallion Award
schools within Purdue University. *See specific disciplines*
Schuck, Cecelia, 58
Science, College of, 113–20, *117*
Science, School of, 22, 46; Department of Household Economics in, 28, 32; Department of Nutrition Science in, 249; Haas, F., at, 145; WISP and, 118
Science Diversity Office, 118
Sciscoe Craig, Susie, 226
Sealtest Laboratory Kitchen, 103
The Search for the Apex of America (Peck), 12

Session, Charles L., 266
sex discrimination suit, 201–2
Sex in Education or A Fair Chance for the Girls (Clarke), 9
Share the Work, 79
Sheldon, W. H., 160
The Shepherd's Guide Through the Valley of Deb and Financial Change (Williams, F.), 189
Shoemaker, Carolyn E., 18, 30, 41, 50
Shortridge, Abraham C., 5, 6
Shrader, Ray Anne, 159
Siems, Ruth M., 96
Sigma Xi Scientific Research Society, 247
Singular Perturbations of an Ordinary Differential Equation (Haas, V.), 144
Smith, Hope M., 157–58
Smith-Lever Act of 1914, 33–34
Smolen, RuthAnn, 176
Soaring Wings (Putnam, G.), 68, 72
Sobrinho, L. Menicucci, 106–7
Society of Western Artists, 18
Society of Women Engineers (SWE), 2, 147
Solomon, Barbara, 278, 282–85, *284*
Solomon, Bruce, 283
Sorcy, Tom, 92–93
Southern Illinois University, 192, 193
Speech, Language, and Hearing Sciences, Department of, 317
Spruce Room, 42, 122–23, 213
Spurgeon, James R. "Rick," 181–82
Staaks, Betty, 202
Stanford University: Brandt at, 191–92; Clifton at, 156; Hyland at, 183–84
Stanley Coulter Hall, 198

Star Behavioral Health Providers (SBHP), 310
Stark, Rachel E. "Betty," 274–78, *275*
State Board of Health, 168
State House, 6–7
Statistics, Department of, 283
Status of Women at Purdue report, 151–53
Steer, Max, 275–76
Stewart, Robert Bruce "R. B.," 51, 121
Stewart Center: Akeley, E., art collection in, 86; Church memorial in, 113; Eliza Fowler Hall in, 64–65; Haas, V., memorial in, 148
Stobaugh, Donita, 202
Stokes, Eoto R., 175–76
Stone, Beverley, 139, 201–3
Stone, Winthrop E., 18, 19, 25, 33, 38, 49
Stone Hall (Home Economics Administrative Building), 121–23, 213; Clark, H., in, 127; Kirksey in, 232; Nutrition and Exercise Clinical Research Center in, 250
stop the tenure clock policy, 3
Storer, Maria Longworth Nichols, 15
Stove Top Stuffing, 96
Stratton, Dorothy C., 69–70, 74, 78
A Streetcar Named Desire (Williams, T.), 111
Strickler, Nancy, 295–99, *298*
Structure and Theme (Church), 113
Suddarth, Betty, 202
suffrage for women, 6, 35
Sullivan, Charlene, 215–21, *218*
Sullivan, Patricia, 292
Sunderlin, Gertrude Laura, 93–97, *96*
Superintendence, Department of, 60

Swanson, Pearl, 125
SWE. *See* Society of Women Engineers

Taft, William Howard, 16
Tarbell, Ida, 75
Taylor, Dave, 289
Taylor, William Watts, 15–16
Teachers Insurance and Annuity Association - College Retirement Equities Fund (TIAA-CREF), 204–7
Teaching Academy, 238–39
Technical Assistance Program, 219
technology: scarcity of women professors in, 202. *See also specific types*
Technology, Department of, 169
Technology, School of, 172, 175, 255, 257, 261–62
Tents in the Clouds (Stark and Jackson), 275, 277
tenure, 3, 85
Terry, Helen Thompson, 63
A Text-Book of Cookery for Use in Schools (Ewing), 14
Theater Arts, 204
Theobald, Sharon, 86–88
therbligs, 77
Thomas Aquinas (Saint), 3, 220, 222, 294
TIAA-CREF. *See* Teachers Insurance and Annuity Association - College Retirement Equities Fund
Tippecanoe County Community Health Clinic, 260
Title IX, 54, 161–64; Bayh and, 201; Chiscon, M., and, 119; Mertler and, 164
Title IX Distinguished Service Award, 162, 268

Title VII, of Civil Rights Act of 1964, 205, 207
Title XII, of US Foreign Assistance Act of 1975, 230
To Love and Learn (Bogan), 198
Torchbearer Award, 120
Trachtman, Leon, 197
transgenders, 284
Trautmann, Joanne, 110
Twin Pines Cooperative House, 181
Tyler, Varro E., 175

Ulysses (Joyce), 111
United States Public Health Service (USPHS), 172, 173, 235, 261
University Athletic Affairs Committee, 164
University Committee on the Status of Women, 128
University Extension Council, 168
University of Alabama, 246
University of California: Clifton at, 157; Williams, F., at 1, 188
University of Chicago: Akeley, E., art collection and, 86; Goble at, 180
University of Colorado, 61
University of Detroit: Haas, V., at, 145; Lauer, J., at, 291–92
University of Houston, 253
University of Illinois, 287
University of Kentucky, 216
University of Maryland, 201
University of Michigan, 9, 101; Haas, V., at, 145; Lauer, J., at, 291; Rupel at, 66; sex discrimination suit at, 201
University of Minnesota, 27, 28; Institute of Child Welfare at, 58; Vail at, 124

University of North Carolina, 234, 235
University of Notre Dame: Mendoza College of Business at, 3; Woo at, 220
University of Oklahoma, 276
University of Oregon, 38–39
University of Texas, 251–52
University of Vienna, 89
University of West Georgia, 93
University of Wisconsin: O'Shea, H., and, 59; Women's Athletic Association at, 49
University Psychological Services, 60–61
University Senate, 119
University Service Flag, 18–19
University Task Force on Women's Issues, 151
Upper Division Baccalaureate Degree Program, 172
UREMG. *See* Rural University of Minas Gerais
US Department of Agriculture (USDA): Agricultural Extension Service of, 105; Bitting, A., at, 23; Clark, H., with, 128; Cooperative Extension Service and, 32, 33–34; Division of Chemistry at, 23; Ferris, V., and, 135–37; Goble and, 181; *National Farm and Home Hour* of, 95; Wiley at, 23; Wood and, 235
US Foreign Assistance Act of 1975, 230
USPHS. *See* United States Public Health Service

Vail, Gladys E., *38*, 107, 123–24; at Department of Foods and Nutrition, 224; Kirksey and, 224; at School of Home Economics, 129–30, 177

Veterinary Medicine, College of, 249; Bitting, A., at, 23; scarcity of women professors in, 202
Vierling, Rick, 140
Vinton, Henry H., 18
Violet Haas Award, 120, 148; to Brooks, 262; to Jamieson, 153; to Ladisch, C., 320
Virginia C. Meredith Home Economics Club, 53, 64
Virginia Meredith Memorial Forest, 53
Virginia R. Ferris Phi Beta Kappa Literary Awards, 139
virtual baby, 269–70
vitamin B-6, 224–30

WAA. *See* Women's Athletic Association
Wabash Award, 120
Walling, John, 262
Wayne State University, 144–45
WBAA Radio, 65, 117, 185
WEAL. *See* Women's Equity Action League
Weaver, Connie M.: at Department of Foods and Nutrition, 240–50, *242*; at National Academy of Medicine, 240, 242, 248; at School of Consumer and Family Sciences (CFS), 243
Weinberg, Bernd, 283
Weiser, Irwin, 292
Weiss, Howard, 307
Weisskopf-Joelson, Edith, 88–93, *90*
Wellesley College: Edgell at, 140; Ferris, V., at, 132–33; nude photos from, 160
West Lafayette Community School Corp. (WLCSC), 99–100
WGHI. *See* Women's Global Health Institute

Whalen, Grover, 60
Wheat Flour Institute, 183
White House Commission on Home Economics, 214
White House Conference on Aging, 186
White House Conference on Food, Nutrition and Health, 128
White Lodging -J. W. Marriott, Jr. School of Hospitality and Tourism Management, 186
WIC. *See* Women, Infants, and Children's Nutrition Program
Widule, Carol J., 204
WIEP. *See* Women in Engineering Program
Wiley, Harvey, 22, 23
Wiley Residence Hall, 198
Williams, Flora Leona Rouch, 187–89
Williams, Helen Bass, 3–4, 190–98, *195*
Williams, Leroy A. H., 192
Williams, Luther S., 139
Williams, Tennessee, 111
Willoughby, Marian, 64
Wilmeth Active Learning Center, 57
Wilson, Woodrow, 33–34, 39
Windsor Halls, 65, 69
Winterowd, Ross, 292
Winter Short Courses, 27
WISP. *See* Women in Science Program
W. K. Kellogg Foundation, 170, 172
WLCSC. *See* West Lafayette Community School Corp.
WO. *See* Writing Opportunity
Woman Faculty Award, 261–62
A Woman's Place Is at the Top (Kimberley), 10

Women, Infants, and Children's Nutrition Program (WIC), 235, 237
Women and the Changing World Conference, 67–68, 75
Women in Engineering Program (WIEP), 2, 147–48, 154, 182
Women in Professions conference, 149
Women in Science Program (WISP), 116, 118
Women in Scientific and Engineering Professions (Haas, V., and Perrucci), 149
Women's Art movement, 14–20, *19*
Women's Athletic Association (WAA), 49, 51, 162
Women's Center on Andrew Place, 148
Women's Equity Action League (WEAL), 201
Women's Global Health Institute (WGHI), 248–49
Women's Health Awareness Month, 261
women's liberation movement, 208–14
Woo, Carolyn Yauyan, 3, 220–23
Wood, Olivia Bennett, 234–39, *236*; at Camp Calcium, 245; in Mary L. Matthews Club, 239–40
Woodson, Randy, 317
Woodward, Bob, 160
Woolf, Virginia, 110
Work Life Legacy Award, 311
workplace triangle, 78
Works Progress Administration, 60
World Bank, 232
World Book Encyclopedia, 59
World Flight (Earhart), 75
World War I: Bitting, K., and, 24; Fry, L, and, 18–19; Gamble and, 40; home economics in, 39–40

World War II: Akeley, A., in, 80–88, *83, 87*; Department of Applied Design in, 63; Diehl in, 98; family life after, 97–101; Gilbreth, L., in, 79; Goble in, 179; Johnson, H., in, 167–68; Memorial Gymnasium in, 54; mental health services in, 61; Purdue Nursery School in, 58; Sunderlin and, 93–97, *96*; Trachtman in, 197; Weisskopf-Joelson in, 88–93, *90*
Wotawa, Edward, 298

Wright, Al, 204
Writing Lab, 286, 288–90
Writing Opportunity (WO), 292–93

X-rays, 82

Yellow Belt Lean, 272
Young, Ernest, 179
Young, Richard, 292

Zeedyk, Mary, 202

ABOUT THE AUTHOR

Author Angie Klink. Photo by Brian Powell.

Angie Klink has authored fourteen books, several about the history and people of Purdue University. She is an independent scholar, essayist, scriptwriter, and advertising copywriter. Klink has written for the American Writers Museum, *Ms. Magazine*, *Traces of Indiana History* magazine, and for documentaries narrated by actor Peter Coyote. She holds sixty-two American Advertising Federation ADDY Awards, including a Lifetime Achievement honor, and an Honorable Mention in the Erma Bombeck Writing Competition. Klink has written about author, poet, and artist Evaleen Stein and procured a 2024 Indiana Historical Bureau marker honoring Stein. Klink is a recipient of the Excellence in Historic Preservation Medal from the National Society of the Daughters of the American Revolution, their most prestigious award honoring dedication to preservation, including the research and writing of books. Klink holds a BA in communication from Purdue University. For more information on Klink and her work, visit www.angieklink.com.

ABOUT THE EDITOR

Jennifer L. Bay, Professor of English, Purdue University. Courtesy Jennifer Bay.

Dr. Jennifer Bay is professor of English in the technical and professional writing program at Purdue University. Her research focuses on community engagement, experiential learning, feminist rhetorics, and rhetorical theory. Her work has appeared in scholarly journals such as the *Journal of Business and Technical Communication*, *Journal of Technical Writing and Communication*, *IEEE Transactions on Professional Communication*, and *Technical Communication Quarterly*.

Dr. Bay has been fortunate to be recognized by Purdue for her community engagement work with Purdue's Service-Learning Award, Faculty Engaged Scholar Award, Faculty Engagement Fellow Award, and Jefferson Award. Whether she is coordinating internships, teaching internship courses, or engaging with the community through service-learning projects, she firmly believes that students learn in deep and unexpected ways through applied experiences.

www.ingramcontent.com/pod-product-compliance
Lightning Source LLC
Chambersburg PA
CBHW071015240426
43661CB00073B/2297